Commentary on Romans

William G. T. Shedd

BAKER BOOK HOUSE
Grand Rapids, Michigan

First published in 1879 by
Charles Scribner's Sons
Reprinted 1980 by
Baker Book House Company
ISBN: 0-8010-8175-0

PHOTOLITHOPRINTED BY CUSHING - MALLOY, INC.
ANN ARBOR, MICHIGAN, UNITED STATES OF AMERICA
1980

PREFACE

The principal purpose I have had in view, in preparing this Commentary upon the Epistle to the Romans, is to promote the critical and doctrinal study of this important portion of the New Testament. It is specially intended for theological students and clergymen. For this reason, the Greek text is printed at the top of the page, so that the reader may refer, by a glance, to the word or the clause that is explained in the notes below. I have adopted the text of Lachmann, with such modifications, chiefly from Tischendorf, as would probably have been made by Lachmann himself, if he had had access to those manuscripts that have been brought to light by the industry and skill of Tischendorf. As an editor, Lachmann, like Bentley, who in the preceding century proposed the same plan of founding the text upon the oldest rather than upon the most numerous manuscripts, possessed a critical tact and sagacity that make his judgment of high value. This is generally acknowledged, especially as exhibited in Lachmann's editorial labors in classical literature. Where the uncial text omits long clauses that appear in the received, I have generally added the received text in brackets; the shorter omitted clauses being given in the notes. The punctuation will be found to vary in some instances from both that of Lachmann and Tischendorf. Punctuation is in reality, exposition; and an editor will of course arrange words and clauses in accordance with his own understanding of their connection.

In respect to the annotations upon the text, I have had in mind the words of Calvin, in his dedicatory epistle to Simon Grynæus. "I remember," he says, "that when three years ago we had a friendly converse as to the best mode of expounding Scripture, the plan which especially pleased you seemed also to me the most entitled to approbation: we both thought that the chief excellence of an expounder consists in *lucid brevity*." The notes are concise, and bear strictly and directly upon the word or clause. Special care has been taken to supply the ellipses, upon which the right understanding of St. Paul so often depends; and to cite the most pertinent Scripture texts that explain the meaning of a word, or sentence. There is little attempt at homiletical expansion of the thought, in order that the actual connection of the reasoning may be kept continually in sight, and not be even temporarily obscured by that more diffuse explanation which sometimes introduces only remotely related matter. At the same time, whenever the case required it, I have not hesitated to enter upon an analytic, and somewhat exhaustive enucleation of the meaning. The reader will find that particular attention has been devoted to the doctrine of original sin, in the 5th chapter; of indwelling sin, in the 7th and 8th chapters; and of election and reprobation, in the 9th, 10th, and 11th chapters. In this way, while the commentary is critical and philological, it is also theological. Under this head, Calvin and Owen have been much consulted, and particularly the exceedingly thorough exposition of David Pareus, who has entirely escaped the notice of such wide readers as De Wette, Meyer, and Philippi.

The history of the exegesis of the Epistle is also given, to a considerable extent, by the mention of the leading advocates, in the Ancient and the Modern Church, of the different explanations of the more disputed passages. This is a task that is not easy to be performed within a short space.

By reason of the ambiguity or hesitation of a commentator, it is sometimes difficult to place him. In citing authorities, I have relied much upon Wolfius, De Wette, Meyer, and Lange.

All the important readings are specified, together with the several manuscripts and versions that support them. I have not, however, deemed it worth while to cite any uncial later than L, or any version later than the Vulgate. This will enable the student to see the manuscript authority down to A.D. 900, and that of versions down to A.D. 400. The manuscripts are cited only a prima manu.

In short, the endeavor of the author has been, to furnish the theological student with an aid to his own conscientious examination of the original text of the Epistle to the Romans, and thereby to the formation of an independent judgment and opinion which he will be ready to announce and maintain. It will be reward enough, if this commentary shall be the means of stimulating any to the close and lifelong study of the most important document in the New Testament, after the Gospels. Demosthenes read Thucydides over and over, seven times, for the sake of forming that concise and energetic style which has been the admiration and the despair of orators. Whoever reads St. Paul's Epistle to the Romans over and over, not seven times only, but seventy times seven, will feel an influence as distinct and definite as that of a Leyden jar. But the study of St. Paul, like that of the speeches in Thucydides, must be patient analysis. The great characteristic of this Epistle is the *closeness* of the reasoning. The line of remark is a concatenation like that of chain-armor, of which each link hooks directly into the next, without intervening matter. The process of an exegete must, consequently, be somewhat similar to that by which a blind man gets a knowledge of a chain. He must do it by the sense of touch. He must handle each link separately, and actually feel the point of contact with the preceding link, and the succeeding.

The Epistle to the Romans ought to be the manual of the theological student and clergyman, because it is in reality *an inspired system of theology*. The object of the writer was to give to the Roman congregation, and ultimately to Christendom, a complete statement of religious truth. It comprises natural religion, the gospel, and ethics; thus covering the whole field of religion and morals. It is sometimes forgotten that the introductory part of this Epistle contains the fullest and clearest account ever yet given, of man's moral and religious nature, and his innate knowledge of God and law. There is no deeper psychology, and no better statement of natural religion, than that in the first and second chapters. St. Paul does not vilify the created endowments of the human intellect, but rates them high; not only because this agrees with the facts, but that he may show the greatness of the sin that has so wantonly misused and abused them. The closing chapters exhibit ethics, or the science of duties, in the same profound and comprehensive manner. And between these two departments of natural religion and ethics, the doctrine of justification, or the gospel, confessedly finds its most complete and exhaustive enunciation. The Epistle to the Romans is therefore encyclopædic in its structure; it is round and full, like the circle of Giotto, and contains all the elements of both natural and revealed religion. The human mind need not go outside of this Epistle, in order to know all religious truth.

UNION THEOLOGICAL SEMINARY.
NEW YORK, Nov. 1, 1879.

NOTE

THE following statement explains the notation of the manuscripts that are cited in the Commentary, mentioning their dates according to Tischendorf and Scrivener. The dates of the versions that are cited are given according to Tischendorf, Scrivener, Mill, and Lightfoot.

MANUSCRIPTS.

א. Codex *Sinaiticus:* A.D. 350, Tischendorf and Scrivener. A. Codex *Alexandrinus:* A.D. 475, Tischendorf; A.D. 450, Scrivener. B. Codex *Vaticanus:* A.D. 350, Tischendorf; A.D. 325, Scrivener. C. Codex *Ephraemi:* A.D. 450, Tischendorf and Scrivener. D. Codex *Claromontanus:* A.D. 550, Tischendorf and Scrivener. E. Codex *Sangermanensis:* A.D. 875, Tischendorf and Scrivener. "A mere transcript of Claromontanus by some ignorant person. It is manifestly worthless, and should long since have been removed from the list of authorities," says Scrivener. F. Codex *Augiensis:* A.D. 875, Tischendorf and Scrivener. G. Codex *Bœrnerianus:* A.D. 875, Tischendorf; A.D. 900, Scrivener. L. Codex *Angelicus:* A.D. 850, Tischendorf and Scrivener.

VERSIONS.

Peshito: A.D. 175, Tischendorf and Scrivener. *Itala,* or *Old Latin:* A.D. 175, Tischendorf; A.D 150, Mill. *Sahidic,* or *Thebaic:* A.D. 250, Tischendorf; A.D. 225, Lightfoot. *Coptic,* or *Memphitic:* A.D. 250, Tischendorf; A.D. 225, Lightfoot. *Æthiopic:* A.D. 350, Tischendorf and Scrivener. *Vulgate:* A.D. 400.

COMMENTARY ON ROMANS

INTRODUCTION

THE church at Rome, at first, was an informal gathering of Christian believers, many of whom had been converted to Christianity in different parts of the Empire, and had subsequently settled at the metropolis. The salutations in chapter xvi. prove that Paul, at the time of writing the Epistle, was acquainted with a considerable number of them. This acquaintance could not have been made at Rome. The list in Acts ii. 9–11 mentions "strangers of Rome" (*ὁί ἐπιδημοῦντες Ῥωμαῖοι*), among the three thousand that were added to the Christian church on the day of Pentecost. These were Jews residing at Rome, who, after their conversion and return to the metropolis, constituted a part of the Roman congregation; the remainder being converted Gentiles. Most of the names mentioned in Rom. xvi. are those of Gentiles.

That the nucleus of a church must have existed very early, is proved by the fact that Paul informs the Romans, that *ἀπὸ πολλῶν ἐτῶν* he had been wishing to visit them and preach to them, xv. 23; i. 10. His engagements elsewhere had hitherto prevented, i. 13; xv. 22. He hoped, however, soon to accomplish his desire, but his visit must be a short one, because he has to carry a charitable collection to the church at Jerusalem, and because Spain and not Italy is to be the terminus of his missionary labors, xv. 23–27; Acts xx. 2 sq. For these reasons, he sends them a written statement of the gospel-plan, as a preparation for a personal visit, making a long stay with them unnecessary. The journey of Phœbe, a deaconess of the church at Cenchrea, the port of Corinth, affords an opportunity of sending the Epistle, xvi. 1.

The Romish tradition, resting mainly upon a vague statement of Eusebius (II. 14, 15), that Peter went to Rome in the reign of Claudius (A.D. 42), and founded a church there, of which he continued to be the bishop for twenty-five years, is incredible for the following reasons: 1. According to Acts xv., Paul finds Peter at Jerusalem as late as the year 50, still laboring with the "apostles and elders" in Palestine and Syria. 2. According to Gal. ii. 11, Peter still finds his field of labor in Western Asia as late as A.D. 55. Paul meets him in Antioch at this date. 3. According to 1 Pet. v. 13, Peter is connected with the church in Babylon as late as A.D. 60. That this is the literal Babylon, is favored by the fact that the first Epistle of Peter was addressed to the dispersed Jewish Christians in Asia Minor (1 Pet. i. 1), whose condition and needs would have much more naturally come under the eye of an apostle on the banks of the Euphrates, than on the banks of the Tiber. 4. Had the church at Rome been founded by Peter in A.D. 42, and been under his presidency from that time onward, it is highly improbable that Paul would have made it any apostolical visit at all, or have written it an apostolic epistle; for, in xv. 20 he states it to be his principle of evangelistic labor, "to preach the gospel not where Christ is named, lest he should build upon another man's foundation." 5. If, in the face of these objections, it still be claimed that Peter was the founder and bishop of the church in Rome, the entire absence in Paul's epistle of any allusion to Peter is inexplicable.

It is generally agreed that Paul wrote the Epistle to the Romans at Corinth, during his third missionary tour. The proofs are these: First, according to xv. 25, the writer is just starting for Jerusalem, with money which has been contributed "for the poor saints which are at Jerusalem;" this collection was completed at Corinth, as appears from 1 Cor. xvi. 1–3; 2 Cor. ix. Secondly, The Epistle is sent by the hands of Phœbe from Cenchrea, the port of Corinth, xvi. 1. Thirdly, Paul's "host" is Gaius, and Gaius was a citizen of Corinth, xvi. 23; 1 Cor. i. 14. Fourthly, Erastus sends a greeting by Paul, xvi. 23, and Erastus lived at Corinth, 2 Tim. iv. 20.

The Epistle to the Romans is the sixth in the series of the Pauline Epistles; having been preceded by 1 and 2 Thessalonians, written from Corinth A.D. 53; by Galatians, written from Ephesus A.D. 54; by 1 Corinthians, written from Ephesus A.D. 55; by 2 Corinthians, written from Ephesus or Macedonia A.D. 56. Guericke's date for the Epistle to the Romans is A.D. 58.

The *authenticity* of the Epistle to the Romans is strongly supported. It is mentioned in the list given in the Muratorian Canon, as early as A.D. 160. The Peshito and Itala Versions of it date at least as far back as A.D. 200. There are citations of, or allusions to it, in Barnabas, Clemens Romanus, Ignatius, Polycarp, Clemens Alexandrinus, Theophilus of Antioch, Tertullian and Origen. These authorities cover the period A.D. 100–250. Chapters xv. and xvi. have been impugned by Semler, Eichorn, and Baur, in support of their individual theories; but they are found entire and complete in the Vatican and Sinaitic manuscripts (A.D. 325–350), as well as in the later ones; and are included in the Peshito version of the Epistle. The diplomatic evidence is as decisive for the genuineness of the last two chapters of the Epistle, as of any.

The *aim* of the Epistle to the Romans is didactic. The main object of Paul is, to furnish the Roman Church with a comprehensive statement of evangelical doctrine. No book of Scripture comes so near to being a body of divinity as this. It is systematic and logical, from beginning to end. Apostasy and redemption are the hinges upon which everything turns, and in discussing these the writer touches, either directly or by implication, upon all the other truths of Christianity. The Epistle to the Romans is, therefore, the Novum Organum of the Christian Religion. "I know," says Jacobi, "no deeper philosophy than that of Paul in the seventh chapter of the Epistle to the Romans. In merely natural men, sin dwells. Regeneration is the foundation of Christianity. He who expels the doctrine of grace from the Bible utterly expunges the Bible."* In a similar manner, Coleridge expresses himself. "I think St. Paul's Epistle to the Romans the most profound work in existence; and I hardly believe that the writings of the old Stoics, now lost, could have been deeper. Undoubtedly it is, and must be, very obscure to ordinary readers; but some of the difficulty is accidental, arising from the form in which the Epistle appears. If we could now arrange this work in the way in which we may be sure St. Paul would himself do, were he now alive, and preparing it for the press, his reasoning would stand out clearer. His accumulated parentheses would be thrown into notes, or extended to the margin."†

Another view of the main design of this Epistle is, that it is polemic against Judaism. Baur maintains that the writer has the early Ebionitism in his eye. The objections to this

* F. H. Jacobi's Fliegende Blätter. Zweite Abtheilung.

† Coleridge's Table Talk, June 15, 1833.

are the following: 1. The matter is addressed to Jewish Christians in common with Gentile. Both divisions are equally regarded as believers in Christianity. Compare ii. 9, 10, 17; iv. 1 sq.; ix. 1 sq. 2. There are no warnings against Judaism as such, as there are in Corinthians and Galatians, which are polemic epistles, to some extent. 3. There is nothing in the Epistle that implies that the Roman church was in danger of apostatizing from evangelical truth, to Jewish ceremonialism. The internal indications, such for example as the Greek names in chapter xvi., go to show that the Gentile Christians were in the majority, and were the controlling power. 4. Whenever there are any injunctions in the way of caution or reprobation, as in xvi. 17–20, they are addressed to the whole church, and have no more reference to Jews than to Gentiles.

That the Epistle has a polemic reference towards legality, as the contrary of evangelical faith, and that this gives a color to it as a whole, is evident. But such polemics as this, is aimed at human nature generally, and not at the Jew particularly. The Gentile equally with the Jew is liable to self-righteousness, and the Epistle combats self-righteousness from beginning to end.

The analysis of the Epistle to the Romans shows that its *plan* is extremely simple and logical. St. Paul discusses the necessity, the nature, the effects, and the individual application of the δικαιοσύνη θεοῦ, or gratuitous justification. Under these four heads, he brings, into the first eleven chapters, the dogmatic substance of the Epistle. He then enunciates, in the remaining five chapters, the principles of Christian ethics and morality, which he deduces from this evangelical method of justification, and connects immediately with it. The Epistle to the Romans, therefore, like the Pauline Epistles generally, combines both theory and practice: the latter being founded upon the former.

The scheme of the whole work, then, is as follows:

I. THE DOCTRINE OF GRATUITOUS JUSTIFICATION: CHAPTERS I.–XI.

1. Necessity of gratuitous justification: Chapters i.–iii. 20.
2. Nature of gratuitous justification: Chapters iii. 21–iv. 25.
3. Effects of gratuitous justification: Chapters v.–viii.
4. Application of gratuitous justification: Chapters ix.–xi.

II. CHRISTIAN ETHICS, AND MORALITY: CHAPTERS XII.–XVI.

1. Duties to God and the Church: Chapters xii. 1–13; xiv. 1–xv. 13; xvi. 17–20.
2. Duties to the State: Chapter xiii. 1–7.
3. Duties to Society: Chapters xii. 14–21; xiii. 8–14.
4. Personal references, greetings, and benediction: Chapters xv. 14–xvi. 16; xvi. 21–27.

CHAPTER I

[1] *Παῦλος δοῦλος Χριστοῦ Ἰησοῦ, κλητὸς ἀπόστολος ἀφωρισμένος εἰς εὐαγγέλιον θεοῦ,* [2] *ὃ προεπηγγείλατο διὰ*

VER. 1. Παῦλος] The apostle's original name was Saul, from שָׁאוּל, "asked for," Acts xiii. 9. Jerome, followed by Bengel Olshausen and Meyer, explains the change to Paul as commemorative of the conversion of Sergius Paulus. But this contradicts the spirit of the maxim, "Without all contradiction, the less is blessed of the better," Heb. vii. 7. The convert might be named for the apostle, but not the apostle for the convert. The opinion of Grotius is better, that Paul is only the Greek form of Saul. δοῦλος] is general, like the Old Testament "servant of the Lord," Josh. i. 1. κλητὸς] denotes the special preparation, by conversion and inspiration. ἀπόστολος] is a person formally commissioned and sent. Compare John i. 6, where ἀπεσταλμένος is not a part of the verb, as in the English Version, but a predicate. ἀφωρισμένος, etc.] explains still more particularly the term κλητὸς; the root, ὁρίζειν, signifies to draw a line around: to horizon; hence, to set apart, or separate. εἰς εὐαγγέλιον] is equivalent to εὐαγγελίζεσθαι. Compare 2 Cor. ii. 12; x. 14. θεοῦ] is the genitive of authorship.

VER. 2. προεπηγγείλατο] This pre-announcement of the gospel is made in the Messianic promises, prophecies, and types of the Old Testament. Paul finds all of the cardinal doctrines of the New Testament, germinally, in the Old, and

τῶν προφητῶν αὐτοῦ, ἐν γραφαῖς ἁγίαις, [3] περὶ τοῦ υἱοῦ αὐτοῦ τοῦ γενομένου ἐκ σπέρματος Δαυεὶδ κατὰ σάρκα,

continually cites the Old Testament in proof of the truths and facts of Christianity. Compare iv. 3 sq.; ix. 7 sq.; x. 5 sq.; xi. 2 sq. γραφαῖς] is anarthrous, because a well-known collection is meant. It is equivalent to a proper noun.

VER. 3. περὶ] refers to προεπηγγείλατο, and not to εὐαγγέλιον. Beza and Wetstein incorrectly make verse 2 a parenthesis. υἱοῦ] is employed theanthropically. The Son here spoken of is the *incarnate* Son, constituted of two natures which are described in the context. γενομένου] implies a birth or γένεσις. Compare Gal. iv. 4; Mat. i. 1. The human nature in the incarnate Son was "born," or "made to become," from "the seed of David." Christ's humanity was not created ex nihilo, but was procreated. It was "made of a woman;" that is, of a woman's nature or substance, Gal. iv. 4. σπέρματος] is equivalent to φύσεως. Though a physical term, it stands here for the whole man, upon both the mental as well as the physical side. σάρκα] is antithetic to πνεῦμα in verse 4, and denotes the humanity of Christ, as the latter denotes his divinity. Though primarily a physical term, like σπέρμα, yet here, like that, σάρξ stands for the *whole* humanity, upon both the side of the soul and body. The apostle is describing Christ with respect to all of his human characteristics, both mental and physical, when he describes him κατὰ σάρκα. Compare ix. 5. The term σάρξ, in this Epistle, commonly denotes sinful human nature. Compare vii. 5, 18, 25; viii. 3–9, et alia. But, in this passage, a sinless humanity is meant. Christ's human nature, having been derived by miraculous conception from Mary who was of the "seed of David," and having been perfectly sanctified by the Holy Ghost, was a sinless birth. It was τὸ γεννώμενον ἅγιον of Luke i. 35. Traducianism finds support in this text, because it is

⁴ τοῦ ὁρισθέντος υἱοῦ θεοῦ ἐν δυνάμει κατὰ πνεῦμα ἁγιωσύνης ἐξ ἀναστάσεως νεκρῶν, Ἰησοῦ Χριστοῦ τοῦ κυρίου

the entire humanity, and not a part of it, only, that was "born," or "made to become," from the "seed of David." The "reasonable soul" as well as the "true body" are both included in the σάρξ, and this is here described as γενομένη ἐκ σπέρματος Δαυεὶδ. Christ was the Son of David mentally, as well as corporally.

VER. 4. ὁρισθέντος] "declared," not "decreed" (Vulgate). Christ's resurrection evinced his divinity, but did not decide or determine it. It was one of the indications of his superhuman nature. In the old grammar, the indicative mood is called ὁριστικός. υἱοῦ] is here employed differently from what it is in verse 3: namely, in the *metaphysical* or trinitarian sense, and denotes the unincarnate Son prior to his assumption of σάρξ. υἱός is here equivalent to the λόγος of John i. 1. Previous to the incarnation, there is only one nature in the Son, and this a divine nature, which the writer describes as τὸ πνεῦμα ἁγιωσύνης. ἐν δυνάμει] is adverbial, and qualifies ὁρισθέντος. The resurrection of Christ from the dead, like the resurrection of Lazarus which preceded it, was an event in which the miracle reached its acme of energy. κατὰ πνεῦμα] is antithetic to κατὰ σάρκα in ver. 3, and refers to the deity in the composite person of Jesus Christ, the incarnate Son (Calvin, Beza, Pareus, Olshausen, Philippi, Hodge). The same antithesis is found in 1 Tim. iii. 16, which teaches that Jesus Christ was manifested to the world by means of his humanity (ἐν σαρκί), and justified and glorified by means of his divinity (ἐν πνεύματι). In 1 Pet. iii. 18, Christ is described as suffering death in his human nature (σαρκί), and overcoming death in his divine nature (πνεύματι). And in John iv. 24, πνεῦμα anarthrous is employed to denote abstract and absolute deity, the divine essence itself. This explanation of πνεῦμα, as signifying divinity when opposed to σάρξ as signifying humanity, was common in the patristic age. In the second Epistle ascribed to Clement of Rome (c. 9), it is said that Christ, ὢν μὲν τὸ πρῶτον πνεῦμα, ἐγένετο σάρξ. Upon this, Hefele remarks, that πνεῦμα is equivalent to τὸ θεῖον ἐν Χριστῷ. In Hermas (Pastor, iii. 5) there is the following statement descriptive of the Son of God "qui creavit cuncta:" "Filius autem spiritus sanctus est." Under this term spiritus sanctus, Grotius, Bull, the Benedictine editors, Ittig, Münscher, Baumgarten-Crusius, and Hefele, understand to be meant the divine nature of Christ, and not the third person of the Trinity. Similarly, Cyprian (De idolorum varietate, 11) describes the incarnation: "Ratio dei in virginem illabitur, carnem spiritus sanctus induitur, Deus cum homine miscetur." Ignatius (Ad Ephesios vii.) remarks, εἷς ἰατρός ἐστιν, σαρκικός τε καὶ πνευματικὸς, γενητὸς καὶ αγένητος, ἐν σαρκὶ γενόμενος θεὸς, ἐν θανάτω ζωὴ ἀληθινὴ, καὶ ἐκ Μαρίας καὶ ἐκ θεοῦ, πρῶτον παθητὸς καὶ τότε ἀπαθὴς [i. e., post resurrectionem], Ἰησοῦς Χριστὸς, ὁ κύριος ἡμῶν. Augustine (Inchoata expositio, Ed. Migne, iii. 2091) comments as follows upon the passage under consideration: Eundem sane ipsum qui secundum carnem factus est ex semine David, predestinatum dicit filium Dei: non secundum carnem, sed secundum spiritum; nec quemlibet spiritum, sed spiritum sanctificationis. That is to say: the "spirit" that is antithetic to the "flesh," in Christ's Person, is not the ordinary finite spirit of man, or angel, but the extraordinary and infinite Spirit. Similarly, Gregory Nazianzen (Oratio xxxviii.) remarks: Προελθὼν δὲ θεὸς μετὰ τῆς προσλήψεως, ἓν ἐκ δύο ἐναντίων, σαρκὸς καὶ πνεύματος, ὧν, τὸ μὲν εθέωσε, τὸ δὲ εθεώθε.

Some commentators, with Beza and Tholuck, refer πνεῦμα to the third person of the Trinity, as the agent by whom the resurrection of Christ was accomplished. But this would require διὰ πνεύματος, as in Heb. ix. 14; to say nothing of the loss of the antithesis between *κατὰ σάρκα*, and *κατὰ πνεῦμα*. Other commentators, like Meyer and De Wette, regard *πνεῦμα* as antithetic to *σάρξ* taken in its *restricted* signification, to denote the sensuous nature only. It is Christ's rational human nature, they assert, as distinguished from his physical human nature: this higher spiritual side of Christ's humanity was filled with the Holy Spirit. But the mere possession of reason in distinction from sense, even though reason be sanctified and inspired by the Holy Spirit, would not be a mighty indication that Jesus Christ was the Son of God. The Old Testament prophets possessed *πνεῦμα* in this sense, and were both sanctified and inspired, so that while there might be a difference in degree between Christ and them, there would be none in kind. Furthermore, the *πνεῦμα* here attributed to Christ was something in respect to which he was *not* "of the seed of David." But, the *πνεῦμα* that constituted his rational soul, in distinction from his animal soul, *was ἐκ σπέρματος Δανεὶδ*. ἁγιωσύνης] is the genitive of origin. This *πνεῦμα*, which is distinguished from Christ's *σάρξ*, is in itself an original fountain of holiness. It does not derive righteousness from a higher source, as all finite *πνεῦμα* does, but possesses self-subsistent righteousness which it can communicate to creatures. Compare 1 Cor. xv. 45, where the "last Adam" is denominated "a quickening spirit." "Paul considers the divine nature of Christ according to the relation it had to, and the great effect that it exercised upon, his other nature. For it was his divinity which sanctified, consecrated, and hypostatically deified his humanity" (South: Sermon on Rom. i. 3, 4). Compare this same force of the genitive of origin in רוּחַ קָדְשׁוֹ, *τὸ πνεῦμα τὸ ἅγιόν* (Sept.), Isa. lxiii. 11, and רוּחַ קָדְשְׁךָ, *τὸ πνεῦμα τὸ ἅγιόν σου* (Sept.), Ps. li. 13. In these, and similar passages, where the third person of the trinity is referred to, the genitive is more than a mere adjective. The Spirit who is thus

ἡμῶν, [5] δι' οὗ ἐλάβομεν χάριν καὶ ἀποστολὴν εἰς ὑπακοὴν πίστεως ἐν πᾶσιν τοῖς ἔθνεσιν ὑπὲρ τοῦ ὀνόματος αὐτοῦ,

described is not only holy, but the eternal ground and source of holiness. In precisely the same manner, this πνεῦμα of Jesus Christ which is distinguished from his σάρξ, is the fountain of holiness, that is to say, is the divine essence itself. ἐξ ἀναστάσεως] This resurrection, which is a mighty indication of Christ's divine Sonship, may be referred to either the first or the second person of the trinity. Sometimes it is the Father who raises Christ, Rom. vi. 4; and sometimes Christ himself rises, 1 Thess. iv. 14. The eternal Logos, being the whole divine essence in a particular trinitarian subsistence, when united to a human nature is the author and cause of all the miraculous experiences of this nature. Hence, the πνεῦμα in Christ's person evinced its own divinity by the resurrection of Christ's human body. It is true, that Christ's resurrection is the particular official work of the Father; but the official work of one person is sometimes attributed in Scripture to another, by reason of the unity of essence. Each person possesses the same entire divine essence, and since it is the essence which wields the infinite power that performs the miraculous work, the work, though eminently belonging to one particular person, may yet be attributed to either one of the trinitarian persons. Thus, creation, though officially and generally ascribed to the Father, is sometimes ascribed to the Son, John i. 3; Coloss. i. 16. Since, however, St. Paul (i. 2) has spoken of God the Father as "promising afore" the gospel of his Son, it is more natural to refer the resurrection here to the first person, as an official act by which he fulfils his promise.

VER. 5. ἐλάβομεν] is the writer's plural for the singular. χάριν] converting and supporting grace. ἀποστολὴν] official authority, together with the inspiration upon which it rests.

6 ἐν οἷς ἐστὲ καὶ ὑμεῖς κλητοὶ Ἰησοῦ Χριστοῦ, 7 πᾶσιν τοῖς
οὖσιν ἐν Ῥώμῃ ἀγαπητοῖς θεοῦ, κλητοῖς ἁγίοις. χάρις
ὑμῖν καὶ εἰρήνη ἀπὸ θεοῦ πατρὸς ἡμῶν καὶ κυρίου Ἰησοῦ
Χριστοῦ.
8 Πρῶτον μὲν εὐχαριστῶ τῷ θεῷ μου διὰ Ἰησοῦ Χριστοῦ περὶ πάντων ὑμῶν, ὅτι ἡ πίστις ὑμῶν καταγγέλλεται
ἐν ὅλῳ τῷ κόσμῳ. 9 μάρτυς γάρ μου ἐστὶν ὁ θεός, ᾧ λα-

εἰς ὑπακοὴν] is like εἰς εὐαγγέλιον in verse 1: "in order to produce obedience." πίστεως] genitive of source; the obedience flows from faith. ὑπὲρ τοῦ ὀνόματος] is to be connected with ἐλάβομεν; "for the glory of Christ's name."

Ver. 6. κλητοὶ] called, not as in verse 1 to the apostolic office, but, to Christian fellowship. Χριστοῦ] the genitive of efficient cause: "by Christ."

Ver. 7. πᾶσιν] is to be connected with Παῦλος in verse 1; the apostle addresses all the saints in Rome. χάρις] begins the salutation that follows the address, which ends with ἁγίοις. Χριστοῦ] the association of Jesus Christ with God the Father, as the source of eternal grace and peace, is a proof of his co-divinity. Ἰησους Χριστος is the name of the Eternal Son, or Logos, after and not before the incarnation, Luke i. 31.

Ver. 8. πρῶτον μὲν] is not followed by any second clause introduced by ἔπειτα δε, because of the rapidity and fullness of thought in the writer's mind. διὰ Χριστοῦ] Christ is the mediator of the prayer. πίστις] in Christ as the object of faith. καταγγέλλεται] a proof that the Roman church had been in existence for some time.

Ver. 9. γάρ] introduces the proof that he "thanks God." ἐν τῷ πνεύματι] denotes sincerity, and is equivalent to ἐν τῇ καρδίᾳ, Eph. v. 19. Though πνεῦμα, in the New Testament,

τρεύω ἐν τῷ πνεύματί μου ἐν τῷ εὐαγγελίῳ τοῦ υἱοῦ αὐτοῦ,
ὡς ἀδιαλείπτως μνείαν ὑμῶν ποιοῦμαι
10 πάντοτε ἐπὶ τῶν
προσευχῶν μου, δεόμενος εἴ πως ἤδη ποτὲ εὐοδωθήσομαι
ἐν τῷ θελήματι τοῦ θεοῦ ἐλθεῖν πρὸς ὑμᾶς.
11 ἐπιποθῶ
γὰρ ἰδεῖν ὑμᾶς, ἵνα τι μεταδῶ χάρισμα ὑμῖν πνευματικὸν
εἰς τὸ στηριχθῆναι ὑμᾶς,
12 τοῦτο δέ ἐστιν συμπαρακληθῆ-
ναι ἐν ὑμῖν διὰ τῆς ἐν ἀλλήλοις πίστεως, ὑμῶν τε καὶ

generally denotes the understanding, and καρδία the heart and will, yet the two are occasionally interchanged, because both constitute one soul. ἐν τῷ εὐαγγελίῳ] in preaching the gospel. Compare verse 1. ὡς] is employed adverbially, denoting degree; it is not equivalent to ὅτι. ἀδιαλείπτως] is the emphatic word, and is to be connected with γάρ.

Ver. 10. ἐπὶ] "upon the occasion, at the time of," Acts xi. 28; 1 Thess. i. 2. It is not equivalent to ἐν. εὐοδωθήσομαι] This verb is employed metaphorically in the passive voice. Hence, it does not mean "to have a prosperous journey" (Eng. Ver.), but, "to be prospered or successful."

Ver. 11. χάρισμα] does not here denote the supernatural gifts spoken of in 1 Cor. xii., but the graces of the Spirit, as the explanation in verse 12 shows.

Ver. 12. συμπαρακληθῆναι] the preposition has its distinctive meaning, denoting mutual comfort. The reference is not to affliction in the restricted modern sense of the word, but to cheer, animation, and strengthening in the Christian race and fight. The connection with στηριχθῆναι, in verse 13, proves this. The old English use of the word "comfort" was founded upon the etymology (con — fortis), and had reference mainly to strength of endurance. Thus Orlando says (As You Like It, ii. 6): "For my sake be comfortable; hold death awhile at the arm's end." To be strengthened

ἐμοῦ. [13] οὐ θέλω δὲ ὑμᾶς ἀγνοεῖν, ἀδελφοί, ὅτι πολλάκις προεθέμην ἐλθεῖν πρὸς ὑμᾶς, καὶ ἐκωλύθην ἄχρι τοῦ δεῦρο, ἵνα τινὰ καρπὸν σχῶ καὶ ἐν ὑμῖν καθὼς καὶ ἐν τοῖς λοιποῖς ἔθνεσιν. [14] Ἕλλησίν τε καὶ βαρβάροις, σοφοῖς τε

with might, by God's Spirit, in the inner man, Eph. iii. 16, is to receive the comfort of the Holy Ghost. In this sense, the Holy Spirit is the only Comforter, because he alone imparts an internal power of endurance, and of submission to the divine will.

VER. 13. οὐ θέλω ἀγνοεῖν] is a weak form of a strong thought; the writer's meaning is: "I wish you to understand very distinctly." This rhetorical figure of litotes, or meiosis, is a favorite one with St. Paul. Compare xi. 25; 1 Cor. x. 1; xii. 1; 2 Cor. i. 8; 1 Thess. iv. 13; Acts xxvi. 19. δὲ] is transitive: "now." καὶ ἐν ὑμῖν] καὶ is repeated pleonastically from the earnestness of the thought. πολλάκις] implies that the Roman church had existed for a considerable time.

VER. 14. βαρβάροις] In Greek authors, βαρβάροι denotes all non-Grecians. The Eleatic stranger, in Plato's Statesman (262) says that "in this part of the world, they cut off the Hellenes as one species, and all the other species of mankind they include under the single name of 'barbarians.'" Xenophon speaks of Greeks and barbarians as composing the army of Cyrus. The Romans are called barbarians by Greek authors (Polybius v. 104); but Roman writers claim classicality for Rome; e.g., Cicero (De finibus ii. 15): "Non solum Græcia et Italia, sed etiam omnis barbaria." It is not probable that St. Paul, with his courtesy and conciliatory method, intended to place the Romans, whom he was addressing, among the barbarians; yet, neither could he call them Greeks. His meaning is, that he was under obli-

καὶ ἀνοήτοις ὀφειλέτης εἰμί· 15 *οὕτως τὸ κατ' ἐμὲ πρόθυ-*
μον καὶ ὑμῖν τοῖς ἐν Ῥώμῃ εὐαγγελίσασθαι. 16 *οὐ γὰρ*
ἐπαισχύνομαι τὸ εὐαγγέλιον· δύναμις γὰρ θεοῦ ἐστὶν εἰς
σωτηρίαν παντὶ τῷ πιστεύοντι, Ἰουδαίῳ τε πρῶτον καὶ
Ἕλληνι. 17 *δικαιοσύνη γὰρ θεοῦ ἐν αὐτῷ ἀποκαλύπτεται*

gation to preach the gospel universally. His second classification of mankind into *σοφόι* and *ἀνοήτοι*, "cultivated and uncultivated," corrects any unfavorable inference that might be drawn, respecting the Romans, from the first classification. The Romans, though not Greeks, were *σοφόι*. *ὀφειλέτης*] sc. *εὐαγγελίσασθαι*. The obligation is to Christ.

VER. 15. *οὕτως*] as an *ὀφειλέτης*, that is. *τὸ κατ' ἐμὲ πρόθυμον*] may be resolved: 1. as equivalent to *ἡ προθυμία ἐμοῦ* (sc. *ἐστιν*); 2. *τὸ κατ' ἐμὲ* (sc. *ἐστιν*) *πρόθυμον*. The construction, *τὸ ἐξ ὑμῶν*, in xii. 18, favors the latter.

Verses 16 and 17 constitute a transition from the preface, to the subject of the Epistle. *ἐπαισχύνομαι*] hints at the scornful treatment which Christianity had received at Athens, Corinth, and Ephesus, the seats of Grecian culture. *δύναμις*] power needs not to be ashamed, and is not generally. In the human sphere it is accompanied with pride; in the divine, with calm confidence. *πρῶτον*] first in the order in which the gospel was to be preached; because "salvation is of the Jews," John iv. 22, and Jerusalem was the natural point of departure. Compare Luke xxiv. 47; Acts i. 8. *παντὶ*] shows that Christianity is a universal religion, and modifies the first impression of *πρῶτον*.

VER. 17. *γὰρ*] introduces the reason for the affirmation in verse 16. *δικαιοσύνη*] the absence of the article denotes that a peculiar and uncommon kind of righteousness is meant: "a righteousness," not "the righteousness" (Eng. Ver.). Two views have been taken. 1. *δικαιοσύνη* denotes an ob-

jective attribute of God: retribute justice (Origen); truth (Ambrose) ; benevolence (Semler). 2. δικαιοσύνη denotes a subjective state or condition of man, in which he is δίκαιος, as in iii. 21, 22. The quotation, in the context, from Hab. ii. 4, favors the second view. The righteousness in question is the personal possession of the believer, through the instrumentality of his faith. That it is an extraordinary righteousness, is proved by the subsequent description of it as χωρὶς νόμου, and χωρὶς ἔργων νόμου, and χωρὶς ἔργων, iii. 21, 28; iv. 6. The common righteousness, known to human ethics, would be described as δικαιοσύνη διά νόμου, or ἐν ἔργοις. It is personal and actual obedience. Viewed from the position of ethics, a "righteousness without works" would be a "righteousness without righteousness:" that is to say, no righteousness at all; because, in the ethical sphere righteousness is work itself, or obedience to law. Consequently, this evangelical righteousness of revealed religion, as distinguished from the ethical righteousness of natural religion, is a solecism and self-contradiction to the ethical philosopher. It is the play of Hamlet, with Hamlet omitted. It is foolishness to the Greek, 1 Cor. i. 23. θεοῦ] is the genitive of source. God, and not man, is the author of this peculiar species of δικαιοσύνη. The ordinary ethical righteousness, on the contrary, has a human author. Personal and actual obedience of the law is man's righteousness. Imputed obedience without actual personal obedience, is God's righteousness. ἀποκαλύπτεται] implies that this extraordinary righteousness is a matter of special revelation. It cannot be derived from the natural operation of the human reason. This would yield only the ethical righteousness of personal obedience. Its only utterance is: "Obey, and live." That "the man which doeth these things shall live," x. 5, is self-evident, and requires no special revelation; but, that "the man who worketh not, but believeth on him that justifieth the ungodly shall live," iv. 5,

ἐκ πίστεως εἰς πίστιν, καθὼς γέγραπται Ὁ δὲ δίκαιος ἐκ πίστεως ζήσεται.

18 Ἀποκαλύπτεται γὰρ ὀργὴ θεοῦ ἀπ' οὐρανοῦ ἐπὶ πᾶσαν ἀσέβειαν καὶ ἀδικίαν ἀνθρώπων τῶν τὴν ἀλήθειαν

is not self-evident, but depends for its credibility upon competent testimony to this effect. The reason why the δικαιοσύνη in question is not deducible by human reason, but must be revealed from God, is: 1. that it is a product of mercy. But, the exercise of mercy is optional, and not necessary. It depends upon the free decision of God, Rom. ix. 15, and this decision cannot be known to man until it is made known to him; and 2. that the compatibility of the exercise of mercy with the indefeasible claims of justice, is a problem insoluble by human reason. The use of the present tense implies that the revelation is not only objective, but subjective also. God revealed this righteousness in the written word, and is still revealing it in the experience of the believer. ἐκ πίστεως εἰς πίστιν] the revelation, from first to last, is made to faith. εἰς is telic; one degree of faith is in order to a succeeding greater degree. Compare the same law of spiritual increase in John i. 16.

§ 1. *The necessity of gratuitous justification.* Rom. i. 18–iii. 20.

In verses 18–32, St. Paul proceeds to prove that man must obtain the δικαιοσύνη θεου in order to future blessedness, by examining the moral condition of the *Pagan* world.

Ver. 18. ἀποκαλύπτεται] looks back to the same word in verse 17. According to the apostle, there are two revelations from God to man; one the written, by which mercy (χάρις) is made known; the other the unwritten, by which retributive justice (ὀργὴ) is made known. He designates them both by one and the same word, ἀποκαλυπτειν, because, in each instance, though in different modes, God is the efficient and man is the recipient. γὰρ] introduces the reason why God has revealed the δικαιοσύνη spoken of: namely, because he had previously revealed his ὀργὴ. This shows that mercy is meaningless except in relation to justice, and that the attempt, in theology, to retain the doctrine of the divine love, without the doctrine of the divine wrath, is illogical. ὀργὴ] not punishment merely (this is an effect of ὀργὴ), but a personal emotion in God which is the necessary antithesis to love. The New Testament, equally with the Old, attributes this feeling to the Supreme Being. Compare Mat. iii. 7; John iii. 36; Rom. ii. 5, 8; v. 9; ix. 22; Eph. ii. 3; v. 6; Col. iii. 6; Rev. vi. 16; xix. 15. Wrath, when ascribed to the deity, must be clarified from all selfishness, in the same manner that love must be. The divine love is not lust, and the divine anger is not rage. Both are energies and effluences from a holy essence; the one terminating upon good, and the other upon evil. The divine ὀργὴ is the wrath of reason and law against their contraries.

Respecting the mode in which this revelation of retributive justice is made, several views may be held. 1. In natural reason and conscience (Ambrose, Reiche); 2. In the day of judgment (Chrysost. Limborch, Philippi); 3. By giving man over to vice, verse 24 sq. (Meyer); 4. In all modes, internal and external (Tholuck, Olshausen). The last is best. πασᾶν] is anarthrous, to denote all kinds and varieties. ἀλήθειαν] is the natural knowledge of God described in verses 19, 20. This knowledge is "truth," because it corresponds to the real and true nature of God. ἐν ἀδικίᾳ] is instrumental; sin is the means by which the rational perceptions of man are rendered inefficacious in life and conduct. κατεχόντων] "holding down or under;" the pagan by self-will and inclination prevents reason and conscience from restraining his lusts and

ἐν ἀδικίᾳ κατεχόντων,
19 *διότι τὸ γνωστὸν τοῦ θεοῦ φανερόν ἐστιν ἐν αὐτοῖς· ὁ θεὸς γὰρ αὐτοῖς ἐφανέρωσεν.*
20 *τὰ γὰρ ἀόρατα αὐτοῦ ἀπὸ κτίσεως κόσμου τοῖς ποιήμασιν*

passions. "Veritas in mente nititur et urget, sed homo eam impedit" (Bengel, in loco). "Video meliora proboque, deteriora sequor" (Ovid, Met. vii. 20).

VER. 19. This verse is not to be separated from verse 18, because it explains why the wrath of God is revealed. *διότι*] is more precise and formal than *ὅτι*: "for the reason that." *τὸ γνωστὸν*] Meyer would render literally: "the known," not, "the knowable;" because all that knowledge which comes from written revelation is excluded, which is, of course, knowable. But the majority of commentators, in accordance with the classical use of the phrase, adopt the signification of *τὸ* scibile. In this sense, *τὸ γνωστὸν* denotes all that is knowable without written revelation, in the manner described in the context; and also implies that there is something absolutely unknowable. Compare xi. 33. *ἐν αὐτοῖς*] in their immediate self-consciousness; it is equivalent to *ἐν ταῖς καρδίαις*, Rom. ii. 15. *θεὸς ἐφανέρωσεν*] the self-consciousness is referred to God as the ultimate cause of it. This, in two ways: 1. God constructed the human mind so that it should have such a form of consciousness; 2. God immediately works upon the human mind as thus constituted. This operation is subsequently described in ii. 15, 16. St. Paul founds the responsibility of the pagan upon his knowledge of God. In proof, compare his own preaching to pagans, in Acts xiv. 13–17; xvii. 22–31. And he founds the guilt of the pagan which necessitates the manifestation of the Divine wrath, upon the abuse or non-use of his knowledge.

VER. 20 is exegetical of *θεὸς ἐφανέρωσεν*, and explains how God "shows" truth to man. *γὰρ*] introduces the explanation. ἀόρατα] the invisible attributes of God: afterwards specified as δύναμις and θειότης. ἀπὸ] "ever since." ποιήμασιν] the visible universe as opposed to the invisible attributes spoken of; the dative is instrumental. νοούμενα] this verb, as its etymon implies, denotes a perception by the reason. It is rational and not sensuous perception; intuitive and not deductive. καθορᾶται] the preposition is intensive. The invisible attributes of God are clearly perceived by the human mind, in the exercise of reason stimulated into activity by the notices of the senses. The merely sensuous vision of the earth and sky by a brute, would not result in the rational ideas of omnipotence (δύναμις) and sovereignty (θειότης), because the brute has not that rational faculty whose operation is properly designated by the verb νοεῖν. Yet the same physical sensations would be experienced by the brute, that are experienced by the man. δύναμις] the first impression produced by the visible creation is that of omnipotence. When all the other divine attributes fail to affect man, owing either to his vicious or his imbruted condition, that of almighty and irresistible power makes itself felt. Horace (Carminum, i. 35) confesses that he was "parcus deorum cultor et infrequens," until "Diespiter, igni corusco, per purum tonantes egit equos, volucremque currum." Says Tertullian (Ad Scapulam, 2) to the pagan: "We Christians worship one God, the one whom you all naturally know, at whose lightnings and thunders you tremble." Aristotle (De Mundo, c. 6) remarks: πάσῃ θνητῇ φύσει γενόμενος ἀθεώρητος, ἀπ' αὐτῶν τῶν ἔργων θεωρεῖται ὁ θεός. Similarly, Cicero (Tusculanarum, i. 23): "Deum non vides, tamen deum agnoscis ex operibus ejus." θειότης] divinity, in the sense of sovereignty or supremacy. The term is wide and somewhat vague, and purposely chosen to denote the general unanalyzed idea of God: a sum total of the divine qualities. It is god*hood*, not god*head* (Eng. Ver.). This latter term would require θεότης, as in Coloss.

νοούμενα καθορᾶται, ἥ τε ἀΐδιος αὐτοῦ δύναμις καὶ θειότης, εἰς τὸ εἶναι αὐτοὺς ἀναπολογήτους, [21] διότι γνόντες τὸν θεὸν οὐχ ὡς θεὸν ἐδόξασαν ἢ εὐχαρίστησαν, ἀλλ' ἐμα-

ii. 9, and would imply the trinitarian distinctions, to which St. Paul has no reference in the verse under consideration. The term θειότης is derived from the adjective θεῖος, and refers to qualities or attributes; the term θεότης is derived from the substantive θεός, and refers to the essence. Augustine (De Civitate, vii. 1) so explains: "Hanc divinitatem, vel, ut sic dixerim, deitatem; nam et hoc verbo uti jam nostros non piget, ut de græco expressius transferant id quod illi θεότητα appellant," etc. εἰς τὸ] is telic. God designed by this revelation of his attributes in human consciousness, that mankind should be inexcusable for any neglect or failure respecting them. St. Paul took the same position in his address to the Lycaonians, Acts xiv. 16, 17, and to the Athenians, Acts xvii. 27. ἀναπολογήτους] without excuse or reply, for not being subject to the divine supremacy and sovereignty.

VER. 21 mentions the ground of the inexcusableness, which is introduced by διότι. γνόντες] having known, in the manner described in verses 19, 20. The participle has a concessive or limitative meaning, as if καίτοι or καίπερ preceded (Kühner § 312; Winer § 45; Acts xxviii. 4). Although they knew God, they did not conduct accordingly. τὸν θεὸν] the article implies the true God. ὡς] denotes proportion; no worship corresponding to the worthiness of the object was rendered. ἐδόξασαν] denotes homage and adoration for what God is in himself. εὐχαρίστησαν] refers to gratitude for what God has done to benefit man. The two feelings of adoration and gratitude cover the whole province of religious feeling. ἐματαιώθησαν] "befooled themselves."

ταιώθησαν ἐν τοῖς διαλογισμοῖς αὐτῶν, καὶ ἐσκοτίσθη ἡ ἀσύνετος αὐτῶν καρδία· [22] φάσκοντες εἶναι σοφοὶ ἐμωράνθησαν, [23] καὶ ἤλλαξαν τὴν δόξαν τοῦ ἀφθάρτου θεοῦ ἐν

The absurdities of the mythologies and cosmogonies of paganism are examples. In the Old Testament, an idol is denominated "vanity," Deut. xxxii. 21; Jer. ii. 5. ἐν] is instrumental: "by means of." Compare ἐν ἀδικίᾳ, verse 18. διαλογισμοῖς]. The word denotes the rational, and not the imaginative faculty, as the rendering "imaginations" (Eng. Ver.) might suggest. The term "speculations" is nearer the meaning. The writer has in mind the great and perverse ingenuity with which the human intellect is employed, in inventing the various schemes of pagan idolatry. In illustration, see Creuzer's Symbolik, passim. ἐσκοτίσθη]. The relation between sin and mental blindness is that of action and re-action. Each is alternately cause and effect. Either, therefore, may be put as the cause. Here, the darkening of the intellect is represented as the effect of the foolish and wicked speculation; the liar comes to believe his own lie. καρδία] is put for πνεῦμα, or νοῦς, as in Mark ii. 6; Rom. ii. 15; 2 Cor. iv. 6.

VERSES 22 and 23 expand and reaffirm the statement made in the latter clause of verse 21. φάσκοντες] signifies an unfounded assumption. Compare Acts xxiv. 9. ἐμωράνθησαν] is the same verb that is employed in Mat. v. 13, to denote the loss of savour in salt. The apostle has in mind the insipidity of the pagan mythology; its flat and spiritless quality. The mythological legends are jejune and puerile. Even when a writer of great genius and great sense, like Bacon, in his "Wisdom of the Ancients," endeavors to discover a solid and valuable meaning in the myths of Greece and Rome, the endeavour is felt to be an effort. The "wisdom" is an im-

ὁμοιώματι εἰκόνος φθαρτοῦ ἀνθρώπου καὶ πετεινῶν καὶ τετραπόδων καὶ ἑρπετῶν. [24] *διὸ παρέδωκεν αὐτοὺς ὁ θεὸς*

portation rather than a deduction. The same remark is true, still more, of an attempt like that of Creuzer and Schelling to rationalize all mythology. ἤλλαξαν, etc.] There is a reference to Ps. cvi. 20. δόξαν] is kindred to ἀλήθειαν in verse 25. That knowledge of God which agrees with his real and *true* being, is also a knowledge of his *glorious* being. ἐν] is either 1. instrumental; or 2. a Hebraism for εἰς. The first is preferable, being favored by the construction of ἐν in the preceding and succeeding context (verses 18, 21, 24, and 25), and is adopted by such grammarians as Fritzsche and Meyer. The second supposes that the writer is quoting closely from the Septuagint version of Ps. cvi. 20, which translates הָמִירוּ בְּ by ἠλλάξαντο ἐν. But it is a free reference, rather than a quotation. ὁμοιώματι] the external figure with particular reference to *outline:* the "shape," as in Rev. ix. 7. εἰκόνος] the form generally: an image, or idol (from εἴδωλον, denoting a form of that which is in itself formless and invisible). ἀνθρώπου] St. Paul mentions the classical idolatry first in the order. The Greek and Roman employed the human form to represent the deity. πετεινῶν] the worship of the storklike bird Ibis. τετραπόδων] that of the bull Apis. ἑρπετῶν] the Serpent-worship. These stand for the more grotesque and hideous idolatries of Egypt and the Orient.

VER. 24. διὸ] introduces the reason for the action indicated by παρέδωκεν, which reason is found in man's abuse of the knowledge of the true God. παρέδωκεν] Chrysostom explains by permission (εἴασε). The permission of sin is a Biblical doctrine. See Acts xiv. 16, where εἴασε is used. But, παρέδωκεν is a stronger word than εἴασε. When God permits sin, he does not restrain, or in any manner counteract the human will. He leaves it to an absolutely free act of *self*-determination. In this instance, God's action is negative merely; he does nothing. But when God "gives up," or "gives over" the human will to sin, he *withdraws* an existing restraint which he had previously applied. In this instance, his action is positive, and privative; he does something. Again, the permission of sin is not necessarily a judicial or punitive act. The first sin of Adam was permitted, but not as a judgment or penalty. And when St. Paul, in Acts xiv. 16, alludes to sin as having been permitted "in times past," he does not bring to view the retributive aspects of sin, so much as the kind forbearance of God in dealing with it. Compare also Acts xvii. 30. But "giving over," or "giving up," man to sin is always and necessarily a judicial act. It is a punishment of sin previously committed. It is needless to remark, that when God "gives up" man to sin, he does not himself cause the sin. To withdraw a restraint, is not the same as to impart an impulse. The two principal restraints of sin are the fear of punishment before its commission, and remorse after it. These are an effect of the divine operation in the conscience; they are the revelation of the divine ὀργὴ in human consciousness. When God "gives over" an individual, he ceases, temporarily, to awaken these feelings. The consequence is, utter apathy and recklessness in sin. The restraint of fear now being withdrawn, the self-determination of the man is unimpeded, and intense. The vices mentioned in the context, to which men were given over, were unaccompanied with either fear or remorse, and were pursued with a cynical and brazen shamelessness. ἐν ἐπιθυμίαις] instrumental dative: the wicked lusts are employed by God as the means whereby the man is given up entirely to his own self-will. No restraint from fear, shame, or remorse is longer put upon them. The consequence is, that they become yet more rampant; and the

ἐν ταῖς ἐπιθυμίαις τῶν καρδιῶν αὐτῶν εἰς ἀκαθαρσίαν τοῦ ἀτιμάζεσθαι τὰ σώματα αὐτῶν ἐν αὐτοῖς, [25] *οἵτινες μετήλλαξαν τὴν ἀλήθειαν τοῦ θεοῦ ἐν τῷ ψεύδει, καὶ ἐσεβάσθησαν καὶ ἐλάτρευσαν τῇ κτίσει παρὰ τὸν κτίσαντα, ὅς ἐστιν*

consequence of this, is a deeper sinking in the filth of sin. The preposition ἐν is a favorite one with St. Paul, and often denotes not only the instrument *by* which, but also the element *in* which, anything occurs, or is done. In these instances, it is best rendered by the two prepositions "in" and "by," together. It has this complex meaning here. For the signification of the important term ἐπιθυμία, see comment on vii. 7. ἀκαθαρσίαν] is anarthrous, because of the peculiarity of the filthiness. τοῦ ἀτιμάζεσθαι] the infinitive is equivalent to a genitive exegetical of ἀκαθαρσίαν, like ποιεῖν in verse 28. The uncleanness was of a species that involved the dishonor of the body; legitimate sexual intercourse does not imply this. See Heb. xiii. 4.

VER. 25 restates the reason for the action in παρέδωκεν. It is of the same general nature with that given in verses 21–23, namely, the abuse of the natural knowledge of God. οἵτινες] denotes a class: "being such as." μετήλλαξαν] they had first changed the truth into error (verse 23), and then *ex*changed the one for the other. ἀλήθειαν] 1. the true and real nature of God (De Wette, Tholuck, Meyer); 2. the truth respecting God revealed in consciousness (Usteri). The first is preferable, because ἀλήθειαν is parallel with δόξαν in verse 23, where the reference is to the divine nature. ἐν τῷ ψευδει] "with the lie" of polytheism, i. e.: the instrumental dative, as in verses 23 and 24. Compare Isa. xxviii. 15; Jer. xiii. 25. ἐσεβάσθησαν] the inward homage of the soul. ἐλάτρευσαν] the outward worship (cultus) in ritual and ceremonies. παρὰ] 1. "beyond," in the sense of "more than"

εὐλογητὸς εἰς τοὺς αἰῶνας, ἀμήν. 26 διὰ τοῦτο παρέδωκεν
αὐτοὺς ὁ ϑεὸς εἰς πάϑη ἀτιμίας· αἵ τε γὰρ ϑήλειαι αὐτῶν
μετήλλαξαν τὴν φυσικὴν χρῆσιν εἰς τὴν παρὰ φύσιν,

(Erasmus, Luther, Vulg., Eng. Ver.); 2. "against," in the sense of opposition to, as in verse 26 (Fritzsche); 3. "instead of" (De Wette, Meyer, Winer). The last is preferable, and is favored by μετήλλαξαν. In the exchange, the creature was taken instead of the creator. The rendering "more than" is objectionable, because it implies that the creator was worshipped in some secondary degree that was exceeded by the worship of the creature. But there was no worship at all of the creator. ὅς ἐστιν, etc.] the doxology is suggested by the dazzling contrast between the true God and the impure idolatry. εὐλογητὸς] is applied only to God; μακάριος is the term for man. Blessing, when God is the object, is not the bestowment of good, but the ascription of honor and praise. The first sense is excluded, because "without all contradiction the less is blessed of the better," Heb. vii. 7.

Ver. 26 again mentions the reprobation. διὰ τοῦτο] refers to the sin described in verse 25. ἀτιμίας] is the genitive of quality. τε] "even" their females, etc. The sex which is naturally most shamefaced is in this instance the most shameless. "A shameless woman is the worst of men" (Young). ϑήλειαι] not γυναῖκες, 1. because the notion of sex is the point of view (Meyer); 2. because of the animalism of the sin (Reiche). Both views may be combined. μετήλλαξαν] has the same meaning as in verse 25. φυσικὴν] "sexual." χρῆσιν] supply τῆς ϑηλείας, because the vice spoken of was that of woman with woman, and because it is suggested by τῆς ϑηλείας in verse 27, which constitutes the second member of the sentence. παρὰ] "against," or "contrary to." Com-

27 ὁμοίως τε καὶ οἱ ἄρρενες ἀφέντες τὴν φυσικὴν χρῆσιν τῆς θηλείας ἐξεκαύθησαν ἐν τῇ ὀρέξει αὐτῶν εἰς ἀλλήλους, ἄρρενες ἐν ἄρρεσιν τὴν ἀσχημοσύνην κατεργαζόμενοι καὶ

pare Acts xviii. 13. φυσιν] "sex." The vice alluded to is that of the tribades: Aristophanes, Lysistrata, 110; Plato, Symposium, 191; Lucian, Amores, xviii., Dialogi Meretricii, v. 2; Juvenal, vi. 311 sq.; Martial, i. 91; vii. 67, 70. The language of Lear (iv. 6) is applicable: "Down from the waist they are centaurs, though women all above: but to the girdle do the gods inherit, beneath is all the fiend's; there's hell, there's darkness, there is the sulphurous pit, burning, scalding, stench, consumption."

VER. 27. τε καὶ] This formula is equivalent to et . . . que, not only . . . but also (Winer, § 53. Compare Acts iv. 27; Rom. i. 14; Heb. xi. 32). Not only did the women practice such vices, but likewise the men, etc. ἄρρενες] not ἄνδρες, for the same reason that θήλειαι is used in verse 26. φυσικὴν] "sexual," as in verse 26. ἐξεκαύθησαν] "burned *out*," or "*up*:" a stronger word than πυροῦσθαι, 1 Cor. vii. 9. The intensity of the appetite inflamed by unnatural instruments is denoted. ἄρρενες ἐν ἄρρεσιν] The vice in question is mentioned in Lev. xviii. 22; 1 Cor. vi. 9; 1 Tim. i. 10. The notices of it are singularly frequent in classical writers. See Herod., i. 135; Plato, Phædrus, 254–256, Symposium, 179–184, 191, 192, 217–219; Plutarch, Moralia, de Amore; Horace, Epodon, xi., Sermonum, I., iv. 27; Catullus, Carminum, xv., xvi.; Martial, Librorum, xi., xii.; Virgil, Bucolicarum, ii.; Suetonius, Nero, xxix. Compare Wuttke's Sittenlehre, I. 100–108. The freedom with which pagan writers speak of this sin contrasts strongly with the reserve of the sacred writers respecting it. St. Paul, Eph. v. 12, remarks, that "it is a shame even to speak of those things which are

τὴν ἀντιμισθίαν ἣν ἔδει τῆς πλάνης αὐτῶν ἐν ἑαυτοῖς ἀπολαμβάνοντες. [28] καὶ καθὼς οὐκ ἐδοκίμασαν τὸν θεὸν ἔχειν ἐν ἐπιγνώσει, παρέδωκεν αὐτοὺς ὁ θεὸς εἰς ἀδόκιμον νοῦν,

done of them in secret." And Sir Thomas Browne says of unnatural vices, that "they should have no registry but that of hell." The freedom and indifference with which even such moral writers as Plato and Plutarch allude to pederasty, illustrate the great difference, in respect to delicacy and purity, between pagan and Christian morality. ἀσχημοσύνην] "indecency." Plato (Symposium, 196) employs the term as the contrary of εὐσχημοσύνη, the graceful and decent. κατεργαζόμενοι] the preposition is intensive. Compare vii. 15, 17, 18. The indecency is unblushingly perpetrated. ἀντιμισθίαν] the recompense is the gnawing unsatisfied lust itself, together with the dreadful physical and moral consequences of debauchery. A celebrated actor, on walking through the syphilitic ward of a hospital, remarked: "God Almighty writes a legible hand." ἔδει] implies the necessity fixed and made certain by the divine appointment. πλάνης] the literal meaning of the word must be kept in mind; they had *wandered* away from the true God, in the manner described in verses 21–23. Compare the Latin and English *error*. ἐν ἑαυτοῖς] the evil consequences are internal: in their own souls and bodies; and mutual: communicated to one another, and received from one another.

VER. 28. The apostle now passes from the sensual to the *mental* sins, to which the retributive justice of God gives the heathen over. καθως] denotes both the cause, and the proportion. God withdrew his restraint, *because* they abused and misused their innate convictions, and *in proportion as* they did so. ἐδοκίμασαν] a paranomasia with ἀδόκιμον: "as they did not think it *worth while* (after trial), God gave

ποιεῖν τὰ μὴ καθήκοντα, [29] πεπληρωμένους πάσῃ ἀδικίᾳ
πονηρίᾳ κακιᾳ πλεονεξίᾳ, μεστοὺς φθόνου φόνου ἔριδος

them over to a *worthless* (after trial) mind." νοῦν] denotes, here, not intellectual perception, but moral disposition, as in Coloss. iii. 17. Νοῦς, in Scripture, like πνεῦμα, is sometimes put for καρδία. Compare Mat. v. 3; xxvi. 41; Rom. viii. 27. In this passage, it signifies the bent or inclination: what is denominated in Eph. iv. 23, the "*spirit* of the mind." The English word "mind," in like manner, sometimes denotes not perception but inclination, as in the question: What is your mind? In the English version of Rom. viii. 6, φρόνημα, which refers to the will, is rendered by "mind." The pagan, because of holding down the truth in unrighteousness, was judicially given over to a disposition, or inclination, that is vile and detestable. The νοῦς in the sense of intellect was still of value, but in the sense of heart and inclination was worthless. ποιεῖν] i. e. τοῦ ποιεῖν. It is equivalent to a genitive exegetical of ἀδόκιμον νοῦν: "an inclination to do." μὴ καθήκοντα] a litotes for detestable. The Greek conception of sin was weaker than the Hebrew, having an undue reference to the idea of the decorous and becoming, τὸ πρέπον. This is seen in the feebleness of some of the terms employed even by St. Paul. Compare ἀσχημοσύνη, i. 27; τὰ οὐκ ἀνήκοντα, Eph. v. 4; τὸ ἀνῆκον, Philemon 8.

VER. 29. πεπληρωμένους] 1. may agree with αὐτοὺς; in which case, the sins mentioned in verses 29–31 are causes of the action denoted by παρέδωκεν; 2. may depend upon παρέδωκεν; in which case they are the consequences of this action. The second is preferable, because πεπληρωμένους, etc., is most naturally to be regarded as epexegetical of ποιεῖν τὰ μὴ καθήκοντα. The sins now to be specified are intellectual and not sensual. Their seat is in the mind, and not in the body.

The Receptus reading, πορνείᾳ, is omitted by ℵABC Copt., Æth., Lachm., Tisch.; and it is improbable that the writer, having previously described the sensual sins of the pagan, should return to them again, and then mention but a single one. These mental sins are 1. general; 2. particular. The former are connected with πεπληρωμένους; the latter with μεστοὺς. πάσῃ] is anarthrous, because all sorts and varieties are meant. ἀδικίᾳ] "unrighteousness" is the most general term possible. πονηρίᾳ] "wickedness" is another general word. By Aristotle it is opposed to ἀρετή, and by Cicero is translated by vitiositas. κακίᾳ] "malice," or "maliciousness" (Eng. Ver.), is the inward temper, "the *leaven* of malice," 1 Cor. v. 8; as κακοηθεία (verse 29) is the temper exhibited in act. Aristotle defines κακία as a disposition to put the worst interpretation upon every thing, ἐπί τό χεῖρον ὑπολαμβάνειν τά πάντα. πλεονεξίᾳ] "covetousness" is not to be limited to the particular vice of avarice, but denotes the general sin of lust, or inordinate desire after creature-good, in preference to the Creator. Hence it is defined to be "idolatry," in Coloss. iii. 5. It is that wide form of sin which is forbidden in the tenth commandment. This latter is rendered by the Septuagint, οὐκ ἐπιθυμήσεις; and St. Paul, in Coloss. iii. 5, associates πλεονεξία with ἐπιθυμία κακή. μεστοὺς] like πεπληρωμένους, implies that the sins mentioned are not shallow and superficial, but deep and central. φθόνου] immediately follows πλεονεξία, because it is a phase of it. He who covets, or lusts after, a created good, envies another who possesses it. φόνου] "murder" naturally comes from envying another's possessions, and lusting after them. ἔριδος] "strife" with another for creature-good occurs in case the extreme of murder is not resorted to. δόλου] "deceit" is employed to aid in the strife. κακοηθείας] "malignity" is the outward manifestation of "malice" (κακία); envy, strife, and deceit, prompt various malignant acts.

δόλου κακοηθείας, [30] ψιθυριστὰς, καταλάλους, θεοστυγεῖς, ὑβριστάς, ὑπερηφάνους, ἀλαζόνας, ἐφευρετὰς κακῶν, γονεῦσιν ἀπειθεῖς, [31] ἀσυνέτους, ἀσυνθέτους, ἀστόργους, ἀνε-

Ver. 30. ψιθυριστὰς] "secret slanderers," or "backbiters." καταλάλους] "open calumniators." θεοστυγεῖς] Suidas gives both the active and passive significations, and assigns the active to St. Paul's use of the word here. The majority of commentators take this view. The classical use is the passive. The Vulgate has deo odibiles. The Peshito gives the active signification. This is favored by the context, in which all the other sins describe man's feeling towards God, and not God's feeling towards man. ὑβριστὰς] "insolent" in word or act. ὑπερηφάνους] "haughty" in temper and spirit. ἀλαζόνας] "boastful" is a term that denotes vanity rather than pride,—which latter is signified by ὑπερηφάνους. The distinction between the two is expressed in Swift's remark, that "the proud man is too proud to be vain." ἐφευρετὰς κακῶν] Tacitus (Ann., iv. 11) describes Sejanus as facinorum omnium *repertor*; and Virgil (Æneid, ii. 163), speaking from the Trojan point of view, styles Ulysses scelerum *inventor*. γονεῦσιν ἀπειθεῖς] As the virtue of filial obedience is placed in the decalogue, so the vice of filial disobedience is placed in this list of heinous sins.

Ver. 31. ἀσυνέτους] is the same term that is employed in verse 21 to describe the effect of sin upon the intellect. The sinner is without understanding in matters of religion. Compare 1 Cor. ii. 14. In the Old Testament, sin is folly, and the sinner a fool. ἀσυνθέτους] the alpha privative may denote: 1. an unwillingness to make a covenant: i. e., "irreconcilable," or "quarrelsome;" 2. a readiness to break a covenant when made: i. e., "treacherous," or "covenant-breakers." Meyer contends for the second signification,

λεήμονας, 32 οἵτινες τὸ δικαίωμα τοῦ θεοῦ ἐπιγνόντες, ὅτι
οἱ τὰ τοιαῦτα πράσσοντες ἄξιοι θανάτου εἰσίν, οὐ μόνον
αὐτὰ ποιοῦσιν, ἀλλὰ καὶ συνευδοκοῦσιν τοῖς πράσσουσιν.

citing Suidas and Hesychius, and asserting that the first has no support in usage. ἀστόργους] wanting even in respect to the στορή, or instinctive affection, of the animal world generally. ἀνελεήμονας] naturally follows the preceding word. If man loses the love of his own offspring, of course he loses all love of his race, and is without any compassion or sympathy. The Receptus, after ἀστόργους, inserts ἀσπόνδους ("without libations:" which were offered when enmities were reconciled); but it is omitted in ℵABDEG Peshito, Copt., Lachm., Tisch. This catalogue of sins is very similar to that given in 1 Tim. iii. 2–4.

Ver. 32. οἵτινες] denotes a class, quippe qui. All such as commit these sins know that they are sins, and that they are damnable. δικαίωμα] has two significations: 1. a statute, or commandment, Luke i. 6; Rom. ii. 26; viii. 4; Heb. ix. 1, 10. 2. a verdict, or decision, either of acquittal or of condemnation, Rom. v. 16, 18; Rev. xv. 4; xix. 8. The second is the signification here. St. Paul does not mean to say, here, that the heathen knew the law itself, as a statute or command of God. This he had already said. But that they knew the decision, or verdict of God respecting such disobedience of the law. ἐπιγνόντες] the preposition is intensive, and the participle is employed concessively: "although they clearly knew," in the manner described in verses 19–21. πράσσοντες] "practising:" frequent action is denoted. θανάτου] From the pagan point of view, this would be the punishments of Tartarus, some of which are represented as endless by Plato (Gorgias, 525). "They who have been guilty of the worst crimes, and are incurable by reason of their crimes, are made examples; for, as they are incurable, the time has passed, at which they can receive any benefit themselves. But others get good, when they behold them forever (τὸν ἀεὶ χρόνον) enduring the most terrible and painful and fearful sufferings, as the penalty of their sins. And Homer describes Tantalus, and Sysiphus, and Tityus as suffering everlasting (τὸν ἀεὶ χρόνον) punishment in the world below." Plutarch also (De sera numinis vindicta) represents the Furies as tormenting forever those whom Pœna in this life, and Diké in the future life, have failed to reform. Guilt is in its own nature endless; and hence the "fearful looking for of judgment," Heb. x. 27, is also in its own nature endless. From St. Paul's point of view, which is that of revealed religion, θάνατος is everlasting. συνευδοκοῦσιν] to take pleasure in seeing another commit a sin implies even greater depravity than to commit it personally. The viciousness is less impulsive, and more cold-blooded and Satanic. Compare 2 Thess. ii. 2.

Respecting the guilt of the heathen, the criterion laid down by St. Paul is also concisely stated in James iv. 17: "To him that knoweth to do good, and doeth it not, to him it is sin." Wherever the individual's character and conduct fail to come up to the individual's knowledge, there is sin. Any rational creature who knows more than he puts in practice is ipso facto guilty. Compare the author's Sermons to the Natural Man, pp. 78–122. Upon the general subject, see Tholuck, On the Nature and Moral influence of Heathenism, Biblical Repository, Vol. II.; Neander's Church History, I. 1–68; Wuttke's Sittenlehre.

CHAPTER II

1 *Διὸ ἀναπολόγητος εἶ, ὦ ἄνθρωπε πᾶς ο κρινων· ἐν ᾧ γὰρ κρίνεις τὸν ἕτερον, σεαυτὸν κατακρίνεις· τὰ γὰρ*

Ver. 1. The apostle now proceeds to consider the moral character and condition of the Jew, for the purpose of evincing that he, likewise, needs the δικαιοσύνη θεοῦ. διὸ] looks back to γὰρ in Rom. i. 18, and refers to the whole line of remark made in Rom. i. 18–32 respecting the connection of moral knowledge with moral obligation. ἀναπολόγητος] is forensic in meaning: without defence before the divine tribunal where the δικαίωμα (i. 32) is pronounced. ἄνθρωπε] is employed universally, but with the intention, in the writer's mind, to apply what is said of man generally to the Jew particularly. πᾶς] is the nominative explanatory of the vocative. Compare Mat. i. 20. κρίνων] denotes not merely the forming of an estimate, but the passing of a sentence. It is a universal trait in man, to sit in judgment upon the conduct of others. This is an additional proof that man possesses the moral knowledge that has been ascribed to him in chapter i.; otherwise he would have no rule to judge by. This propensity was stronger in the Jew than in the Gentile, because of his possession of the written as well as the unwritten law. It is rebuked by Christ, in Mat. vii. 1–5. ἐν ᾧ] 1. instrumental: the sentence that is passed is the very means by which the one passing it is himself sentenced; 2. supply χρόνῳ; 3. supply πράγματι. The last is simplest. τὸν ἕτερον] the article singles out the individual. κατακρίνεις] the prepo-

αὐτὰ πράσσεις ὁ κρίνων. 2 *οἴδαμεν δὲ ὅτι τὸ κρῖμα τοῦ*
θεοῦ ἐστὶν κατὰ ἀλήθειαν ἐπὶ τοὺς τὰ τοιαῦτα πράσσοντας·
3 *λογίζῃ δὲ τοῦτο, ὦ ἄνθρωπε ὁ κρίνων τοὺς τὰ τοιαῦτα*
πράσσοντας καὶ ποιῶν αὐτά, ὅτι σὺ ἐκφεύξῃ τὸ κρῖμα τοῦ

sition is intensive. The sentence which man passes upon his fellow-man comes back upon himself in yet severer form. τὰ αὐτὰ] not necessarily all the particular vices mentioned in the preceding chapter, but the same in principle. πράσσεις] denotes habitual practice, as in i. 32. ὁ κρίνων] is repeated for the sake of emphasizing the inconsistency of condemning a sin and yet practising it.

VER. 2. οἴδαμεν] Not the Jews particularly, but a general truth. Every one knows. δὲ] marks the beginning of the argument: "now" we know. This reading is supported by ABDEG Peshito, Recept., Lachm. The reading γὰρ is supported by ℵC Copt., Vulg., Tisch. κρῖμα] the judicial verdict. κατὰ ἀλήθειαν] impartiality is particularly intended, as the context shows. ἐπὶ] the sentence comes down upon them. τοιαῦτα] such as have been spoken of in Rom. i. 18–32.

VER. 3. λογίζῃ] is kindred in meaning to διαλογισμοῖς in Rom. i. 21: "Do you imagine?" δὲ] is correlative to δὲ in verse 2: "Now, we know, etc., . . . and, do you imagine, etc." ποιῶν αὐτὰ] For proof, see the terms in which Christ speaks of the Jews, Mat. iii. 7; xii. 39; xvi. 4; Mark viii. 38. τοῦτο] is contemptuously emphatic. ἐκφεύξῃ] the word denotes exemption rather than acquittal. The person addressed is supposed to imagine that he will escape the trial to which others will be brought. At this point, the Jew, though not named, is brought into view, and henceforth kept in view; for, exemption from the tests and punishments to which the Gentiles are liable was thought by the

θεοῦ; [4] ἢ τοῦ πλούτου τῆς χρηστότητος αὐτοῦ καὶ τῆς ἀνοχῆς καὶ τῆς μακροθυμίας καταφρονεῖς, ἀγνοῶν ὅτι τὸ χρηστὸν τοῦ θεοῦ εἰς μετάνοιάν σε ἄγει; [5] κατὰ δὲ τὴν σκληρό-

Jew to be his national prerogative. The Jewish feeling is indicated in Mat. iii. 7–9.

VER. 4. ἢ] "or," in case thou dost not thus imagine, "dost thou despise," etc. The particle introduces a new case. πλούτου] is emphatic by collocation. It is a frequent word with St. Paul: not a Hebraism, but a common term for abundance. Plato (Euthyphro, 12) speaks of πλοῦτος τῆς σοφίας. χρηστότητος] "goodness," in the sense of good-will, or kindness: not the attribute by which God is good (holiness), but by which he does good (benevolence). It is a general term, under which ἀνοχή and μακροθυμία are species. For the meaning of these, see comment on iii. 25. καταφρονεῖς] the contempt is in the disregard of the tendency of the divine goodness to produce repentance. ἀγνοῶν] "not recognizing." The word implies an action of the will along with that of the understanding. It is that culpable ignorance which results: 1. from not reflecting upon the truth; and 2. from an aversion to the repentance which the truth is fitted to produce. It is the "*willing* ignorance" spoken of in 2 Pet. iii. 5. Compare also the use of ἀγνοεῖν in Acts xvii. 23; Rom. x. 3. μετάνοιάν] sorrow for, and turning from, the sins that have been mentioned, and charged home. ἄγει] the present tense denotes the natural tendency and influence of the divine attribute of goodness. The context shows that this tendency was resisted and thwarted. The apostle is not speaking, here, of the effectual operation of special grace upon the human will, but only of common influences.

VER. 5. Not a continuation of the question, but an emphatic affirmative sentence stating the actual fact in the

τητά σου καὶ ἀμετανόητον καρδίαν θησαυρίζεις σεαυτῷ ὀργὴν ἐν ἡμέρᾳ ὀργῆς καὶ ἀποκαλύψεως δικαιοκρισίας τοῦ

case. κατὰ] denotes that the consequence, namely the wrath, is according or proportionate to the cause, namely the hardness and impenitency. καρδίαν] the heart, in the biblical psychology, includes the will. It *inclines*, Ps. cxix. 112; *seeks*, Deut. iv. 29; *lusts*, Rom. i. 24; *trusts*, Prov. xxxi. 11; *purposes*, 2 Cor. ix. 7; *turns*, Luke i. 17; *believes*, Rom. x. 9, 10; *repents*, Rom. ii. 5. An impenitent heart, consequently, is culpable, and merits the wrath of God. Compare Acts viii. 21, 22. θησαυρίζεις] the wrath accumulates, like waters at a dam, by being held back by the divine ἀνοχή and μακροθυμία. σεαυτῷ] denotes the individuality and voluntariness of the process. ἐν ἡμέρᾳ] "in," or "on," the day when the accumulated wrath will burst the limits of forbearance and long-suffering. This day is the great day of final judgment. ὀργῆς] defines the day of judgment, in reference to the wicked. ἀποκαλύψεως δικαιοκρισίας] defines the judgment day in reference to both the wicked and the good. The latter word is found only here in the New Testament. It is employed in patristic Greek, and in an anonymous translation of Hos. vi. 5, where the Sept. has κρίμα.

Verses 6–16 constitute a paragraph, in which there is a train of thought (suggested by the allusion to the day of doom in ver. 5) respecting: 1. The ethical ground of the judgment, namely, the character and conduct of men; 2. The subjects, Jews and Gentiles; 3. The rule of judgment, namely, the moral law, written and unwritten. In this connection, the apostle was not called upon to say anything about righteousness by faith, and therefore it is not mentioned. He speaks of law only, not of the gospel. He describes the legal position upon which man stands by creation,

θεοῦ, 6 ὃς ἀποδώσει ἑκάστῳ κατὰ τὰ ἔργα αὐτοῦ, 7 τοῖς
μὲν καθ' ὑπομονὴν ἔργου ἀγαθοῦ δόξαν καὶ τιμὴν καὶ

irrespective either of apostacy or redemption, in order to exhibit the principles upon which reward and penalty are distributed under the divine government. This answers the objection of those who allege that St. Paul here teaches legalism, or righteousness by works. The apostle no more contradicts himself here, than when he cites from Moses the ethical principle, "The man that doeth those things shall live by them," Rom. x. 5; or when he affirms that, "To him that worketh is the reward not reckoned of grace, but of debt," Rom. iv. 5. In this paragraph, the writer merely enunciates the principles of a universal legislation for moral beings. Whether disobedient man can attain salvation by them, is a question by itself, abundantly answered in the Epistle as a whole.

VER. 6. ἀποδώσει] applies to the recompense either of reward, or of punishment; either to remunerative, or retributive justice. κατὰ] denotes proportion, as in verse 5. ἔργα] the actions are the exponent of the heart, as in Christ's account of the last judgment, in Mat. xxv.

VER. 7. καθ'] "in proportion to," as in verses 5 and 6. ὑπομονὴν] denotes patient perseverance, and implies an abiding disposition. Compare Luke viii. 15. It is applied to hope, faith, and other graces, 1 Thess. i. 3; 2 Thess. i. 4; James i. 3. δόξαν] 1. the heavenly glory; 2. the divine approbation, as in John xii. 43. The latter meaning is favored by the context. The class of persons spoken of patiently labor after an approving sentence in the final judgment: after the plaudit, "Well done," Mat. xxv. 21. τιμὴν] is the honor that comes from the divine approbation. ἀφθαρσίαν] is the *blessed* immortality consequent upon the divine verdict

ἀφθαρσίαν ζητοῦσιν ζωὴν αἰώνιον· [8] τοῖς δὲ ἐξ ἐριθείας καὶ ἀπειθοῦσι τῇ ἀληθείᾳ, πειθομένοις δὲ τῇ ἀδικίᾳ, ὀργὴ

of approval. The theory of the annihilation of the wicked receives no support from this text, because that "glorious" immortality is here intended, in which the body of the believer alone is raised, 1 Cor. xv. 43; which he "inherits," 1 Cor. xv. 50; which he "puts on," 1 Cor. xv. 53; to "attain unto" which, he toils and suffers, Philip. iii. 11; and which he "seeks for," Rom. ii. 6. It is not that common immortality which is neither sought for, nor toiled after, but belongs to man merely as man. According to Acts xxiv. 15, both the just and the unjust are to be raised from the grave; but the resurrection-body of the believer is discriminated from that of the unbeliever by the epithet ἐπουράνιον, 1 Cor. xv. 40. All human bodies at the resurrection are "spiritual" bodies, in the sense that they are adapted to a spiritual world; but only the bodies of the redeemed are "celestial." The latter are raised "in glory" and "in power," 1 Cor. xv. 43; the former "awake to shame and everlasting contempt," Dan. xii. 2; the latter come forth from the grave to the "resurrection of life;" the former to the "resurrection of damnation," John v. 29. ζωὴν] sc. ἀποδώσει. This is a general term denoting all forms of felicity, as θάνατος, its contrary, denotes all forms of misery. The preceding context shows that it includes the glorification of the body, as well as the blessedness of the soul. αἰώνιον] There being no motive to deny that this term when used in connection with the happiness of heaven signifies endlessness, it is not denied.

VER. 8. τοῖς δὲ] sc. οὖσιν. ἐξ] with the genitive ἐριθείας, describes the trait with reference to its being a root or source of action. It is stronger than an adjective. Meyer compares ἐκ πίστεως, iii. 26; ἐκ περιτομῆς, iv. 12; ἐξ ἔργων νόμου, Gal. iii.

καὶ θυμός. [9] θλῖψις καὶ στενοχωρία ἐπὶ πᾶσαν ψυχὴν ἀνθρώπου τοῦ κατεργαζομένου τὸ κακόν, Ἰουδαίου τε πρῶ-

10; ἐξ ἀγάπης, Philip. i. 17. ἐριθείας] is not derived from ἔρις, as is proved by 2 Cor. xii. 20 and Gal. v. 20, but from ἔριθος, a laborer for hire; hence, "mercenary" or "self-seeking." The signification of the term is further explained by the following clause: καὶ ἀπειθοῦσι, etc. The persons spoken of do not follow after the truth, for the truth's sake, but from selfish and partisan motives, and there is, consequently, no true obedience. The Jew, more than the Gentile, it should be noticed, is now in the eye of the writer, and this hireling and partisan advocacy of the truth was a characteristic trait of the Jew: like the trait, previously mentioned (ii. 3), of fancied exemption from the trial to which the Gentile was liable. The passionate and impatient temper of the partisan is also the exact contrary of the ὑπομονή. πειθομένοις] there is no indifference in the will, or negative state of the moral disposition. Those who do not obey, positively disobey. ὀργὴ καὶ θυμός] sc. ἀποδώσεται, suggested by ἀποδώσει in verse 6. ὀργή, "wrath," is the inward feeling, and θυμός, "indignation," is the external manifestation. Both are free from selfish passion. See explanation of Rom. i. 18.

VER. 9. In this and the following verse, the writer concisely repeats, for emphasis, the principles of distributive justice enunciated in verses 6–8. θλῖψις καὶ στενοχωρία] sc. ἀποδώσεται. The former term refers more to the cause of the feeling, and the latter to the feeling itself. The latter is the more intense word, as 2 Cor. iv. 8 shows. The etymology (a tight or close place) denotes that the feeling is accompanied with a sense of helplessness. ψυχὴν] denotes the whole man, as in Rom. xiii. 1; the higher spiritual part being naturally put for the total person; particularly as the punishment,

τον καὶ Ἕλληνος· 10 *δόξα δὲ καὶ τιμὴ καὶ εἰρήνη παντὶ*
τῷ ἐργαζομένῳ τὸ ἀγαθόν, Ἰουδαίῳ τε πρῶτον καὶ Ἕλληνι.
11 *Οὐ γάρ ἐστιν προσωποληψία παρὰ τῷ θεῷ.* 12 *ὅσοι*

though not exclusively yet principally, falls upon the soul. κατεργαζομένου] the participle is intensive: "perpetrating." πρῶτον] first in order, as in Acts iii. 26, and first in degree: pre-eminence in privileges, if abused, carries pre-eminence in condemnation.

VER. 10. δόξα καὶ τιμὴ] See comment on Rom. ii. 7. εἰρήνη] is opposed to στενοχωρία. It is the term specially chosen by Christ to denote the spiritual blessedness of the redeemed. Compare John xiv. 27; xvi. 33. Christian peace is twofold: 1. the pacification of the remorseful conscience, through atonement; 2. the removal of the violent antagonism between will and conscience and the restoration of the serene equilibrium of the soul, through sanctification.

Ver. 11 assigns the reason of the procedure mentioned in verses 9 and 10, and is aimed at the Jew, who claimed special privileges before God. προσωποληψία] "partiality," or greater favor to one person than to another, when both have equal claims: as in the instance of parent and child, or of the government and the citizen. It is impossible that there should be partiality in the exercise of *mercy*, because there cannot be an obligation or claim of any kind, in this case. God may do as he will with "his own," that is, with that which is not due in justice. See Mat. xx. 10–15. But there may be partiality in the administration of *justice*. A reward equally due to two persons may be arbitrarily given to one, and arbitrarily refused to the other; one of two criminals may be arbitrarily sentenced, and the other arbitrarily released, by an earthly judge. No such "respect of persons" is found in God.

γὰρ ἀνόμως ἥμαρτον, ἀνόμως καὶ ἀπολοῦνται· καὶ ὅσοι
ἐν νόμῳ ἥμαρτον, διὰ νόμου κριθήσονται. 13 οὐ γὰρ οἱ

VER. 12. The apostle proceeds to prove his statement that God is impartial in the administration of justice, by considering the case of the Jew and the Greek respectively. γὰρ] introduces the argument. ἀνόμως] without the written or Mosaic law. Compare 1 Cor. ix. 21. ἥμαρτον] denotes an act deserving of condemnation, and implies the existence of an unwritten law; for, sin is impossible without law of some kind, according to iv. 15; v. 13. Plato (De Legibus, viii. 838) and Xenophon (Memorabilia, IV. iv. 19) speak of νόμος ἄγραπτος. The unwritten law has already been mentioned by implication, in τὸ γνωστὸν τοῦ θεοῦ φανερόν ἐν αὐτοῖς, i. 19. An unwritten revelation of the Supreme Being himself involves an unwritten revelation of his law. The law of conscience compared with the written law, differs from and is inferior to it, in the following respects: 1. It is less specific; 2. It is more exposed to honest doubts in particular cases; 3. It is much more liable to corruption and alteration; 4. Its sanctions are less explicit. Notwithstanding these deficiencies, however, the unwritten law is sufficiently clear to be transgressed; and sufficiently authoritative to constitute its transgression a sin. καὶ] emphasizes not ἀνόμως, but ἀπολοῦνται; the verbs are the emphatic words: "as many as have *sinned* shall also *perish*." ἀπολοῦνται] denotes the contrary of σωτηρία, i. 16; of ζήσεται, i. 17; of ζωὴ αἰώνιος, ii. 7; and consequently implies endless perdition. See comment on θανάτος, Rom. i. 32. ἐν] "in the sphere of," or "under." νόμῳ] is the written law: it is anarthrous, because the Mosaic law is meant. The phrase ἐν νόμῳ is the contrary of ἀνόμως. κριθήσονται] denotes a judgment or sentence of condemnation, as in Luke xix. 22; John iii. 17: "shall be condemned," rather than "shall be judged" (Eng. Ver.). St. Paul here

ἀκροαταὶ νόμου δίκαιοι παρὰ θεῷ, ἀλλ' οἱ ποιηταὶ νόμου δικαιωθήσονται [14] (ὅταν γὰρ ἔθνη τὰ μὴ νόμον ἔχοντα

represents the difference between the "perdition" of the Gentile and the "condemnation" of the Jew, as one of degree, not of kind. Both result from a decision in the last day (verse 16), from which there is no appeal. Hopelessness characterizes both. But the measure of guilt is greater in one case than in the other, and the degree of suffering is so likewise. Compare Christ's statement of the case, in Mat. xi. 21–24; xii. 41, 42; Luke xii. 47, 48. That servant which knew his lord's will clearly, and did it not, shall be beaten with many stripes; and he who knew it not clearly, but knew it dimly, and did it not, shall be beaten with few stripes.

VER. 13. ἀκροαταὶ] refers to the synagogue-reading of the Mosaic law. There is no such partiality in God as would declare a mere auditor of the law to be righteous. Compare James i. 22. δίκαιοι and δικαιωθήσονται] signify *pronounced* just, not made just, Luke vii. 29; Rom. iii. 4. Both terms denote a declaration or verdict merely, and suppose that the righteousness has already been wrought, or produced, upon the ground of which the person is "justified." ποιηταὶ] St. Paul here states an obvious principle of ethics. He who obeys the law will of course be denominated obedient, and declared to be a just person. It must be carefully noted, however, that the action denoted by ποιηταὶ is *perfect* and *complete* action. It is like that indicated by ὁ ἐργαζομένος in Rom. iv. 4, and intended in Gal. iii. 10, 12. A partial obedience is insufficient. Sinlessness in the inward disposition, and perfection in every outward act, are requisite to constitute a ποιητής. This would exclude all such obedience as is spoken of in the context, ii. 15, which is accompanied with alternations of self-reproach and self-acquittal. δικαιωθήσονται] is best connected with εν ἡμέρα, in verse 16; because the verdict is one pronounced by the Great Judge upon the great day. There is no conflict, here, with the doctrine of justification by faith. The writer cites an axiom in ethics, namely, that perfect personal obedience will be recognized and rewarded by that impartial Judge who is no respecter of persons, and that nothing short of this will be. That any man will actually appear before this tribunal with such an obedience, is neither affirmed nor denied, in the mere statement of the principle. The solution of this question must be sought for elsewhere in the Epistle.

VER. 14. With Lachmann and Meyer, we regard this and the following verse as parenthetical. St. Paul interrupts his course of thought, in order to illustrate the self-evident principle, that only doers and not hearers of the law shall be justified, by a reference to acts of morality and immorality, and the consequent workings of conscience, in the case of a pagan. Whenever the heathen obeys the monitions of conscience, in a particular instance, and performs an external virtuous act, his conscience "excuses" him. This is analogous to God's justifying the doer of the law, before his tribunal on the last day. Whenever, on the contrary, the heathen disobeys the command of conscience and does a vicious act, his conscience "accuses" him. In this case, he is a hearer only, and not a doer, and is condemned, and not justified. "Every man's conscience," says Tillotson, "is a kind of God to him, and accuseth or absolves him, according to the present persuasion of it." By the phrase: "do by nature the things contained in the law," the writer does not mean that sinless and perfect obedience which he has in view in *οἱ ποιηταὶ νόμου*, of verse 13, but only something resembling it, which serves to confirm the particular truth that he would enforce. The exegesis of the passage will prove this.

φύσει τὰ τοῦ νόμου ποιῶσιν, οὗτοι νόμον μὴ ἔχοντες ἑαυτοῖς εἰσὶν νόμος, [15] *οἵτινες ἐνδείκνυνται τὸ ἔργον τοῦ νό-*

ὅταν] "Whenever," denotes a hypothetical case, but one that may and does occur. γὰρ] introduces the analogous instance in which the principle is illustrated, that not the hearer but the doer is justified. ἔθνη] is anarthrous, to denote the heathen generally. The adjunct, τὰ μὴ νόμον ἔχοντα, shows that no particular pagan is intended. νόμον] the written law. φύσει] "by nature:" that is, from the operation of a natural impulse. The term implies that the action in question is founded upon something innate. Compare ii. 27; Gal. ii. 15; iv. 8. St. Paul has in view that spontaneous attempt to follow the law of conscience which is seen in every act of pagan morality. Whether the act is morally perfect or imperfect, holy or selfish, depends upon its motive, and must be decided by other considerations than the mere signification of φύσει. Both right and wrong, perfect and imperfect actions may be done "by nature," that is, from a natural impulse. τὰ τοῦ νόμου] is not equivalent to ὁ νόμος, in ii. 13, 27. It is fractional, denoting only some particular parts of the law, and not the law as a whole. Individual statutes, such as relate to external morality, are meant. The pagan does not obey the law in its entirety. That the Apostle has not in his mind such a spiritual and perfect obedience as is attributed to the ποιηταὶ of verse 13, and such as would be a ground of justification "in the day when God shall judge the secrets of men by Jesus Christ," is proved by ii. 15, where he speaks of an "*accusing*" conscience as still characterizing these very persons who "do by nature the things contained in the law;" and by iii. 9–12, where he affirms that Jews and Gentiles are "all under sin," and that "there is none righteous, no not one;" and also by iii. 20, where he asserts that "no flesh shall be justified by the deeds of the law," that is

μου γραπτὸν ἐν ταῖς καρδίαις αὐτῶν, συμμαρτυρούσης αὐτῶν τῆς συνειδήσεως καὶ μεταξὺ ἀλλήλων τῶν λογισμῶν

to say, by personal character and conduct. The doctrinal unity of the Epistle to the Romans forbids any other interpretation, to say nothing of the teaching of the Pauline Epistles generally, as well as of the other Scriptures. ἑαυτοῖς νόμος] The voice of conscience is authoritative, and menacing. Hence it is naturally denominated a *law*. Compare Aristotle's νόμος ὢν ἑαυτῷ, and Cicero's ipse sibi lex est.

VER. 15. οἵτινες] denotes the class. ἐνδείκνυνται] "show *out*," by the actions designated in ποιῶσιν. Whenever a pagan hears the voice of conscience he is an ἀκροατὴς νόμου. If he disobeys its command, and practises vices like those which St. Paul has previously spoken of, he is a hearer and not a doer. He is not "justified," but condemned by his "accusing" conscience. If, on the contrary, he refrains from a vicious act when tempted, he is a doer as well as a hearer of the law. His conscience "excuses." And although fear, or self-interest in some form or other, be the ruling motive of the act, it still has its justifying force. Though the act, in this case, does not spring from love, and is not a spiritual and perfect act, yet the conscience does not "accuse" the man of yielding. It does not impute a vicious act to him. On the contrary, it "excuses," or "justifies" him, *quo ad hoc*. ἔργον τοῦ νόμου] the particular work which the law enjoins: the "prescript" of the law. This term, also, like τὰ τοῦ νόμου, denotes only an individual statute, in distinction from the law as a totality. γραπτὸν] Compare i. 19; and νόμος ἄγραφος (Plato, Laws, viii. 838), νόμοι ἄγραφοι (Thucydides, ii. 37), and νόμιμα ἄγραπτα (Sophocles, Antigone, 454, 455). καρδίαις] is here put for πνεύματι or νοΐ, as in i. 28 νοῦς is put for καρδία, and in i. 9 πνεῦμα is put for καρδία.

See comment on i. 9, 28. The apostle has in mind, here, the understanding and not the heart; the intellectual perception of law and not the affectionate love of it. He is not speaking of that writing of the law in the human heart which is effected in regeneration, alluded to in Jer. xxxi. 33, 34; Heb. x. 16, 17; 2 Cor. iii. 3; but of that engraving of it in the human conscience which is effected in creation. That this is so, is proved by the substitution, in the context, of συνείδησις for καρδία. συμμαρτυρούσης] conscience *co*-testifies with the prescript of the law, respecting the agreement or disagreement of the act with the prescript. The statute says: "Thou shalt." Conscience replies, "Thou hast," or, "Thou hast not." There may also be a reference to the fact that conscience, by reason of its rigorous impartiality, seems to be an alter ego, objective to the man, bearing witness to his guilt or innocence as if it were a third party. Compare ix. 1. συνειδήσεως] con-scientia: the preposition in composition here, again, brings to view the dualism in the self-consciousness. In every act of self-acquittal or self-condemnation, there is an apparent duplication of the unity of the ego; that is to say, there are two psychological distinctions, one of which is the *subject* acquitting or condemning, and the other is the *object* acquitted or condemned. μεταξὺ] governs ἀλλήλων, so that the clause is equivalent to ἐναλλάξ, "alternately." ἀλλήλων] refers to λογισμῶν. The writer has in view *self*-condemnation or *self*-acquittal, and not a heathen's blame or praise of another heathen. λογισμῶν] "reflections;" the term denotes the reflex action of the mind whereby it turns in upon itself, and reviews its own agencies. κατηγορούντων] supply ἑαυτοις: the individuals themselves are the objects of the accusation. St. Paul mentions the accusing action of conscience first in the order, because this constitutes the major part of the heathen consciousness. There is vastly more of self-reproach than of self-acquittal in the pagan experience. Self-condemnation and remorse are the rule, because sin is the rule. For descriptions of this constitutional action of conscience, see Plato's Republic, i. 330; ix. 579. Even when there is a greatly imbruted moral state, there is often great remorse. Tiberius says to the Roman Senate: "Quid scribam vobis, patres conscripti, aut quomodo scribam, aut quid omnino non scribam hoc tempore, dii me deæque pejus perdant, quam perire me quotidie sentio, si scio." And upon this Tacitus remarks: "Adeo facinora atque flagitia sua ipsi quoque in supplicium verterant. Neque frustra præstantissimus sapientiæ firmare solitus est, si recludantur tyrannorum mentes, posse aspici laniatus et ictus; quando, ut corpora verberibus, ita sævitia, libidine, malis consultis, animus dilaceretur: quippe Tiberium non fortuna, non solitudines protegebant, quin tormenta peccatoris suasque ipse pœnas fateretur" (Taciti Ann., vi. 7). See also Ann., xiv. 10; xv. 36. καὶ] whether this be rendered "even," or "also," the implication is, that the "excusing" action of conscience is something *extraordinary*; more uncommon, certainly, than the "accusing" action. Had the writer deemed the one to be as common as the other, and both to be upon a parity, he would not have introduced καὶ. ἀπολογουμένων] this word is negative, denoting non-accusation or mere non-imputation, rather than positive praise and commendation: self-acquittal rather than self-approval. The best pagan life, as described in this passage, is not uniform. It is an alternation of vicious and virtuous actions, accompanied with an alternating experience of self-reproach and self-acquittal. And in the alternation, the "accusing" far outruns the "excusing," because the vice springs from an abiding disposition, while the virtue springs merely from a momentary volition. The former is the index of the real inclination, while the latter is the exceptional product of the will under the influence of fear or some prudential motive. Consequently, the "excusing" action of conscience, in the case referred to, is not equivalent to "the answer of a good conscience toward God," 1 Pet. iii. 21. This non-imputation of sin, or "justification" of the pagan, is relative only. It is not absolute and perfect, like that of the unfallen angels, which is founded upon sinless perfection, or like that of redeemed sinners, which is founded upon the righteousness of Christ. But though only an imperfect and relative justification, it furnishes an analogue by which to illustrate the dictum, that not the mere hearer but the doer is justified.

The defects in pagan virtue are the same that are seen in the legality, or morality of the nominal Christian. 1. It is fragmentary: not the ruling and steady disposition of the person, but a fractional and intermittent activity. 2. It springs from the impulse of self-interest, and not from the love and adoration of God. 3. It is vitiated by the pride of egotism. True and perfect virtue, like that of the seraphim, and of Christ, is meek and lowly. See Isa. vi. 2, 3; Mat. v. 5; xi. 29. An extreme instance is mentioned by Plutarch (On the Contradiction of the Stoics). Chrysippus remarks: "As it well beseems Jupiter to glory in himself and his life, to magnify himself, and, if we may so say, to bear up his head and have a high conceit of himself, so the same things do not misbeseem all good men, who are in nothing exceeded by Jupiter." Of the same spirit is the demand, attributed to Marcus Aurelius, addressed to the deity: "Give me my dues." It was in this reference, and as tested by spiritual tests, that Augustine denominated the virtues of the pagans, *splendida vitia*. In looking, therefore, for hopeful indications in paganism, the search should be to discover a sense of sin, rather than an assertion of virtue. The virtue of Socrates, as delineated in the Platonic Dialogues, though lofty and attractive, judged by a human standard, is defective. He himself acknowledges that the philosophic ideal of

κατηγορούντων ἢ καὶ ἀπολογουμένων) 16 *ἐν ἡμέρᾳ ὅτε κρινεῖ ὁ θεὸς τὰ κρυπτὰ τῶν ἀνθρώπων κατὰ τὸ εὐαγγέλιόν*

character is not reached by any man. His own moral estimates of some of the horrible vices of his time were indulgent, and deficient in ethical energy. And that cutting, contemptuous irony, and sense of superiority, with which Socrates often deals with the faults and transgressions of his fellow men, evinces that he had not attained to the gentle and compassionate virtue of St. Paul, as expressed in Gal. vi. 1. Moreover, the Socratico-Platonic view of sin, which makes it to be ignorance, and, sometimes at least, represents it to be involuntary, is theoretically unfavorable to virtue.

VER. 16. ἐν ἡμέρᾳ] has been connected with δικαιωθήσονται (Lachmann, Meyer); with κριθήσονται (Beza, Grotius, Griesbach, Winer); with ἐνδείκνυνται (Bengel, Tholuck); with ἀπολογουμένων (Rosenmüller, Koppe). Either κριθήσονται or δικαιωθήσονται may naturally be connected with ἡμέρα, because the condemnation or the justification alike denote an objective judicial decision, such as is passed on the day of judgment. But δικαιωθήσονται, being the nearer antecedent, is preferable. The action, on the other hand, denoted by the clause κατηγορούντων ἢ καὶ απολογουμένων is subjective, occurs as much upon one day as another, and is sometimes favorable and sometimes adverse. There is alternate accusation and excuse. But no such alternation in consciousness is possible on the day when God shall pass a final judgment. κρινεῖ] may denote a judicial sentence, either favorable or unfavorable; the context must decide which it is. κρυπτὰ] this term most naturally refers to sins. Men do not keep their righteousness secret from others. The sentence intended, consequently, is that of condemnation. κατὰ τὸ εὐαγγέλιόν] the day of judgment, and the mode of judicial procedure, are particularly

μου διὰ Χριστοῦ Ἰησοῦ. [17] *εἰ δὲ σὺ Ἰουδαῖος ἐπονομάζῃ*
καὶ ἐπαναπαύῃ νόμῳ καὶ καυχᾶσαι ἐν θεῷ [18] *καὶ γινώσκεις*

revealed in the New Testament, and in connection with the doctrine of redemption. Compare Mat. xxv.; John v. 28, 29; Acts xvii. 31; 1 Cor. iv. 5. μου] is used officially, here, and in xvi. 25. St. Paul speaks as an ambassador of Christ, "in Christ's stead." Compare 2 Cor. vi. 20. διὰ Χριστοῦ] "all judgment is committed to the Son," John v. 22, 27; Acts xvii. 31, et alia. The Redeemer of man is officially the Judge of man.

Ver. 17. St. Paul, in verses 17–24, now applies the maxim that not mere hearers but doers of the law shall be justified, to the Jew. In an anacoluthon (verses 17–20), and an antithetic interrogative sentence (verses 21–24), which taken together are equivalent to protasis and apodosis, he charges them with hearing and not doing. The same charge is virtually made by St. James, i. 22, 23. εἰ δὲ] is supported by ℵABD Peshito, Copt., Æthiop., Griesb., Lach., Tisch. δὲ is transitive: "Now," the case being so, that a mere hearer shall not be justified, "if thou art," etc. Ἰουδαῖος] a name denoting theocratic honor: "Judah, thou art he whom thy brethren shall *praise*;" יְהוּדָה אַתָּה יוֹדוּךָ, Gen. xlix. 8. Compare also Gen. xxix. 35; Rev. ii. 9. ἐπονομάζῃ] "art styled;" perhaps the middle signification is preferable. ἐπαναπαύῃ] denotes entire confidence. The Jew had no doubt that the decalogue was an infallible rule of conduct, and the Mosaic economy a divine institution. And this confidence had degenerated into a blind trust, as if the mere possession of such a law were enough. νόμῳ] anarthrous (ℵABD Lach., Tisch.), because, as in verse 14, the Mosaic law is meant, which is equivalent to a proper name. καυχᾶσαι] the Jew had reason to glory in the God of Israel, in the good sense,

τὸ θέλημα καὶ δοκιμάζεις τὰ διαφέροντα, κατηχούμενος ἐκ τοῦ νόμου, [19] πέποιθάς τε σεαυτὸν ὁδηγὸν εἶναι τυφλῶν,

of adoration and praise (v. 11; 1 Cor. i. 31), but the feeling had become mere boasting (2 Cor. x. 15; Gal. vi. 13).

VER. 18. τὸ θέλημα] the will of God as revealed in the Jewish scriptures. δοκιμάζεις τὰ διαφέροντα] compare Phil. i. 10. This clause will be explained, according as the several significations of the words are chosen and combined. δοκιμάζειν may mean: 1. to examine, or test, as in Luke xiv. 19, 1 Cor. iii. 13, 1 John iv. 1; 2. to understand, or discern (a result of the act of examining), as in Luke xii. 56, Rom. xii. 2, 2 Cor. viii. 22, Eph. v. 10; 3. to approve of, or to like (another result of examining), as in 1 Cor. xvi. 3, Rom. i. 28, xiv. 22. διαφέρειν may mean: 1. to differ, merely, as in Gal. ii. 6, iv. 1; 2. to differ for the better, i. e. to excel, as in Mat. vi. 26, xii. 12, 1 Cor. xv. 41. Hence, several renderings of the clause: 1. "Thou approvest the things that are more excellent" (Eng. Version); 2. "Thou discernest the things that are obligatory" (Peshito); 3. "Thou testest the things that differ" (Erasmus); 4. "Thou discernest the things that differ." The last is preferable, because the reference is to casuistry, or the settlement of nice questions in morals, upon which the Jew plumed himself. This is, also, the better rendering of the parallel passage in Phil. i. 10, because in verse 9 the writer mentions "knowledge" and "judgment" as the particular means by which his readers were δοκιμάζειν τὰ διαφέροντα. κατηχούμενος] this ethical discernment was the fruit of catechetical and synagogical instruction in the Old Testament, particularly the decalogue. The participle has an explanatory force: "*because* thou art instructed in the law" (Peshito).

VER. 19. πέποιθάς] implies personal assurance and un-

φῶς τῶν ἐν σκότει, [20] παιδευτὴν ἀφρόνων, διδάσκαλον νηπίων, ἔχοντα τὴν μόρφωσιν τῆς γνώσεως καὶ τῆς ἀληθείας ἐν τῷ νόμῳ, [21] ὁ οὖν διδάσκων ἕτερον σεαυτὸν οὐ

bounded confidence. τε] "furthermore:" the particle directs attention to a feature that adds decidedly to the description. ὁδηγὸν] this term, together with φῶς and παιδευτὴν and διδάσκαλον, refers both to the original intention of God that the salvation of the world should come out of the Jewish nation, and to the proselytizing disposition of the Jew. τυφλῶν] together with σκότει, and ἀφρόνων, denotes the Gentile or pagan world. Compare Isa. lx. 2; xlix. 6; Mat. xv. 14; Luke ii. 32; John i. 5.

Ver. 20. νηπίων] novitiates introduced probationally into the Jewish congregation. μόρφωσιν] the particular prescripts of the written law constitute a *form*, or *scheme*, corresponding to the inward essence of the law. Law requires to be embodied in statutes. γνώσεως and ἀληθείας] denote two phases of the same thing: the moral and religious truth contained in the law is something to be cognized by the human mind. Truth should be knowledge, and knowledge should be truth; and in knowing the decalogue, the two things were secured to the Jew.

Ver. 21. The casting of the apodosis into an interrogative form brings out more vividly than would an affirmative proposition, the contrast between the Jew's knowledge and the Jew's conduct, and shows clearly that he is a mere hearer and not a doer of the law. κλέπτειν] this infinitive, like μοιχεύειν, does not require δεῖν to be supplied, because the notion of a command is contained in the governing verbs. Compare Winer, § 44 b. St. James, v. 4, charges the sin of defrauding the laborer upon the Jew; and Asaph accuses the people of theft and adultery, Ps. l. 18.

διδάσκεις; ὁ κηρύσσων μὴ κλέπτειν κλέπτεις; [22] ὁ λέγων μὴ μοιχεύειν μοιχεύεις; ὁ βδελυσσόμενος τὰ εἴδωλα ἱεροσυλεῖς; [23] ὃς ἐν νόμῳ καυχᾶσαι, διὰ τῆς παραβάσεως τοῦ νόμου τὸν θεὸν ἀτιμάζεις; [24] τὸ γὰρ ὄνομα τοῦ θεοῦ δι' ὑμᾶς βλασφημεῖται ἐν τοῖς ἔθνεσιν, καθὼς γέγραπται.

VER. 22. μοιχεύεις] Christ frequently charges this sin upon the Jews, Mat. xii. 39; xvi. 4; Mark viii. 38. The ancient prophets often make the charge, Jer. v. 7; vii. 9; Mal. iii. 5. Compare James iv. 4. βδελυσσόμενος] the term denotes the disgust caused by a bad odor. ἱεροσυλεῖς] 1. Robbing pagan temples, which was forbidden, lest the people should be corrupted by the spoil, Deut. vii. 25; Acts xix. 37; 2 Mac. iv. 42; Josephus, Antiq., IV. viii. 10 (Chrysostom, De Wette, Fritzsche, Meyer). 2. Withholding of tithes, and thus robbing the Jewish temple, Mal. iii. 8, 9. There is also, perhaps, a reference to the desecration of the temple rebuked by Christ, Mat. xxi. 13; John ii. 16 (Grotius, Michaelis, Ewald). 3. Irreverence toward God, and profanation of the Divine majesty, Ezek. xxxvi. 33 (Luther, Calvin, Bengel, Hodge). Either the second or third is preferable to the first view, because the instances in which pagan temples were robbed by Jews were too infrequent to found a general charge upon. καυχᾶσαι] compare comment on ii. 17. τὸν θεὸν] the article denotes the true God, the author of the law. ἀτιμάζεις] the dishonor is described in the following verse.

VER. 24. γὰρ] introduces the proof that God is dishonored. δι' ὑμᾶς] "on account of your conduct." βλασφημεῖται] when applied to man, denotes calumny, Rom. iii. 8; and contempt, or blasphemy, when applied to God. γέγραπται] in 2 Sam. xii. 14; Neh. v. 9; Isa. lii. 5; Ezek. xxxvi. 23.

VER. 25. A new objection begins here. The failure of the Jew, like the Gentile, to keep the law has been proved.

25 *περιτομὴ μὲν γὰρ ὠφελεῖ, ἐὰν νόμον πράσσῃς· ἐὰν δὲ παραβάτης νόμου ᾖς, ἡ περιτομή σου ἀκροβυστία γέγονεν.*

The thought now occurs to the Jew that he is in special covenant-relations with God. The apostle takes this point into consideration: "You speak of circumcision: this is a benefit, if you keep the law; otherwise you have no advantage over the uncircumcised." μὲν] "Circumcision, indeed, if *that* is in your mind." ὠφελεῖ] how it profits is stated in iii. 2; iv. 11. 1. Circumcision, like a seal upon a document, formally authenticates the fact that the Jews alone, of all peoples, have been taken into covenant by the invisible God, and are under his special protection, for a certain particular purpose which he intends to accomplish by them. 2. This covenant puts the Jews in possession of a written revelation, which the Gentile world did not have. St. Paul (iii. 2) states that this is the principal benefit (πρῶτον ὅτι) accruing to them from the covenant. ἐὰν πράσσῃς] The benefits of the covenant of circumcision, between Jehovah and Israel, were conditioned upon "keeping his statutes, and his commandments, and his judgments," Deut. xxvi. 17. The word πράσσῃς denotes here a perfect performance, like ποιητής in ii. 13. Only in case of a complete fulfilment of the terms of the covenant upon his own side, was the Jew legally entitled to the blessings promised upon God's side. "Every man that is circumcised is a debtor to do the *whole* law," Gal. v. 3. This is how the matter stands upon principles of justice, with which alone St. Paul is concerned at this point. The Jewish objector appeals to justice. He claims justification before God, because God has made a covenant with him and sealed it with circumcision. Upon this ground he maintained that a Jew would not be condemned at the last day. Meyer quotes from a Jewish Rabbi, the assertion: "Quandoquidem circumcisi sumus, in infernum non descendimus." νόμον] is frequently employed by St. Paul to denote the Old Testament economy as a whole. This economy was two-fold, having a legal and an evangelical phase: the former preparatory to the latter, Gal. iv. 24–26. The apostle here has the legal phase in view. He is considering the covenant of circumcision as a covenant of works. As such, its benefits depended upon the *perfect* performance of the conditions. "Circumcision is nothing, but the keeping of the commandments of God," 1 Cor. vii. 19. Compare Gal. v. 6; vi. 15. These conditions were never perfectly performed by any Jew whatsoever. Two courses might be taken. 1. The Jew might assume the attitude of the "Jew outwardly," Rom. ii. 28, and demand the fulfilment of the covenant upon God's part, because of the circumcision of the flesh, without the circumcision of the heart (Deut. x. 16; Jer. iv. 4; Coloss. ii. 11), and because of moral and ceremonial obedience. This was formalism and legality, and to be met, as St. Paul meets it here, by a strict application of the principles of justice as involved in the covenant itself. 2. The Jew might take the attitude of the "Jew inwardly," Rom. ii. 29, who knowing that his obedience though sincere and spiritual was yet imperfect, and therefore not sufficient to found a claim for justification upon, cast himself upon the Divine promise made to Abraham and to faith in the Messiah. In this case, the legal covenant of circumcision prepared the way for the evangelical covenant of grace: both covenants being comprised in the Old Economy. περιτομή ἀκροβυστία γέγονεν] Since, according to 1 Cor. vii. 19, "circumcision is nothing, and uncircumcision is nothing, but the keeping of the commandments of God" [is everything], it follows that the absence of obedience will render the first of these "nothings," or non-essentials, as valueless as the second. The Jew, if disobedient, derives no benefit from the covenant. The written revelation does not profit him, and the abused bless-

[26] ἐὰν οὖν ἡ ἀκροβυστία τὰ δικαιώματα τοῦ νόμου φυλάσσῃ,
οὐχ ἡ ἀκροβυστία αὐτοῦ εἰς περιτομὴν λογισθήσεται, [27] καὶ

ings of the theocracy increase his condemnation. He is no better off than a Gentile.

VER. 26. ἡ ἀκροβυστία] is put for οἱ ἀκρόβυστοι. δικαιώματα] the statutes severally of the νόμος. ἐὰν φυλάσσῃ] perfect keeping of the law is meant, as in i. 13, 25. That it is only a hypothesis, for the sake of the argument, and not an actual case, is evident from the context. It is improbable that St. Paul concedes instances of perfect obedience amongst the pagans, in the very midst of an argument to prove that there are none such among the Jews. αὐτοῦ] instead of αὐτῆς, because the concrete person is meant by ἡ ἀκροβυστία. λογισθήσεται] This passage clearly illustrates the meaning of gratuitous imputation. There is no circumcision, confessedly, in the case of the Gentile, yet it is reckoned, or regarded, as belonging to the Gentile. This may be done for the same reason that "circumcision becomes uncircumcision" (verse 25); namely, because the perfect obedience of the law which is supposed in the case is the essential thing, and makes the non-essential of uncircumcision to be as good as the non-essential of circumcision.

VER. 27. This verse may be regarded: 1. as continuing the question (Eng. Version, Fritzsche, Olshausen, Lachmann, Philippi, Wordsworth); 2. as categorical (Chrysost., Erasmus, Luther, Bengel, De Wette, Tholuck, Meyer, Tisch.). According to this latter view, the question ends with verse 26, and the affirmative "yes," is mentally supplied at the beginning of verse 27. The interrogative construction is the simpler of the two, and κρινεῖ may have the emphatic force indicated by its position, as easily as with the categorical construction. κρινεῖ] denotes condemnation, the

κρινεῖ ἡ ἐκ φύσεως ἀκροβυστία τὸν νόμον τελοῦσα σὲ τὸν διὰ γράμματος καὶ περιτομῆς παραβάτην νόμου; 28 οὐ γὰρ ὁ ἐν τῷ φανερῷ Ἰουδαῖός ἐστιν, οὐδὲ ἡ ἐν τῷ φανερῷ ἐν

contrary of εἰς περιτομὴν λογισθήσεται, which stands for justification. If a Gentile should perfectly obey the law, he would thereby demonstrate, positively, the justice of his own acquittal, and, negatively, that of the condemnation of the disobedient Jew. ἐκ φύσεως] "by birth:" Gal. ii. 15. τελοῦσα] the participle has a conditional force: "If it fulfil" (Eng. Ver.). Had the writer intended to assert an actual fulfilment of the law, he would have written ἡ τελοῦσα. διὰ γράμματος] the instrumental genitive. The Jew, by a perverted use of them, converts the written law and the rite of circumcision, into the means and instruments of sin. It is an instance in which disobedience and death are wrought out by means of "that which is good," vii. 13. There is no need of attributing to διὰ the "loose" sense of "being in possession of" (Winer, p. 379).

VER. 28. In the first proposition, the ellipsis is in the subject: οὐ γὰρ ὁ ἐν τῷ φανερῷ [Ἰουδαῖος], Ἰουδαῖός ἐστιν. In the second proposition, the ellipsis is in the predicate: οὐδὲ ἡ ἐν τῷ φανερῷ ἐν σαρκὶ περιτομή [περιτομή ἐστιν]. Other arrangements multiply the ellipses, by finding them in both subject and predicate together. γὰρ] introduces a statement which is to confirm the positions that have been taken in verses 26 and 27. φανερῷ] denotes what is visible to the eye of sense, namely, circumcision, fasting, phylacteries, attendance upon ceremonies, etc. Ἰουδαῖός] is emphatic by position, and does not require ἀληθινός to be supplied. The same truth is taught in ix. 6, 7. ἐν σαρκὶ] is explanatory of ἐν τῷ φανερῷ. It is here employed as the opposite of πνεῦμα. As thus antithetic to each other, σάρξ denotes what is pretended and for-

σαρκὶ περιτομή, 29 *ἀλλ' ὁ ἐν τῷ κρυπτῷ Ἰουδαῖος, καὶ περιτομὴ καρδίας ἐν πνεύματι οὐ γράμματι, οὗ ὁ ἔπαινος οὐκ ἐξ ἀνθρώπων ἀλλὰ ἐκ τοῦ θεοῦ.*

mal, and πνεῦμα what is genuine and true. Compare John iv. 23; Rom. i. 9. περιτομή] merely physical circumcision does not comprise all that God intended, when he established the rite. It is therefore not real and full circumcision.

VER. 29. The ellipsis is in the predicate in both propositions (Beza, De Wette, Tholuck): ὁ ἐν τῷ κρυπτῷ Ἰουδαῖος [Ἰουδαῖος ἐστιν], καὶ περιτομὴ καρδίας ἐν πνεύματι οὐ γράμματι [περιτομὴ ἐστιν]. ἐν κρυπτῷ] the contrary of ἐν φανερῷ, referring to the inward disposition which is hidden from the eye of man. Compare τὰ κρυπτὰ in ii. 16. The Jew was marked off from the Gentile by the rite of circumcision, and by the observance of the Mosaic law. If these marks were outward merely, he was a Jew outwardly; if inward, that is, if the heart was circumcised and the obedience spiritual, he was a Jew inwardly. περιτομὴ καρδίας] is explanatory of ἐν κρυπτῷ Ἰουδαῖος. The Jew inwardly is one whose circumcision is not a mere surgical operation (χειροποιήτος, Coloss. ii. 11), but that of the heart (Deut. x. 16; Jer. iv. 4). ἐν πνεύματι] explains καρδίας. It denotes, here, the inner man, as opposed to the outer. Compare 2 Cor. iv. 16. Some commentators (Calvin, De Wette, Fritzsche, Meyer, Hodge) refer πνεῦμα to the Holy Spirit as producing this inward circumcision and obedience, in sanctification. The objections to this are: 1. that καρδίας does not have this signification; 2. that ἐν πνεύματι is employed as the contrary of ἐν σαρκὶ, in a technical manner; and, 3. that the introduction of the Person of the Holy Spirit in his office of sanctification at this point in the epistle would be premature. St. Paul reserves this topic, until after he has discussed justification. Compare v. 5; vi.–

viii. That this inward and spiritual Judaism is the work of the Holy Spirit is a truth subsequently taught. οὐ γράμματι] defines, negatively, the meaning of ἐν πνεύματι. Merely external circumcision was obedience of the letter of the law; merely external obedience is the same thing. Language is an imperfect medium of ideas, especially of religious ideas. It suggests more than it says. He who sticks in the letter (in the phrase of Horace), loses the deeper spiritual meaning. Hence, obedience of the mere letter of a law may be not only failure to obey, but actual disobedience itself. Conquently ἐν γράμματι denotes the same as ἐν φανερῷ and ἐν σαρκὶ. For the technical antithesis between spirit and letter, see vii. 6; 2 Cor. iii. 6. οὗ] the masculine is employed, because the concrete person is meant. Compare αὐτοῦ, in ii. 26. ἔπαινος] is, perhaps, an allusion to Gen. xlix. 8: "Judah, thou art he whom thy brethren shall *praise*." Compare Gen. xxix. 35.

CHAPTER III

[1] *Τί οὖν τὸ περισσὸν τοῦ Ἰουδαίου, ἢ τίς ἡ ὠφέλεια τῆς περιτομῆς;* [2] *πολὺ κατὰ πάντα τρόπον. πρῶτον μὲν*

The objection occurs that if the Jew, equally with the Gentile, is a hearer and not a doer of the law, and like the Gentile cannot be justified by the law, then Judaism has no superiority of any kind over Paganism. The first eight verses of this chapter contain an answer to this objection.

Ver. 1. *οὖν*] introduces the objection. What "then," in view of what has been said respecting the Jew, in chapter ii. It is immaterial, whether the objection be regarded as made by the Jew, or by St. Paul from the logical movement of his own thought. *τὸ περισσὸν*] the *plus*, or overplus: something additional to the natural religion and ethics described in i. 19, 20; ii. 14–17. *ἢ*] "or, in other words." *ὠφέλεια τῆς περιτομῆς*] explains *περισσὸν*. Whatever superiority there was, was connected with the Abrahamic covenant of circumcision.

Ver. 2. *πάντα τρόπον*] "in whatever manner it be viewed." *πρῶτον μὲν*] "first," with no secondly. Compare i. 8; 1 Cor. xi. 18. Calvin and Beza render præcipue; Eng. Ver. "chiefly." The fact that the particular which he is about to mention is first in order, implies that it is first in importance. The possession of the written revelation is the principal prerogative of the theocracy. Tischendorf and Meyer, following ℵADL, insert *γάρ* ("namely") after *μὲν*;

ὅτι ἐπιστεύθησαν τὰ λόγια τοῦ θεοῦ. 3 *τί γάρ, εἰ ἠπίστησάν τινες; μὴ ἡ ἀπιστία αὐτῶν τὴν πίστιν τοῦ θεοῦ καταρ-*

we omit it, following Lachmann BDEG Peshito, Copt., Æthiop., Vulg. ἐπιστεύθησαν] "were intrusted with." See Winer, p. 229, Thayer's Ed. A formal bestowment, and a solemn commission, are intended. The Jews were the depositaries of revelation by divine appointment. λόγια] "oracles:" the term denotes special disclosures from God. This is the meaning in classical writers. For the Biblical usage, compare Acts vii. 38; Heb. v. 12; 1 Pet. iv. 11. These oracles comprise supernatural instruction: 1. respecting the moral law and man's disobedience of it; 2. respecting God's mercy. The revelation intrusted to the Jewish theocracy contained the decalogue, and the Messianic promises and prophecies: the law and the gospel together. The latter, especially, constituted a high prerogative. As the depositary of the only certain and authentic information possessed by man respecting the forgiveness of sin and a blessed immortality, the Jew had a great περισσὸν over the Gentile.

VER. 3. γὰρ] introduces an argument to answer an objection that is not formally stated, but is implied in the answer: namely, that the Jews have not believed these oracles. The argument is, that disbelief of the promise does not invalidate the promise. ἠπίστησάν] the unbelief, though covering the whole revelation yet related more to the gospel than to the law; more to the Messiah than to the decalogue. The Jews, previous to the Advent, had misinterpreted the Messianic prophecies, and had desired a merely temporal prince and savior; and since the Advent, they had positively rejected Jesus Christ. τινες] "some:" not all. Says God: "I have reserved to myself seven thousand men who have not bowed

γήσει; 4 μὴ γένοιτο· γινέσθω δὲ ὁ θεὸς ἀληθής, πᾶς δὲ ἄνθρωπος ψεύστης, καθάπερ γέγραπται Ὅπως ἂν δικαιωθῇς
ἐν τοῖς λόγοις σου καὶ νικήσῃς ἐν τῷ κρίνεσθαί σε. 5 εἰ

the knee to Baal;" and St. Paul adds: "Even at this present time, also, there is a remnant according to the election of grace," xi. 4, 5. Up to the time of St. Paul, the majority of the people of Israel had been unbelievers in the true Messiah, yet he speaks of them as τινες. The remark of Lange (in loco) explains this: "In view of the certain final fulfilment of the Divine promise, this mass of apostate Jews is only a small crowd of individuals, *some*." See xi. 25, 26. μὴ] the subjective negative implies an answer in the negative. πίστιν] with θεοῦ in the subjective genitive, means "credibility," or trustworthiness. Compare 2 Tim. ii. 13; 1 Cor. i. 9. καταργήσει] is a strong word, denoting total destruction, or annihilation. It is frequently used by St. Paul; and in the New Testament is found outside of the Pauline Epistles only in Luke xiii. 7: a linguistic evidence for the Pauline supervision of this gospel.

VER. 4. μὴ γένοιτο] a denial accompanied with abhorrence: absit, "far be it;" "God forbid" (Eng. Ver.). It is equivalent to חָלִילָה, which the Septuagint (Gen. xiiv. 17) translates μὴ γένοιτο. Compare the Latin ad profana, and the English, "To the devil." γινέσθω] is equivalent to φανερούσθω. The notion of a development, or manifestation, is expressed by γίνομαι. ψεύστης] Compare Ps. cxvi. 11. γέγραπται] in Ps. li. 4. δικαιωθῇς] the forensic meaning here is indisputable. God cannot be made just. κρίνεσθαί] is best taken in the middle signification: "in thy litigating, or contest" (Beza, Bengel, Tholuck, Meyer). In the court, before which God is represented as condescending to implead, he is victor. It should be noticed, that St. Paul does not here

δὲ ἡ ἀδικία ἡμῶν θεοῦ δικαιοσύνην συνίστησιν, τί ἐροῦμεν; μὴ ἄδικος ὁ θεὸς ὁ ἐπιφέρων τὴν ὀργήν; κατὰ ἄνθρωπον λέγω. [6] μὴ γένοιτο· ἐπεὶ πῶς κρινεῖ ὁ θεὸς τὸν

resort to syllogistic reasoning to prove God's veracity, but to the idea of God, as that of a necessarily perfect Being. Even if, by so asserting, all finite beings should be proved to be false, yet the assertion that the Infinite Being is true must be maintained. The conception of the Infinite necessitates this.

Ver. 5 contains an objection from a confessed transgressor. It may be raised by both Jew and Gentile convicted of sin by the previous reasoning, or by the apostle for them. The use of ἡμῶν, and the interrogative form, favors the latter view. The objection is suggested by δικαιωθῇς and νικήσεις: "Granting the fact of sin, since sin results in the glory of God why should it be punished?" ἀδικία] is more generic than ἀπιστία (verse 3), and comprises unrighteousness of every kind. δικαιοσύνην] is also generic, embracing righteousness of every kind. συνίστησιν] "evinces," or "demonstrates." The word denotes a thorough and complete proof. Compare v. 8; 2 Cor. vii. 11; Gal. ii. 18. μὴ] the subjective negative implies not only a negative answer, but a hesitation in even putting the question. The objecter does not feel that the objection is a strong one, as the τί ἐροῦμεν also indicates. κατὰ ἄνθρωπον] "as men are wont to speak." Tholuck observes that this phrase, like τί ἐροῦμεν, is characteristic of Rabbinical argumentation, and shows the apostle's training.

Ver. 6. ἐπεὶ] "since," if this were true, i. e. πῶς κρινεῖ] The emphasis is to be placed upon κρινεῖ. If to punish the wicked is injustice, how can God exercise the office of a *judge?* κόσμον] not the pagan world, whom the Jew ac-

κόσμον; [7] εἰ γὰρ ἡ ἀλήθεια τοῦ θεοῦ ἐν τῷ ἐμῷ ψεύσματι ἐπερίσσευσεν εἰς τὴν δόξαν αὐτοῦ, τί ἔτι κἀγὼ ὡς ἁμαρτωλὸς κρίνομαι; [8] καὶ μὴ καθὼς βλασφημούμεθα καὶ

knowledged could be justly punished (Reiche, Olshausen), but the whole world (De Wette, Tholuck, Meyer).

Ver. 7 returns to the objection stated in verse 5; restating and expanding it. This makes the sentiment of verse 6 somewhat premature, logically considered. The apostle, in the energy of his conception, repels the objection with abhorrence and argues against it, before he has fully concluded the statement of it. The reading εἰ γὰρ is preferable, being supported by BDEGL Peshito, Vulg., Rec., Lachm., Tisch., 1859. The reading εἰ δὲ is supported by ℵA Copt., Tisch., 1872. γὰρ resumes the statement of the objection: "for, the sinner might say, 'If,' etc." ἀλήθεια] refers back to ἀληθής in verse 4. ψεύσματι] is one form of the ἀδικία of verse 5, by which the righteousness of God is "commended." ἐπερίσσευσεν] "*appears* more abundant." δόξαν] corresponds to δικαιοσύνην συνίστησιν of verse 5: that which evinces God's righteousness promotes God's glory. κἀγὼ] is correlative to τῷ ἐμῷ. κρίνομαι] denotes a condemning judgment.

Ver. 8 continues the restatement and expansion of the objection: "Why should not we not only be free from punishment, but also continue to sin, in order to cause God's glory to abound still more?" After καὶ] supply τί. With μὴ] supply either λέγωμεν (Calvin), or ποιήσωμεν (Luther, Bengel), or regard ὅτι as a recitative particle and construe μὴ with ποιήσωμεν (Vulg., Erasmus, Beza). The last is simplest. βλασφημούμεθα] when applied to man signifies calumny, or slander. φασίν] the difference between this and λέγειν is exemplified in 1 Cor. x. 12. The first denotes affirmation, the last recital merely. The attribution, by the Jews, of this

καθώς φασίν τινες ἡμᾶς λέγειν ὅτι ποιήσωμεν τὰ κακὰ ἵνα ἔλθῃ τὰ ἀγαθά; ὧν τὸ κρῖμα ἔνδικον ἐστίν.

9 Τί οὖν; προεχόμεθα; οὐ πάντως· προῃτιασάμεθα γὰρ Ἰουδαίους τε καὶ Ἕλληνας πάντας ὑπὸ ἁμαρτίαν εἶναι,

maxim of the Jesuits to the early Christians, probably sprung from the Christian's neglect of the ceremonial law and ordinances. ὧν] those, namely, who adopt such a principle. St. Paul does not condescend formally to argue in proof that such a principle is false, but dismisses it as intuitively damnable.

VER. 9. τί οὖν] supply ἔστιν: "what, then, is the state of the case?" The connection of thought, through οὖν, is with iii. 1, 2. The apostle, in these verses, speaks of a particular "advantage" possessed by the Jew. He now raises the inquiry whether it is of such a nature as to imply moral superiority. προεχόμεθα] 1. the middle voice for the active: "do we excel?" (Peshito, Vulg., Eng. Ver., Theophylact, Luther, Calvin, Beza, Grotius, Bengel, De Wette, Alford, Hodge); 2. the middle voice: "can we screen or defend ourselves?" or, "have we anything for a pretext?" against the charge of being sinners, i. e. (Venema, Fritzsche, Meyer); 3. the passive voice: "are we [Jews] surpassed" [by the Gentiles]? or, "are we [Gentiles] surpassed" [by the Jews]? (Œcumenius, Wetstein, Olshausen). The first is by far preferable. The only objection to it is, that there is no instance in the classics of the active use of προέχομαι. But the interchange of the middle and active voices occurs occasionally in the New Testament. See Winer, p. 255. οὐ πάντως] a decided negative: "not at all." προῃτιασάμεθα] St. Paul has established the fact of sin, in reference to the Gentiles, in i. 18 sq.; and in reference to the Jews, in ii. 1 sq. παντάς] implies that there is not a single exception:

10 καθὼς γέγραπται ὅτι οὐκ ἔστιν δίκαιος οὐδὲ εἷς, 11 οὐκ ἔστιν ὁ συνίων, οὐκ ἔστιν ὁ εκζητῶν τὸν θεόν· 12 πάντες

"no not one," as the next verse explains it. ὑφ' ἁμαρτίαν] is stronger than ἁμαρτωλούς: they are under sin as a burden of guilt and penalty.

Ver. 10. The apostle now proceeds (verses 10–18), to prove his assertion that the Jews are hearers and not doers of the law, by quotations from the Old Testament. This is an additional and conclusive proof for the Jew, who conceded the divine authority of the Old Testament. ὅτι] is recitative. This quotation is taken from Ps. xiv. 1. δίκαιος] signifies perfect and complete conformity to law: the ποιητής νόμου of ii. 13, or ὁ ἐργαζομένος of iv. 4. οὐδὲ εἷς] denotes that there are no exceptions. Compare John i. 3; 1 Cor. vi. 5; Plato's Symposium, 214. d.

Ver. 11 is quoted from Ps. xiv. 2. St. Paul changes the original interrogative form into the negative. The article ὁ], accompanying the two participles, marks the species or class. συνίων] describes righteousness upon the side of the understanding. It is the "spiritual discernment" mentioned in 1 Cor. ii. 14, and the "knowledge" spoken of in John viii. 19; xvii. 3; Jer. ix. 24; Prov. ix. 10; Ps. cxix. 34, et passim. εκζητῶν] describes righteousness in the same reference. It is inquiry and search in order to knowledge. Compare 1 Pet. i. 10; Acts xv. 17; Heb. xi. 6. At the same time, this word hints at the other side of righteousness: namely, its relation to the will and affections. The reason why men do not inquire and search after God is, because they do not incline towards, or desire Him.

Ver. 12. Quoted from Ps. xiv. 3. ἐξέκλιναν] this word describes righteousness with reference to the will: "all have

*ἐξέκλιναν, ἅμα ἠχρειώθησαν· οὐκ ἔστιν ὁ ποιῶν χρηστό-
τητα, οὐκ ἔστιν ἕως ἑνός.*
13 *τάφος ἀνεῳγμένος ὁ λάρυγξ
αὐτῶν, ταῖς γλώσσαις αὐτῶν ἐδολιοῦσαν, ἰὸς ἀσπίδων ὑπὸ
τὰ χείλη αὐτῶν.*
14 *ὧν τὸ στόμα αὐτῶν ἀρᾶς καὶ πικρίας*

inclined away" from the rule or law of righteousness. In Aristotle (Politics), ἐκκλινεῖν εἰς ὀλιγαρχίαν denotes an inclination towards oligarchy, and away from democracy. Sin, in its first and deepest form, is the inclination or disposition of the will, and hence the apostle mentions it first in order. ἅμα] "in one body or mass." ἠχρειώθησαν] the uselessness and worthlessness of the sinner in relation to all good objects is apparent. He is an "unprofitable (ἀχρεῖος) servant," Mat. xxv. 30. ποιῶν] sin in the form of actions, springing from the inclination, is next mentioned. ἕως ἑνός] like οὐδὲ εἷς, in verse 10, is sweeping, excluding any exception. The standard of judgment is sinless perfection. No man does good spiritually, perfectly, and without a single slip or failure from first to last.

VER. 13. Quoted from Ps. v. 10 and Ps. cxl. 3, in the Septuagint version. λάρυγξ] their words uttered through the larynx (not throat) are like the odor of a tomb. Compare the "rotten communication out of the mouth," of Eph. iv. 29. This description is applicable to written as well as spoken words. Little is known of Jewish literature, other than the Old Testament Scriptures; but some portions of Greek and Roman literature stink like a newly-opened grave. ἐδολιοῦσαν] (for ἐδολιοῦν, Winer, 77) false words naturally accompany licentious words. The imperfect tense denotes habitual action. ἰὸς ἀσπίδων] is explanatory of ἐδολιοῦσαν.

VER. 14. Quoted from Ps. x. 7: freely from the Septuagint. The character is still described from the language uttered: the libidinous and false words end in bitter curses.

γέμει. 15 ὀξεῖς οἱ πόδες αὐτῶν ἐκχέαι αἷμα, 16 σύντριμμα
καὶ ταλαιπωρία ἐν ταῖς ὁδοῖς αὐτῶν, 17 καὶ ὁδὸν εἰρήνης οὐκ
ἔγνωσαν. 18 οὐκ ἔστιν φόβος θεοῦ ἀπέναντι τῶν ὀφθαλμῶν
αὐτῶν. 19 οἴδαμεν δὲ ὅτι ὅσα ὁ νόμος λέγει τοῖς ἐν τῷ νόμῳ

πικρίας] denotes intense hatred. Compare Eph. iv. 31; Acts viii. 23; James iii. 14.

VERSES 15–17 are a condensation of Isa. lix. 7, 8, in the Septuagint version. ἐκχέαι αἷμα] murder swiftly follows the cursing. σύντριμμα] an utter destruction which bruises and grinds down to the very substance and fibre, is the result of such murderous hatred. ὁδοῖς] the word is employed literally, here: "wherever they go." ὁδὸν] the word is employed figuratively, here: "way" in the sense of "method." They do not understand the mode of diffusing the blessings of peace. Compare Acts xix. 9, 23.

VER. 18. Quoted exactly from the Septuagint rendering of Ps. xxxvi. 1, excepting the substitution of αὐτῶν for αὐτοῦ. φόβος] "reverential fear." ἀπέναντι ὀφθαλμῶν] the eye is not directed towards God as the object of holy awe. The lack of this feeling accounts for the sins that have been mentioned. This text of scripture constitutes the preface to the judicial sentence to capital punishment. In this description of the Jewish character, original sin is mentioned in verses 10–12 (to ἠχρεώθησαν), and in verse 18; and actual transgression in verses 12–17. Melanchthon speaks of it as a delineation in qua magna est verborum atrocitas.

VER. 19. The apostle now sums up, and draws a conclusion from these Old Testament quotations: namely, that all men are sinful and guilty, and consequently that no man can be justified in the ordinary mode of justification, that is, by personal obedience. οἴδαμεν] Not the Jews particularly:

λαλεῖ, ἵνα πᾶν στόμα φραγῇ καὶ ὑπόδικος γένηται πᾶς ὁ κόσμος τῷ Θεῷ. [20] διότι ἐξ ἔργων νόμου οὐ δικαιωθήσεται

"everybody knows." Compare ii. 2. δὲ] is transitive: "now." ὁ νόμος] the written law, primarily, because St. Paul has been speaking, last, of the Jew; yet not the written law exclusively, because the Gentiles are included in πᾶν στόμα and πᾶς ὁ κόσμος. The written law contains the unwritten, by implication, and hence may be put for all law, or law generally. λέγει] to say, merely. λαλεῖ] to say in the way of description. The first refers only to the matter (λόγοι); the last to the application and enforcement of the matter. Compare John viii. 43; Mark i. 34. ἵνα] is telic, denoting a purpose of God, and not a chance event. πᾶν] is emphatic, and exclusive of exceptions. φραγῇ] complete and entire silence under the accusation of the law, is meant. The accused is ἀναπολόγητος, ii. 1. ὑπόδικος] "liable to punishment," or "guilty." πᾶς ὁ κόσμος] the universality of sin is here taught. This passage throws light upon the true interpretation of ii. 14, 15; ii. 26, 27. Compare Gal. iii. 10. In the Apocryphal book entitled the "Prayer of Manasses," Abraham, Isaac, and Jacob are described as sinless: "Thou, therefore, O Lord, that art the God of the just, hast not appointed repentance to the just, as to Abraham, and Isaac, and Jacob, which have not sinned against thee; but thou hast appointed repentance unto me that am a sinner." The Council of Trent rejected this book from the Apocrypha.

Ver. 20. διότι] introduces the reason for the assertion in the preceding verse, that every man must be silent when accused by the law, and must stand guilty before it. The reason is, that no man's obedience of the law is adequate to justify him. ἔργων νόμου] is a frequent phrase with St. Paul. Compare iii. 28; iv. 2, 6; ix. 11, 32; xi. 6; Gal. ii. 16; iii. 2,

πᾶσα σὰρξ ἐνώπιον αὐτοῦ· διὰ γὰρ νόμου ἐπίγνωσις ἁμαρτίας.

5, 10; Eph. ii. 9. The νόμος here is the same as in the preceding verse, namely, the written law primarily, yet as inclusive of the unwritten. The decalogue has in it all the law of conscience, and may, therefore, stand for law generally. That νόμος has this comprehensive signification is proved by the fact, that "the knowledge of sin" is produced by it. This is a universal consciousness, caused sometimes by the written, and sometimes by the unwritten law. Two explanations have been given of ἔργα νόμου: 1. Works *prescribed* by the law: i. e. sinless obedience (Calvin, Beza, De Wette, Fritzsche, Meyer, Hodge); 2. Works *produced* by the law: i. e. human morality (Augustine, Aquinas, Luther, Usteri, Neander, Olshausen, Philippi). The choice between the two explanations depends upon whether the phrase is employed by St. Paul in a good, or a bad sense: whether it denotes an obedience that is spiritual and perfect, and which if performed would justify (according to ii. 13, 25; iv. 4); or whether it denotes an obedience that is heartless and formal, and which if performed would not justify (according to Gal. iii. 10). The objection to the second view is, that the "works of the law," in this sense, would be defective and sinful works, and therefore would not naturally take their denomination from the "law," which is "holy, and just, and good," vii. 12. The "work," in this case, is the product of the fallen will unmoved by the Holy Spirit, and is not performed from love, but from fear or some other selfish motive. It is unspiritual and insincere work: the "dead work" alluded to in Heb. vi. 1; ix. 14. But such a "work" as this is forbidden, rather than enjoined, by that law which requires love in all obedience, Deut. vi. 5; Mat. xxii. 37, 38. It is unlawful, rather than lawful, and should not, consequently, be associated with the law in any manner. To say that "no flesh shall be justified" by such a work as this, would be a truism rather than a truth. The first explanation, therefore, is preferable. The "works of the law" are those which are commanded by the law of God. This law is "spiritual," vii. 14. It requires a "work," or obedience, that is actuated by the Holy Spirit, issues from the inmost depths of the human spirit, is completely conformed to the law which is spiritual, and is performed without intermission from first to last. The "works of the law," then, are sinless obedience, and not human morality. It must furthermore be noticed, that, according to this explanation, the spiritual but imperfect obedience of the regenerate man would not come up to the meaning of τὰ ἔργα νόμου. The obedience of faith is very different from human morality, and far nearer to what the law requires. But it is not an absolutely perfect obedience of the law, and, therefore, upon the principle that "whosoever shall keep the whole law, and yet offend in one point is guilty of all" (James ii. 10), the believer can no more be justified by his "works," or obedience, than the moralist can be by his. Both are failures, when tested by the ideal of the law. The law calls nothing obedience, but perfect obedience. οὐ] qualifies δικαιωθήσεται: if it were intended to qualify πᾶσα, a different collocation would have been employed. Compare 1 Cor. xv. 39; Mat. vii. 21. δικαιωθήσεται] to pronounce, or declare, just: as in ii. 13; iii. 4, 24, 26, 28; iv. 2, 5; v. 9; vi. 7, et alia. For the Classical, Septuagint, and New Testament use of δικαιοῦν, see the exhaustive discussion of Wieseler, in his comment on Gal. ii. 16; the substance of which is given by Schaff, in Lange on Rom. iii. 20. This impossibility of man's justification by the "works of the law" is not absolute and intrinsic, but only relative. The apostle has distinctly affirmed, that "the doers of the law shall be justified," ii. 13. If there actually were sinless obedience, in the case of man, it would justify him. The impossibility arises from the fact, that no such "work" as is prescribed by the law is performed by man. The law, instead of having been perfectly and completely obeyed, has been disobeyed by the Gentile, in the manner described in i. 18–32; by the Jew, in the manner described in ii. 1–10, 17–29; and by both Jew and Gentile, in the manner described in iii. 10–19. γὰρ] assigns the reason why no man shall be justified by the "works of the law," or perfect obedience; namely, because he has not rendered such obedience. When the test of the law, either written or unwritten, is applied, sin is disclosed, instead of sinless perfection. ἐπίγνωσις] the law detects sin, but does not remove it; as the Levitical sin-offering reminded of guilt, but did not take it away, Heb. x. 3. This revelatory work and office of the law is fully described in vii. 7–12. See comment in loco.

§ 2. *The nature of gratuitous justification.* Rom. iii. 21–iv. 25.

St. Paul now begins the second division of the Epistle, which discusses the *nature* of gratuitous justification. Verses 21–30 contain an account of the extraordinary righteousness that was alluded to in i. 17,—the apostle having, from that point in the Epistle up to this, been occupied with proving that the common and ordinary righteousness known to human ethics, namely, personal and exact conformity to the law and obedience of it, is out of the question, for both Jew and Gentile.

VER. 21. νυνὶ] 1. an adverb of time: nostris temporibus. Compare iii. 26; Gal. iv. 4; 2. an adverb of relation: "in this state of things." The latter is preferable, because the writer is engaged in a process of reasoning and not in a historical narrative. χωρὶς] "apart," or separate from: *entire*

21 *Νυνὶ δὲ χωρὶς νόμου δικαιοσύνη θεοῦ πεφανέρωται,*
μαρτυρουμένη ὑπὸ τοῦ νόμου καὶ τῶν προφητῶν, 22 *δικαιο-*

separation is intended. νόμου] is anarthrous, to denote law generally, either written or unwritten. The law is here put for the "works of the law," or obedience. The clause χωρὶς νόμου qualifies πεφανέρωται. God, in revealing and manifesting this peculiar kind of righteousness, makes no use of man's work of obedience. He employs only the work of Christ. δικαιοσύνη θεοῦ] for the meaning of this phrase, see comment on i. 17. πεφανέρωται] is equivalent to ἀποκαλύπτεται in i. 17. Both terms imply a supernatural disclosure of something otherwise unknown. The perfect tense is here the present of a completed action: this righteousness has been objectively revealed, and is still revealed subjectively to faith. μαρτυρουμένη ὑπὸ, etc.] this is said, to show that this peculiar species of righteousness, though "without the law," is nevertheless not antinomian. There is no intrinsic hostility between this "righteousness of God," and the law of God. Law and justice are completely maintained in this method of gratuitous justification. Compare iv. 31. νόμου] in connection with προφητῶν denotes the Old Testament scriptures. Compare Mat. v. 17; vii. 12. In this use, it is more comprehensive than in either of the instances of its use in verse 20; because it includes the *gracious* as well as the legal elements of the Old Economy. The Old Testament reveals both law and gospel, justice and mercy. See John v. 39; Acts x. 43; xxviii. 23; Luke xxiv. 27. The testimony which the "law and the prophets" bear to the δικαιοσύνη θεοῦ is contained in the Messianic matter of the Old Testament, some of which St. Paul soon proceeds to cite. See iv. 3–10. These passages prove that a righteousness that does not consist of perfect personal obedience, is known to the Old Testament. See comment on x. 6–10.

σύνη δὲ θεοῦ διὰ πίστεως Ἰησοῦ Χριστοῦ, εἰς πάντας τοὺς πιστεύοντας. οὐ γάρ ἐστιν διαστολή· [23] πάντες γὰρ ἥμαρ-

VER. 22. δὲ] is adversative: not the common ethical righteousness, "*but* a righteousness," etc. Compare Phil. ii. 8; θανάτου δὲ: no ordinary death "*but* a death," etc. δικαιοσύνη θεοῦ] sc. ἐρχόμενη. See comment on i. 17. διὰ] is instrumental. Faith is the act upon the part of man by means of which this righteousness comes upon him. Χριστοῦ] the genitive of the object, Mark xi. 22; Acts iii. 16; Gal. ii. 16; xx. 3, 22; Eph. iii. 12; Phil. iii. 9; James ii. 1. εἰς πάντας] without the addition of καὶ ἐπὶ πάντας, is supported by ℵABC Copt., Æthiop., Lachm., Tisch. The additional clause is supported by DEF Peshito, Vulg., Recept. When retained, the thought is, that this righteousness not merely comes up to (εἰς) the person, but overflows and covers (ἐπὶ) him. πιστεύοντας] sc. τῷ Χριστῷ. The radical notion contained in this important and frequent word is that of confiding trust (fiducia). γάρ] introduces the reason why this righteousness comes upon "all who believe." διαστολή] there is no difference between Jew and Gentile, in respect both to sin and to faith. Both alike are sinners, and both alike are invited to believe in Christ.

VER. 23. γὰρ] introduces the reason why there is no difference between Jew and Gentile. πάντες ἥμαρτον] "all sinned:" the aoristic meaning is to be retained. The apostle has in his mind a particular historical event: the same, namely, with that alluded to in πάντες ἥμαρτον of v. 12, the sin in Adam. It is the one original sin of *apostasy*, more than any particular transgressions that flow from it, that puts Jew and Gentile upon the same footing, so that there is no "difference" between them. The fall in Adam, like the recovery in Christ, is a central and organizing idea in

τον καὶ ὑστεροῦνται τῆς δόξης τοῦ θεοῦ, [24] δικαιούμενοι δωρεὰν τῇ αὐτοῦ χάριτι διὰ τῆς ἀπολυτρώσεως τῆς ἐν

the Epistle to the Romans, and therefore it is alluded to here under the historical tense, and without any further description, as a well-known truth and fact. With this primary and principal reference to the Adamic transgression, have also been connected, the corruption of nature, and actual transgressions, as is done by Bengel (in loco): "Both the original act of sin in paradise, is denoted, and the sinful disposition, as also the acts of transgression flowing from it." Others select a single particular: corruption of nature (Luther and Calvin); individual transgressions (Tholuck, Meyer, Philippi). ὑστεροῦνται] with the genitive, signifies: "to be destitute of:" compare Luke xxii. 35; Mat. xix. 20. The present tense denotes the present and continuing consequence of that act in the past designated by ἥμαρτον. δόξης] is the approbation or praise which God bestows, John v. 44; xii. 43; Rom. ii. 29 (Grotius, De Wette, Fritzsche, Meyer, Hodge). Other explanations: self-approbation before God (Luther, Rosenmüller); the glory of heaven (Beza); the image of God (Olshausen); the honor of God (Eng. Ver.).

VER. 24. δικαιούμενοι] for the signification, see comment on ii. 13; iii. 4. The participle, here, is not equivalent to a finite verb stating another fact additional to those specified by the preceding verbs, but mentions a proof of these facts: "they sinned and were destitute of the divine approbation, *because*, or *since*, they are justified," etc. The fact that they are justified in this extraordinary way proves that they must have sinned; otherwise they would have been justified in the ordinary ethical way. For this use of the participle, compare 2 Cor. iv. 13; Col. i. 3; Heb. vi. 6, 8; 2 Pet. ii. 1. Winer, p. 352. δωρεὰν] gratis (the contracted form of gratiis, implying that nothing but thanks is expected for the favor done). Compare John xv. 25; Mat. x. 8; 2 Thess. iii. 8; Rom. v. 17; Eph. ii. 3. The justification is δωρεάν, in respect to the believer. He pays nothing for it: it is "without money and without price," Isa. lv. 1. In reference to Christ, however, it is not δωρεὰν. He purchases it at a costly price, which he pays, 1 Cor. vi. 20; Mat. xx. 28; 1 Pet. i. 18, 19. τῇ] is separated from its noun by αὐτοῦ, in order to put emphasis upon the fact that it is *God's* grace that accomplishes the object spoken of, without man's co-operation. χάριτι] designates the feeling in God that inclines him to show favor to the guilty. διὰ τῆς, etc.] denotes the medium or instrument through which the grace is exerted. This implies that an instrument is requisite, so that without it there could be no manifestation of grace. ἀπολυτρώσεως] deliverance, or release, from claims, by the payment of a price (λύτρον). In classical usage, the word denotes the release of prisoners and slaves by the payment of money. In Biblical usage, it denotes the release of sinners from the claims of divine justice, by the vicarious sufferings of Christ. These are a price paid for the release. Compare 1 Cor. vi. 20; vii. 23; Gal. iii. 13; Acts xx. 28; Titus ii. 14; Mat. xx. 28; Eph. i. 7; 1 Tim. ii. 6; 1 Pet. i. 18. Inasmuch as these passages, as well as the explanation given in verse 25 of the "redemption," connect the deliverance or release with the *blood*, or *atonement*, of Christ, the reference in ἀπόλύτρωσις must be more to the guilt of sin than to its corruption; or more to justification than to sanctification. Though, of course, the latter is comprised in the redemption considered as a whole. "Every mode of explanation which refers redemption and the forgiveness of sins, not to a real atonement through the death of Christ, but subjectively to the dying and reviving with him guaranteed and produced by that death (Schleiermacher, Nitzsch, Hofmann, and others), is opposed to the New Testament,—

Χριστῷ Ἰησοῦ, [25] *ὃν προέθετο ὁ θεὸς ἱλαστήριον διὰ τῆς πίστεως ἐν τῷ αὐτοῦ αἵματι, εἰς ἔνδειξιν τῆς δικαιοσύνης αὐτοῦ, διὰ τὴν πάρεσιν τῶν προγεγονότων ἁμαρτημάτων*

a mixing-up of justification and sanctification." Meyer in loco. ἐν Χριστῷ] in and by his person and work. The particular manner is described in verse 25.

VER. 25. προέθετο] "publicly set forth:" Plato (Phædo, 115) employs the word to describe the laying out of the corpse of Socrates; Herodotus, to denote the display of gold and silver utensils (iii. 148). This setting forth is in and by the crucifixion pre-eminently, yet not exclusively. The entire humiliation and suffering of the God-man, from the instant of the miraculous conception to the τετελέσται (John xix. 30), is included. Perhaps the force of the middle voice should be insisted upon: "God set forth for himself." The atonement of Christ is a *self*-satisfaction for the triune God. It meets the requirements of that divine nature which is equally in each person. "God hath reconciled us to *himself* (ἑαυτῷ)," 2 Cor. v. 18, 19; Coloss. i. 20. In the work of vicarious atonement, the Godhead is both subject and object, active and passive. God holds the claims, and God satisfies the claims; he is displeased, and he propitiates the displeasure; he demands the atonement, and he provides the atonement. It should be noticed that προέθετο does not signify the making of the ἱλαστήριον. This idea is expressed by ἔδωκεν, John iii. 16; παρέδωκεν, Eph. v. 2; προσφέρειν, Heb. v. 1, 3. Chrysostom, who is followed by Fritzsche and Eng. Ver. (margin), takes προέθετο in the sense of purpose, or decree. This interpretation is favored by the fact that in the only other instances in which the word is used (Rom. i. 13; Eph. i. 9), it has this signification; and, moreover, it agrees well with St. Paul's general system. But the fact that in the context a "manifestation" is spoken of as being accomplished by the act defined by προέθετο, is conclusive for the explanation most generally adopted. ὁ θεὸς] God the Father. The trinitarian persons are objective to each other. One sends another (John v. 37; x. 36; xvi. 7; xiv. 26); and one addresses another (John xvii. 5; Heb. i. 8). Each has his official work. Yet, since the whole essence is in each person (for a trinitarian person is not a fraction of the essence), this official work cannot be attributed to the particular person in an *exclusive* sense. The unity and identity of essence, after all, necessitates that each person have a common participation and honor in the official work of the others. Hence, the official work of one is occasionally attributed to another: e. g. the Son creates, Coloss. i. 16; the Father sanctifies, John xvii. 17. ἱλαστήριον] Explanations: 1. supply ἐπίθεμα, so that it is the כַּפֹּרֶת (which the Sept. translates by ἱλαστήριον, Ex. xxv. 17), the lid of the ark of the covenant, upon which the blood was sprinkled: the "propitiatory" (Aug., Theodoret, Theophylact, Erasmus, Luther, Calvin, Grotius, Olsh., Tholuck, Philippi, Lange); 2. supply θῦμα: a "propitiatory sacrifice" (De Wette, Fritzsche, Meyer, Alford, Wordsworth, Hodge); 3. ἱλαστήριον is taken as a noun (a frequent use in later Greek writers), so that it is equivalent to ἱλασμός, 1 John iv. 10: the "propitiation" (Vulg., Eng. Ver., Hilary, Usteri, Rückert). Either the second or third explanation is preferable to the first, because it agrees better with προέθετο; and because this would be the only instance in which Christ is compared to the sprinkled lid of the ark of the covenant: a comparison, which upon the face of it seems incongruous. διὰ πίστεως ἐν τῷ αὐτοῦ αἵματι] Explanations: 1. a comma is to be placed after πίστεως, so that προέθετο will have two adjuncts: God sets forth Christ as a propitiatory sacrifice, first, by means of (διὰ) the believer's faith in this sacrifice, and, secondly, by means of (ἐν) the blood of Christ: *by* the believer's faith, and *in* Christ's blood (De Wette); 2. the same punctuation, but so that προέθετο shall have but one adjunct: the clause διὰ πίστεως qualifying ἱλαστήριον: God sets forth Christ as a propitiatory sacrifice (effective through faith), by means of (ἐν) the blood of Christ (Meyer); 3. the whole clause is an adjunct of προέθετο: God sets forth Christ as a propitiatory sacrifice, by means of (διὰ) the believer's faith in this sacrifice, and this faith rests upon (ἐν) the blood, or death, of the sacrifice (Luther, Calvin, Beza, Olshausen, Tholuck, Hodge). This is the most natural interpretation. The objection that the preposition should have been εἰς instead of ἐν, if the writer had intended to connect πίστεως with αἵματι, has no force in view of such texts as John viii. 31; Acts v. 14; xviii. 8; 1 Tim. iii. 13; 2 Tim. i. 13; iii. 15. The thought of the writer is, that the propitiatory sacrifice of Christ is *completely* set forth and exhibited, only when it is effectually applied by the Holy Spirit, and appropriated by faith. The full virtue of the atonement is not understood except by a believer. The believer's faith, of course, adds nothing to the piacular value of Christ's sacrifice, which is infinite and a fixed quantity, but it helps to reveal its real nature, and to explain the mystery to men and angels (1 Pet. i. 12). εἰς] is telic, denoting the design of God in the act designated by προέθετο. ἔνδειξιν] the purpose of the action in προέθετο is a disclosure of something otherwise unmanifested. It is anarthrous, to distinguish it from the other and more important ἔνδειξις mentioned in verse 26. δικαιοσύνης] judicial or punitive righteousness (De Wette, Meyer, Tholuck, Philippi, Wordsworth, Alford, Hodge). The context settles it. It is a righteousness that is manifested in and through the ἱλαστήριον, or piacular offering. But this is correlated to retributive justice. διὰ] "on account of." The implication is that the πάρεσις ἁμαρτημάτων, in itself considered, is inconsistent with the δικαιοσύνη, and requires to be explained and set right. πάρεσιν] "pretermission," (Beza, Cocceius, Bengel, Hammond, Meyer, Trench, Synonyms, 33, Philippi), not "remission." "Sins temporarily passed by may be subsequently punished (compare 2 Sam. xvi. 10–12; xi. 21–23, with 1 Kings ii. 8, 9, 44–46), but not sins absolutely forgiven." Philippi in loco. The marginal rendering of the Eng. Ver. is correct: "passing over." The act of God here intended is not that of forgiveness, or remission proper. This is denoted by ἄφεσις: the term πάρεσις being found in the New Testament only in this passage. This divine act of "passing over," or temporarily omitting to punish, is described as "overlooking" (ὑπεριδὼν, "winking at," Eng. Ver.), Acts xvii. 30; "suffering to walk in their own ways," Acts xiv. 16; "forbearance," and "long-suffering," Rom. ii. 4; ix. 22. Compare Ps. lxxxi. 12; cxlvii. 20. The sin, in these instances, is not pardoned. It still stands charged against the sinner, but there is a delay of punishment. This delay, in itself considered, is an irregular act, according to the principle of retributive justice which demands instant and exact infliction of penalty; and hence it requires to be legitimated by some method. On account of (διὰ) this irregularity, and conflict with justice, it was necessary that there should be a vindication of this attribute of God by a propitiatory sacrifice. All temporary delay of penalty, as well as all full remission of penalty, in the history of mankind, occurs through the ἱλαστήριον τοῦ θεοῦ. The atonement of Christ, says Tholuck, is the divine theodicy for the past history of the world, in which there is so much of forbearance and delay to punish. It is needless to remark, that this pretermission of sin, as distinguished from its remission, is only a secondary end of Christ's atonement. It is a benefit which the lost, as well as the redeemed, receive from Christ. The great and primary design of Christ's death is the actual pardon of sin which is

26 ἐν τῇ ἀνοχῇ τοῦ θεοῦ, πρὸς τὴν ἔνδειξιν τῆς δικαιοσύνης αὐτοῦ ἐν τῷ νῦν καιρῷ, εἰς τὸ εἶναι αὐτὸν δίκαιον καὶ δικαιοῦντα τὸν ἐκ πίστεως Ἰησοῦ.

designated by the phrase εἰς ἄφεσιν ἁμαρτιῶν. προγεγονότων] "previously or already committed." It is antithetic to τῷ νῦν καιρῷ, and denotes the sin of man before the Advent, like "the times of ignorance," Acts xvii. 30; and the "times past," Acts xiv. 16. This ante-Christian sin, though not forgiven, was treated with indulgence. The passage also may have an individual application. At any point of time, the past sins of a man though not pardoned, have been treated with forbearance upon the ground of the atonement. The Romanist explanation of πάρεσις, according to which it is a quasi-pardon granted to Old Testament saints, to be followed by a full remission (ἄφεσις) after Christ's "descent into hell" for their deliverance, is refuted by the fact that the πάρεσις relates to all men alike who lived before the advent.

VER. 26. ἀνοχῇ] is connected with πάρεσιν, and signifies indulgence, or forbearance to punish, and must not be confounded with grace (χάρις). This latter, alone, is the ground of the full and real remission of sin. ἀνοχή agrees with the sentimental, as distinguished from the ethical idea of God. Indulgence is not the same as grace or mercy. Mercy has a moral basis. It is willing, if need be, to suffer self-sacrifice for its object. It is good ethics. Indulgence, on the contrary, recoils from all suffering, and is easy good-nature. It is bad ethics, and requires to be set right by some method which satisfies that principle of justice which indulgence has interfered with. This explanation and legitimation of the irregularity of "overlooking" sin, and "suffering all nations to walk in their own ways," St. Paul finds in the sacrifice of Christ who in this way "tasted death for every man." And the implication is, that apart from this sacrifice, the justice of God would have no more allowed ἀνοχή, and delay of penalty, in the instance of mankind, than it did in that of the fallen angels. πρὸς] "with a view to;" "for the sake of." It denotes an aim or purpose with more particularity than does εἰς. See Vigerus in voce. τὴν ἔνδειξιν] the article (supported by ℵABCD, Lachm., Tisch.) is associated with the noun, in this instance, to indicate that *this* "manifestation" is the great and principal one. It is not that incidental ἔνδειξις, or display of retributive righteousness, spoken of in verse 25, which merely explains the delay to inflict the penalty of sin, but that which relates to and explains its complete and absolute non-infliction. The apostle now has in view the pardon and justification of believers, and not the mere forbearance of God towards unbelievers. δικαιοσύνης] punitive justice, as in verse 25. τῷ νῦν καιρῷ] is antithetic to προγεγονότων: the Christian, in distinction from the ante-Christian era. This particular manifestation of retributive justice in vicarious atonement does not actually occur until the advent and crucifixion of Christ. εἰς τὸ εἶναι] is epexegetical of τὴν ἔνδειξιν alone, and not of ἔνδειξιν anarthrous in verse 25. This latter ἔνδειξις is associated with the justification of the believer; the other only with the delay of punishment in the instance of the unbeliever. Christ is set forth a propitiatory sacrifice, principally for the sake of disclosing how God can be strictly just, and at the same time justify the unjust. δίκαιον καὶ δικαιοῦντα] καὶ has an adversative force: "and yet:" implying that there is a natural incompatibility between the two things. To pronounce the ungodly to be just (iv. 5), is an unjust verdict, taken by itself without explanation, and without any ground being laid for it. St. Paul implies that if God had justified the ungodly without the ἱλαστήριον, he would not have been δίκαιος. That a judge can be just, and at the same time not inflict punishment

27 *Ποῦ οὖν ἡ καύχησις; ἐξεκλείσθη. διὰ ποίου νόμου; τῶν ἔργων; οὐχί, ἀλλὰ διὰ νόμου πίστεως.* 28 *λο-*

where it is due, is in itself self-contradictory. This contradiction is removed by *vicarious* atonement, or the infliction of penalty upon a substitute. τὸν ἐκ πίστεως]. Compare οἱ ἐξ ἐριθείας, ii. 8. The preposition implies that faith is the principle *out of* which the whole life and conduct issues.

Ver. 27 contains an inference from the statements in verses 21–26. ποῦ] is scornful in its tone. Compare 1 Cor. i. 20. The reply is: "It is nowhere." οὖν] is inferential in its force, and looks back to the reasoning in verses 21–26. καύχησις] is not used in its bad sense of "boasting" (Eng. Ver.), but its good sense, as in iv. 2; xv. 17; 2 Cor. i. 12. It signifies, here, that proper self-approbation which rests upon perfect obedience. Had man completely fulfilled the law of God, he would have been justified upon this ground, and might have gloried and rejoiced in the fact that he had been an obedient subject of the divine government. His consciousness, in this case, would have been like that of the holy angels, who do not "boast" of their virtue, yet know that they have kept the commandment. ἐξεκλείσθη] says Theodoret, οὐκ ἔτι χώραν ἔχει: it has no ποῦ at all. νόμου] supply ἐξεκλείσθη. The term νόμος, here, has the secondary meaning of a rule of procedure, or of judgment, in a particular case. The apostle asks, upon what "principle" is καύχησις excluded. ἔργων] is the same as ἔργων νόμου in iii. 20. The whole clause would be, διὰ νόμου τῶν ἔργων νόμου: in which the term νόμος would be employed in two significations. The "works of the law" are sinless obedience, which, of course, if rendered, would not (οὐχί) shut out self-approbation and the consciousness of personal rectitude. πίστεως] supply ἐν τῷ Χριστοῦ αἵματι, as in iii. 25. Faith is

γιζόμεθα γὰρ δικαιοῦσθαι πίστει ἄνθρωπον χωρὶς ἔργων νόμου. [29] ἢ Ἰουδαίων ὁ θεὸς μόνων; οὐχὶ καὶ ἐθνῶν;

confidence in another's merit, and of course excludes confidence in personal merit.

VER. 28. λογιζόμεθα] "We are certain; it is our fixed opinion." Compare ii. 3; viii. 18; xiv. 14; 2 Cor. xi. 5. St. Paul, after this course of reasoning, regards the case as made out, and feels warranted in expressing his confidence in the correctness of his position respecting gratuitous justification. γὰρ] is supported by ℵADE Vulg., Copt., Griesb., Lach., Tisch. οὖν is the reading in BCL Peshito, Receptus. The weight of authority is in favor of γὰρ. St. Paul assigns this confident certainty of the truth of gratuitous justification as a reason (γὰρ) why καύχησις is excluded, and not as an inference (οὖν) from the previous investigation. δικαιοῦσθαι] "declared to be just," as in iii. 20. πίστει] is the instrumental dative; the clause ἐν τῷ Χριστοῦ αἵματι is to be supplied from iii. 25. Faith justifies in the same sense that eating nourishes. It is not the act of mastication, but the food, that sustains life; and it is not the act of believing, but Christ's death, which delivers from the condemnation of the law. "In justification, man, indeed, does something; but the act of taking, viewed as an act, does not justify, but that which is taken or laid hold of," Bengel on Rom. v. 17. This is taught in the common statement, that the atonement of Christ is the meritorious or procuring cause of justification, while faith is only the instrumental cause. Viewed as an act merely, and apart from its relation to the oblation of Christ, there is no more reason why a man should be justified by his faith, than by his hope, or by his charity,—as the Tridentine doctors assert he is. Charity is said by St. Paul to be greater than faith or hope (1 Cor. xiii. 13). But it is plain, that no act of man, internal or external, however excellent, can be a sufficient reason why the punishment of sin should be remitted to him. χωρὶς] entirely separate and apart from: without a single deed; faith only, and alone. ἔργων νόμου] good and perfect works such as are prescribed by the law. See comment on iii. 20. St. Paul is speaking of justification, or the deliverance from penalty, in distinction from sanctification, or the production of holiness; and asserts that good works contribute nothing towards justification. That a man has performed a good action, is not a reason why he should be released from the punishment due for having done a bad one. There is nothing of the nature of an atonement in sinless obedience, because there is nothing of the nature of *suffering* in it. Obedience is happiness, but happiness is not expiatory. Good works do not bleed; and without shedding of blood there is no remission of punishment (Heb. ix. 22). The Romanist attempt to produce justification by sanctification, to obtain the pardon of sin upon the ground of either internal or external obedience, is not an adaptation of means to ends. It is like the attempt to quench thirst with bread, instead of water. The true correlate to guilt is atoning suffering, and to substitute anything in the place of it, however excellent and necessary in other respects the substitute may be, must be a failure.

VER. 29. ἢ] "or," granting that justification is by faith alone, and that καύχησις is excluded, in the case of the *Jew*, is it so with the *Gentile?* ὁ θεὸς] The universality of this method of justification is proved by the fact of one God for all men, who has but one course of action for all.

VER. 30. εἴπερ] "since" (ℵABC Lachm., Tisch.) is stronger than ἐπείπερ (DEL Recept.), and introduces an assertion that is indisputable. εἷς] "one and the same." The doctrine of the divine unity implies that God is not the deity of the

ναὶ καὶ ἐθνῶν, [30] *εἴπερ εἷς ὁ θεός ὃς δικαιώσει περιτομὴν ἐκ πίστεως καὶ ἀκροβυστίαν διὰ τῆς πίστεως.* [31] *νό-*

Jews only; in which case there must be another for the Gentiles. δικαιώσει] the future, as in iii. 20, denotes a uniform rule without exceptions. ἐκ and διὰ] are used as equivalents. Compare Gal. iii. 8; Eph. ii. 8. The former preposition presents faith more as a principle of action in the person. Compare ἐξ ἐριθείας, ii. 8; ἐκ περιτομῆς, iv. 12; ἐξ ἀγάπης, Phil. i. 17. τῆς πίστεως] the article signifies that the emphasis must be laid upon faith: "the very same *faith*."

Ver. 31. De Wette and Meyer regard this verse as belonging to chapter iv., and announcing the theme of the discussion in this chapter; but it is preferable (with Aug., Beza, Calvin, Bengel, Tholuck, Lange, Wordsworth, Hodge) to consider it as the conclusion of chapter iii. It is a bold and confident affirmation, followed up only indirectly by an argument in chapter iv., because St. Paul has already (iii. 21) shown that the doctrine of gratuitous justification is not antinomian, by referring to the Old Testament where it is taught; and because all that he has said respecting Christ as the ἱλαστήριον proves that the law as retributive is maintained. νόμον] is emphatic by position. It is primarily the moral law as stated in the Mosaic decalogue (iii. 28; Acts xxi. 28; Gal. iv. 21); yet as this includes the unwritten law, by implication, νόμος here stands for law universally. Neither the decalogue nor the human conscience are "made void" by faith in Christ's atonement. οὖν] refers to the foregoing statements regarding a righteousness that is without works, which upon the face of it looks like a nullification of the moral law. καταργοῦμεν] "to make useless:" a frequent word with St. Paul, who often employs it in the sense of utterly abolishing, or nullifying. τῆς πίστεως] the article

μον οὖν καταργοῦμεν διὰ τῆς πίστεως; μὴ γένοιτο, ἀλλὰ νόμον ἱστάνομεν.

directs attention to that peculiar faith spoken of, which is "without works." μὴ γένοιτο]. See comment on iii. 4. ἀλλὰ] "on the contrary." ἱστάνομεν] (ℵABCD Lach., Tisch.) for ἵσταμεν. The reading ἱστῶμεν is supported by E Receptus. It signifies, to make firm what otherwise would be tottering. The apostle has already done this in iii. 21, and by what he has said respecting the connection between the propitiation of Christ and retributive justice. In the following chapter, however, he incidentally strengthens the proof, by what is said in the Old Testament concerning the justification of Abraham.

CHAPTER IV

[1] Τί οὖν ἐροῦμεν εὑρηκέναι Ἀβραὰμ τὸν προπάτορα ἡμῶν κατὰ σάρκα; [2] εἰ γὰρ Ἀβραὰμ ἐξ ἔργων ἐδικαιώθη,

Ver. 1. οὖν] i. e., with reference to this doctrine of gratuitous justification. The question is one raised by St. Paul himself, for the purpose of finding in its answer a proof, additional to that already given in chapter iii., that justification by faith does not conflict with the Old Testament. εὑρηκέναι] "to acquire," or "obtain." Compare Luke i. 30. This collocation of εὑρηκέναι is supported by ℵACDEF Vulg., Copt., Æthiop., Lachm., Tisch. The Receptus, with L Peshito, places it after ἡμῶν. B omits it. Ἀβραὰμ] The case of the head and father of the Jewish nation would be a crucial test of the doctrine, so far as the Jew was concerned. κατὰ σάρκα] is to be construed with εὑρηκέναι (Peshito, De Wette, Tholuck, Meyer, Alford, Wordsworth, Hodge), and not with προπάτορα (Origen, Ambrose, Chrys., Calvin, Eng. Ver.). This is evident, for the following reasons: 1. σάρξ is employed by St. Paul to denote human nature: the entire man, both soul and body, Rom. i. 3; iii. 20; vi. 19; vii. 5, 18; viii. 12 et alia. But there is no other mode than this, in which Abraham could have been the forefather of the Jews; and hence it would not require to be specially mentioned. If it be said, that Abraham was the forefather of a Jew with respect to the body, in distinction from the soul, this would make σάρξ synonymous with σῶμα, which is contrary to the Pauline use of terms. 2. The phrase κατὰ σάρκα is expressly explained in verse 2, by ἐξ ἔργων. The question, then, which St. Paul asks is: What merit before God did Abraham acquire, in the use of his natural human faculties, or, in other words, by his own works? The view of Meyer, that σάρξ here is antithetic to πνεῦμα or νοῦς, and that St. Paul asks what Abraham obtained in the use of his lower physical, in distinction from his higher rational and spiritual nature, is incompatible with the Pauline use of σάρξ as comprehending the whole man, and is connected with that un-Pauline theory of sin which places its seat in the sensuous in distinction from the rational nature. Compare Müller, On Sin, I. 321. Urwick's Translation.

VER. 2. γὰρ] implies that the answer to the question is, that Abraham acquired no merit at all by this method. ἐξ ἔργων] supply νόμου: perfect sinless obedience is meant, as in iii. 20, 27, 28, and as the connection with ἐδικαιώθη involves. καύχημα] *materies gloriandi*, "matter or ground for self-approbation." "Paul calls that glorying, when we profess to have anything of our own to which a reward is supposed to be due at God's tribunal." Calvin in loco. Like καύχησις in iii. 27, it is employed here in a good sense. Compare 1 Cor. ix. 15; Gal. vi. 4; Phil. iii. 3. According to 1 Cor. v. 6, there is a true and a false "glorying." Had Abraham perfectly kept the moral law, he might have had confidence in this obedience as the basis of justification before God. πρὸς] "with reference to." If Abraham were pronounced just upon his own merits, then he was not justified δωρεὰν (iii. 24), and consequently his καύχημα, or ground of confidence, would not have reference to God's ἱλαστήριον. He would glory in, and rest upon personal righteousness, and could not glory and trust in free grace, as St. Paul does in v. 2, 11; 1 Cor. i. 31. His consciousness would be like that of an unfallen angel, and not that of a redeemed man. Some

ἔχει καύχημα, ἀλλ᾽ οὐ πρὸς θεόν. [3] τί γὰρ ἡ γραφὴ λέγει; Ἐπίστευσεν δὲ Ἀβραὰμ τῷ θεῷ, καὶ ἐλογίσθη αὐτῷ

explain the phrase as meaning that Abraham could not have confidence in the presence of God, because God searches the heart. But if Abraham had really rendered a perfect obedience, the Searcher of hearts would have seen it.

Ver. 3. γὰρ] introduces the reason for the assertion in οὐ πρὸς θεόν. The Old Testament (γραφὴ) asserts that Abraham was justified by the imputation of faith for righteousness (Gen. xv. 6); this would lead Abraham to glory, not πρὸς ἑαυτόν but πρὸς θεόν: i. e., with respect to God's grace in Christ. Compare v. 11. ἐπίστευσεν] Abraham believed the divine promise that the "Seed of the Woman" (Gen. iii. 15) should be born of him. This was faith in the divine Redeemer of man; which was, of course, accompanied with the sense of needing a Redeemer; which, of course, excluded self-approbation (καύχησις). That Abraham's faith was an act of confiding trust in the divine mercy through a mediator, and the same in kind with that of the Christian believer, is proved by the fact, that Christ distinctly affirmed that Abraham's faith terminated on Himself (John viii. 56); and that St. Paul denominates Christian believers "the children of Abraham" (Rom. iv. 11; Gal. iii. 7). δὲ] is transitive: "now." ἐλογίσθη] the Hebrew is וַיַּחְשְׁבֶהָ, "he imputed." St. Paul quotes from the Septuagint. The word signifies to "account," or "reckon." Righteousness may be reckoned to man, as Rom. iv. 4 explains, in either of two ways: 1. *meritoriously* (κατὰ ὀφείλημα); 2. *graciously* (κατὰ χάριν). The imputation may rest upon personal obedience. In this case, it is meritorious, and due upon principles of justice. Or the imputation may rest upon the obedience of another, there being no personal obedience for it to rest upon. In this case, the imputation is not a debt, but gracious (κατὰ χάριν), or gratuitous (δωρεὰν, χωρίς ἔργων). It should be carefully noted, that St. Paul is speaking here only of the imputation, to fallen man, of *righteousness.* Sin cannot, like righteousness, be imputed to fallen man, in *two* modes, one of which is meritorious, and the other gratuitous. Sin is imputable to man, in only one way. The phrases employed to describe the second of these two imputations prove this. Sin is never represented as charged to man δωρεὰν, or χωρίς ἔργων, or κατὰ εὐδοκίαν θεοῦ. The imputation of sin, both original and actual, is κατὰ ὀφείλημα, *only.* "Gratia dat beneficium immerenti, justitia pœnam non irrogat nisi merenti. Nam in imputatione Adæ, justitia dei non irrogat pœnam immerenti, sed merenti, si non merito proprio et personali, at participato et communi, quod fundatur in communione naturali et fœderali, quæ nobis cum Adamo intercedit." Turretini Institutio IX., ix. 24. This arises from the absolute contrariety between holiness and sin. The former has the creator for its ultimate author; the latter is the work of the creature. The former, consequently, may be reckoned to the account of man, gratuitously, but the latter cannot be. Man can be pronounced innocent when he is not; but he cannot be pronounced guilty when he is not. Merit may be bestowed gratis, but not demerit. Justification may be a gift of God; but damnation cannot be. Eternal life is χάρισμα, but eternal death is ὀψώνια (vi. 23). εἰς] the telic use of the preposition ("in order to") implies that righteousness was wanting in Abraham. δικαιοσύνην] signifies a condition in which the person is δίκαιος in every respect. This, in the case of Abraham, as in that of sinful man universally, would require the fulfilment of the law both as penalty and precept.

Ver. 4. St. Paul, founding his reasoning upon the state-

εἰς δικαιοσύνην. 4 *τῷ δὲ ἐργαζομένῳ ὁ μισθὸς οὐ λογίζεται*
κατὰ χάριν, ἀλλὰ κατὰ ὀφείλημα· 5 *τῷ δὲ μὴ ἐργαζομένῳ,*
πιστεύοντι δὲ ἐπὶ τὸν δικαιοῦντα τὸν ἀσεβῆ, λογίζεται ἡ

ment which he has quoted from the Old Testament, argues that Abraham could not have been justified meritoriously (κατὰ σάρκα, or ἐξ ἔργων), but must have been justified graciously (δωρεάν). δὲ] is transitive: "now." τῷ ἐργαζομένῳ] "the worker:" *perfect* work is meant, such as is rendered by the ideal and sinless workman. Neither the dead work of the moralist, nor the imperfect work of the Christian, comes up to that absolute perfection which is demanded by the law. "There is no righteousness, according to St. Paul, but what is perfect and absolute. Were there such a thing as half-righteousness, it would nevertheless deprive the sinner of all glory." Calvin on Rom. iii. 23. μισθὸς] the reward which the workman has earned by perfect service. κατὰ χάριν] wages actually earned cannot be either tendered, or accepted as a gift. Grace is out of the question, in such a case. "The judge," remarks Socrates (Apologia, 35), "does not sit upon the bench to make a present of justice (τῷ καταχαρίζεσθαι τὰ δίκαια)." Says Coriolanus (Act ii., sc. 3):

> "Better it is to die, better to starve,
> Than crave the hire which first we do deserve."

κατὰ ὀφείλημα]. The indebtedness of God to man, or angel, for service rendered, is only *relative.* This is taught by Christ in Luke xvii. 7–10. (Compare 1 Chron. xxix. 14; Rom. xi. 35, 36; 1 Cor. iv. 7.) No creature can make himself a "profitable" servant to the creator, in the sense of meriting his "thanks," and bringing him under an original and absolute obligation. This for three reasons: 1. God creates from nothing the faculties by which the service is rendered; 2. He upholds them in existence while the service is being rendered; and, 3. He influences and assists in the service itself. Consequently, the merit of the creature before the creator is *pactional.* It is founded upon a promise or covenant, and not upon the original relation between the finite and Infinite. God as creator, preserver, and sanctifier, is not obligated to promise a reward for a holiness derived from Himself; but having promised, he is then bound by his own word, and in case of perfect obedience there is a relative indebtedness upon his part. Having established by a covenant this ground for a reward, it is as firm and immutable as if it depended upon the original and necessary relation of the Creator to the creature ("for he is faithful that promised," Heb. x. 23), and any perfect service that has been rendered by man or angel will be rewarded, not κατὰ χάριν, but κατὰ ὀφείλημα.

VER. 5. μὴ ἐργαζομένῳ] the idea of *perfect* work is still in view: he who fails to render such a sinless obedience as the law requires. This would include the regenerate as well as the unregenerate man. The imperfect obedience of the believer, equally with the disobedience of the unbeliever, fails to come up to what is demanded in order that the reward may be "reckoned of debt." The spiritual man is as entirely dependent upon grace for justification, as is the natural man. πιστεύοντι δὲ] the particle is adversative, and denotes that the act of believing is different from the act of working: the person has failed in "work," and betakes himself to another species of activity, that of trust and reliance. ἐπὶ] this preposition, like εἰς and ἐν, is associated with πιστεύειν, to signify the recumbence and rest of the soul upon the object of faith. δικαιοῦντα] is forensic, as ἀσεβῆ shows: the man is taken as ungodly, "just as he is," and is forgiven. He is not first made perfectly holy, and then pronounced just. Neither is he first made imperfectly holy or partially

πίστις αὐτοῦ εἰς δικαιοσύνην. [6] καθάπερ καὶ Δαυεὶδ λέγει τὸν μακαρισμὸν τοῦ ἀνθρώπου ᾧ ὁ θεὸς λογίζεται δι-

sanctified, and then pardoned. Pardon and justification is the very first act (after election, viii. 30) which God performs in reference to the "ungodly." ἀσεβῆ] does not refer to any uncommon sin, like the worship of idols, which Abraham, according to Philo and Josephus (compare Joshua ii. 2, 14), practised before his call. The English version "ungodly" is misleading; since it suggests heinous depravity. The term is to be explained by Rom. i. 25, where the common sin of mankind is described as the worshipping (ἐσεβάσθησαν) of the creature, instead of the creator. Every man is idolatrous. Covetousness is idolatry, Coloss. iii. 5. Every man, consequently, is ἀσεβής in reference to God. He fails to worship him. Hence, the term denotes the universal corruption of human nature, as seen in the disinclination to honor and glorify God. Compare Rom. v. 6. λογίζεται, etc.] See comment on iv. 3. The fact that Abraham's faith was counted to him for righteousness proves that he was not a "worker."

VER. 6. St. Paul strengthens his position by a reference to the statements of David. καθάπερ] denotes the agreement of what is to be said, with what has just been said. καὶ] "also:" the addition of David's testimony would be very weighty, in the eye of a Jew. λέγει] in Ps. xxxii. μακαρισμὸν] (not μακαρία) the felicitation, rather than the felicity; pronouncing blessed. λογίζεται] See comment on iv. 3. χωρὶς ἔργων]. See comment on iii. 21, 28. "This righteousness is not ours; otherwise God would not gratuitously impute it, but would bestow it as matter of right. Nor is it a habit, or quality, for it is 'without works;' but it is a gratuitous remission, a covering over, a non-imputation of sins." Pareus in loco.

καιοσύνην χωρὶς ἔργων, [7] Μακάριοι ὧν ἀφέθησαν αἱ ἀνομίαι καὶ ὧν ἐπεκαλύφθησαν αἱ ἁμαρτίαι· [8] μακάριος ἀνὴρ

VER. 7 contains a definition and description of the righteousness that is imputed "without righteousness" (χωρὶς ἔργων). The description is taken from Ps. xxxii. 1, 2. ἀφέθησαν] "are forgiven" (Eng. Ver.). This word, by which the Septuagint translates סָלַח (of which the primary idea seems to be that of *lightness, lifting up,* Gesenius) signifies, to "let go," or "release." Forgiveness, in the Biblical representation, is *remission of penalty;* the non-infliction of judicial suffering upon the guilty. The key to the idea is given in Lev. vi. 2–7. "If a soul commit a trespass, he shall bring his trespass offering, and the priest shall make an atonement for him before the Lord, and it shall be forgiven him" (ἀφεθήσεται αὐτῷ, Sept.). The punishment due to his sin shall be *dismissed,* or *let go,* because it has been endured for him by the substituted victim. Sin is a debt (Mat. vi. 12). As, to forgive a debt is, not to collect it, so, to forgive a sin is, not to punish it. Accordingly, everywhere in the New Testament, ἀφιέναι (release) is the term for forgiveness. Compare Mat. vi. 12; ix. 2; Acts xiii. 38; James v. 15; 1 John i. 9; ii. 11. ἐπεκαλύφθησαν] is the Septuagint translation of כָּסָה, to "cover over," so as to conceal from view. This idea, or representation, of the action of mercy, is common in the Old Testament, but not in the New. This is the only instance of its use. ἁμαρτίαι] this term, like ανομια, is most commonly employed in the singular, to denote sin as a principle. But both are occasionally used in the plural, to denote the manifestations of sin; ἁμαρτία defines sin with reference to the true *end* of man's action; ἀνομία defines it with reference to the true *rule* of his action.

VER. 8. οὗ] is supported by ℵBDE Tisch.: AC Receptus, Lachm. read ᾧ. λογίσηται] the subjunctive is hypothetical, implying that the person is blessed in case that God shall not have imputed. The double negative is noticeable: the fact that there is *certainly* no imputation of sin must first be established, before there can be the felicitation. In verse 7, St. Paul defines the imputation of righteousness to be the remission of sin; and in verse 8, to be the non-imputation of sin. This brings to view again the intrinsic difference, already noticed in the comment upon iv. 3, between the imputation of righteousness, and the imputation of sin. The imputation of righteousness to sinful man can be defined as the non-imputation of sin; but the imputation of sin to sinful man cannot be defined as the mere non-imputation of righteousness. The imputation of sin is a positive, and not a negative act. The imputation of righteousness to the sinner supposes the total absence of righteousness, but the imputation of sin to the sinner does not suppose the total absence of sin. It can be said: "Blessed is the man to whom the Lord imputeth righteousness without righteousness;" but it cannot be said: "Cursed is the man to whom the Lord imputeth sin without sin." It is also to be observed, that while St. Paul in this place describes the imputation of righteousness as being the remission, covering, and non-imputation of sin, it does not follow that this is the *whole* of imputation. Christ's righteousness comprises two parts: his sufferings, or passive obedience of the law as penalty; and his active obedience of the law as precept. Both of these are imputed: the one, to deliver the believer from condemnation, and the other to entitle him to eternal reward. St. Paul, at this point, however, is concerned with the imputation of the passive obedience. Guilt and condemnation have thus far been chiefly in his eye, and he defines accordingly. The other side of imputation he presents subsequently. Compare v. 10, 17, 19; 1 Cor. i. 30; 2 Cor. v. 21.

οὗ οὐ μὴ λογίσηται κύριος ἁμαρτίαν. 9 *ὁ μακαρισμὸς οὖν οὗτος ἐπὶ τὴν περιτομήν, ἢ καὶ ἐπὶ τὴν ἀκροβυστίαν; λέγομεν γὰρ Ἐλογίσθη τῷ Ἀβραὰμ ἡ πίστις εἰς δικαιοσύνην.* 10 *πῶς οὖν ἐλογίσθη; ἐν περιτομῇ ὄντι, ἢ ἐν ἀκροβυστίᾳ; οὐκ ἐν περιτομῇ, ἀλλ' ἐν ἀκροβυστίᾳ.* 11 *καὶ*

VER. 9. St. Paul now proceeds to show, in verses 9–13, that gratuitous justification is as entirely separate from circumcision, as it is from obedience of the moral law. οὖν] introduces the ensuing reasoning as it is related to the fact that Abraham, who possessed the righteousness described by David, was a *circumcised* person. οὗτος] supply λέγεται, from λέγει in verse 6; in which case, ἐπὶ means "concerning," as in Mat. iii. 7; Mark ix. 12; Heb. vii. 13. καὶ] shows that περιτομὴν denotes the Jews to the exclusion of the Gentiles; DE and Vulgate add μόνον, which is probably an explanatory gloss. λέγομεν] looks back to verse 3. γὰρ] implies an affirmative answer to the second of the two questions. ἐλογίσθη] though emphatic by position is not to be emphasized; neither is Ἀβραὰμ, nor πίστις. The whole sentence is only the recital, a second time, of a quotation; and the stress lies upon the quotation as a whole, and not upon any particular word. To place the emphasis upon Ἀβραὰμ, as De Wette, Fritzsche, Lange, and Alford maintain, is to contemplate Abraham as a circumcised person. But this is premature. At this point, in the reasoning, Abraham's circumcision must be an open question.

VER. 10. πῶς] in what condition, or status. οὐκ ἐν, etc.] the faith of Abraham and its imputation are mentioned in Gen. xv., and his circumcision in Gen. xvii. The latter occurred about fourteen years after the former.

VER. 11. σεμεῖον] denotes an external token evident to the senses. This term, like σφραγίς, gives the key to the notion

σημεῖον ἔλαβεν περιτομῆς, σφραγῖδα τῆς δικαιοσύνης τῆς πίστεως τῆς ἐν τῇ ἀκροβυστίᾳ, εἰς τὸ εἶναι αὐτὸν πατέρα πάντων τῶν πιστευόντων δι' ἀκροβυστίας, εἰς τὸ λογισθῆναι

of a sacrament. A sacrament being a "sign" or "seal," is *sensuous.* It appeals, in some form or other, to the senses. Consequently, no efficiency can be attributed to it; because the sensuous cannot energize the spiritual, matter cannot move mind. A sacrament, therefore, never operates of itself (*ex opere operato*). A sign requires a signer, and a seal a sealer. περιτομῆς] ℵBDEF Vulg., Copt., Rec., Lachm., Tisch. The reading περιτομήν is supported by AC Peshito, Griesbach. The sense is the same in either case, since περιτομῆς is the genitive of apposition: "he received circumcision, as a sign." σφραγῖδα] the impression of a seal upon a document is an official certification. Compare John iii. 33. This term is explanatory of σημεῖον. The mark of circumcision authentically certified that Abraham was in covenant with Jehovah. In Gen. xvii., circumcision is represented as the seal of a *covenant*; but the covenant implied a promise on the part of Jehovah, and this promise was appropriated by Abraham by faith. Hence, St. Paul speaks of circumcision as the sign and seal of gratuitous justification. εἰς τὸ] denotes the intention of God, who designed by the fact that Abraham believed *previous* to circumcision, that he should be the spiritual father of believing Gentiles, as well as believing Jews. πατέρα] is anarthrous, to denote a father in a particular sense. δι' ἀκροβυστίας] the preposition here has the "loose" sense of "denoting the circumstances and relations under which one does something" (Winer, p. 379). καὶ] is supported by CDEL Vulg., Peshito, Æth., Rec., Meyer, and omitted by ℵAB Copt., Lachm., Tisch. It is favored by the connection of thought. It was the divine purpose that righteousness should be imputed to the Gen-

καὶ αὐτοῖς τὴν δικαιοσύνην, 12 καὶ πατέρα περιτομῆς, τοῖς οὐκ ἐκ περιτομῆς μόνον, ἀλλὰ καὶ τοῖς στοιχοῦσιν τοῖς

tiles *also*, equally with the Jews. The clause εἰς τὸ λογισθῆναι, etc., is explanatory of the preceding clause εἰς τὸ εἶναι αὐτὸν, etc., and shows that spiritual and not carnal paternity was intended by God. Abraham was to be a father to this class of Gentiles, because they exercised the same faith that he did, and had the same kind of righteousness imputed to them. Christ had previously taught this truth in Mat. iii. 9; John viii. 39; and St. Paul returns to it again in Rom. ix. 8 sq., and Gal. iii. 7 sq. τὴν δικαιοσύνην] is supported by BCEL. Rec., Lachm.: the article is omitted by ℵD Tisch.

VER. 12. καὶ] is to be mentally followed by εἰς τὸ εἶναι αὐτὸν. περιτομῆς] is anarthrous, to denote some, not all of the circumcised. Abraham was, of course, to be the spiritual father of circumcised Jews, as well as of uncircumcised Gentiles; yet not from the mere fact of circumcision and carnal descent, as he proceeds to state. τοῖς] "those namely:" the dative either of advantage, or of relation (Luke vii. 12; Rev. xxi. 7). St. Paul now specifies what class of the Jews are the spiritual children of Abraham. μόνον] is connected with οὐκ: who are "not only" circumcised, but who, etc. καὶ] denotes that in addition to circumcision, the persons spoken of *also* "walk in the steps," etc. τοῖς στοιχοῦσιν] the article is not superfluous, but employed for emphasis. Theodoret, Luther, and others, take τοῖς οὐκ for οὐ τοῖς, so that two classes, namely, Jews and Gentiles, would be mentioned, in verse 12, as having Abraham for their father. But, the apostle has already, in the preceding verse, affirmed that Abraham is the spiritual father of believing Gentiles. Hence, the clause τοῖς στοιχοῦσιν, etc., must refer to the same class that τοῖς οὐκ, etc., refers to. It mentions a characteris-

ἴχνεσιν τῆς ἐν ἀκροβυστίᾳ πίστεως τοῦ πατρὸς ἡμῶν Ἀβραάμ. [13] *οὐ γὰρ διὰ νόμου ἡ ἐπαγγελία τῷ Ἀβραὰμ ἢ τῷ σπέρματι αὐτοῦ, τὸ κληρονόμον αὐτὸν εἶναι κόσμου,*

tic in *addition* to that of circumcision, by virtue of which this class of the Jews are the spiritual children of Abraham. ἴχνεσιν] conveys the notion of exact following after: the feet are carefully put in the tracks of the leader: "I follow here, the footing of thy feete" (Spenser). The dative is rather local, than normative. τῆς ἐν ἀκροβυστίᾳ πίστεως] is a much simpler reading than τῆς πίστεως τῆς ἐν τῇ ἀκροβυστίᾳ (L Rec.), and is supported by ℵABCDEFG Lachm., Tisch.

Ver. 13 confirms the position that Abraham was to be the father of all believing Gentiles, by considering the nature of the *promise* that was made to him. γὰρ] introduces the point. νόμου] denotes the moral law, yet unwritten in the day of Abraham. The "law" is here put for the "works of the law," and is equivalent to perfect obedience. The promise did not come to Abraham through the instrumentality (διὰ) of this. ἐπαγγελία] supply ἐγένετο. The promise is that mentioned in Gen. xxii. 17, 18. σπέρματι] not carnal, but spiritual offspring. Gal. iii. 7, 16; Rom. ix. 7–9; John vii. 39. κληρονόμον] spiritual inheritance, like that in Mat. v. 5; Dan. vii. 27. κόσμου] implies the universality of the Divine intention: "In thy seed, all the nations of the earth shall be blessed." Abraham was promised only the land of Canaan (Gen. xvii. 8); but this, in Scripture, is represented as the centre of departure for the Messiah's universal kingdom (Acts i. 4; John iv. 22), and often stands for the Church universal. Compare Mat. xix. 28; Luke xxii. 30. δικαιοσύνης πίστεως] trust and confidence in God's gracious justification, and not in personal and perfect obedience, was the condition (διὰ) of the promise to Abraham and his seed,

ἀλλὰ διὰ δικαιοσύνης πίστεως. [14] εἰ γὰρ οἱ ἐκ νόμου κληρονόμοι, κεκένωται ἡ πίστις καὶ κατήργηται ἡ ἐπαγγελία.
[15] ὁ γὰρ νόμος ὀργὴν κατεργάζεται· οὗ δὲ οὐκ ἔστιν νόμος,

that they should have a universal dominion, and be a universal blessing to mankind. The evangelical promise is made to faith, and not to works.

VER. 14 continues the proof that the promise to Abraham and his spiritual seed was not διὰ νόμου ἀλλὰ διὰ πίστεως. ἐκ] denotes the source and ground of the heirship. Compare ii. 8; iv. 12; Acts x. 45; Gal. iii. 10. νόμου] as in verse 13, is put for ἔργα νόμου, and signifies obedience of the law. St. Paul does not mean by οἱ ἐκ νόμου, those who *desire* or *attempt* to be justified by the law, but who actually are. They are a class who can claim the inheritance upon the ground of desert. If there were any such class among men, they would have nothing to do with either faith or a gracious promise. The "law" spoken of here is not the Mosaic law particularly, since Abraham lived before this was given, but law in the abstract. κατήργηται] perfect obedience nullifies faith, and vice versa. If the inheritance is to rest upon a complete fulfilment of the command, then it cannot rest upon a gracious promise. Compare the similar reasoning in xi. 6, 7.

VER. 15. A confirmation of the statement in the preceding verse, introduced by γὰρ. ὀργὴν] the personal displacency of God towards sin, manifested subjectively in remorse of conscience, and objectively in the penal evils of this and the future life. The moral law, in relation to sinful man, operates in the mode of retribution, and therefore cannot be the medium of a promise of good. For the transgressor, the law is a threat and a terror. This is the very contrary of a promise. οὗ δὲ οὐκ, etc.] (ℵABC Pesh., Copt., Lachm., Tisch.

οὐδὲ παράβασις. 16 *διὰ τοῦτο ἐκ πίστεως, ἵνα κατὰ χάριν, εἰς τὸ εἶναι βεβαίαν τὴν ἐπαγγελίαν παντὶ τῷ σπέρματι, οὐ τῷ ἐκ τοῦ νόμου μόνον, ἀλλὰ καὶ τῷ ἐκ πίστεως Ἀβραάμ,*

read δὲ; DEF Rec. read γὰρ). The logical connection of this clause with the preceding is somewhat obscure, owing to its negative form, and the ellipses. The reasoning of the apostle in verse 15 is this: The law works wrath [wherever there is sin]; but [among men] there is sin wherever there is law. The second of these positions is stated in a negative form, and requires the positive part to be supplied. The complete sentence would run thus: οὗ δὲ ἔστιν παράβασις, ἐκεῖ νόμος· οὗ δὲ οὐκ ἔστιν νόμος, οὐδὲ παράβασις. The sin is as wide as the law; and the law has been shown to be as wide as the race (ii. 12–16).

VER. 16. διὰ τοῦτο] a conclusion from verses 14, 15. ἐκ πίστεως] supply οἱ κληρονόμοι εἰσίν, from verse 14; since ἐκ πίστεως is antithetic to ἐκ νόμου. κατὰ χάριν] supply ἡ ἐπαγγελία γένηται, from the subsequent ἐπαγγελίαν. εἰς τὸ] the divine purpose. βεβαίαν] is opposed to κατήργηται in verse 14: "firm," because depending upon God's word, and not upon man's obedience. The evangelical promise secures human obedience, and consequently does not rest upon it. σπέρματι] spiritual and not carnal descent is meant, as in iv. 13. οὐ τῷ] sc. σπέρματι. ἐκ τοῦ νόμου] describes the Jew, but the *believing* Jew, because he is a part of πᾶν τό σπέρμα. The Jew as merely carnally descended from Abraham, was no part of the "seed" here spoken of: "for they are not all Israel which are of Israel; neither because they are the seed of Abraham are they all children," ix. 6, 7. Hence, νόμου, in this place, is not put for ἔργα νόμου, or perfect legal obedience, as it is in verses 13, 14, and elsewhere. It stands for the Mosaic economy simply. Compare Heb. vii. 19; x. 1. καὶ τῷ] sc.

ὅς ἐστιν πατὴρ πάντων ἡμῶν 17 (καθὼς γέγραπται ὅτι πατέρα πολλῶν ἐθνῶν τέθεικά σε) κατέναντι οὗ ἐπίστευσεν

σπέρματι. ἐκ πίστεως Ἀβραάμ] qualifies τῷ σπέρματι. This class were believing Gentiles, having Abraham's faith, but not Abraham's blood. The other class had both the faith and the blood; and both united made up the whole spiritual seed. The comment of Theophylact is excellent: "To all the seed, that is to say, to all *believers:* not only those believers who are of the law, that is, who are circumcised, but those believers also who are uncircumcised, who are a seed of Abraham begotten to him by faith." The phrase ἐκ πίστεως Ἀβραάμ is antithetic to ἐκ τοῦ νόμου, only for the purpose of distinguishing the *circumcised* believer from the *uncircumcised.* The antithesis must not be pressed so far as to imply that those Jews who constituted a part of the total seed alluded to were not also ἐκ πίστεως Ἀβραάμ. ὅς ἐστιν, etc.] a repetition of verses 11 and 12. ἡμῶν] "us believers."

VER. 17 cites from the Old Testament (Gen. xvii. 5), in proof that Abraham is the father of all believers, both Gentile and Jewish. The quotation is best regarded as parenthetical, so that κατέναντι, etc., is immediately connected with ὅς ἐστιν πατὴρ, etc. (Eng. Ver., Lachm., Meyer, Tholuck, Alford, Hodge). πολλῶν ἐθνῶν] Abraham could have been the father of only one nation, if carnal paternity were meant. τέθεικά] "appointed," or "constituted." The word denotes that the paternity spoken of was the result of a special arrangement or economy. It would not be used to denote the merely physical connection between father and son. No one would say that Philip was appointed to be the father of Alexander. κατέναντι] *coram:* "in the presence of" (Mark xi. 2). The eternity of God precludes sequences in his con-

θεοῦ τοῦ ζωοποιοῦντος τοὺς νεκροὺς καὶ καλοῦντος τὰ μὴ ὄντα ὡς ὄντα. [18] *ὃς παρ' ἐλπίδα ἐπ' ἐλπίδι ἐπίστευσεν,*

sciousness, and implies that all things and events are simultaneous in his intuition. The full construction is: κατέναντι τοῦ θεοῦ, κατέναντι οὗ ἐπίστευσεν. Compare the similar structure in Luke i. 4: περὶ ὧν κατηχήθης λόγων, for περὶ τῶν λόγων, περὶ ὧν κατηχήθης (Meyer). νεκροὺς] the primary reference is to the circumstances of Abraham mentioned in verse 19, but this for the purpose of illustrating the agency of God in the act of gratuitous justification. The word that blots out sin is a creative word. This is implied in Christ's question: "Whether is easier to say, Thy sins be forgiven thee: or to say, Rise up and walk?" Luke v. 23. καλοῦντος] the creative call of the Almighty. Isa. xl. 4; xlviii. 13. τὰ μὴ ὄντα] the subjective negative is employed, because the non-entity is relative, and not absolute. It may be displaced by entity, if God so please. The phrase, καλεῖν τὰ μὴ ὄντα ὡς ὄντα, is equivalent to creare ex nihilo. The same exertion of infinite power, though not under precisely the same form of statement, is described in 1 Cor. i. 28; 2 Cor. iv. 6; Heb. xi. 3; Coloss. i. 16; Gen. i. 3. In 2 Maccabees vii. 28, it is said that God "made the heaven and the earth, and all that is therein, ἐξ οὐκ ὄντων." Philo (De creatione, 728 b) employs phraseology like that of St. Paul: τὰ μὴ ὄντα ἐκάλεσεν εἰς τὸ εἶναι. The primary reference of τὰ μὴ ὄντα is to the posterity of Abraham who were not yet born; the secondary reference is to the justification of the *ungodly* (iv. 5). When God imputes righteousness without righteousness (χωρὶς ἔργων), he calls that which is not, as though it were.

VER. 18. St. Paul now (verses 18–21) gives a more particular description of Abraham's faith. παρ' ἐλπίδα] "beyond," or "contrary to" hope considered objectively: hope

εἰς τὸ γενέσθαι αὐτὸν πατέρα πολλῶν ἐθνῶν κατὰ τὸ εἰρη-
μένον Οὕτως ἔσται τὸ σπέρμα σου, 19 *καὶ μὴ ἀσθενήσας*
τῇ πίστει κατενόησεν τὸ ἑαυτοῦ σῶμα νενεκρωμένον, ἑκα-
τονταετής που ὑπάρχων, καὶ τὴν νέκρωσιν τῆς μήτρας
Σάρρας, 20 *εἰς δὲ τὴν ἐπαγγελίαν τοῦ θεοῦ οὐ διεκρίθη τῇ*
ἀπιστίᾳ, ἀλλὰ ἐνεδυναμώθη τῇ πίστει, δοὺς δόξαν τῷ θεῷ,

in all external respects. ἐπ' ἐλπίδι] the preposition has the signification of "because of," "on the ground of," as in Mat. xix. 9; Luke i. 59; Phil. i. 3; Heb. vii. 11; viii. 6. Hope, in this case, is viewed subjectively. Abraham was inwardly hopeful, when all was outwardly hopeless. Contrary to hope, he yet, on account of his hope, believed the promise. εἰς τὸ] denotes the divine purpose. In the plan of God, Abraham believed in order that he might become the father of all believers. εἰρημένον] in Gen. xv. 5. οὕτως] i. e., like the stars in multitude.

VER. 19. μὴ ἀσθενήσας τῇ πίστει] is a meiosis for ἰσχυρὰν πίστιν ἔχων (Theophylact). See comment on i. 13. κατενόησεν] (the reading of ℵABC Copt., Lachm., Tisch.; DEFL Peshito, Vulg., Rec. read οὐ κατενόεσεν) denotes distinct notice and observation, Heb. iii. 1; x. 24; Luke xii. 24. Abraham plainly saw the physical impossibility in the case, Gen. xvii. 17. The retention of οὐ makes the clause οὐ κατενόεσεν, etc., nearly equivalent to the clause οὐ διεκρίθη, etc., and also destroys the adversative force of δὲ.

VER. 20. δὲ] is adversative; Abraham distinctly perceived the deadness, etc., *but yet*, etc. διεκρίθη] has the middle signification (compare 1 Cor. xi. 31): "he did not scrutinize into" (εἰς). Meyer renders: "he did not doubt in reference to" (εἰς). ἐνεδυναμώθη] "became, or grew, strong," Heb. xi. 34. πίστει] instrumental dative. δοὺς] "since he gave." δόξαν] honor to God's power and promise.

21 καὶ πληροφορηθείς, ὅτι ὃ ἐπήγγελται δυνατός ἐστιν καὶ
ποιῆσαι. 22 διὸ καὶ ἐλογίσθη αὐτῷ εἰς δικαιοσύνην. 23 οὐκ
ἐγράφη δὲ δι' αὐτὸν μόνον, ὅτι ἐλογίσθη αὐτῷ, 24 ἀλλὰ
καὶ δι' ἡμᾶς, οἷς μέλλει λογίζεσθαι, τοῖς πιστεύουσιν ἐπὶ
τὸν ἐγείραντα Ἰησοῦν τὸν κύριον ἡμῶν ἐκ νεκρῶν, 25 ὃς
παρεδόθη διὰ τὰ παραπτώματα ἡμῶν καὶ ἠγέρθη διὰ τὴν
δικαίωσιν ἡμῶν.

VER. 21. πληροφορηθείς] denotes complete conviction. Compare xiv. 5. If Gen. xvii. 17 be compared with Gen. xv. 6, there is an apparent contradiction. The latter, however, implies only a momentary wavering of Abraham's faith, like that of John the Baptist. See Mat. xi. 2 sq. Neither Abraham nor John fell away into absolute unbelief. ἐπήγγελται] is middle.

VER. 22. The summary conclusion from the whole narrative in verses 18–21, and looking back to verse 3. διὸ] "on this account."

VER. 23. The paragraph in verses 23–25 exhibits the relation of the Old Testament testimony concerning Abraham, to all believers. δι' αὐτὸν μόνον] merely for the purpose of showing the way and manner of Abraham's justification, alone.

VER. 24. δι' ἡμᾶς] i. e., to show how we are justified. μέλλει] denotes the continuing purpose of God. λογίζεσθαι] sc. πίστις. ἐγείραντα] this particular exertion of divine power is chosen with reference to the νεκροὺς and νέκρωσιν of verses 17 and 19, and because it is the highest exercise of power.

VER. 25. παρεδόθη] to death. Compare viii. 32. διὰ παραπτώματα] on account of their guilt, which is expiated by the ἱλαστήριον (iii. 25). ἠγέρθη] Christ's resurrection was indispensable in order to the act of faith in Christ's death. Compare v. 1; 1 Cor. xv. 17. The death constitutes the atonement for guilt, but had Christ never risen from the dead, no man could have appropriated it, because there would have been no evidence that he had conquered death, and no living person in whom to believe. δικαίωσιν] the state of justification, as distinguished from the act, which is denoted by δικαιώμα (v. 18).

CHAPTER V

1 *Δικαιωθέντες οὖν ἐκ πίστεως εἰρήνην ἔχομεν πρὸς τὸν θεὸν διὰ τοῦ κυρίου ἡμῶν Ἰησοῦ Χριστοῦ,* 2 *δι᾽ οὗ καὶ*

§ 3. *The effects of gratuitous justification.* Rom. v.–viii.

ST. PAUL has described the *necessity* of the righteousness by faith, in Rom. i. 18–iii. 20; and the *nature* of it, including its harmony with the Old Testament, in iii. 21–iv. 25. He now proceeds to describe the *effects* of this righteousness, in v.–viii.

VER. 1. δικαιωθέντες] See comment on iii. 20. οὖν] draws a conclusion from the matter in iii. 21–iv. 25. εἰρήνην] justification, rather than sanctification, is intended by this word. It is the subjective pacification of the conscience resulting from the objective satisfactiòn of divine justice. Paul does not begin to discuss sanctification, as one of the effects of the gratuitous righteousness of God, until chapter vi. He begins with the first and more immediate effect, namely, the removal of remorse, and mental tranquillity before the offended law. The justified person is no longer an ἐχθρός (v. 10), and no longer under ὀργή (iv. 15; v. 9). Compare John xiv. 27; xvi. 33; Eph. ii. 14. ἔχομεν] we retain this reading upon dogmatic grounds, with the majority of commentators, although the subjunctive ἔχωμεν is by far the most strongly supported (ℵABCDL Pesh., Copt., Æth., Vulg., Lachm., Tisch., Tregelles). The writer now mentions an actual and

τὴν προσαγωγὴν ἐσχήκαμεν εἰς τὴν χάριν ταύτην ἐν ᾗ ἑστήκαμεν, καὶ καυχώμεθα ἐπ' ἐλπίδι τῆς δόξης τοῦ θεοῦ.

necessary effect of justification, namely, peace with God. This requires the indicative. The subjunctive mode, in the *hortatory* signification certainly, is entirely out of place here. The connection between God's act of justification and peace of conscience is that of cause and effect, and it would be illogical in the highest degree to exhort a person who has experienced the operation of the cause, to labor that the effect may follow. Given the cause, the effect follows of course. Perhaps, however, the *concessive* signification of the subjunctive might be defended here, by one who should insist upon taking the reading which has such a strong diplomatic support: "Being justified, we may have peace." The subjunctive, in this signification, approximates to the future (Winer, p. 285); and the Peshito (Murdock's Trans.) renders: "Because we are justified by faith, we shall have peace." The reading ἔχωμεν would in this case yield a sense as consistent, both logically and doctrinally, as the reading ἔχομεν. πρὸς] denotes relation: "in respect to." τὸν θεὸν] the article denotes God in his trinitarian plenitude: the Godhead. The divine Being, irrespective of Christ's ἱλαστήριον, is displacent towards man as sinful, and man as sinful is hostile towards the divine Being. Peace between the holy nature of God and the guilty will of man, is mediated by an act and work of one of the persons of the Godhead incarnate: διὰ Ἰησοῦ Χριστοῦ.

VER. 2. καὶ] "also." Christ is not only the atonement, but he is the access to it. John xiv. 6; Acts v. 31; Eph. iii. 12; Heb. xii. 2. χάριν] the grace that imputes faith for righteousness. ἑστήκαμεν] the present of a completed action. Compare 1 Cor. xv. 1. καυχώμεθα] i. e., ἐν ᾗ καυχώμεθα. Self-

3 οὐ μόνον δέ, ἀλλὰ καὶ καυχώμεθα ἐν ταῖς θλίψεσιν, εἰδότες ὅτι ἡ θλῖψις ὑπομονὴν κατεργάζεται, 4 ἡ δὲ ὑπομονὴ
δοκιμήν, ἡ δὲ δοκιμὴ ἐλπίδα· 5 ἡ δὲ ἐλπὶς οὐ καταισχύνει,

congratulation in the good sense is meant; for examples see Rom. viii. 36 sq.; 2 Cor. xi. 30; Mat. v. 10. Joy is combined with self-congratulation in possessing the blessing of justification. ἐπ'] "over," or "on account of." Winer, p. 408, Thayer's Ed. δόξης] a comprehensive term for all the divine attributes in their celestial manifestation. Compare Ex. xxxiii. 18; Mat. xvi. 27; John xvii. 5. θεοῦ] subjective genitive: "God's heavenly glory."

VER. 3. οὐ μόνον δέ,] sc. καυχώμεθα ἐπ' ἐλπίδι. καυχώμεθα] See comment on verse 2. ταῖς] "those well-known afflictions." εἰδότες] "since we know." ὑπομονὴν] the *power* of patient endurance is the result. κατεργάζεται] "works *out*."

VER. 4. δοκιμήν] denotes: 1. the act of trying: the experiment, 2 Cor. viii. 2; 2. the result of the trial: the experience, 2 Cor. ii. 9. The latter is the meaning here. ἐλπίδα] the hope of seeing the divine glory which accompanies justification is strengthened by the experience of afflictions.

VER. 5. ἡ ἐλπὶς] the hope of heavenly glory thus tried. καταισχύνει] to make ashamed (or to terrify) by failure. Perhaps the latter is the better rendering. Compare Ps. xxii. 5, where the Septuagint translates בּוֹשׁוּ (of which, according to Gesenius, the primary meaning is not to blush from shame, but to turn pale from terror) by κατῃσχύνθησαν. ὅτι] introduces the reason why the hope does not disappoint. θεοῦ] 1. subjective genitive: God's love towards us (Orig., Chrys., Ambrose, Luther, Calvin, Grotius, Olsh., De Wette, Meyer); 2. objective genitive: our love to God (Theodoret, Aug., Anselm, and the Papal divines, from dogmatic considera-

ὅτι ἡ ἀγάπη τοῦ θεοῦ ἐκκέχυται ἐν ταῖς καρδίαις ἡμῶν διὰ πνεύματος ἁγίου τοῦ δοθέντος ἡμῖν. 6 ἔτι γὰρ Χριστὸς, ὄντων ἡμῶν ἀσθενῶν ἔτι, κατὰ καιρὸν ὑπὲρ ἀσεβῶν ἀπέθα-

tions). Verse 8 shows that the first interpretation is the correct one. ἐκκέχυται] denotes an exuberant communication. Compare Acts ii. 17; x. 45; Tit. iii. 6. ἐν ταῖς καρδίαις] the dative denotes motion in place: "within our hearts." πνεύματος] the Holy Spirit produces in the believer an immediate and overflowing consciousness that he is the object of God's redeeming love; and this is the guaranty that his hope will not disappoint him.

VER. 6. ἔτι γὰρ] ℵACD Rec., Lach., Tisch. (εἴ γε: B). γὰρ introduces the death of Christ as the evidence of God's love. Χριστός] separates ἔτι from ὄντων, to which it belongs, by reason of emphasis and the crowd of thoughts. Meyer, in loco, cites similar instances from Plato. ἀσθενῶν] Sin is helplessness (α privative, and σθενός), especially contemplated as guilt. Man is powerless to atone for sin. ἔτι] repeated after ἀσθενῶν seems superfluous, but is strongly supported by ℵABCD Lachm., Tisch. It would agree better with the Vatican reading, εἴ γε: "If, surely, we being still without strength, etc." κατὰ καιρὸν] "at the appointed time." It is to be construed with ἀπέθανεν. Compare Gal. iv. 4; Eph. i. 10. ὑπὲρ] as verse 7 shows, has here the signification of ἀντί. Compare Luke xxii. 19, 20; John xi. 50; 1 Cor. i. 13; 2 Cor. v. 14, 15, 20, 21; 1 Pet. iii. 18. Winer (Thayer's Ed., p. 383) remarks that "ὑπὲρ is sometimes nearly equivalent to ἀντί, *instead*, *loco* (see, especially, Eurip., Alcest., 700; Philemon, 13; Thuc. i. 141; Polyb., 3, 67, 7)." He adds, however, in a note, somewhat inconsistently with the above remark: "Still, in doctrinal passages relating to Christ's death (Gal. iii. 13; Rom. v. 6, 8; xiv. 15; 1 Pet. iii. 18), it is not justifiable to render ὑπὲρ ἡμῶν, and the like, rigorously by *instead of*, on account of such parallel passages as Mat. xx. 28 (Fritzsche, Rom. i. 267). Ἀντί is the more definite of the two prepositions. Ὑπὲρ signifies merely *for* men, for their deliverance; and leaves undetermined the precise sense in which Christ died *for* them." But, the fact, conceded by Winer, that ὑπὲρ "is sometimes nearly equivalent to ἀντί," shows that it has a *twofold* sense, and therefore it must be left to the context to determine the meaning. The same ambiguity is found in the English preposition *for*. To die "for" a man may mean either to die in his place, or for his benefit. In which sense the preposition is to be taken, must be decided by the connection. But either signification is possible. De Wette (com. on Rom. v. 7) says, "ὑπὲρ kann *anstatt* und *für* heissen: 1 Cor. v. 20." Baur (Paulus der Apostel, s. 165) remarks: "Wenn auch in vielen Stellen das ἀποθανεῖν ὑπὲρ nur ein Sterben zum Besten Anderer ist, so kann doch wohl in den Stellen, Rom. iv. 25; Gal. i. 4; Rom. viii. 3; 1 Cor. xv. 3; 2 Cor. v. 14, der Begriff der Stellvertretung, wenigstens der Sache nach, nicht zurückgewiesen werden." Compare, also, Magee On Atonement, Dissertation xxx. The reason why St. Paul employs ὑπὲρ, not exclusively, but more frequently than ἀντί, when speaking of the vicariousness of Christ's death, is this: ὑπὲρ having two meanings can teach the two facts that Christ died in the place of, and for the benefit of, the believer; while ἀντί, having but one signification, can mention but one of them. The more comprehensive of the two prepositions is preferred in the majority of instances. ἀσεβῶν] See the explanation of this word in the comment on iv. 5.

VER. 7. ὑπὲρ] See comment on verse 6. δικαίου] a strict and exactly just man who gives to every one his due; no more, and no less. The term excludes compassionate benev-

νεν· [7] μόλις γὰρ ὑπὲρ δικαίου τις ἀποθανεῖται· ὑπὲρ γὰρ τοῦ ἀγαθοῦ τάχα τις καὶ τολμᾷ ἀποθανεῖν· [8] συνίστησιν

olence, which bestows more than is due. Justice is venerable and admirable, but not winning. Though abstractly possible, yet it would be altogether improbable (μόλις), that an ordinary imperfect man should be so impressed by this rigorous and exact attribute, as to lay down his life for it. Only the perfect God-man has done this. ἀποθανεῖται] the future here expresses something that is never likely to occur (Winer, p. 279). γὰρ] in both instances in this verse assigns an explanatory reason, with reference to the statement in verse 6 that Christ died for the *ungodly*. This is an extraordinary thing, and not to be expected, for two reasons: 1. *for* one would hardly die for a strictly upright man; 2. *for*, possibly, one would venture to die for a man who had been compassionate to him. The English rendering, "yet," is erroneous. τοῦ ἀγαθοῦ] the article denotes the particular individual of this class, and implies that such men are rare. δικαίου is anarthrous, because only the class is thought of, and this class is more numerous than the other. Men are more inclined to be exactly just, than to be generous and compassionate: to give what is due, than to give more than is due. ἀγαθοῦ is antithetic to δικαίου, and denotes the benefactor: the kind and compassionate man. "Vir bonus est, qui prodest, quibus potest, nocet nemini." Cicero, De Officiis, iii. 15. Compare Luke xviii. 18; xxiii. 50; Rom. vii. 12; and the Hebrew צַדִּיק and חָסִיד. The Rabbins explain these words thus: "The just man says to his neighbor, All mine is mine and all your's is your's. The good man says, All your's is your's alone, and all mine is your's also." It is remarkable that a passage containing a contrast so sharp as that between justice and benevolence, and a meaning so plain, should have called out such a variety of interpreta-

δὲ τὴν ἑαυτοῦ ἀγάπην εἰς ἡμᾶς ὁ θεὸς ὅτι ἔτι ἁμαρτωλῶν ὄντων ἡμῶν Χριστὸς ὑπὲρ ἡμῶν ἀπέθανεν· ⁹ πολλῷ οὖν μᾶλλον δικαιωθέντες νῦν ἐν τῷ αἵματι αὐτοῦ σωθησόμεθα

tions. *τάχα*] in the classics, expresses possibility, yet accompanied with doubt.

VER. 8. *συνίστησιν*] "sets (*ἵστσιν*) in a strong light." Compare iii. 5. The position of the verb is emphatic. *ἑαυτοῦ*] reflexive for emphasis: "his own." *ἔτι*] the benefit conferred by the divine compassion is prior to all excellence or merit, as well as to all strength (*ἀσθενῶν*, ver. 6) upon man's part. *ὑπὲρ*] the connection implies substitution, as in v. 6; viii. 32. *ἀπέθανεν*] as an *ἱλαστήριον*, iii. 25.

VER. 9. *πολλῷ μᾶλλον*] expresses the great certainty of the believer's salvation, in view of what has been said in verses 7 and 8. A man might perhaps be willing to die for his benefactor, but not for an exactly upright man who pays all debts, but confers no benefits. But God makes a self-sacrifice for the positively *wicked*, who are neither just nor benevolent, and while they are still in this state of wickedness. It is certain, consequently, that those who are the chosen objects of such compassionate love as this will be saved. Compare v. 15, 17. *νῦν*] if justified now in time, we shall be saved hereafter in eternity. *αἵματι*] the life-blood when poured out in death is expiatory; typically, in the instance of the Levitical lamb, actually, in the instance of the Lamb of God. John i. 36. *ὀργῆς*] for the explanation of this word, see comment on i. 18, and the author's Theological Essays, pp. 268–284. It denotes a personal emotion, and not merely an abstract attribute. A divine emotion is a divine attribute in energy. In relation to it, the oblation of Christ is called a "propitiation" (*ἱλασμός*), 1 John ii. 2; iv. 10. The feeling of anger towards sin, is not incompatible with the feeling of

δι' αὐτοῦ ἀπὸ τῆς ὀργῆς. [10] εἰ γὰρ ἐχθροὶ ὄντες κατηλλά-
γημεν τῷ θεῷ διὰ τοῦ θανάτου τοῦ υἱοῦ αὐτοῦ, πολλῷ μᾶλ-

compassionate benevolence (ἀγάπη, ver. 7) towards the sinner. The very Being who is displeased, is the very same Being who, though a placatory atonement of his own providing, saves from the displeasure. The supplication of the litany: "From thy wrath, Good Lord deliver us," implies that it is God's compassion (ἀγάπη) that saves from God's anger (ὀργή), and, consequently, that both feelings co-exist in the divine nature.

VER. 10. A confirmatory explanation of verse 9. ἐχθροὶ] the passive signification (the holy God displeased with wicked man) is the meaning here (Calvin, De Wette, Tholuck, Fritzsche, Meyer). This is corroborated by the ὀργή τοῦ θεοῦ, from which the believer is saved by Christ's ἱλαστήριον. It is not the wrath of man toward God, but of God toward man, that requires the reconciliation. It is true, that the subjective wrath of the human conscience (not toward God, but toward the man himself) requires appeasement and pacification, and obtains it through this same vicarious atonement of the Son of God; but this point is not brought into view here. The co-existence and compatibility of ἀγάπη and ὀργή in the Supreme Being is seen in the fact here spoken of by St. Paul, that God's compassion for the soul of man prompts him to appease or "propitiate" his own wrath at the sin of man. The highest form of love, that, namely, of self-sacrifice, prompts the triune God to satisfy his own justice, in the room and place of the sinner who has incurred the penalty of justice. In the work of vicarious atonement, God himself is both the offended and the propitiating party. This is taught in 2 Cor. v. 18: "God hath reconciled us to *himself*;" Coloss. i. 20: "to reconcile all things to *himself*."

λον καταλλαγέντες σωθησόμεθα ἐν τῇ ζωῇ αὐτοῦ, [11] *οὐ μόνον δέ, ἀλλὰ καὶ καυχώμενοι ἐν τῷ θεῷ διὰ τοῦ κυρίου ἡμῶν Ἰησοῦ Χριστοῦ, δι' οὗ νῦν τὴν καταλλαγὴν ἐλάβομεν.*

God, in the person of Jesus Christ, is judge, priest, and sacrifice, all in one Being. The common objections to the doctrine of the propitiation of the divine anger, rest upon the unitarian idea of the deity. According to this view, which denies personal distinctions in the Essence, God, if propitiated, must be propitiated by *another* being than God. Christ is merely a creature. The influence of the atonement upon God is, therefore, a foreign influence from the sphere of the finite. But, according to the trinitarian idea of the Supreme Being, it is God who propitiates God. Both the origin and the influence of the atonement are personal, and not foreign, to the deity. The transaction is wholly in the divine Essence. The satisfaction of justice, or the propitiation of anger (whichever terms be employed, and both are employed in Scripture), is required by God, and made by God. And the infinite and everlasting benefits of such a trinitarian transaction are graciously and gratuitously bestowed upon the guilty creatures for whom, ἀσθενεῖς ἔτι (ver. 6), and ἔτι ἁμαρτολοι ὄντες (ver. 8), the transaction took place. καταλλάγημεν] is used in the passive signification: "so that God is no longer unreconciled with man" (Meyer). ζωῇ] If the *death* of Christ effects the conciliation of God's justice to man, certainly the *life* of the glorified Christ will not leave redemption incomplete.

VER. 11. οὐ μόνον δέ] supply σωθησόμεθα (compare v. 3). ἀλλὰ καὶ] supply σωθησόμεθα. καυχώμενοι] is used in the good sense, denoting a union of joy and triumphant self-congratulation. It qualifies σωθησόμεθα, understood. καταλλαγὴν] This important word is rendered "atonement," in the English version. At the time when the version was made, atonement = at-one-ment, or reconciliation. The present use of the word atonement makes it equivalent to expiation, or satisfaction. This latter is the true meaning of καταλλαγή, in this passage. The term denotes, primarily, that which is paid in *exchange*, in the settlement of a disagreement or difference between two parties. Parties are "reconciled" with each other, by one paying to the other a stipulated sum: the καταλλαγή (the "balance"). Then, the effect is put for the cause; and καταλλαγή comes to have the secondary signification of reconciliation itself. There is an allusion to these two meanings of the term, in Athenæus, x. 35. "Why do we say of a tetradrachma that καταλλάττεται, when we never speak of its getting into a passion?" A coin can be "exchanged," but not "reconciled." The same metonymy of effect for cause is seen in the Saxon word *bot*, from which the modern "boot" is derived. This, primarily, signifies the compensation paid to the injured party by the offender; then, secondly, the harmony or reconciliation effected between the parties by such compensation; and, lastly, the repentance itself of the offending party (Bosworth's Anglo-Saxon Dictionary, in loco). Through Christ, the believer "*receives* the atonement:" namely, that expiation for sin which settles the difference between God and man. The result is reconciliation and harmony between the two parties. ἐλάβομεν] If the sinner himself made this expiation, he would not "receive" it, but would give it. This would be personal atonement. He cannot make it himself; and it is graciously made for him. This is vicarious atonement, which he "accepts" and "receives," by faith.

Verses 12–21 describe the parallel between the condemnation in Adam, and the justification in Christ. Verses 12, 18, 19 contain the substance of the parallel, namely, the protasis

[12] Διὰ τοῦτο ὥσπερ δι' ἑνὸς ἀνθρώπου ἡ ἁμαρτία εἰς τὸν κόσμον εἰσῆλθεν, καὶ διὰ τῆς ἁμαρτίας ὁ θάνατος, καὶ

and apodosis of the proposition. Verses 13–17 are parenthetic and explanatory. Verses 20, 21 exhibit the relation of the Sinaitic law to the justification in Christ.

VER. 12. διὰ τοῦτο] a conclusion from the whole previous reasoning respecting gratuitous justification. ὥσπερ, etc.] has no correlative clause regularly expressed. Some, like Tholuck, regard the clause ὅς ἐστιν τύπος τοῦ μέλλοντος as a substitute for it. But it is simplest to regard the clause introduced by ὥσπερ as suspended by the parenthetic explanation, and then repeated in verse 18, where the ὡς finds its correlative in οὕτως. δι' ἑνὸς ἀνθρώπου] through one man, in distinction from a multitude of individuals. In 2 Cor. xi. 3; 1 Tim. ii. 13, 14 (compare Sirach xxv. 24), Eve is joined with Adam in the first transgression; as she is, also, in the narrative in Genesis. Hence εἷς ἄνθρωπος, here, stands for *both Adam and Eve*, including their posterity. The two, as taken together, are denominated "man," in Gen. v. 2: "God called *their* name Adam, in the day when they were created." Similarly, Hosea vi. 7: "They, like men (marg. Adam) have transgressed." In 1 Cor. xv. 22, the article is employed, in order to denote the species as male and female: "In Adam (τῷ 'Αδὰμ) all die." In Rom. vii. 1, the "man" includes the woman, as verse 2 shows. Compare Mat. xii. 12; 1 John iii. 15; Coloss. i. 2. St. Paul does not mean that sin entered into the world by Adam *exclusive* of Eve: by the man, in distinction from the woman. He employs the term "man" as it is employed in Gen. v. 2, to denote the human *species* which God created bi-sexual, in two individuals, "male and female." The work of creating "man" was not finished until Eve had been created; and the apostasy of "man" was not complete until Adam as well as Eve had eaten of the tree of knowledge. Augustine (De Civitate, xv. 17) notices this use of the term "man." "Enos (אֱנוֹשׁ) signifies 'man' not as Adam does, which also signifies man but is used in Hebrew indifferently for man and woman; as it is written, 'male and female created he them, and blessed them, and called their name Adam' (Gen. v. 2), leaving no room to doubt that though the woman was distinctively called Eve, yet the name Adam, meaning man, was *common to both*. But Enos means man in so restricted a sense, that Hebrew linguists tell us it cannot be applied to woman." Compare the use of ἄνθρωπος and ἀνὴρ in the Greek language. In accordance with this, Augustine (De Civitate, xi. 12) calls Adam and Eve *primos homines*. The Formula Concordiæ (Hase, p. 643) expressly mentions both individuals as concerned in the apostasy: "In Adamo et Heva, natura initio pura, bona, et sancta, creata est: tamen, per lapsum, peccatum ipsorum naturam invasit." De Moore in Marckium (Caput xv. § 10) remarks respecting Paul's statement in 1 Tim. ii. 14: "Nec negat ab altera parte apostolus mulieris peccatum, cum *unum hominem*, quem ceu τύπον τοῦ μέλλοντος Christo opponit, peccati propagati auctorem, in quo peccavimus et morimur omnes, esse docet, quem expresse quoque *Adamum* vocat: coll. Rom. v. 12–19 cum 1 Cor. xv. 21, 22." De Moore (xv. § 10) also cites Pareus, as making Adam to include Eve, by community of nature, and by the fact that husband and wife are one flesh (Gen. ii. 24). Witsius (Covenants, II. iv. 11) approvingly quotes Cloppenburg as saying, that "the apostle Paul in Rom. v. 12 did not so understand one man Adam as to exclude Eve: which is here the error of some." ἡ ἁμαρτία] original sin (Calvin); the sinful habitus (Olshausen); the principle of sin (De Wette, Meyer, Philippi). The latter is preferable. Compare v. 21; vi. 12, 14; vii. 8, 9, 17. κόσμον] the human world; it had

οὕτως εἰς πάντας ἀνθρώπους ὁ θάνατος διῆλθεν, ἐφ' ᾧ πάντες ἥμαρτον·

previously entered the angelic world by the fall of Satan and his angels. θάνατος] supply εἰς τὸν κόσμον εἰσῆλθεν. Both physical and spiritual death is meant. That it is physical, is plain from v. 14; Gen. iii. 19; that it is spiritual, is evident from Rom. v. 18, 21, 23, where ζωή is the contrary of θάνατος, and from 2 Tim. i. 10, where the same contrast appears. Chrysostom, Augustine, and Meyer confine the term to physical death. Pelagius confined it to spiritual death. De Wette, Tholuck, Olshausen, Philippi, Lange, Alford, Stuart, and Hodge regard it as including physical and spiritual death. Death is stated to be the penalty of sin, in Gen. ii. 17; Ezek. xviii. 4; Rom. vi. 23; viii. 13. From Gen. ii. 17; iii. 22 the inference is, that man's body would have been immortal in case he had not sinned; he would have been permitted "to eat of the tree of life, and live forever." Compare Rev. ii. 7. οὕτως] "consequently:" death is an effect, of which sin is the cause. πάντας ἀνθρώπους] denotes universality: it is equivalent to the antecedent κόσμον. διῆλθεν] corresponds to εἰσῆλθεν: sin entered *in*, and death passed *through*. ἐφ' ᾧ] is equivalent to ἐπὶ τούτο ὅτι = διότι, 2 Cor. v. 4; Phil. iii. 12; iv. 10. It mentions a reason, with particularity: "for the reason that." The patristic rendering, which makes it equivalent to ἐν ᾧ, in quo (Aug., Pelag., Beza, Owen), is incorrect, because: 1. the preposition ἐπὶ will not bear it; and 2. the supposed antecedent, ἑνὸς ἀνθρώπου, is too remote. πάντες] all without exception, infants included, as verse 14 teaches. ἥμαρτον] mentions the particular reason why all men died: viz., because all men sinned. ἥμαρτον is a verb active, and has an active signification (Aug., Beza, Owen, Edwards, Olshausen, Fritzsche, Tholuck, De Wette, Meyer, Philippi, Haldane). This is proved: 1. by the uniform use, in the New Testament, of the verb ἁμαρτανεῖν, Mat. xxvii. 4; Luke xv. 18; John ix. 2; Acts xxv. 8; Rom. ii. 12; iii. 23; v. 14, 16; vi. 15; 1 Cor. vii. 28; Eph. iv. 26; 1 Tim. v. 20; Tit. iii. 11; Heb. x. 26; 1 Pet. ii. 20; 1 John i. 10; 2. by the uniform signification of the substantive ἁμαρτία, Rom. v. 12, 13, 14, 15 et passim; 3. by the interchange of παράπτωμα with ἁμαρτία, v. 16–21; vi. 1, 13; 4. by the fact, that the clause ἐφ' ᾧ πάντες ἥμαρτον explains the clause διὰ τῆς ἁμαρτίας, in the preceding context. "The meanings, 'peccati pœnam subire' (Grotius), or 'peccatores facti sunt' (Melanch.), do not at all belong to ἥμαρτον. The word cannot mean: '*became sinful*,' or: '*were sinful*,' for ἁμαρτανεῖν is not = ἁμαρτωλὸν γίγνεσθαι, or εἶναι. Still less does it mean: '*bore the penalty of sin*.' Rather, ἥμαρτον is nothing but = *sinned*." Philippi, in loco. The force of the aorist is to be retained. A particular historical event is intended: "all sinned, when sin entered into the world by one man." See comment on iii. 23. Ἥμαρτον, then, denotes, in this place, the first sin of Adam. This is proved by the succeeding explanatory context, verses 15–19, in which it is reiterated five times in succession, that *one*, and *only* one sin is the cause of the death that befalls all men. Compare 1 Cor. xv. 22. Accordingly, some commentators supply ἐν Ἀδὰμ, after ἥμαρτον (Bengel, Olshausen, Koppe, Meyer, Philippi, Delitzsch), suggested by ἑνὸς ἀνθρώπου (v. 12), and by Ἀδὰμ (bis) in verse 14. And that large class of exegetes who explain the clause by the Adamic union, virtually supply ἐν Ἀδὰμ.

The explanation of Pelagius, adopted by De Wette, Fritzsche, Tholuck, Baur, Stuart, that ἥμαρτον denotes the actual sin of each individual subsequent to birth, is contradicted: 1. by Rom. v. 14, in which it is asserted that certain persons who are a part of πάντες, the subject of ἥμαρτον, and who suffer the death which is the penalty of sin, did not commit sins *resembling* Adam's first sin: i. e., individual and conscious transgressions; and, 2. by v. 15–19, in which it is asserted, repeatedly, that only one sin, and not millions of sins, is the cause of the death of all men. If St. Paul had intended to teach that death passes upon all men, because of their multiplied *repetition* of Adam's first sin, he would have written ἐφ' ᾧ πάντες ἁμαρτάνουσιν,—employing the present tense, to denote something continually going on.

A qualified and passive signification has been given to ἥμαρτον, by commentators who differ from each other in their exegesis of the passage, as well as in their general dogmatic position: 1. "became sinful:" Calvin (pravitatem ingenitam et hereditariam), Melanchthon, Flatt. 2. "were accounted to have sinned:" Chrysostom (γεγόνασιν παρ' ἐκείνου πάντες θνητοί), Theodore Mops., Theophylact, Grotius (frequens est Hebræis dicere peccare pro pœnam subire), Limborch, Locke, Whitby, Wahl, Bretschneider, John Taylor, Macknight, Hodge. The objections to the passive signification of ἥμαρτον, in either of these forms, are the following: 1. It is contrary to uniform usage in the New Testament, and is particularly incompatible with the meaning of ἁμαρτία, in the clause διὰ τῆς ἁμαρτίας which it explains. If this interpretation be correct, it is the only instance in Scripture in which this active verb, in the active voice, has a passive signification. Passages cited from the Old Testament, in support of the signification "to account to have sinned," are Gen. xliii. 9; xliv. 32, where חָטָאתִי is translated by the Seventy ἡμαρτηκώς ἔσομαι ("I shall bear the blame," Eng. Ver.); and 1 Kings i. 21, ἔσομεθα ἁμαρτολοι ("We shall be counted offenders," Eng. Ver.). But, if St. Paul had intended to teach, in Rom. v. 12, that all men were regarded or reckoned as sinners, he would have adopted the same complex form of the verb, and have written ἐφ' ᾧ πάντες ἡμαρτηκότες ἦσαν. 2. This passive signification excludes Adam (i. e., Adam and Eve) from the πάντες who "sinned." Death, certainly, did not pass upon the first pair, the "one man," because they were *reckoned* to be sinners. And, since the πάντες who sinned are identical with the κόσμον into which sin entered, this interpretation of ἥμαρτον also excludes Adam from the "world:" thus destroying the unity of Adam and his posterity. 3. The passive signification makes ἥμαρτον to denote God's action, and not man's. It designates only the treatment, or estimate, which men receive from God, and not an act of their own. But an act of God would not be a proper ground for the infliction of punishment upon man, or angel. The clause ἐφ' ᾧ πάντες ἥμαρτον is introduced to justify the infliction of death, temporal and eternal, upon all men. But it makes such an infliction more inexplicable, rather than less so, to say that it is visited upon those who did not commit the sin that caused the death, but were fictitiously and gratuitously regarded as if they had. 4. The passive signification, if given to ἥμαρτον, destroys the logical force of the passage in its connection, because it amounts only to the proposition: All men die, for the reason that they are reckoned to deserve death. This is one reason for death, but not the reason that is required by the nature of St. Paul's argument. This demands a reason founded upon the act of the *criminal*, and not of the judge. 5. The passive signification tends to evacuate θάνατος of its plenary biblical signification. If the sin in question is only hypothetical and putative, then it is natural to infer that the punishment inflicted on account of it should be mitigated and moderate. Hence, of those who hold that Adam's posterity were "reckoned" to have sinned in him, but really did not, a portion deny altogether, that penalty properly so called is inflicted upon the posterity for Adam's sin; while another portion teach that only the *privative* part of the penalty denominated θάνατος falls upon the posterity considered merely as descendants of Adam,—the positive part of it being visited only upon the actual transgressions of the individual. The latter class hold, that because of the first sin of Adam, the Holy Spirit is withdrawn from every individual man at birth; but the pains of hell, the positive part of the penalty of sin, they assert, are not inflicted upon the ground of Adam's first sin, but of subsequent individual action. But Rom. v. 14 teaches that θάνατος, in the same *plenary* signification that it has throughout the chapter, comes upon those "that had not sinned after the similitude of Adam's transgression." Adam's first sin, even without actual transgression, according to St. Paul, merits death, physical, spiritual, and eternal.

Historically, the passive signification, in its second form, was first forced upon ἥμαρτον by those who denied that Adam's first sin was immediately and literally imputed to his posterity, and that original sin is truly and properly sin. Compare Chrysostom on Rom. v. 12 sq. The Semi-Pelagian and Arminian exegetes, generally, explain ἥμαρτον, in this place, in the sense of "peccati pœnam subire." The lexicographers Wahl and Bretschneider have given currency to this explanation. Exegetes like De Wette and Meyer, though doctrinally favoring the Semi-Pelagian view of original sin, are prevented by philological considerations from giving this signification to ἥμαρτον.

This signification of ἥμαρτον is defended by a reference to the parallelism in v. 12–19. Men, it is argued, are confessedly justified by the righteousness of Christ without any merit of their own, and hence it follows that they are condemned by Adam's sin without any demerit of their own (Hodge, in loco). The answer to this is: 1. St. Paul teaches that the parallel between Adam and Christ does not hold in every particular, v. 15–17. 2. If it holds in reference to the particular under consideration, then as justification in

Christ is described as "gratuitous" (δωρεὰν), and "without works" (χωρὶς ἔργων), condemnation in Adam must be described in the same manner. See the comment on iv. 3. But the doctrine that the posterity of Adam are gratuitously condemned would be both absurd and impious. 3. The gratuitous imputation of sin, by which the sin of his people was reckoned to Christ, and "He who knew no sin was made to be sin," 2 Cor. v. 21, was for the purpose of *expiating* sin. This is totally different from the imputation of Adam's sin to his posterity, which has nothing to do with the vicarious atonement for sin. Christ was charged with a sin that he did not participate in, or commit, in order that he might come under the *reatus* without the *culpa* peccati, the punishment without the guilt. Hence, this gratuitous imputation of sin to the Redeemer cannot be cited to prove that there is also a gratuitous imputation of sin to the race of mankind. Sin is charged to them in order to its personal punishment, and not its vicarious atonement. There is nothing in this locus classicus respecting Adam's sin, that implies that the connection between ἁμαρτία and θάνατος is any other than the common ethical connection between real guilt and merited punishment: between *culpa* and *reatus*. Unless there is culpa there is no reatus, for the human race. All men die for the first sin, because all men committed the first sin; or, in St. Paul's words, "all die, because all sinned."

The doctrine of the imputation of the first sin to all men, and of their punishment therefor, rests upon the doctrine of the *natural* and *substantial unity* of Adam and his posterity in the first act of sin. This doctrine of the Adamic unity is taught in the Old Testament, Gen. v. 2; Job xxxi. 33; Hosea vi. 7. It passed from the Old Testament into the Jewish theology, 2 Esdras iii. 7, 21; vii. 11, 46, 48; ix. 19; Wisdom ii. 23, 24; Sirach xxv. 32. The Rabbins (excepting the Cabalists, who were emanationists, and referred evil to God) referred the origin of sin to Adam. See, especially, Wolfius, ad Rom. v. 12; also Wetstein, Olshausen, Tholuck, Meyer, and Philippi, on Rom. v. 12 sq. The Chaldee paraphrase on Ruth iv. 22 is as follows: "Because Eve ate the forbidden fruit, all the inhabitants of the earth are subject to death." The doctrine of the Adamic unity, thus dimly revealed in the Old Testament, was confirmed and more fully developed by St. Paul, as the Logos-doctrine, which also appears dimly in the Old Testament and passed into the Jewish theology, was by St. John: the former dogma being the key to anthropology, and the latter to trinitarianism. Christ hints at the doctrine in John viii. 44, where he denominates Satan ἀνθρωποκτόνος, "a slayer of man*kind*." Compare Acts xvii. 26, where God is said to have made all nations of men ἐξ ἑνὸς αἵματος (ℵBA Vulg., Lachm., Tisch., omit αἵματος).

In constructing a dogmatic scheme that shall agree with the exegesis of St. Paul's teaching respecting the origin of sin, in man, and its imputation, some method must be adopted, by which, without logical contradiction, though not without a mystery, it can be made to appear that all men can act *en masse*, and at once, and commit that "one offence" against the probationary statute of which the apostle speaks. There are only two methods: 1. that of real existence in Adam; 2. that of representation by Adam. The elder Calvinism followed Augustinianism, in adopting the former; the later Calvinism has favored the latter.

The following extracts from the commentary of Pareus upon Rom. v. exhibit the views of the elder Calvinism (and Lutheranism also), respecting the union of Adam and his posterity, and the imputation of the first sin. "Assumptio apostoli consideratione indiget, quomodo omnes peccaverint. Loquitur haud dubie de peccato illo primo, per quod mors transiit ad omnes. Non (inquit) ita fuit unius, quin et omnium fuerit. In uno, omnes illud admiserunt: alioqui mors in omnes transire non potuisset. Qui enim non peccant, hoc est nulla culpa et reatu tenentur, ut sancti angeli, in eos mors nil juris habet. Quia vero mors in omnes transiit, omnes igitur peccaverunt, hoc est culpa et reatu tenentur. Hoc est, enim, peccare apostolo: *omnes*, inquam, non adulti tantum, sed et parvuli." Pareus explains how all sinned in one man, as follows: 1. "*Participatione culpæ*, quia omnes posteri seminali ratione fuerunt in lumbis Adami. Ibi, igitur, omnes in Adamo peccante peccaverunt: sicut Abraham in lumbis Levi dicitur decimatus. Et liberi sunt pars parentum. Culpa, igitur, parentum participatione est liberorum. 2. *Imputatione reatus*, quia primus homo ita stabat in gratia, ut si peccavet, non ipse solus, sed tota posteritas ea excideret, reaque cum ipso fieret æternæ mortis, juxta interminationem: *morte morieris:* nempe, tu cum tua sobole et posteritate: sicut feuda tali conditione dantur vasallis, ut si ea per culpam perdant parentes, parentum reatu involvantur et liberi. Atque hoc est, quod primum Adæ peccatum nobis imputari dicitur. 3. *Naturali* denique *propagatione* seu generatione, horribilis naturæ deformitas cum tristi reatu in omnes posteros sese diffudit. Nam qualis Adam post lapsum fuit, tales filios genuit: unde dicitur *genuisse filium ad imaginem suam.* Sic tria sunt in peccato originis: participatio culpæ, imputatio reatus, et propagatio naturalis pravitatis.

Peccatum originale dicitur ambigue, tam peccatum *originans*, hoc est, primum peccatum Adami qua fuit personalis transgressio, quam peccatum *originatum*, qua idem peccatum Adami fuit totius generis humani prævaricatio. Utroque sensu, peccatum originale, tam in Adamo quam in posteris, tria lethifera mala includit: *culpam actualem; reatum legalem* seu mortis pœnam; et *pravitatem habitualem* seu deformitatem naturæ. Hæc enim, simul in parente et posteris, circa peccatum primum concurrerunt: eo solum discriminatione, quod Adam peccans fuit principale agens, admittens culpam, promerens reatum, abjiciens imaginem dei, seque depravens; posterorum hæc omnia sunt participatione, imputatione, et generatione ex vitioso parente. Sic frustra disputatum est a Sophistis, an peccatum originale sit culpa prima, an tantum reatus, an tantum morbus, vel macula, vel labes, vel vitium naturæ. Est enim *hæc omnia.*" See, also, the extract from Turretine, in the comment on iv. 3.

The following particulars are noteworthy, in this statement of Pareus: 1. The imputation of Adam's sin rests upon *participation*, as its first ground and cause. The later Calvinism, in some of its representatives, has departed from this position, by throwing out participation, entirely, and making the sole ground of imputation to be the sovereign will of God. 2. To sin in Adam means, to incur *both* guilt and liability to punishment: "omnes peccaverunt: hoc est *culpa* et *reatu* tenentur" (Pareus). The later Calvinism, in some instances, has departed from the elder, by explaining the guilt of Adam's sin to be merely *reatus* without *culpa*. This modification of the earlier view burdens the problem of original sin with grave difficulties of an ethical nature; because it implies that sin and guilt, precisely like righteousness and innocence, may be imputed *gratuitously*, by an act of sovereignty.

Verses 13 and 14 are parenthetical, and explain the statement in verse 12, that all men sinned that one sin of "one man," which brought the penalty of death upon all men. Such an extraordinary statement as this requires explanation; but the statement that death passes upon all men because of their many individual transgressions, would require no explanation at all.

VER. 13. *ἄχρι γὰρ νόμου*] St. Paul first shows, that the sin meant in the clause *πάντες ἥμαρτον*, is not one that was com-

13 ἄχρι γὰρ νόμου ἁμαρτία ἦν ἐν κόσμῳ, ἁμαρτία δὲ
οὐκ ἐλλογεῖται μὴ ὄντος νόμου. 14 ἀλλὰ ἐβασίλευσεν ὁ

mitted against the Mosaic law. Sin was in the world prior to the decalogue: the fact of death previous to the time of Moses proves this. All violations of the decalogue must, therefore, be excluded from the account, when looking for the particular sin that brought death into the world of mankind. ἦν] "was, that is, really was, or truly existed; not, 'was counted,' as if Adam's posterity had his sin counted to them, though it was not really theirs. It was their sin, as truly as it was that of Adam, otherwise the justice of God would not have required that they should suffer for it." Haldane, in loco. ἁμαρτία δὲ . . . νόμου] Sin necessarily supposes a law against which it is committed. Although the decalogue was not yet promulgated, there must, nevertheless, have been some law of some kind against which πάντες ἥμαρτον; otherwise sin could not have been charged to them. Compare iv. 15. ἐλλογεῖται] "put into the account," for punishment, i. e. See Philemon, 18, for the meaning of the word.

VER. 14 is an explanatory clause, introduced by ἀλλὰ, the object of which is, to prevent the reader from inferring from the statement that "sin is not imputed when there is no law," that individual transgressions against the *unwritten* law are intended in the clause, "sin was in the world." This is the actual inference of some commentators. Wolfius (in loco) so interprets: "regnavit mors ab Adamo usque ad Mosen, ac proinde necesse est, primum, hominibus imputatum fuisse, deinde vero etiam legem aliquam fuisse, nempe *naturalem* illam, de qua cap. i. & ii." The apostle prohibits this explanation, by mentioning a class of persons who did not sin against the unwritten law, who, nevertheless, suffer

θάνατος ἀπὸ Ἀδὰμ μέχρι Μωυσέως καὶ ἐπὶ τοὺς μὴ ἁμαρτήσαντας ἐπὶ τῷ ὁμοιώματι τῆς παραβάσεως Ἀδάμ,

the penalty of death. ἀλλὰ] Winer (p. 442) remarks, that ἀλλὰ is used when a train of thought is interrupted by a correction, or explanation, and is equivalent to "yet," or "however." "*But although*" sin is not imputed when there is no law, "*yet* death," etc. ἐβασίλευσεν] denotes the despotic sway of sin. ἀπὸ Ἀδὰμ μέχρι Μωυσέως] the ante-Mosaic period. καὶ] whether rendered "even," or "also," implies that it would not have been expected that death should reign over the class of persons spoken of, and that their case is the difficult one to explain. The implication also is, that if these persons *had* sinned "after the similitude of Adam's transgression," it would not have been strange that they should die. τοὺς μὴ ἁμαρτήσαντας] viz.: infants (Augustine, Aquinas, Melanch., Beza, Pareus, Owen, Justification, Chap. xviii., Edwards, Original Sin, Ch. iv., § 2). Respecting these persons, three facts are incontestable: 1. they constitute a part of the πάντες of verse 12, and therefore sinned; 2. they must have been under a law of some kind, or sin could not have been imputed to them (verse 13); and 3. they die (verse 14). ἐπὶ τῷ ὁμοιώματι . . . Ἀδάμ] B reads ἐν τῷ ὁμοιώματι. ἐπὶ signifies, "after:" used of the rule, or model, Luke i. 59 (Winer, p. 394). ὁμοιώματι is emphatic, in the clause. It signifies "shape," or "form:" Rom. i. 23; viii. 3; Phil. ii. 7; Rev. ix. 7. These persons, says the writer, did not commit a sin *resembling* (of the same shape, or form, with) the sin that brought death upon all men. A sin resembling Adam's first sin would have been a particular act of transgression, either of the written, or the unwritten law. This kind of sin, the apostle asserts, these persons had not committed. Neither the law of conscience, nor the decalogue, is the law which they transgressed, when, as part of the πάντες, they "sinned."

The sin, consequently, which the apostle has in mind is Adam's first sin itself; and the law which these persons transgressed, and without which sin could not be imputed to them, was the command: "Thou shalt not eat of the tree of the knowledge of good and evil," Gen. ii. 17. This class of persons sinned, then, not after the similitude of Adam's transgression, by violating the unwritten law, but they sinned the very same sin itself, by transgressing the Eden statute. The relation between their sin and Adam's is not that of resemblance, but of *identity*. Had the sin by which death came upon them been one *like* Adam's, there would have been as many sins to be the cause of death, and to account for it, as there were individuals. Death would have come into the human world by millions of men, and not "by one man" (ver. 12); and judgment would have come upon all men, to condemnation, by millions of offences, and not "by one offence" (ver. 18).

The object, then, of the parenthetical digression in verses 13 and 14 is to prevent the reader from supposing from the statement that "all men sinned" ("have sinned:" Eng. Ver.), that the *individual* transgressions of all men are meant, and to make it clear that only the one first sin of the one first man is intended. In order to this, the apostle begins by remarking that the existence of sin does not depend upon the Mosaic law; and yet it depends upon the existence of some law or other. The only other laws conceivable in the case, are the unwritten law previously spoken of by the apostle (ii. 14, 15), and the commandment given in Eden (Gen. ii. 16, 17). The former of these, rather than the latter, would most naturally come into the mind of the reader, and he might explain the proposition that "all men have sinned," by reference to the unwritten law. The apostle precludes this explanation, by the statement that some who are included in the πάντες did not violate the unwritten law,

by a transgression similar to that of Adam. And yet they die, as all other persons do. Death supposes sin, and sin supposes a law. They must, therefore, have committed a sin of some kind, against a law of some kind. The Mosaic law and the law of conscience have been ruled out of the case. These persons must, therefore, have sinned against the commandment in Eden, the probationary statute; and their sin was not similar (ὁμοιως) to Adam's, but Adam's *identical* sin: the very same sin, numerically, of the "one man." They did not sin *like* Adam; but they "sinned *in* him, and fell *with* him in that first transgression" (Westminster Larger Catechism, 22).

St. Paul, in this verse, alludes to adults between Adam and Moses only by implication, and not directly: καὶ implies that there were some between Adam and Moses who *had* sinned after the similitude of Adam's transgression (viz.: adults); but the penalty of death which they suffer is not founded upon their actual and individual transgressions, but upon the one sin of the one man. If responsibility for the first sin is established in the case of infants, it is established for adults; for all adults were once infants. τύπος] anarthrous: "*a* type." The word denotes a copy taken by impressing a seal, John xx. 25. Adam, by reason of his unity with his posterity, is a type of Christ who is one with his people. The two unities are alike in some particulars, but not in all; as the following verses show. "This passage clearly represents the human race, not only with respect to its physical and mental but also its spiritual powers, as wrapped up in Adam; inasmuch as sin, not merely as a corruption of body and soul, but as an apostasy of the spirit from God and rebellion of the will against his commandment, is expressly traced back to Adam's fall." Philippi, on Rom. v. 13, 14.

Verses 15–17 exhibit the *dissimilarity* between the con-

ὅς ἐστιν τύπος τοῦ μέλλοντος. [15] ἀλλ' οὐχ ὡς τὸ παράπτωμα, οὕτως καὶ τὸ χάρισμα. εἰ γὰρ τῷ τοῦ ἑνὸς παραπτώματι οἱ πολλοὶ ἀπέθανον, πολλῷ μᾶλλον ἡ χάρις τοῦ

demnation in Adam and the justification in Christ. The writer is led to this, by the remark that Adam is the type of Christ. See Owen on Justification, Ch. xviii.; Howe's Oracles of God, Lecture xxi.

VER. 15. ἀλλ'] has the same force as in verse 14: "*But although* Adam is a type of him who is to come, *yet* not as the offence, so, etc." τὸ παράπτωμα] sc. ἐστι: the sin of the one man; the single special instance of ἁμαρτία spoken of in verse 12. τὸ χάρισμα] sc. ἐστι: the gift of righteousness mentioned in iii. 21; iv. 5. εἰ ἀπέθανον] the indicative denotes an actual instance: "if, as is the fact." τοῦ ἑνὸς] viz.: Adam and Eve, including their posterity, as in verse 12. οἱ πολλοὶ] is put for the πάντες of verse 12, for the sake of antithesis with τοῦ ἑνός. ἀπέθανον] became subject to the θάνατος mentioned in verse 12. πολλῷ μάλλον ἐπερίσσευσεν] Compare v. 10; James ii. 13; Isa. lv. 7. If God exhibited exact justice, in punishing all men without exception, infants included, for that first sin which all men, infants included, committed, he has exhibited great mercy in the extraordinary method of *gratuitous* justification. The justice in the former case is apparent, because it is κατὰ τὰ ἔργα; but the mercy in the latter case is still more apparent, because it is entirely χωρὶς ἔργων. Adam's sin is the act of Adam and his posterity *together*. Hence, the imputation to the posterity is just and merited. Christ's obedience is the work of Christ *alone*. Hence, the imputation of it to the elect is gracious and unmerited. The latter imputation is for nothing (δωρεάν). The former is for something. The difference between the merited condemnation, and the unmerited justification is that

θεοῦ καὶ ἡ δωρεὰ ἐν χάριτι τῇ τοῦ ἑνὸς ἀνθρώπου Ἰησοῦ
Χριστοῦ εἰς τοὺς πολλοὺς ἐπερίσσευσεν. 16 καὶ οὐχ ὡς δι'
ἑνὸς ἁμαρτήσαντος τὸ δώρημα· τὸ μὲν γὰρ κρῖμα ἐξ ἑνὸς εἰς

of *degree*, or *quality:* "where sin abounded, grace superabounded," v. 20. ἡ χάρις] the principle itself, of compassion in the divine mind. ἡ δωρεὰ] sc. θεοῦ: the effect of the principle. ἐν χάριτι . . . Χριστοῦ] this clause qualifies ἐπερίσσευσεν (Meyer), and not δωρεὰ (Tholuck, Eng. Ver.); because the article is not repeated after δωρεὰ, and because ἐν χάριτι, etc., is the correlate in the apodosis to τῷ παράπτωματι in the protasis. τοὺς πολλοὺς] is not of equal extent with οἱ πολλοὶ in the first clause, because other passages teach that "the many" who die in Adam are not co-terminous with "the many" who live in Christ. Compare Mat. xxv. 46. ἐπερίσσευσεν] denotes an ample and overflowing abundance. Compare Eph. i. 8; Rom. iii. 7. The aorist indicates an accomplished fact in the past.

VER. 16. The differentiating of the condemnation and the justification is continued, and a numerical difference is now noticed. Condemnation results from one offence; justification delivers from many offences. The dissimilarity here relates to *quantity.* καὶ οὐχ ὡς] supply τὸ κρίμα ἐστὶν, suggested by κρίμα in the succeeding clause. τὸ δώρημα] (i. e., οὕτως καὶ ἐστὶν τὸ δώρημα) means the same as τὸ χάρισμα, in verse 15. The former denotes the gratuitous righteousness as an object; the latter denotes it in its subjective reference to compassion (χάρις) in God. τὸ κρῖμα] sc. ἐστὶν: the judicial sentence, or verdict, after the examination and trial. ἑνὸς] supply παραπτωμάτος, suggested by παραπτωμάτων in the succeeding clause. εἰς κατάκριμα] defines the intention and result of the sentence as a *condemning* one: a verdict (κρίμα) might be one of acquittal, if the examination and trial of the

κατάκριμα, τὸ δὲ χάρισμα ἐκ πολλῶν παραπτωμάτων εἰς
δικαίωμα. [17] εἰ γὰρ τῷ τοῦ ἑνὸς παραπτώματι ὁ θάνατος
ἐβασίλευσεν διὰ τοῦ ἑνὸς, πολλῷ μᾶλλον οἱ τὴν περισσείαν
τῆς χάριτος καὶ τῆς δωρεᾶς τῆς δικαιοσύνης λαμβάνοντες
ἐν ζωῇ βασιλεύσουσιν διὰ τοῦ ἑνὸς, Ἰησοῦ Χριστοῦ. [18] ἄρα

person so resulted. χάρισμα] sc. ἐστὶν. πολλῶν παραπτωμάτων] denotes the first sin, and all the sins that result from it: both original sin, and actual transgression. The condemnation in Adam relates to one sin only; the justification in Christ relates to that sin and millions of sins besides. δικαίωμα] is the contrary of κατάκριμα, and denotes justification as a declarative *act* of God (Fritzsche, Meyer). Compare i. 32; ii. 26; viii. 4. Luther and Tholuck say that it denotes the subjective *state* of justification.

Ver. 17. A further enforcement and explanation of verse 16, introduced by γὰρ. τοῦ ἑνὸς] sc. ἀνθρώπου: the same as in verse 12. Codices AFG read ἐν ἑνὶ παραπτώματι. διὰ τοῦ ἑνὸς] is repeated for the sake of emphasis. Compare 2 Cor. xii. 7. πολλῷ μᾶλλον] qualifies βασιλεύσουσιν, and relates to certainty, not to quantity (Chrysostom). "The issues of a *divine* act working salvation are much more sure, than the issues of a *human* act working ruin." Philippi in loco. If the union with Adam in his sin was certain to bring destruction, the union with Christ in his righteousness is yet more certain to bring salvation. οἱ λαμβάνοντες] the participle for a substantive: "the recipients." Compare Mat. ii. 20. περισσείαν] is used with reference to ἐπιρίσσευσεν in verse 15. Compare ii. 4. χάριτος and δωρεᾶς] are distinguished from each other as in verse 15. B omits τῆς δωρεᾶς. τῆς δικαιοσύνης] the article denotes that gratuitous righteousness which has been so fully described. ζωῇ] eternal life, the contrary of the θάνατος mentioned in verse 12.

οὖν ὡς δι' ἑνὸς παραπτώματος εἰς πάντας ἀνθρώπους εἰς κατάκριμα, οὕτως καὶ δι' ἑνὸς δικαιώματος εἰς πάντας

VER. 18 resumes the parallel between Adam and Christ, which was commenced in verse 12, but interrupted by the explanatory parenthesis in verses 13–17. ἄρα οὖν] "accordingly then;" a very frequent phrase in the Pauline epistles. Compare vii. 3, 25; viii. 12; ix. 16, 18; xiv. 12, 19. It is contrary to pure Greek usage, at the beginning of a proposition (Meyer). ὡς] corresponds to ὥσπερ in verse 12. ἑνὸς] is better rendered in the neuter with παραπτώματος. Were it masculine, the article would have preceded it, as in verses 15 and 17 (Meyer). The masculine without the article, but with the substantive ἀνθρώπου, is used in verse 12. It is, however, regarded as masculine by the Vulgate, Eng. Ver., Theodoret, Erasmus, Luther, Calvin, Tholuck; and this view is favored by the antithesis πάντας ἀνθρώπους. The elliptical words in the first clause are τὸ κρίμα ἦλθεν (ἦλθεν suggested by διῆλθεν in verse 12); and in the second clause, τὸ χάρισμα ἦλθεν. πάντας ἀνθρώπους] the same as in verse 12. εἰς κατάκριμα] denotes the tendency and result of the judicial sentence (κρίμα). ἑνὸς] as in the preceding clause, is to be rendered in the neuter. δικαιώματος] denotes, here, the act of justification, considered as a decision or declaration of God, as in i. 32; v. 16. It is correlated to δικαίωσιν. It is sometimes employed in a subjective sense, to denote righteousness itself, as in Rev. xix. 8. πάντας ἀνθρώπους] i. e., all οἱ λαμβάνοντες, of verse 17. The meaning of πάντες, equally with that of πολλοί, must be determined by the context. Compare xi. 32; 1 Cor. xv. 22. The efficacy of Christ's atonement is no more extensive than faith; and faith is not universal (2 Thess. iii. 2). δικαίωσιν] the state and condition of justification, in which the person is pronounced complete before the law, both in respect to penalty and precept. See

ἀνθρώπους εἰς δικαίωσιν ζωῆς· [19] ὥσπερ γὰρ διὰ τῆς
παρακοῆς τοῦ ἑνὸς ἀνθρώπου ἁμαρτωλοὶ κατεστάθησαν οἱ

the explanation of δίκαιος, in verse 19. ζωῆς] the genitive of quality; or, perhaps, of apposition: "justification which is life."

VER. 19 merely repeats, in corroboration, the statement in verse 18. ὥσπερ] instead of ὡς (ver. 18), is the same form employed in verse 12. παρακοῆς] the ἁμαρτία spoken of in verse 12, and descriptive of it as an unwillingness to *hear* (ἀκοή) the divine command. ἁμαρτωλοὶ] real and not reputed sinners. This is the universal signification in the New Testament. Compare Mat. ix. 10; Mark ii. 17; Luke vii. 39; John ix. 31; Rom. iii. 17; Heb. vii. 26. κατεστάθησαν] denotes that οἱ πολλοί were "set down in a class, or under a category." The verb καθίστημι never signifies "to make." Causation is not implied by it. Even in passages like James iii. 6, iv. 4 (where the English version translates by "is"), and 2 Pet. i. 8, the word signifies, "to place in the class of." And in Acts xvii. 15, where it signifies, "to conduct," it is because the conductor "sets down," or appoints, all the movements of the person conducted. The meaning then is, that "the many were placed in the class, or category, of sinners," for a reason that has been specified in the preceding statements concerning the connection between the one man and all men, in the first act of sin. Meyer explains thus: "The many were set down and classified as sinners, because, according to verse 12, they sinned in and with Adam in his fall." The word κατεστάθησαν denotes merely a *declarative* (not a causative) act upon the part of God; founded, however, upon a foregoing causative act upon the part of man. This foregoing causative act is the first sin of Adam. Because all sinned in Adam, God placed all in the list or catalogue of

πολλοί, οὕτως καὶ διὰ τῆς ὑπακοῆς τοῦ ἑνὸς δίκαιοι κατασταθήσονται οἱ πολλοί.

sinners. He pronounced them to be what they had already become by their own act in Adam. The action denoted by this verb, which is ambiguously rendered by "made" in the English version, supposes the fact of *natural union* between those to whom it relates. All men are declared to be sinners, on the ground of the "one offence;" because, when that one offence was committed, all men were one man (omnes eramus unus ille homo, Augustine),—that is, were one common nature in the first human pair,—and in this first original mode of their existence committed the original offence. The imputation of the first sin rests upon the fact of a created unity of nature and being. All mankind commit the first sin, and therefore all mankind are chargeable with it. The ethical principle, consequently, upon which original sin is imputed is the same as that upon which actual transgressions are imputed. It is imputed because it is committed. All men are punished with death, because they literally sinned in Adam; and not because they are metaphorically reputed to have done so, but in fact did not. οἱ πολλοί] are the same as the πάντες of verse 12. It is used rather than πάντες, in order to make a verbal antithesis to τοῦ ἑνὸς ἀνθρώπου. ὑπακοῆς] denotes the entire agency of Christ, both in obedience and suffering. δίκαιοι] denotes those upon whom justice has no claims, either with respect to the penalty or the precept of the law, because both the penalty and the precept have been fulfilled, either personally, or vicariously. Under the law, a man is δίκαιος who has *personally* obeyed the precept. In this case there is no penalty to be fulfilled. Under the gospel (which is the status of the persons here spoken of), a man is δίκαιος who, by faith in Christ, has *vicariously* suffered the penalty, and *vicariously* obeyed the precept. καταστaθήσονται] has, of course, the same signification as in the first part of the verse. The declaration that these persons are righteous, and the placing of them in this class, supposes, as in the other instance, the fact of a *union* between ὁ εἷς and οἱ πολλοί: i. e., between Christ and believers. But this union differs in several important particulars, from that between Adam and his posterity. It is not natural and substantial, but moral, spiritual, and mystical; not generic and universal, but individual and by election; not caused by the creative act of God, but by his regenerating act. All men without exception are one with Adam; only believing men are one with Christ. The imputation of Christ's obedience, like that of Adam's sin, is not an arbitrary act, in the sense that if God so pleased he could reckon either to the account of any beings whatever in the universe, by a volition. The sin of Adam could not be imputed to the fallen angels, for example, and be punished in them; because they never were one with Adam by unity of substance and nature. The fact that they have committed actual transgression of their own, would not justify the imputation of Adam's sin to them; any more than the fact that the posterity of Adam have committed actual transgressions of their own would be a sufficient reason for imputing the first sin of Adam to them. Nothing but a real union of nature and being can justify the imputation of Adam's sin. And, similarly, the obedience of Christ could no more be imputed to an unbelieving man, than to a lost angel, because neither of these is morally, spiritually, and mystically one with Christ. οἱ πολλοί] not all mankind, but only those persons who are described in verse 17, as "they which receive abundance of grace, and of the gift of righteousness." Compare 1 Cor. xv. 22. At the close of this paragraph, in which St. Paul presents the parallel between Adam and Christ, with respect both to the resemblance and the dissimilarity, we recapitulate the more important points: 1. At the time when Adam disobeyed, all men were one nature or species in him, and participated in his disobedience. Adam's disobedience, consequently, is imputed to all men upon the ground of their race-participation in it. 2. At the time when Christ obeyed, all men were not one nature or species in Him, and did not participate in his obedience. Christ's obedience, therefore, is imputed without race-participation in it. 3. The natural or substantial union between Adam and his posterity was established in creation, prior to Adam's disobedience. Consequently, when Adam disobeyed, he did not disobey alone, and by himself. The agency, in this instance, was a common one. 4. The spiritual union between Christ and his people is established subsequently to creation, in regeneration. This union does not exist until after Christ's obedience has been accomplished; for it supposes the finished work of the Mediator. Consequently, Christ suffers and obeys alone and by himself (Isa. lxiii. 3). The agency, in this case, is an individual one, only. 5. The imputation of Adam's disobedience is necessary. All men have participated in it, and hence all men must be charged with it. 6. The imputation of Christ's obedience is optional. No man has participated in it, and whether it shall be imputed to any man, depends upon the sovereign pleasure of God. 7. The imputation of Adam's sin is universal: no man escapes it. 8. The imputation of Christ's righteousness is particular: only those who are chosen of God are the subjects of it. 9. The imputation of Adam's sin is an act of justice, and a curse. 10. The imputation of Christ's righteousness is an act of grace, and a blessing. 11. The imputation of Adam's sin is merited, and not gratuitous. 12. The imputation of Christ's righteousness is gratuitous, and not merited.

20 *νόμος δὲ παρεισῆλθεν, ἵνα πλεονάσῃ τὸ παράπτωμα· οὗ δὲ ἐπλεόνασεν ἡ ἁμαρτία, ὑπερεπερίσσευσεν ἡ χάρις,*

VER. 20 assigns the reason for the promulgation of the Mosaic law. The question naturally arises: If sin and death occurred in the way that has been described, *previous* to the Mosaic law, and without its use, then why its subsequent introduction? The answer is, that it was introduced in order to develop and manifest the sin of man originated in Adam's fall. The object was not to prevent the apostasy: it was too late to do this. Neither was salvation from sin the object; for the law can do nothing but condemn to death. *νόμος*] the written law of Moses. *δὲ*] is adversative, and supposes an objection to be mentally supplied: viz.: that if these representations respecting Adam's sin are correct, then it is strange that a written law should have been promulgated so long a time after the apostasy and ruin of mankind. *παρεισῆλθεν*] "came in alongside of." The decalogue entered the world centuries after sin had entered it. Erasmus finds the notion of stealth, or secrecy (subintravit). *ἵνα*] telic. It was the distinct purpose of God. *πλεονάσῃ*] The decalogue was not promulgated with any expectation that it would, of itself, gradually diminish sin, and recover man from the ruin of the fall; but, on the contrary, with the intention that it should elicit and intensify human depravity, in order to its removal not by law, but by the Holy Ghost. The effect of law upon a sinful soul is to detect sin, and bring it into consciousness. Law makes sin "abound:" 1. apparently: by directing attention to it, and disclosing its nature. Compare vii. 9; Gal. iii. 19; 1 Cor. xv. 56. 2. really: by stimulation through checks (not stimulation by enticements, as in the case of temptation). The effect, upon the sinner, of the legal prohibition, coupled with the threat of punishment, is, to provoke to anger, and to intensify the self-will. "Niti-

21 *ἵνα, ὥσπερ ἐβασίλευσεν ἡ ἁμαρτία ἐν τῷ θανάτῳ, οὕτως καὶ ἡ χάρις βασιλεύσῃ διὰ δικαιοσύνης εἰς ζωὴν αἰώνιον διὰ Ἰησοῦ Χριστοῦ τοῦ κυρίου ἡμῶν.*

mur in vetitum." παράπτωμα] is the same as the ἁμαρτία of verse 12, but viewed as a concrete working principle in men. οὗ] local (Meyer); temporal (De Wette). ὑπερπερίσσευσεν] compare comment on v. 15–17.

VER. 21. ἵνα] denotes the purpose of νόμος δὲ παρεισῆλθεν; showing that the cumulation, and "abounding" of sin in the consciousness of the sinner, is in order to its removal. Augustine (in Ps. cii.) remarks: "Non crudeliter hoc fecit deus, sed concilio medicinæ. Augetur morbus, crescit malitia, quæritur medicus et totum sanatum." ἐβασίλευσεν] entire sway and domination. ἐν τῷ θανάτῳ] the sphere in which, and the instrument by which. δικαιοσύνης] that gratuitous and imputed righteousness described in chapter iv. αἰώνιον] absolute endlessness. It is not expressed, here, with the contrary term θάνατος, but is implied. When a qualifying word belongs equally to two substantives that are antithetic to each other, it may be omitted in the protasis to be suggested by the apodosis, or omitted in the apodosis, to be suggested by the protasis. Were the death temporal, the life being eternal, the writer would have qualified θάνατος with some word denoting temporary duration (e. g. πρόσκαιρος, Mat. xiii. 21), in order to prevent the reader from putting it under the same category with ζωή, as by the laws of grammar he would. διὰ Ἰησοῦ] both the medium and the mediator.

CHAPTER VI

[1] *Τί οὖν ἐροῦμεν; ἐπιμένωμεν τῇ ἁμαρτίᾳ, ἵνα ἡ χάρις πλεονάσῃ;* [2] *μὴ γένοιτο. οἵτινες ἀπεθάνομεν τῇ ἁμαρτίᾳ,*

THIS chapter continues the description of the effects of gratuitous justification. The particular effect now to be mentioned is *progressive sanctification.* Faith in Christ's atonement is the vital and spontaneous source of morality and piety. The peace of conscience spoken of in chapter v. 1 sq., as the immediate effect of the application of Christ's blood, is naturally connected with holy living. A justified person, though regenerated, is imperfectly sanctified. He has remnants of original corruption. Owing to these, he may lapse into sin, and sin mixes with his best experience; but he cannot contentedly "*continue* in sin," without any resistance of it and victory over it. St. Paul teaches, with great cogency and earnestness, that trust in Christ's atoning blood is incompatible with self-indulgence and increasing depravity. The two things are *heterogeneous*, and cannot exist together. The proof of this is derived: 1. from the unity of the believer with Christ, in respect to Christ's work of atonement, verses 1–14; 2. from the nature of the human will and of voluntary agency, verses 15–22.

VER. 1. *οὖν*] in accordance with what has been said in v. 20, 21. *ἐπιμένωμεν*] is the reading of ABCDEFG Griesb., Lachm., Tisch. The word denotes a permanent abiding in sin, in distinction from a temporary lapse into it; a supine indulgence of inward lust, in distinction from a steady struggle with and conquest of it. τῇ ἁμαρτίᾳ] the article denotes sin as a state and condition: that sin which came into the world by the one man, and which has been the subject of examination in the preceding chapter. ἡ χάρις] the grace that justifies without works.

VER. 2. μὴ γένοιτο] See comment on iii. 4. οἵτινες] denotes a class. Compare i. 25. The relative clause is placed first for emphasis, in order to impress the absurdity of the proposition. ἀπεθάνομεν τῇ ἁμαρτίᾳ] Contrary to the view of the great majority of commentators, we regard this as objective in its meaning: "We who died *for* sin." (Storr, Flatt, Nitzsch: with these are to be associated Venema, Haldane, Chalmers, who explain by: "dead to the guilt of sin.") St. Paul still has in view his previous line of remark respecting Christ's ἱλαστήριον. This, confessedly, is not a death to sin, but for sin. Believers, he has said, by their union with Christ, appropriate this death for sin, and make it their own, for purposes of justification. Believers, consequently, through their vicar and substitute, die *for* sin. In this *vicarious* manner they atone for their sin, as really as if they died personally for it. By this method they are "justified gratuitously through the redemption that is in Christ Jesus, whom God hath set forth to be a propitiation" in their room and stead. Such is the teaching and argument of St. Paul, up to this point in the Epistle. The objection then is raised, that this method, so easy to the believer (though so costly to the Redeemer), is likely to produce self-indulgence. Believers will continue to sin, because an ample atonement has been made for them, and they have nothing to do but to rely upon it. The Christian life will, thus, be a course of perpetual sinning and perpetual trusting in vicarious atonement. Gratuitous justification will result in increasing depravity and license. It is with reference to such an objection as this, that the apostle asks the question: How can we who have died *for* sin live any longer therein? How can persons who are vicariously making an *atonement* for their transgression, continue to transgress? The ideas of expiation and license are incongruous. As states of mind they cannot co-exist. It is impossible at one and the same time to act faith in Christ's blood, and indulge sinful lust. The one excludes the other. In proportion as the believer has a clear discernment of Christ's expiatory work, and penitently trusts in it, he resists sin, and is kept from sin. In this way, gratuitous justification is not antinomian, but the very contrary (iii. 31). This interpretation is favored by the following considerations. 1. The subjective meaning: "dying *to* sin," yields nothing but a truism. To ask: How shall one who is dead to sin, live in sin? is like asking: How shall one who is growing better, grow worse? This is too obvious to be argued. To say that death to sin is incompatible with living in sin, is merely to say that sanctification is incompatible with unsanctification,—which is so self-evident that no one would even think of the contrary. But to say that justification is incompatible with unsanctification is not so evident as to be a mere truism, and affords ground for an argument,—which St. Paul furnishes, by examining the intrinsic relation of atonement to self-indulgence, of justification to sanctification. 2. Both the preceding and the succeeding context favors the objective meaning. In v. 3–5, the apostle has already alluded to the sanctifying effect of justification. "Being justified by faith," the believer has, as a consequence, *hope* of eternal blessedness, *patience* and even *joy* in the midst of affliction, the *wisdom* that comes from experience of earthly trials, and glowing *love* for God. These are graces of sanctification, that spring out of the sense of the divine forgiveness and acceptance in Christ.

Again, in v. 18, the writer describes gratuitous justification as a "justification unto *life:*" that is, one that aims at, and results in holiness. In this chapter, he resumes the same topic, by answering the objection that gratuitous justification must be destructive of morality and piety. The exegesis of verses 3–11 will show that, with the exception of verse 6, whenever "death" is spoken of, an *atoning* death for sin is meant. In this entire paragraph, the sanctification of the believer is directly connected with his appropriation of Christ's vicarious sacrifice. It is not the *believer's* death *to* sin, that prevents him from continuing in sin; but it is *Christ's* death *for* sin, trusted in and appropriated, that prevents this. 3. The notion of dying *to* sin, or the mortification of sinful lusts, is expressed by νεκρόω, rather than by ἀποθνήσκω. See Coloss. iii. 5. 4. The idea that believers are one with Christ in his atoning death for sin, and that such a union is sanctifying, is taught in many other passages. Compare Coloss. ii. 20. Here, the "death with Christ" which the believer "dies," is Christ's atoning death for sin. The preposition ἀπὸ (in ἀπεθάνετε) indicates the believer's liberation from the claims of the moral and ceremonial law (στοιχεῖα τοῦ κόσμου), by means of Christ's expiation. The believer's personal dying to sin, or sanctification, would not have this effect. The same idea is expressed in Gal. ii. 19, 20. Upon the phrase νόμῳ ἀπέθανον, Ellicott, in loco, remarks that "ἀπέθανον is not merely 'legi valedixi,' but expresses generally, what is afterward more specifically expressed in verse 20 by συνεσταύρωμαι. Νόμῳ is not merely the dative of 'reference to,' but a species of dative 'commodi.' The meaning is: 'I died not only as concerns the law, but as the law required.' The whole clause, then, may be thus paraphrased: 'I, through the law, owing to sin, was brought under its curse; but having undergone this curse, with, and in the person of, Christ, I died to the law, in the fullest and deepest sense: being both free from its claims, and having satisfied its curse.'" Similarly, Meyer, in loco, explains. After quoting Bengel's remark, that the clause, "I am crucified with Christ," is "summa ac medulla Christianismi," he says: "By the crucifixion, the curse of the law was inflicted upon Christ (Gal. iii. 13). Whoever, therefore, is crucified *with* Christ, on him also is the curse of the law inflicted, so that by means of his ethical participation in the death of Jesus, he is conscious of having died *διὰ νόμου*." Bengel (Rom. vi. 3) remarks that "when one is baptized in reference to Christ's death, it is the same thing as if, at that moment, Christ suffered, died, and was buried for such a man, and as if such a man suffered, died, and was buried with Christ."

Some commentators explain St. Paul's co-crucifixion with Christ, to be his own personal sufferings in the cause of Christ. But St. Paul's own sufferings would not be the reason why he is "dead to the law." Christ's atoning suffering is the reason of this. Again, in 2 Cor. v. 14, 15, the death for sin is presented as a motive for the death to sin, precisely as in the paragraph under consideration: "If one died for all, then all died" (in and with him, i. e.). The clause *οἱ πάντες ἀπέθανον* affirms that all believers die that expiatory death which Christ died *ὑπὲρ πάντων*. And the purpose of this is, that they "should not henceforth live unto themselves." The same sentiment is also taught in 2 Tim. ii. 11. These passages abundantly prove that the doctrine of the believer's unity with Christ in his vicarious death for sin is familiar to St. Paul, and is strongly emphasized by him.

VER. 3. *ἢ*] "or, if this is not perfectly clear." *ὅσοι*] "all we who." *εἰς*] "with respect to." The rite of baptism is referential, merely. "The formula *βαπτίζεσθαι εἰς* designates

πῶς ἔτι ζήσομεν ἐν αὐτῇ; 3 *ἢ ἀγνοεῖτε ὅτι ὅσοι ἐβαπτίσθημεν εἰς Χριστόν Ἰησοῦν, εἰς τὸν θάνατον αὐτοῦ ἐβαπτίσ-*

the object in respect to which the baptism is received, Mat. xxviii. 19; 1 Cor. i. 13; x. 1, 2. Hence the equivalent formula, *βαπτισθῆναι ἐπ' ὀνόματι* (Acts ii. 38), and *ἐν τῷ ὀνόματι* (Acts x. 48)." Tholuck, in loco. So also, Bengel, Meyer, Hodge. Believers are not baptized in order to bring about a union with Christ, but because such a union has been brought about. The rite has reference to this fact of union, and is the sign, and not the cause, of it. Baptism presupposes regeneration, and does not produce it. Χριστόν] The God-man here represents the Trinity, with reference to whom Christ commanded the rite to be administered. Compare Gal. iii. 27. Such texts prove the deity of Christ. Baptism in the name of Christ alone (involving an alteration of the baptismal formula given in Mat. xxviii. 19) is not valid, according to the decision of the Church, in the controversy between Cyprian and Stephen: the latter of whom contended that baptism might be administered in the name of Jesus Christ simply. It would have been equally irregular to baptize in the name of the Father alone, or of the Holy Spirit alone. The meaning and efficacy of baptism are indicated in Coloss. ii. 11, 12. St. Paul here describes Christian baptism as a Christian circumcision: "the circumcision of Christ." And the meaning and efficacy of circumcision are indicated in Rom. iv. 11. It is a sign and seal of an already existing faith in the promised Redeemer. Abraham's faith preceded his circumcision, and therefore was not produced by it. Similarly, faith precedes baptism, and is not the effect of it. In the case of infants, faith is involved and latent in regeneration; and infant baptism, like infant circumcision, is the sign and seal of regenerating grace already bestowed, or to be bestowed. εἰς τὸν θάνατον] "with

θημεν; [4] συνετάφημεν οὖν αὐτῷ διὰ τοῦ βαπτίσματος εἰς τὸν θάνατον, ἵνα ὥσπερ ἠγέρθη Χριστὸς ἐκ νεκρῶν διὰ

reference to his death:" which certainly was a death for sin, not to sin. Baptism, it is true, has a reference to the pollution of sin, as well as the guilt of it (compare Eph. v. 26; Titus iii. 5); but the Apostle does not here allude to this part of the significance of the rite. He singles out only its reference to the atoning work of Christ, the objective dying for sin, because he is occupied particularly with this side of the subject. The question of the Apostle really is: "Know ye not, that so many of us as were baptized with reference to Jesus Christ, were baptized with reference to his *atonement?*"

VER. 4. Compare Coloss. ii. 12. συνετάφημεν] "We were entombed." This word, contrary to the opinion of many commentators, has no reference to the rite of baptism, because the burial spoken of is not in water, but in a sepulchre. "Θάπτω signifies: *to pay the last dues to a corpse;* and so, at first, *to burn* it, as in Od. xii. 12; then, as the ashes were usually inurned and put under ground, *to bury, inter, entomb,* as Od. xi. 52." Liddell and Scott in voce. Burial and baptism are totally diverse ideas, and have nothing in common. In order to baptism, the element of water must come into *contact* with the body baptized; but in a burial, the surrounding element of earth comes into no contact at all with the body buried. The corpse is carefully protected from the earth in which it is laid. Entombment, consequently, is not the emblem of baptism, but of death. Entombment would be even a more inappropriate term by which to describe the rite of baptism, than would "ingrafting" which follows as another emblem of the believer's union with Christ, and which has never been associated, by

commentators, with the rite of baptism. Συνετάφημεν must, therefore, be referred back to ἀπεθάνομεν, in verse 2, and not forward to βαπτίσματος. "We died and were entombed with Christ, by means of the baptism that refers to his death." The preposition denotes *co*-burial of the believer with the atoning Redeemer. Compare συνεσταύρωμαι, in Gal. ii. 20. The rite of baptism, which the believer has received, is a sign and authenticating seal that by faith he has been made one with Christ, in respect to (εἰς) Christ's death *for* sin. Baptism signifies, that by faith he has been laid in the tomb with Christ; and Christ was laid in the tomb as an atonement. Συνετάφημεν αὐτῷ, being thus exegetical of ἀπεθάνομεν τῇ ἁμαρτίᾳ, in verse 2, makes it certain that this latter clause is objective in its meaning. It is indisputable, that Christ when laid in the tomb did not die to sin, but for sin; and consequently a co-burial with him in this *same reference* (εἰς τὸν θάνατον) cannot mean the mortification of lust, or dying to sin. οὖν] introduces an inference from the fact that these believers were baptized with special reference to Christ's expiatory death. διὰ τοῦ βαπτίσματος] the preposition denotes a secondary agency only. Baptism is not the efficient cause of that union with Christ whereby the believer dies with him in his atoning death, and is buried with him. The efficient cause is the Holy Spirit, in regeneration. It is here that the spiritual and the sacramentarian theories of baptism find their point of divergence. Baptism is a sign that the soul is already united to Christ, and has already died with him. The article denotes the peculiarity in the baptism. εἰς τὸν θάνατον] qualifies βαπτίσματος. The baptism has particular reference to the atoning death of Christ. The piacular element is singled out, and distinguished from the rest of Christ's redemptive agency. ἵνα] indicates the purpose intended by God, by the believer's death and burial with Christ: viz.: that he may "walk in newness of life." This

τῆς δόξης τοῦ πατρός, οὕτως καὶ ἡμεῖς ἐν καινότητι ζωῆς περιπατήσωμεν. [5] εἰ γὰρ σύμφυτοι γεγόναμεν τῷ ὁμοιώματι τοῦ θανάτου αὐτοῦ, ἀλλὰ καὶ τῆς ἀναστάσεως ἐσόμεθα,

is an additional proof that dying for sin is incompatible with living in sin. The divine purpose puts things together, that agree together. And here, again, the subjective explanation results in a truism. To say that the believer dies *to* sin, in order that he may "walk in newness of life," is equivalent to saying that the purpose of the believer's sanctification, is that he may be sanctified. δόξης] is a general term, including all the attributes of God; but is sometimes put for a particular attribute. It stands here for the attribute of omnipotence. Compare 1 Cor. vi. 14; Eph. i. 19, 20. καινότητι ζωῆς] a new order or structure of life; it is stronger than ζωή καινή.

VER. 5. γὰρ] introduces a corroborative explanation of the statement made in the preceding verse. σύμφυτοι] sc. Χριστῷ. A new figure, derived from the kingdom of vegetable life, follows the previous figure taken from the realm of death. The rendering, "planted together," as if the term were derived from σύν and φυτεύω (Vulg., Luther, Eng. Ver.), is incorrect. The root is σύν and φύω: "grown together," or "ingrafted." Christ's comparison of the vine and the branches, John xv. 1 sq., explains the term. ὁμοιώματι] denotes the "form," or "shape," as in Rom. i. 23; v. 14; viii. 3; Phil. ii. 7; Rev. ix. 7. It is best construed with σύμφυτοι, as the dative of manner (Vulg., Chrys., Calvin, Tholuck, Olsh., De Wette, Meyer). θανάτου] denotes, as in the preceding verses, an expiatory death for sin. ἀλλὰ] is employed often, in the classics, to introduce the apodosis of a conditional proposition in a bold and emphatic manner: "then, certainly, all the more shall, etc." ἀναστάσεως] supplying the

[6] τοῦτο γινώσκοντες, ὅτι ὁ παλαιὸς ἡμῶν ἄνθρωπος συνεσταυρώθη, ἵνα καταργηθῇ τὸ σῶμα τῆς ἁμαρτίας, τοῦ

ellipses, the clause runs thus: ἀλλὰ καὶ τῷ ὁμοιώματι τῆς ἀναστάσεως αὐτοῦ σύμφυτοι Χριστῷ ἐσόμεθα. Growing together in the "form" of death, involves growing together in the "form" of life. Resurrection is often the symbol of regeneration and sanctification. Compare John v. 24, 25; Coloss. iii. 1; Eph. v. 14.

VER. 6. This verse is immediately connected with the preceding, and constitutes a part of the total proposition begun in verse 5. τοῦτο γινώσκοντες] "since we know:" the participle assigns a reason. St. Paul adduces the personal experience of the believer, in proof that dying for sin with Christ is accompanied with rising with Christ to newness of life. The believer himself is conscious that the sense of forgiveness and acceptance with God is sanctifying; that faith in the atonement "works by love" (Gal. v. 6), "purifies the heart" (Acts xv. 9), and "overcomes the world" (1 John v. 4). παλαιὸς ἄνθρωπος] denotes the sum-total of human powers and faculties before regeneration. Compare Eph. iv. 22; Coloss. iii. 9. It is equivalent to corrupt human nature: the "old leaven" of 1 Cor. v. 7, 8. συνεσταυρώθη] is employed, here, in the subjective reference, and not objectively as in Gal. ii. 20, because the apostle is now describing an effect of justification as found in the actual experience of the believer. The idea of expiation is not now in view, but of *mortification;* because this crucifixion and death is that of the "old man," and not, as in the preceding context, that of the Lord Jesus Christ. ἵνα] denotes the purpose of this personal crucifixion of the believer, or dying *to* sin. καταργηθῇ] is a strong word frequently used by St. Paul: it signifies a complete abolishing, and verges in its meaning upon annihilating. σῶμα τῆς

μηκέτι δουλεύειν ἡμᾶς τῇ ἁμαρτίᾳ· [7] ὁ γὰρ ἀποθανὼν δεδικαίωται ἀπὸ τῆς ἁμαρτίας. [8] εἰ δὲ ἀπεθάνομεν σὺν

ἁμαρτίας] 1. The body as ruled by sin; as described in verses 12 and 13 of the context (De Wette, Meyer, Alford). 2. The body as the seat and source of sin (Semler, Usteri, Rückert). 3. The equivalent of παλαιὸς ἄνθρωπος (Augustine, Luther, Hodge). 4. The total mass of sin: "body," in the figurative sense (Origen, Chrysostom, Grotius, Calvin, Philippi). The third explanation is preferable, because the "destruction of the body of sin" is the result of the "crucifixion of the old man;" and because σῶμα is subsequently put for σάρξ, or corrupt nature, in Rom. viii. 12, and the bodily "members" are made to represent the faculties of both body and soul, in vi. 12, 13, 19; vii. 5. The second of the interpretations is objectionable, because it ascribes a merely sensuous origin to sin. δουλεύειν] Sin is the bondage of the will, John viii. 34.

VER. 7. The apostle returns, after the reference in verse 6 to the actual experience of the believer, to his argument concerning the connection of dying for sin to dying to sin, or of justification to sanctification. γὰρ] is introductory only. ἀποθανὼν] supply σὺν Χριστῷ, as in verse 8, and suggested by it: "he who died with Christ," in the manner described in verses 2–5. δεδικαίωται ἀπὸ] "is justified from." Compare Acts xiii. 39. The rendering: "freed from" (Eng. Ver.) is misleading, unless it be explained as "freed from the guilt of." Freedom from sin, in the sense of cessation from sin, would require πέπαυται, as in 1 Pet. iv. 1. The apostle's meaning is, that he who has died with Christ for sin, is thereby justified, and delivered from the curse and condemnation of sin. When Christ's atonement has been made the believer's atonement, by faith and the mystical union, then "all

Χριστῷ, πιστεύομεν ὅτι καὶ συνζήσομεν αὐτῷ, ⁹ εἰδότες ὅτι Χριστὸς ἐγερθεὶς ἐκ νεκρῶν οὐκέτι ἀποθνήσκει· θάνατος

Christ's sufferings and obedience are as certainly the believer's own, as if he had himself suffered and done all in his own person" (Heidelberg Catechism, 79); and then acquittal follows naturally and necessarily, according to both the Rabbinical and the legal maxim: "The criminal when executed has atoned for his crime." This verse is conclusive in respect to the meaning of the phrase ἀπεθάνομεν τῇ ἁμαρτίᾳ, in verse 2. For, to affirm that "he who has died *to* sin is thereby "justified from sin," would be making subjective holiness the ground of pardon, or sanctification the procuring cause of justification,—than which, nothing could be more antagonistic to the Pauline doctrine.

VER. 8. δὲ] is transitive to the inference, that union with Christ in his atonement involves union with him in spiritual life and sanctification. ἀπεθάνομεν] in the piacular manner described in verses 2, 3, 4, 7, and Gal. ii. 20. πιστεύομεν] expresses the confident expectation of the believer. συνζήσομεν] the future denotes the natural consequence. As Christ's revivification naturally followed his crucifixion, so the believer's sanctification naturally follows his justification. It is the same thought which has been presented in verse 5. Compare also Heb. x. 5, where believers are said to be "*sanctified* by means of the *offering of the body* of Jesus Christ."

VER. 9. εἰδότες] the same use of the participle as in verse 6: "since we know." οὐκέτι ἀποθνήσκει] Christ's piacular death occurs but once, Heb. x. 10. κυριεύει] Christ's conquest of and dominion over death, is taught in Acts ii. 24; 1 Cor. xv. 54–57; 2 Tim. i. 10; Rev. i. 18.

αὐτοῦ οὐκέτι κυριεύει. 10 ὃ γὰρ ἀπέθανεν, τῇ ἁμαρτίᾳ ἀπέθανεν ἐφάπαξ· ὃ δὲ ζῇ, ζῇ τῷ θεῷ. 11 οὕτως καὶ ὑμεῖς λογίζεσθε ἑαυτοὺς εἶναι νεκροὺς μὲν τῇ ἁμαρτίᾳ, ζῶντας

VER. 10. γὰρ] introduces a reason why death no longer has dominion over Christ. ὃ] 1. κατὰ ὅ: "as respects his death." 2. the direct object of ἀπέθανεν: "that (namely death) which he died;" like ὅ ζῶ, in Gal. ii. 20 (Meyer). ἁμαρτίᾳ] "for the guilt of sin." ἐφάπαξ] Compare Heb. vii. 27; ix. 12; x. 10. ὃ] is to be resolved like the preceding ὃ. θεῷ] the dative of advantage: for God's service and glory.

VER. 11 applies the foregoing statement that Christ died once for sin, and then forever after lives for God, to believers. οὕτως] introduces the application. λογίζεσθε] to "reckon," or "account," as in iv. 3–10. The employment of this word here confirms the explanation given of ἀπεθάνομεν τῇ ἁμαρτίᾳ, in verses 2, 7, 8. The notion of reckoning, or imputing, is congruous with dying for sin and justification, but incongruous with dying to sin and sanctification. Believers can "reckon" or "account" themselves to have died fully and completely *for* sin, in and with Christ; but they cannot "reckon" or "account" themselves to have died fully and completely *to* sin. They may regard themselves to be completely justified, but not completely sanctified. ἑαυτοὺς] reflexive: "your ownselves." νεκροὺς] denotes the state and condition resulting from the act denoted by ἀποθνήσκειν. τῇ ἁμαρτίᾳ] "for sin," as above. Believers are exhorted to be mindful of Christ's atoning death, and to "reckon" it as their own (ἑαυτοὺς) death for the guilt of their own sin. ζῶντας] those who possess that ζωὴ αἰώνιος which is the contrary of θάνατος αἰώνιος, and which is the gift (χάρισμα) of God, vi. 23. It does not denote complete sanctification, though it will finally result in this. It is a complex idea,

δὲ τῷ Θεῷ ἐν Χριστῷ Ἰησοῦ. [12] *μὴ οὖν βασιλευέτω ἡ ἁμαρτία ἐν τῷ θνητῷ ὑμῶν σώματι εἰς τὸ ὑπακούειν ταῖς ἐπι-*

including regeneration, justification or the imputation of both the active and passive righteousness of Christ, and progressive sanctification. Believers are to regard themselves as in this state and condition. As "alive for and in reference to God," they are free from condemnation, have a title to heavenly blessedness, are renewed in the spirit of their minds, are dying to sin, and increasing in the love and knowledge of God. *τῷ Θεῷ*] the dative of advantage: "for God;" for his honor and service. *ἐν Χριστῷ*] qualifies both *νεκροὺς* and *ζῶντας*: this "reckoning" is possible, and allowable, only in case the person is united to Christ, "a man in Christ," 2 Cor. xii. 2.

VER. 12. St. Paul has concluded his argument to prove that dying for sin is incompatible with living in sin; or trust in vicarious atonement with self-indulgence. Having shown the natural and homogeneous connection between justification and sanctification, he now proceeds to urge believers, *by motives drawn from their justification*, to resist their remaining corruption. *οὖν*] "therefore," in accordance with the previous reasoning. Because they are no longer in the state and condition of death (*θάνατος*), but of life (*ζωὴ*), they have inducement and encouragement to withstand the sin that lingers in them. Were they still under condemnation, they would have no motive for such a struggle, and could not succeed in it. An unforgiven man is powerless against sin. The fear of condemnation paralyzes him. *βασιλευέτω*] sin exists in the believer, but it must not be allowed to be the ruling principle within him. Holiness must be *βασιλεύς*. *ἡ ἁμαρτία*] remaining sin, personified. *θνητῷ*] "per contemptum vocat mortale." Calvin, in loco. *σώματι*] is not to

ϑυμίαις αὐτοῦ, 13 μηδὲ παριστάνετε τὰ μέλη ὑμῶν ὅπλα ἀδικίας τῇ ἁμαρτίᾳ, ἀλλὰ παραστήσατε ἑαυτοὺς τῷ ϑεῷ

be taken here, in its restricted sense; but as standing for σάρξ, or the entire man as corrupt. The "lusts of the body" include mental as well as physical desires. The succeeding use of μέλη, which in the restricted sense means only corporal members, proves this. See comment on viii. 13. εἰς τὸ ὑπακούειν] denotes the tendency of the domination or kingship of sin. ἐπιϑυμίαις] is a general term, comprehending both mental and physical lusts. St. Paul gives a list of lusts, in Gal. v. 19–21. Among them are the sensual cravings of fornication and drunkenness, and the intellectual cravings of envy and emulation. The distinguishing characteristic in ἐπιϑυμία is, that it is *forbidden* desire. Those desires that are permitted and allowed by God cannot be denominated "lusts." Provision is made for them in creation, and they are innocent cravings. But those desires, either of the body or the mind, that issue from corrupt human nature (i. e., human nature, not as made by God, but as vitiated by man) are prohibited cravings, and are sinful and guilty. All such desires, or lusts, are forbidden by the tenth commandment, which, in the original reads: "Thou shalt not lust." St. Paul includes all the varieties of them under the term ἐπιϑυμία. It is to be noticed, that the inward rising of lust is itself sin, apart from the external act; otherwise it would not be forbidden. See Christ's decision of the question, in Mat. v. 22, 28. See the comment on Rom. vii. 7.

VER. 13 continues the exhortation to resist indwelling sin. παριστάνετε] is here employed in the military sense of presenting in line, and before officers. μέλη] includes the mental faculties, as well as the bodily organs; just as ἐπιϑυ-

ὡς ἐκ νεκρῶν ζῶντας καὶ τὰ μέλη ὑμῶν ὅπλα δικαιοσύνης τῷ θεῷ. [14] ἁμαρτία γὰρ ὑμῶν οὐ κυριεύσει· οὐ γάρ ἐστε ὑπὸ νόμον, ἀλλὰ ὑπὸ χάριν.

μία includes mental as well as physical lusts. Compare Coloss. iii. 5, where the "members which are upon the earth" comprise "covetousness which is idolatry," as well as "fornication and uncleanness." ὅπλα] the weapons by which sin would maintain its dominion. τῇ ἁμαρτίᾳ] the dative of the object: antithetic to θεῷ. παραστήσατε] the change from the present to the aorist denotes the energy and instantaneousness of the action enjoined. ἑαυτοὺς] explains μέλη, and shows that the latter cannot be confined to physical appetites merely. The whole self is included, both soul and body. ὡς] denotes the quality of the persons spoken of: "being such as." We retain this reading, with Meyer, although ὡσεὶ is more strongly supported (ℵABC Lachm., Tisch.). If ὡσεὶ is accepted, it must be restricted to a connection with ἐκ νεκρῶν, to the exclusion of ζῶντας. δικαιοσύνης] not in the technical meaning of justification, but as the contrary of ἀδικίας in the preceding clause. Compare verse 16.

VER. 14. An encouragement to obey the exhortation in verses 12 and 13. κυριεύσει] sin, although not extinct in the believer, nevertheless, shall not have lordship (κύριος) and controlling sway. The "strong man" is still within the house, but a stronger than he has entered and bound the occupant, and is spoiling his goods, Mat. xii. 28, 29. The principle of holiness, in the believer, is mightier than the remnants of the principle of sin. Sin in fragments is weaker than holiness in mass. γὰρ] introduces the reason of this fact. οὐ ἐστε ὑπὸ νόμον] this is said relatively, not absolutely. As rational creatures simply, the subjects of God's moral government merely, they are still under law. Compare Gal. iv. 4, 5, 21. In this reference, it cannot be said of any man or angel that he is not under law. But, as trusting in Christ's atonement,—as those who in and with Christ have died an expiatory death for sin,—they are not under law viewed as retributive and punitive. By means of Christ's death, believers have discharged their obligation to satisfy the law by their own death, and are no longer under it, in this particular. An unbeliever, on the contrary, is under law and not under grace, in that he is obligated to suffer in his own person the punishment which the law threatens against sin. Having rejected the vicarious endurance of the penalty by a third person, he must endure it in the first person.

Again, believers are not "under the law" in regard to their title to eternal blessedness. The law promises this future reward, upon the condition that a perfect personal obedience has been rendered. The believer is not discouraged by this condition, so impossible of fulfilment by him. He has a full title to this great reward, although his own personal obedience has been very imperfect, because Christ as his vicar (in this case also, as in that of the endurance of penalty) has rendered an absolutely perfect obedience for him. His conviction, therefore, that eternal reward is awaiting him, does not rest upon his own imperfect sanctification, but upon Christ's sinless obedience, and perfect righteousness.* χάριν] the grace that justifies in this complete manner, "without works," or perfect personal obedience.

* While this effect of Christ's active righteousness belongs to an exhaustive exegesis of St. Paul's affirmation that believers are "not under law but under grace," the principal reference, thus far in the Epistle, has been to the passive righteousness—to the negative deliverance from condemnation, rather than to the positive title to life.

15 *Τί οὖν; ἁμαρτήσωμεν, ὅτι οὐκ ἐσμὲν ὑπὸ νόμον
ἀλλὰ ὑπὸ χάριν; μὴ γένοιτο.* 16 *οὐκ οἴδατε ὅτι ᾧ παριστάνετε ἑαυτοὺς δούλους εἰς ὑπακοήν, δοῦλοί ἐστε ᾧ*

VER. 15 contains an objection similar to that in verse 1: viz., that the doctrine of grace and justification is antinomian. Τί οὖν] sc. ἐροῦμεν, as in verse 1. ἁμαρτήσωμεν] is the reading of ℵABCDEL Lachm., Tisch. ὑπὸ νόμον, etc.] is repeated, for emphasis.

VER. 16. Compare 2 Pet. ii. 19. The argument, here, is derived from the nature of the human will, and of voluntary agency. Purpose and inclination in one direction are incompatible with purpose and inclination in the contrary direction. It is the argument of Christ in Mat. vi. 24; vii. 18. No man can serve two masters, at one and the same moment. A good tree cannot bring forth evil fruit, neither can a corrupt tree bring forth good fruit. The connection of thought is as follows: "Because you have died with Christ for sin, and are delivered from condemnation, and have a full title to eternal reward, you are obligated, by such gracious treatment, not to yield yourselves to the lusts that still remain, but to yield yourselves to the holy law of God (verses 12, 13). This you have done. You are obeying from the heart (verse 17). Your wills are surrendered to Christ and righteousness. Such being the facts of the case, the proposition to 'sin because we are not under law, but under grace' is self-contradictory. The nature of the will and of voluntary agency forbids it. You cannot do these two contrary things at one and the same time." παριστάνετε] looks back to verse 13. ἑαυτοὺς] the reflexive pronoun denotes the spontaneity and willingness of the agency. There is no compulsion in an inclination, be it good or evil. δούλους] signifies total subjection. The self-surrender of the

ὑπακούετε, ἤτοι ἁμαρτίας εἰς θάνατον ἢ ὑπακοῆς εἰς δικαιοσύνην; [17] χάρις δὲ τῷ θεῷ ὅτι ἦτε δοῦλοι τῆς ἁμαρ-

will is complete. The will is not in equilibrio, and able to do right as easily as wrong, or wrong as easily as right. The will has a decided bias. εἰς ὑπακοήν] indicates the purpose of the action in παριστάνετε. δοῦλοί] sc. ἐκεινοῦ. The collocation is emphatic. ὑπακούετε] implies that the slavery is voluntary. It arises from the action of the human will itself, and not from any external cause or arrangement. ἤτοι] shows that this species of bondage may be connected with either sin or holiness; and this, because it is the bondage of a bias, or inclination. ἁμαρτίας] Compare 2 Pet. ii. 14; John viii. 34. For an explanation of the latter text, see the author's Sermons to the Natural Man, pp. 202–230. εἰς] indicates the terminus and issue of sin. Compare verse 21. θάνατον] death physical, spiritual, and eternal, as in v. 12. This proves that the bondage in question is culpable, and punishable. δικαιοσύνην] is best regarded, here, as subjective righteousness, the opposite of ἀδικία, as in verse 13. This is what personal obedience results in. Personal obedience is not εἰς δικαιοσύνην in the sense of gratuitous justification. So, Philippi, Hodge.

Ver. 17. ἦτε] the tense is emphatic: "ye *were*," but are no longer. The apostle thanks God that their total and helpless bondage to sin is a fact of the past, and not of the present. ἐκ καρδίας] willingly, and not by compulsion. In the Biblical psychology, heart and will are interchangeable. Compare Luke i. 17; 2 Cor. ix. 7; Rom. x. 9, 10; Prov. xxxi. 11; Ps. cxix. 112. εἰς ὃν, etc.] is best resolved by τῷ τύπῳ τῆς διδαχῆς εἰς ὃν παρεδόθητε. παρεδόθητε] the passive: "were intrusted." τύπον] that plan of salvation which they had received from those who had first taught them the Christian

τίας, ὑπηκούσατε δὲ ἐκ καρδίας εἰς ὃν παρεδόθητε τύπον διδαχῆς. [18] ἐλευθερωθέντες δὲ ἀπὸ τῆς ἁμαρτίας ἐδουλώ-

religion, and which St. Paul is now restating for them. It is what he denominates elsewhere "my gospel," xvi. 25. The term is similar to μόρφωσις in ii. 20. See the comment. This verse is not connected with the following, but with the preceding. It merely states the fact that they whom he is addressing are servants of righteousness, after the preceding statement that they must be either one thing or the other; either servants of sin, or of righteousness.

VER. 18 reaffirms the fact of obedience from the heart, asserted in verse 17, and mentions a necessary consequence of it: viz., slavery to righteousness. This consequence goes to prove that reckless and unresisted sinning is incompatible with grace (verse 15). ἐλευθερωθέντες] freed not perfectly and absolutely, from all remainders of sin, but substantially and virtually, from sin as a dominant disposition. Compare verse 22. Believers are free from the condemning power of sin, and from its enslaving power. They are not under the curse of the law, and their wills are not, as in the days of unregeneracy, in total and helpless bondage to the principle of evil. "The converted," says Leighton (Sermon ix.), "are delivered from the dominion of original sin, though not from the molestation and trouble of it. Though it is not a quiet and uncontrolled master, as it was before, yet it is in the house still as an unruly servant or slave, even vexing and annoying them: and this body of death they shall still have cause to bewail, till death release them. And it is this, more than any other sorrows or afflictions of life, that makes the godly man not only content to die, but desirous: longing 'to be dissolved, and be with Christ which is far better.'" As a man is physically free whose fetters have been broken, although their fragments may not have been removed, and he be much impeded by them in his movements, so a man is spiritually free, in whom sin as a nature or principle has been slain, although its remnants still hinder him in holy living. Compare John viii. 32, 36; Ps. cxix. 45; James i. 25; ii. 12; Gal. v. 1; Rom. viii. 2; Is. lxi. 1. δὲ] is transitive: "now." ἐδουλώθητε] Freedom from sin is slavery to holiness. There is no liberty of indifference, so that the will is equally facile to sin and holiness. If there were, then believers might "sin, because they are not under law but under grace" (verse 15); and might "continue in sin, that grace may abound" (verse 1). Bias to holiness implies the absence of bias to sin; and vice versa. But without bias, or inclination, no moral act can be performed in either direction. Hence, inclination in one direction is impotence in the other. St. Paul has asserted that the persons whom he is addressing are, as matter of fact, positively inclined to holiness. They are obeying ἐκ καρδίας (verse 17). Consequently, by their holy inclination, and because of it, they are slaves in respect to holiness, and freedmen in respect to sin. It must be carefully observed, that the term "slavery" when employed by St. Paul in connection with sin and holiness, is used in a relative signification; as he implies in his assertion, ἀνθρώπινον λέγω (verse 19). In the absolute and unqualified signification, slavery is *compulsion.* A slave in this sense is not voluntarily inclined, or self-determined, in his enslavement. He is forced into it by another. In this sense, neither the sinner nor the believer is a slave; neither sin nor holiness is slavery. But in the relative sense, in which St. Paul here employs the term, slavery is an *inability to the contrary resulting from a foregoing activity of the will.* A man, for illustration, is physically a slave, who, instead of being forced into slavery, has sold himself into this condition. He cannot now recover himself from a self-determined status, and is in as real and complete a bondage, as the slave captured in war or kidnapped in peace. Such is the slavery of sin. And the other phrase of St. Paul: "slaves of righteousness," is to be explained in the same way. This also is an inability to the contrary resulting from a foregoing act and state of the will. Holy inclination is inability to sin. It is true, that inclination of the will upon the side of holiness differs greatly from inclination upon the side of sin, in respect to the ultimate *origin* of it. The former originates in the operation of the Holy Spirit upon the human faculty, while the latter is self-determination pure and simple, without any internal efficiency of the Holy Ghost. Yet the former is as really and truly the will's *inclination* as the latter; and inability to the contrary accompanies the former as it does the latter. There is, consequently, a "slavery to righteousness," as well as a "slavery to sin." A will which, by regeneration, has been "powerfully determined" (Westminster L. C., 67) and inclined to holiness, is unable to sin, in the sense in which Christ intends, when he says that "a good tree cannot bring forth evil fruit" (Mat. vii. 18); and in which St. John intends, when he asserts that the regenerate "cannot sin, because he is born of God" (1 John iii. 9.) This does not mean, that the regenerate, while here upon earth, is sinlessly perfect, committing no actual transgression, and having no remainders of sinful inclination. See 1 John i. 8. But it means that the regenerate will is unable to sin in the manner of the unregenerate will: i. e., *impenitently* and *totally*. The good man cannot feel and act as he did in the days of impenitency. He is "enslaved to righteousness." "Old things have passed away, and all things have become new." And when the ultimate consequence of regeneration, namely, perfect sanctification, shall be reached in the heavenly state, the believer will be unable to sin, even in the manner in which he did while upon earth. The *posse peccare* of imperfect

θητε τῇ δικαιοσύνῃ. 19 ἀνθρώπινον λέγω διὰ τὴν ἀσθέ-
νειαν τῆς σαρκὸς ὑμῶν. ὥσπερ γὰρ παρεστήσατε τὰ μέλη

sanctification will become the *non posse peccare* of sinless perfection.

This minor element of difference between the "slavery to sin," and the "slavery to righteousness," arises from a difference between the effects of apostasy, and the effects of regeneration. The apostasy of the human will resulted immediately and instantaneously in *total* depravity: viz., a sinful inclination, with no *remainders* of the previous holy inclination. But the regeneration of the will does not result immediately and instantaneously in *total* sanctification: viz., a holy inclination with no *remainders* of the previous sinful inclination. A holy inclination is originated, but remnants of sin are left. These fragments, though moribund, continue to show a lingering vitality, in the manner described by St. Paul in Rom. vii. 14–25. See comment.

No portion of Scripture has more psychological value than this, in determining the true nature of the human will. Compare Aristotle's Ethics, iii. 5, and Plato's Alcibiades, i. 135; where the same view is taken of the "slavery to evil," though nothing is said of the "slavery to good."

VER. 19 is explanatory of the terms freedom and slavery, in the preceding verse. The phrase "enslaved to righteousness" is an unusual one. ἀνθρώπινον] borrowed from human relationships: those, namely, of master and slave. ἀσθένειαν] infirmity in spiritual perception. σαρκὸς] denotes unspiritual human nature which does not discern the things of the Spirit. See the explanation in 1 Cor. ii. 6–14. Believers have remainders of this ignorance which obscure their full spiritual understanding. Hence, the need of illustrations, to explain spiritual freedom and spiritual bondage. ὥσπερ γὰρ] looks

ὑμῶν δοῦλα τῇ ἀκαθαρσίᾳ καὶ τῇ ἀνομίᾳ εἰς τὴν ἀνομίαν, οὕτως νῦν παραστήσατε τὰ μέλη ὑμῶν δοῦλα τῇ δικαιο-

back to verse 18, and introduces an explanation of the statement there; especially the statement in the last clause. The particular expression most needing to be explained, in the illustration drawn from human relations, is, "enslavement to righteousness." This, upon the face of it, looks as if holiness were compulsion. It is not so; "*for* (γὰρ) as you once willingly and entirely surrendered yourselves to sin, and were in *this* way slaves of sin, so now willingly and entirely surrender yourselves to righteousness, and be in *this same* voluntary manner slaves of righteousness." St. Paul, by thus repeating the phraseology already twice employed by him, in verses 13 and 16, shows his readers plainly what he means by the terms "slavery" and "freedom," in this connection. It is a slavery, and a freedom, that is founded in the nature of the human will, and not in physical causes. μέλη] See comment on verse 13. δοῦλα] the adjective has the full signification of the substantive δοῦλοί. ἀκαθαρσίᾳ] instead of ἁμαρτία (verse 13), to denote sin in its relation to man, and in its sensuous aspect: "impurity." ἀνομίᾳ] sin in its spiritual aspect, and as related to law and God. εἰς τὴν ἀνομίαν] 1. the purpose: in order that iniquity as a principle may go into outward act (Meyer, Stuart, Hodge). 2. the result: the principle issues in an abiding state (De Wette, Tholuck, Lange, Alford). The latter is preferable, because of the antithetic term ἁγιασμός. δικαιοσύνῃ] is used in the subjective sense, as the contrary of ἀκαθαρσίῃ and ἀνομίᾳ. ἁγιασμόν] sanctification, as the state of the soul. Compare vi. 22; 1 Cor. i. 30; 1 Thess. iv. 3, 4, 7; 2 Thess. ii. 13; Heb. xii. 14; 1 Pet. i. 2.

VER. 20. This verse teaches the same doctrine of the will

σύνῃ εἰς ἁγιασμόν. [20] *ὅτε γὰρ δοῦλοι ἦτε τῆς ἁμαρτίας ἐλεύθεροι ἦτε τῇ δικαιοσύνῃ.* [21] *τίνα οὖν καρπὸν εἴχετε*

with verse 18, but in a reversed form. Verse 18 affirms that freedom from sin is slavery to righteousness; verse 20 affirms that freedom from righteousness is slavery to sin. ὅτε] denotes a time gone by. The slavery to sin is not in the present, but in the past. St. Paul thanks God for this fact (verse 17). γὰρ] connects this verse with the preceding, as a part of the total explanation of the statement in verse 18. ἐλεύθεροι] In proportion as the will is surrendered to sin, it is released from holiness. It is not free from holiness as matter of *right*, but as matter of *fact:* as when we say, "free from disease," or "free from pain." When viewed *ethically*, however, as a question of right, and not of fact merely, this kind of freedom is found to be a false freedom. Man has no right to it, and to have it is guilt. This proves that it is only a spurious liberty. Real and true freedom is something that man needs not to be ashamed of; something which he is obligated to have, and the possession of which is praiseworthy.

> True liberty always with right reason dwells
> Twinn'd, and from her hath no dividual being."
>
> PARADISE LOST, xii. 83.

This difference between freedom in sin, and freedom in holiness, is referred to by Christ, in John viii. 32–36. The freedom of the will, in our Lord's use of the term in this passage, is simply the inclination of the will. Whoever is inclined is *ipso facto* free, be the inclination right or wrong. But, holy inclination is *true* freedom (ὄντως ἐλεύθεροι, John viii. 36), because it agrees with the prescript of the moral law. •Sinful inclination (which is as really *inclination* as holy inclination) is *false* freedom, because it conflicts with

τότε ἐφ' οἷς νῦν ἐπαισχύνεσθε; τὸ μὲν γὰρ τέλος ἐκείνων θάνατος. 22 *νυνὶ δὲ ἐλευθερωθέντες ἀπὸ τῆς ἁμαρ-*

the moral law, and is forbidden by it. But the law never forbids the real, and the true; only the unreal, and the false.

VER. 21. St. Paul strengthens his exhortation to yield the members to righteousness, by a reference to the consequences of the contrary course. Two views of the structure of the verse are possible: 1. The interrogation ends with *τότε*, and the remaining clause contains the answer (Theodoret, Luther, Melanch., De Wette, Tholuck, Olshausen, Lachmann, Tischendorf). 2. The interrogation ends with *ἐπαισχύνεσθε* (Chrys., Beza, Calvin, Grotius, Wetstein, Bengel, Fritzsche, Winer, Meyer, Murdock's Peshito, Eng. Ver.). This latter arrangement, which is preferable, requires either *ἐκείνων*, or *ἐν τουτοῖς*, to be supplied before *ἐφ' οἷς*. *καρπὸν*] gain, or advantage. *ἐφ'*] "over," or "on account of." *ἐπαισχύνεσθε*] This word gives, indirectly, a part of the answer to the question which, by the punctuation we have adopted, receives no direct answer. If they were ashamed of yielding their members to impurity, they obtained no advantage. *τέλος*] This clause indirectly gives the remainder of the answer, and the most important part of it. The final termination of such conduct being endless perdition, there can be no *καρπός*. *θάνατος*] is the contrary of *ζωή αἰώνιος* in verse 22, to which it is antithetic. See comment on v. 12.

VER. 22. *νυνὶ*] now, as Christians, i. e. *ἐλευθερωθέντες*] the same description of believers as that in verse 18, and involving the same view of the will. See comment on verse 18. *δουλωθέντες τῷ θεῷ*] See the explanation of *ἐδουλώθητε τῇ δικαιοσύνῃ*, in verse 18. St. Paul is not shy of the unusual phrase, "slavery to righteousness." This is the fourth time he has

τίας, δουλωθέντες δὲ τῷ θεῷ, ἔχετε τὸν καρπὸν ὑμῶν εἰς ἁγιασμόν, τὸ δὲ τέλος ζωὴν αἰώνιον. [23] τὰ γὰρ ὀψώνια

used it. His favorite title, as descriptive of himself, is δοῦλος Χριστοῦ. Rom. i. 1; 1 Cor. vii. 22; 2 Cor. x. 7; Gal. i. 10; Phil. i. 1; Tit. i. 1, et alia. Compare also עֶבֶד יְהוָה, Josh. xxiv. 29; Job i. 8; Ps. cv. 6; Jer. xxxiii. 21, et alia. εἰς] denotes the tendency of the καρπός. ἁγιασμόν] as in verse 19. τέλος] denotes the termination of the καρπός. Liberation from sin and subjection to righteousness *tends* to perfect sanctification, and *ends* in eternal felicity. ζωὴν] comprehends all good, in relation to body, soul, and spirit. αἰώνιον] denotes endlessness, here; because of the nature of the αἴων spoken of. The Scriptures know of but two αἰῶνες: the present αἰών, and the future αἰών; ὁ νῦν αἰών, and αἰών ὁ μέλλων (Mat. xii. 32; Luke xvi. 8; Heb. vi. 5; Eph. i. 21). The doctrine of an indefinite series of αἰῶνες, or cycles, is Gnostic and not Biblical. Christianity recognizes but two ages, or worlds: the temporal and the eternal. Accordingly, in Scripture, anything that is αἰώνιος belongs either to one world, or the other; either to the present temporal age (Philemon, 15), or to the future endless age (2 Cor. v. 1). The ζωή here spoken of is, indisputably, a good that belongs to the future αἰών, and will therefore endure as long as that does. Since ζωή in this verse is the antithesis to θάνατος in verse 21, the epithet αἰώνιος belongs to the latter also, though it is not expressed. The "death" occurs in the same future αἰών with the "life." Both have precisely the same duration; and the duration is endless because the future "age" or "world" is endless.

VER. 23. γὰρ] introduces further proof in corroboration of the doctrine taught in verses 21 and 22. ὀψώνια] "rations" (ὄψον: cooked meat). The word looks back to ὅπλα, in verse

τῆς ἁμαρτίας θάνατος, τὸ δὲ χάρισμα τοῦ θεοῦ ζωὴ αἰώνιος ἐν Χριστῷ Ἰησοῦ τῷ κυρίῳ ἡμῶν.

13. Sin, unlike holiness, originates solely in the finite will. God does not "work" in man "to will and to do" (Phil. ii. 2; Eph. iii. 20; Coloss. i. 29), when man transgresses the moral law. Consequently, sin is absolute demerit or guilt, and its recompense is "wages," in the strict sense. The sinner, if he pleased, could demand eternal death as his due upon principles of exact justice. He has earned it by his own action alone. τῆς ἁμαρτίας] sin personified pays wages for military service. θάνατος] as in verses 16 and 21. The adjective αἰώνιος is omitted with θάνατος, because it is expressed with its antithesis ζωή; in accordance with the grammatical principle, that when two clauses are antithetic to each other, an epithet may be suggested in the first clause by its expression in the second, or suggested in the second clause by its expression in the first. The epithet αἰώνιος is expressed with κόλασις and πύρ, in Mat. xxv. 41, 46. χάρισμα] St. Paul does not say ὀψώνια τῆς δικαιοσύνης, as the antithesis of ὀψώνια τῆς ἁμαρτίας; because the imputed righteousness of a believer is a gratuity, and his inherent righteousness is the product of the Holy Spirit moving and inclining his will. Righteousness, unlike sin, is not self-originated, and consequently its reward must be gracious, and only relatively merited. The recompense of righteousness is χάρισμα, and not ὀψώνια. ἐν Χριστῷ] in Christ, as both the ground and the cause. Only as man is one with Christ, is this gift of eternal life possible.

CHAPTER VII

[1] Ἢ ἀγνοεῖτε, ἀδελφοί, (γινώσκουσιν γὰρ νόμον λαλῶ)
ὅτι ὁ νόμος κυριεύει τοῦ ἀνθρώπου ἐφ᾽ ὅσον χρόνον ζῇ;
[2] ἡ γὰρ ὕπανδρος γυνὴ τῷ ζῶντι ἀνδρὶ δέδεται νόμῳ· ἐὰν
δὲ ἀποθάνῃ ὁ ἀνήρ, κατήργηται ἀπὸ τοῦ νόμου τοῦ ἀν-

VER. 1. St. Paul continues the consideration of the connection between justification and sanctification, which he began in chapter vi. 1. He does so, by still further explaining the assertion made in vi. 14, that believers "are not under law but under grace." He illustrates by the marriage relation. ἢ ἀγνοεῖτε] compare vi. 3. ἀδελφοί] all Christians, i. 13; xii. 10. νόμον] the Old Testament law; which, as the base from which the gospel proceeded, was known by Gentile as well as Jewish Christians. ἀνθρώπου] is generic: including woman as well as man, the female as well as male. This is plain from verse 2, where it is asserted in illustration of the legal principle that "man is bound by the law as long as he lives," that "the *woman* is bound by the law." See the explanation of ἄνθρωπος in v. 12.

VER. 2. γὰρ] introduces a proof of the proposition in verse 1, derived from the marriage relation. δέδεται] has been, and still is bound. νόμῳ] the Mosaic law, yet as agreeing with the law of nature, in this case. κατήργηται] in the active, signifies to nullify; in the passive, to free from. Compare vi. 6; 2 Cor. iii. 11. In the illustration, the woman stands for the believer, and the first husband for the law.

δρός. [3] ἄρα οὖν ζῶντος τοῦ ἀνδρὸς μοιχαλὶς χρηματίσει, ἐὰν γένηται ἀνδρὶ ἑτέρῳ· ἐὰν δὲ ἀποθάνῃ ὁ ἀνήρ, ἐλευθέρα ἐστὶν ἀπὸ τοῦ νόμου, τοῦ μὴ εἶναι αὐτὴν μοιχαλίδα γενομένην ἀνδρὶ ἑτέρῳ. [4] ὥστε, ἀδελφοί μου, καὶ ὑμεῖς ἐθανατώθητε τῷ νόμῳ διὰ τοῦ σώματος τοῦ Χριστοῦ, εἰς τὸ γενέσθαι ὑμᾶς ἑτέρῳ, τῷ ἐκ νεκρῶν ἐγερθέντι, ἵνα

VER. 3. ἄρα οὖν] "accordingly, then." Compare v. 18. χρηματίσει] Shall be "formally denominated," or "styled." Acts xi. 26. γένηται] to "belong to," as the wife to the husband. Compare 2 Cor. xi. 2; Eph. v. 25 sq.

VER. 4. ὥστε] is illative: "wherefore." Compare Mat. xii. 31. καὶ ὑμεῖς] "ye too," like the woman, in verse 2. ἐθανατώθητε] the aorist signification is to be retained: "ye became dead to the law" (when ye believed, i. e.), so that the law no longer κυριεύει (verse 1). If the figure had been regularly carried out, the writer would have said that the *law* became dead. The Receptus reading, ἀποθανόντος, in verse 6, would favor this. τῷ νόμῳ] The Mosaic law both ceremonial and moral, but eminently the latter. σώματος] the body offered as an ἱλαστήριον, Rom. iii. 25. Through the instrumentality of Christ's atonement, in reference to which the believer has been baptized as the sign of his faith (vi. 3), he is dead to the law considered as a means of justification, and the law is dead to him. So far as forgiveness and acceptance with God are concerned, the believer and the law have no more to do with one another, than one corpse has to do with another. εἰς τὸ] indicates the purpose of this deadness to the law. The justification is in order to sanctification. γενέσθαι] as in verse 3. The marriage union is the emblem of the spiritual union between Christ and the believer. Isa. lxii. 5; Eph. v. 23–32. ἐγερθέντι] union with Christ in his atoning death, involves union with him in his resurrection. See

καρποφορήσωμεν τῷ θεῷ. [5] ὅτε γὰρ ἦμεν ἐν τῇ σαρκί, τὰ παθήματα τῶν ἁμαρτιῶν τὰ διὰ τοῦ νόμου ἐνηργεῖτο ἐν

comment on vi. 3–5. καρποφορήσωμεν] the figure of marriage is still kept up. Faith in atoning blood is fruitful of good works.

VER. 5 contains a confirmation of the preceding statement respecting the believer's fruitfulness in holiness, by a reference to the effect of the law upon an unbeliever. The former is freed from the curse of the law, and for this reason obeys the law from love, with spontaneity, and gladness of heart. The latter is under the curse of the law, and by reason of servile fear, and the bondage of his will, is driven more and more into sin. For him, "the law is the strength (instead of the destruction) of sin," 1 Cor. xv. 56. ὅτε] implies a state of things that has passed away. Compare vi. 17, 20, 21; vii. 9. σαρκί] here denotes: 1. the *entire* man, as "spirit, soul, and body" (1 Thess. v. 23); and 2. the entire man as *corrupt*. Compare Rom. iv. 1; vi. 19; vii. 18, 25; viii. 3, 5; 2 Cor. x. 3, et alia. The phrase ἐν σαρκί is equivalent to the "natural man" of 1 Cor. ii. 14. παθήματα] "passions:" from *patior*. Both the mental and the physical passions are marked by a degree of passiveness. They are the effects of exciting and stimulating objects, to which the soul and body supinely yield. The English version renders the word by "motions," in the sense of "emotions:" "drugs, or minerals, that waken motion," Othello, i. 2. Cogan (On the Passions, i. 1) thus defines: "Emotions, according to the genuine signification of the word, are the sensible and visible effects which particular passions produce upon the frame, in consequence of some particular agitation of the mind." ἁμαρτιῶν] the plural denotes the acts, in distinction from the principle of sin. See the analysis in James

τοῖς μέλεσιν ἡμῶν εἰς τὸ καρποφορῆσαι τῷ θανάτῳ· [6] νυνὶ δὲ κατηργήθημεν ἀπὸ τοῦ νόμου, ἀποθανόντες ἐν ᾧ κα-

i. 15, where the principle of sin is denominated ἐπιθυμία, and the particular act ἁμαρτία. διὰ τοῦ νόμου] through the law as an occasional (not efficient) cause. The explanation of this important statement is given, at length, by the Apostle, in vii. 7–13. ἐνηργεῖτο] "energized:" the passions, or emotions, operate inwardly and dynamically. ἐν τοῖς] in them as the seat, and by them as the instruments. μέλεσιν] includes the mental faculties, as well as the bodily organs. The sinful passions, or emotions, operate in and by the human understanding and the human will, as well as in and by the fleshly members and the five senses. Envy, malice, emulation, pride, and avarice, are "passions," in St. Paul's sense, equally with the physical appetites that show themselves in gluttony, drunkenness, and fornication. All are alike the "motions of sin." See the comment on vi. 13. καρποφορῆσαι] is correlative to the same word in verse 4. The figure of marriage is still in view. θανάτῳ] the dative of advantage.

VER. 6. νυνὶ] is opposed to ὅτε in verse 5. It denotes the present believing and justified state. κατηργήθημεν] See comment on verse 2. ἀπὸ τοῦ νόμου] the believer is delivered from the law as penalty, and as the instrument of justification. ἀποθανόντες] is the reading of ℵABCL Erasmus, Mill, Griesb., Scholz, Hahn, Lachm., Tisch. The English Version, Elzevir, and Beza read ἀποθανόντος. The first is preferable diplomatically and logically, though not rhetorically ; as it does not carry out the figure in verse 1. As the law stands for the first husband, the law should die, rather than the woman, who stands for the believer. But St. Paul may have wished to avoid the phrase: "death of the law." He has previously said that believers die to the law, in verse 4. ἐν ᾧ] i. e., τούτῳ

τειχόμεθα, ὥστε δουλεύειν ἡμᾶς ἐν καινότητι πνεύματος καὶ οὐ παλαιότητι γράμματος.

ἐν ᾧ; the reference is to the antecedent τοῦ νόμου. κατειχόμεθα] the law as condemning and pronouncing a curse "holds down," and keeps under, the criminal, as in a dungeon. Compare i. 18, where the criminal is represented as holding down the truth, and keeping it underneath. This latter suppression differs from the former, by being only temporary; because it is a "holding down in *unrighteousness;*" the former is a holding down in righteousness. ὥστε] denotes the actual effect, or consequence. The death to the law, and deliverance from it, result in a more perfect and better obedience of the law, instead of a "continuance in sin," vi. 1, 15. δουλεύειν] the present tense denotes constant and habitual action. καινότητι] the obedience that is rendered to the law by the believer is that of a "new creature" (2 Cor. v. 17; Gal. vi. 15) and of a "new man" (Col. iii. 10; Eph. ii. 15). It is "new," also, in respect to the principle from which it flows: viz., love instead of fear, which was the old principle (Ezek. xi. 19; xxxvi. 26). In 2 Cor. x. 5, it is denominated "the obedience of Christ." πνεύματος] denotes, here, not the Holy Spirit, which is never a "new" spirit, but the human spirit enlightened, enlivened, and actuated by the divine: a new spirit in man, compared with the previous one. Service that originates in "newness of spirit" is spontaneous, genial, and free (ἐκ καρδίας, vi. 17). Such being the nature of the obedience rendered by one who has "died with Christ for sin," and has "become dead to the law by the body of Christ," it is plain that there is nothing licentious, or antinomian, in the doctrine of vicarious atonement. παλαιότητι] the legal precedes the evangelical (1 Cor. xv. 46); the "natural man" is the "old man" (Rom. vi. 6; Eph. iv. 22; Col. iii. 9). γράμματος] denotes the law in its written and external form. Compare Rom. ii. 20; 2 Cor. iii. 6. Service that is performed in the "oldness of the letter" originates in fear instead of love, in spasmodic struggle instead of living impulse, in volitionary effort instead of inward inclination, has reference merely to the letter instead of the intent of the law, is forced out by the threat and penalty of the law instead of drawn out by its excellence and beauty (Ps. cxix. 97). These two kinds of obedience are exact contraries. In the one case, the law is external to the will: it is written *on* the heart (Rom. ii. 15), but not *into* the heart (Jer. xxxi. 33). Consequently, the obedience is mechanical and false. In the other case, the law through regeneration is internal to the will: is no longer a threat but an impulse; no longer a statute but a force (Ps. xxxvii. 31; xl. 8; Is. li. 7). Consequently, the obedience is vital and real. In the moralist and legalist, will and conscience are separate and antagonistic. In the believer, they are one and harmonious.

VER. 7 begins a new paragraph, which raises an objection suggested by the words *τὰ διὰ τοῦ νόμου ἐνηργεῖτο*, in verse 5 of the preceding paragraph, and replies to it. The reply constitutes another proof, in addition to that already given, that justification is necessarily connected with sanctification, and that they who are trusting in Christ's vicarious atonement cannot "continue in sin that grace may abound," v. 1. The paragraph is divided into two sections: the first, consisting of verses 7–13, which describes the unbeliever, first as unconvicted (status securitatis), and then as under conviction (status sub lege); the second, consisting of verses 14–25, which delineates the experience of the believer contending victoriously with remaining depravity (status regenerationis). Augustine, Luther, Calvin, Pareus, Chemnitz, Gerhard, Wolfius, Owen, Delitzsch, Philippi, Haldane, and Hodge take this

7 *Τί οὖν ἐροῦμεν; ὁ νόμος ἁμαρτία; μὴ γένοιτο· ἀλλὰ τὴν ἁμαρτίαν οὐκ ἔγνων εἰ μὴ διὰ νόμου· τήν τε γὰρ ἐπιθυμίαν οὐκ ᾔδειν, εἰ μὴ ὁ νόμος ἔλεγεν Οὐκ ἐπιθυμήσεις·*

view. The opposite view, which refers the entire paragraph to the unregenerate, but in a convicted and transitional state, is supported by Chrysostom, the Arminian exegetes generally, Bengel, De Wette, Meyer, Tholuck, Hengstenberg, Neander, Nitzsch, Müller, Stuart. τί οὖν ἐροῦμεν] introduces the new objection, as in iii. 9; iv. 1; vi. 1, 15. ὁ νόμος ἁμαρτία;] is the law, in its very nature and essence, sin? It is stronger than ἁμαρτίας διάκονος, in Gal. ii. 17. ἀλλὰ] introduces the exactly contrary position: "on the contrary, I," etc. τὴν ἁμαρτίαν] the article is specific: the principle of sin, originated in the manner described in v. 12 sq., latent in every man (v. 14), and elicited by temptation alluring and law prohibiting. ἔγνων] the aorist signification is to be retained: "I had not known," in the days of unbelief, i. e.; the time denoted by ποτέ, in verse 9. The omission of ἂν with both ἔγνων and ᾔδειν strengthens the conditional force of the verbs, making the affirmation more positive (Winer, p. 305). The knowledge meant is that of clear and painful consciousness: what is technically denominated "conviction of sin." εἰ μὴ] supply ἔγνων. νόμου] the Old Testament written law, which, however, includes natural ethics. St. Paul, in this passage, is describing his own past experience, as representative of that of every convicted person, either Jew or Gentile, under revelation or outside of it. The application of the unwritten as well as the written law, elicits the sense of sin (ii. 15). τε] "even:" it qualifies ᾔδειν: "for, lust I should not have even *known*, still less, have *resisted*, unless," etc. ἐπιθυμίαν] lust generically: mental as well as physical, yet with a reference to bodily appetite, as that species of forbidden evil desire which is most patent to human observation. The catalogue of lusts, both physical and mental, is given in Gal. v. 16–21. Fletcher, in his Purple Island (Canto vii.), has analysed and delineated each. See, also, Eph. ii. 3, where αἱ ἐπιθυμίαι are characterized as voluntary inclination (θελήματα); and are classified as "desires of the flesh, and of the *mind.*" Compare, also, 2 Tim. iii. 6, 7; iv. 3, where the hankering after false doctrine, and the itch for sensational preaching, are placed among the "lusts." That ἐπιθυμία is truly and properly sin, is proved by the interchange, in this verse, between it and ἁμαρτία. St. Paul regards the two as synonymes. The clause ἐπιθυμίαν οὐκ ᾔδειν is the equivalent of the preceding ἁμαρτίαν οὐκ ἔγνων. To "know lust" is the same thing as to "know sin." That lust is sin, is proved, also, by the prohibition of it in the tenth commandment. The moral law forbids nothing but sin; and the closing statute in the decalogue forbids inward lust. The Lawgiver, having in previous statutes prohibited particular forms of sin, as exhibited in particular acts of transgression,—theft, adultery, murder,—finally sums up all individual sins under the one generic denomination of "lust," because all have their source and root in evil desire. Compare James i. 14, 15. The Septuagint translates לֹא־תַחְמֹד (Exod. xx. 17) by οὐκ ἐπιθυμήσεις. The English version: "Thou shalt not covet," is inadequate, because covetousness now denotes only one form of lust. Upon the meaning of the tenth commandment as understood by St. Paul in this place, Rivetus (Explicatio Decalogi, vers. xv.) remarks: "Patet Paulum extendere præceptum ad eam concupiscentiam, adversus quam Spiritus pugnat (Gal. v. 17), quæ repugnat legi mentis (Rom. vii. 23), quam mens regenita non approbat (vii. 15), quam non vult (vii. 16, 19). Eam tamen expressè *peccatum* dicit. Nam quinquies (vii. 13, 14, 17, 20, 21) *peccatum* appellat legem in membris suis rebellantem, et obnoxium eum reddentem legi peccati." Respecting the

relation of lust to the will, Rivetus remarks that "concupiscentia est inclinatio voluntaria." "The concupiscence forbidden in the tenth commandment," says Leighton (Exposition of the Ten Commandments), "is an inordinate desire, or the least beginning of such a desire. This commandment is broken by the least envious look upon any good of others, or the least bendings of the mind after it for ourselves, and by that common mischief of self-love, as the very thing that gives life to all such undue desires, and by that common folly of discontent at our own estate, which begets a wishing for that of others. This very concupiscence itself, though it proceed no further than the rising of it in the mind, pollutes and leaves a stain behind it." Similarly Owen (Saints' Perseverance, Ch. xv.) remarks, that "though a man should abstain from all actual sins, or open commission of sin, all his days, yet if he have any habitual delight in sin, and defileth his soul with delightful contemplations of sin, he liveth to sin and not to God, which a believer cannot do, for he is 'not under law, but under grace.' To abide in this state, is to 'wear the garment spotted with the flesh.'" The term ἐπιθυμία sometimes, but not often, denotes *holy* desire, as in Gal. v. 17; Luke xxii. 15. οὐκ ἐπιθυμήσεις] The *negative* form of the law is always exasperating. It implies an existing inclination contrary to law, and sets up a barrier against it. It is the form of law for *fallen* creatures. "The law [in this negative form] is not made for a righteous man, but for the lawless and disobedient, for the ungodly, and for sinners," 1 Tim. i. 9. Hence, the "Thou shalt *not*," awakens the consciousness of inward and slumbering lust; and, "by the law, is the knowledge of sin," iii. 20. This examination of the operation of the law makes it plain that the law is not sin (verse 7). That which detects and prohibits sin, cannot be of the nature of sin.

8 ἀφορμὴν δὲ λαβοῦσα ἡ ἁμαρτία διὰ τῆς ἐντολῆς κατειργάσατο ἐν ἐμοὶ πᾶσαν ἐπιθυμίαν. χωρὶς γὰρ νόμου ἁμαρ-

Ver. 8 continues the explanation, with the introductory particle δὲ. ἀφορμὴν] from ἀπὸ and ὁρμάω: a departure; a start, rather than an "occasion" (Eng. Ver.). The simple *nisus* of the will is meant. "Sin taking a start, wrought," etc. ἡ ἁμαρτία] sin in the form of inward lust (ἐπιθυμία), and showing itself, after its start, in the passions or emotions (παθήματα) spoken of in verse 5. διὰ τῆς ἐντολῆς] is best connected with κατειργάσατο (Bengel, De Wette, Fritzsche, Meyer, Tholuck). Compare διὰ τοῦ ἀγαθοῦ κατέργαζομένη, in verse 13. Meyer asserts that ἀφορμὴν λαβεῖν is never connected with διὰ, but often with ἐκ. τῆς ἐντολῆς] the article denotes the particular tenth commandment, οὐκ ἐπιθυμήσεις. κατειργάσατο] is supported by ℵACFGL Rec., Lachm.; κατηργάσατο is the reading of BDE Tisch. The preposition is intensive: "wrought *out*." πᾶσαν] anarthrous: "every kind of;" lust in all the varieties of its emotions (παθήματα, ver. 5). The law produces this irritating and stimulating effect, it must be observed, only in those who are ἐν τῇ σαρκί (verse 5): only in the unregenerate. In the unbeliever (who has not died and been intombed with Christ with respect to his atoning death, and risen again with him to newness of life), conscience and will are antagonistic (viii. 7). As a consequence, the moral law terrifies him by its threat of punishment, and irritates him by its strict requirement. Law is hateful and exasperating to all who do not love it; and in this way is the occasional cause of sin. Ovid (Amorum, iii. 4) notices this effect of the law: "Desine vitia irritare vetando. Nitimur in vetitum semper, cupimusque negata." Horace also: "Audax omnia perpeti gens humana ruit per vetitum nefas" (Carminum, i. 3). Compare Livy, xxxiv. 4; Seneca, De Clementia, i. 23; Euripidis, Medea, 1077. χωρὶς] "separate and apart

from." Lachmann's punctuation is preferable, which places only a comma between this clause and verse 9, because νεκρά is antithetic to ἔζων. γὰρ] looks back to the assertion in verse 7, "I had not known sin but by the law." "*For*, apart from the law," etc. νόμου] anarthrous: law generally; as this is a general truth. ἁμαρτία] supply ἔστιν (not ἦν), as no particular time is intended. νεκρά] unconvicted: without remorse (Chrys., Calvin, Olsh.); inactive (Tholuck, Meyer). The first is preferable. Sin was active, because it had taken a start and wrought all manner of concupiscence (verse 8); but it was not known in painful self-consciousness. νεκρά certainly cannot have the absolute meaning which it has in James ii. 17, 26; Heb. ix. 14. Only a seeming death is meant; like the death of sleep. Compare Shakspeare's: "We were dead of sleep," Tempest, v. 1.

VER. 9. ἐγὼ δὲ] in contrast with ἁμαρτια: "sin apart from law is dead, but I was alive." ἔζων] 1. I seemed, to myself, to live (August., Erasmus, Calvin). 2. I was without fear or apprehension (Melanch., Beza, Bengel). Both explanations are kindred, and should be combined. It is a seeming life, antithetic to the seeming death of sin in the preceding verse. The enjoyment of sin, and the absence of remorse, make up a false and counterfeit life which is the characteristic of the unconvicted sinner. "Absentia legis faciebat, ut viviret, hoc est, inflatus justitiæ suæ fiducia, vitam sibi arrogaret, quum tamen esset mortuus." Calvin in loco. The life intended here, in ἔζων, is the same with that expressed in the second member of the epicure's dictum: "dum vivimus, *vivamus*," or in the common phrases: "high life," and "seeing life." χωρὶς] here, as in the preceding clause, is used in a qualified sense only. In the strict sense, neither sin nor the sinner can be separated from law. Wherever there is sin and a sinner, there is law (iv. 15; v. 13).

τία νεκρά, 9 ἐγὼ δὲ ἔζων χωρὶς νόμου ποτέ· ἐλθούσης
δὲ τῆς ἐντολῆς ἡ ἁμαρτία ἀνέζησεν, 10 ἐγὼ δὲ ἀπέθανον,

But there is not always the distinct consciousness of the claims of the law; and in this sense, sin and the sinner are separate and apart from the law. But this separation can be only temporary. ποτέ] "formerly:" in the days of unregeneracy and unbelief, when sin was enjoyment without remorse or fear. This word is important, showing that this false and seeming life is not the writer's present moral state. It is an "old thing" that has "passed away" (2 Cor. v. 17). ἐλθούσης] "coming" into my consciousness. The law has been away (χωρὶς) from consciousness, and now returns. Compare the common phrase: "He has come to;" descriptive of recovery from the loss of consciousness in a fainting-fit, or swoon. Compare Luke xv. 17. The position of ἐλθούσης is highly emphatic: the energy and onset with which the law comes in, and bears down upon the previously happy and careless soul, are expressed by the collocation. τῆς ἐντολῆς] viz.: "thou shalt not lust" (verse 7). The tenth commandment is more searching, and productive of the consciousness of sin, than either the sixth, seventh, or eighth, because it goes behind the outward act, to the secret and inward desire. Hence, our Lord, in his interpretation and application of the moral law in the Sermon on the Mount, discussed sin chiefly in the form of evil desire (Mat. v. 20–24). "He asserts, that the inmost thoughts of the heart, and the first motions of concupiscence therein, though *not consented to*, much less *actually accomplished* in the outward deeds of sin, and all the occasions leading unto them, are directly forbidden in the law. This he doth in his holy exposition of the seventh commandment. He declares the penalty of the law, on the least sin, to be hell fire, in his assertion of causeless anger to be forbidden in the sixth

commandment." Owen, On Justification, Ch. xvii. ἀνέζησεν] revived from that state denominated νεκρά, in verse 8. As the "death" of sin alluded to is the absence of the painful conviction of sin, so the "reviving" of sin, here intended, is the presence of such conviction.

VER. 10. δὲ] denotes a contrast in ἀπέθανον to ἀνέζησεν. But the contrast is verbal only, and not logical and real; because the "reviving" of sin in consciousness is the same thing, essentially, with the "death" here spoken of. Remorse is a main element in spiritual death. ἀπέθανον] does not imply that previously he was not dead, any more than the reviving of sin implies that previously there had been no sin. As the "coming" of the commandment brought him to the consciousness of a sin that was latent, so it brought him to the consciousness of a death that was already within him, and resting upon him. Compare John iii. 18. This text proves that spiritual death is not annihilation, because it implies consciousness. Physical death, confessedly, is not annihilation. It is only a peculiar mode of existence. In 1 Cor. xv. 36, and John xii. 24, the physical "death" of the corn of wheat is not the extinction of its substance, but the metamorphosis of it. Spiritual death, in like manner, supposes existence; because it is a vivid and distressing *experience.* Compare Luke xvi. 23–27; Mat. xxv. 30; 1 Thess. iv. 13; 1 Tim. v. 6; Rev. iii. 3; xx. 10. Both spiritual life and spiritual death imply a spiritual substance existing in the highest degree of energetic action, and possessing consciousness at its greatest intensity. The one is conscious blessedness; and the other is conscious misery. εὑρέθη] "*found:*" not originally constituted so by the divine arrangement. Compare ἐγένετο in verse 13. The death which has been spoken of as resulting from the moral law, is the consequence of human action, and not of the design of God in

καὶ εὑρέθη μοι ἡ ἐντολή ἡ εἰς ζωήν, αὕτη εἰς θάνατον.
11 ἡ γὰρ ἁμαρτία ἀφορμὴν λαβοῦσα διὰ τῆς ἐντολῆς ἐξηπά-
τησέν με καὶ δι' αὐτῆς ἀπέκτεινεν. 12 ὥστε ὁ μὲν νόμος

laying down the moral law. εἰς ζωήν] the original aim and object of the divine command is life, and not death; happiness, and not misery. αὕτη] "even *this*," in itself considered, beneficent thing. εἰς θάνατον] the actual, but not primarily designed result. See the author's discourse upon, "The original and the actual relation of man to law." Sermons to the Natural Man, pp. 231–248.

VER. 11. γὰρ] introduces the explanation of the statement in the preceding verse. ἀφορμὴν] See comment on verse 8. διὰ τῆς ἐντολῆς] is connected with ἐξηπάτησεν: the commandment is the occasional cause. ἐξηπάτησέν] The convicted man betakes himself to the law, expecting by it to obtain life and blessedness. Instead of this, he "finds," by it, only death and misery. See Gal. iii. 1–3, 21; v. 2–4. This, the apostle represents as a deception by the law; though, in reality, it is the sinner's self-deception. The deception in the case is two-fold. 1. The law curses and condemns the transgressor, instead of pardoning him, Gal. iii. 10. 2. The law elicits and exasperates, instead of removing his sin, Rom. iii. 20. Neither the guilt nor the pollution of sin is removable by the law; yet, man mistakenly hopes for its removal by means of "the works of the law," i. e., personal attempts at obedience. αὐτῆς] "the very law itself," which had been ordained to life. ἀπέκτεινεν] is suggested by ἀπέθανον in verse 10.

VER. 12. ὥστε] introduces the logical conclusion from the reasoning in verses 7–11. A law having such characteristics, and operating in such a manner, cannot be sin. μὲν] implies an adversative δὲ which is not expressed: "The law, indeed,

ἅγιος, καὶ ἡ ἐντολὴ ἁγία καὶ δικαία καὶ ἀγαθή. [13] τὸ οὖν ἀγαθὸν ἐμοὶ ἐγένετο θάνατος; μὴ γένοιτο, ἀλλ' ἡ ἁμαρτία, ἵνα φανῇ ἁμαρτία, διὰ τοῦ ἀγαθοῦ μοι κατεργαζομένη

is good, but sin misuses it." νόμος] the written Mosaic law, but inclusive of the unwritten law. ἡ ἐντολὴ] denotes the particular commandment forbidding evil desire. Three distinct and separate epithets are applied to this, while only one is applied to the law generally, because this particular statute has been spoken of as particularly occasioning the activity of sin. ἁγία καὶ δικαία καὶ ἀγαθή] The cumulation of the epithets, and their careful connection by the copulative, are highly negative to the question, "Is the law sin?"

VER. 13 presents another objection, the reply to which is a reaffirmation of the excellence of the law. The question is equivalent to: Is the law *death?* corresponding to the question in verse 7: Is the law sin? ἀγαθὸν] this is the last of the epithets applied to the law, in the preceding verse. ἐμοὶ] refers to the apostle as he was ποτέ (verse 9). He would not think of asking such a question in reference to himself in his present moral status, as "a man in Christ Jesus." ἐγένετο] is the reading of ℵABCDE Lachm., Tisch. The Receptus, KL read γέγονε. The word denotes a transformation by gradual development. The question is: Did the good law become death, the greatest of evils, by a *divine* arrangement, so that *God* is the author of this bad result of a good thing? μὴ γένοιτο] the question is negatived in the strongest form. ἡ ἁμαρτία] supply ἐμοι ἐγένετο θάνατος. ἵνα] denotes God's purpose and arrangement. φανῇ] is emphatic by its position, and refers to the exhibition of the inward nature of sin. The object of God is to show forth the malignant quality of sin, which converts a good into an evil.

θάνατον, ἵνα γένηται καθ' ὑπερβολὴν ἁμαρτωλὸς ἡ ἁμαρτία διὰ τῆς ἐντολῆς.

ἁμαρτία] is the predicate of the verb. κατεργαζομένη] the participle assigns a reason: "since it works out." ἵνα] repeats a second time, and with strong emphasis, the divine purpose in this arrangement. γένηται] is equivalent to φανῇ in the preceding clause, and has a kindred meaning. The development of sin, in the manner that has been described, reveals its exceeding wickedness. διὰ τῆς ἐντολῆς] is connected with γένηται. By means of the law, as the instrument, the disclosure is made.

The section contained in verses 7–13, as thus interpreted, will read as follows, by supplying the ellipses. "What shall we say then [in view of the statement, that the motions of sins are by the law]? Is the law [in its very nature] sin? God forbid. On the contrary, I had not become convicted of sin, but by the law; for I had not even known lust [to be sin], unless the law had said, 'Thou shalt not lust.' But sin [as a latent and unconscious principle] taking a start, wrought in me, through the instrumentality of the law, evil desires of every kind. For, without [the disclosures of] the law, sin is dead (latent and unconscious); but, I [an unconvicted sinner] was formerly alive (happy and fearless in sin) without [the disclosures of] the law. But when the commandment came [to my consciousness], sin revived (became remorse); but I died [with fear of death and hell], and the law, ordained to life [for a holy being], I [a sinner] found to be unto death. For, sin taking a start [as already said], deceived me through the commandment [by suggesting justification by works], and slew me [with pangs of conscience, and fears of perdition]. So that the law is [neither sin, nor death, but] holy, just, and good. Does it follow, then, that that which is good [in its own nature] was made death to me [by God's agency]? God forbid. [On the contrary, this must be charged upon sin.] For, sin [became death to me], in order that it might be seen to be [dreadful and malignant] sin, since it works death by means of a law that is good and beneficent."

Verses 14–25 contain still further proof that the law, in its own nature, is neither sin nor death, by a reference to the experience of the *believer*. Having evinced this, in the preceding section, by examining the experience of the unregenerate, both as unconvicted and convicted, St. Paul now turns to the experience of the regenerate. The sudden and striking change, in verse 14, and continuing through the entire section, from the past to the present tense, together with ποτέ in verse 9, indicates this. Calvin's statement of the relation of Rom. vii. 1–13 to vii. 14–25 is as follows: "Initio, nudam naturæ et legis comparationem proponit apostolus. Deinde exemplum proponit hominis regenerati: in quo sic carnis reliquiæ cum lege Domini dissident, ut spiritus ei libenter obtemperet." Calvin ad Romanos, vii. 14.

The clue to the meaning of this important and disputed section is in Owen's remark (Holy Spirit, III. vi.), that "in the unregenerate convicted man, the conflict is merely between the *mind* and *conscience* on the one hand, and the *will* on the other. The will is still absolutely bent on sin, only some head is made against its inclinations by the light of the mind before sin, and rebukes of conscience after it. But in the case of the regenerate man, the conflict begins to be *in the will itself*. A new principle of grace having been infused thereinto, opposes those habitual inclinations unto evil which were before predominant in it. This fills the soul with amazement, and in some brings them to the very door of despair, because they see not how nor when they shall be delivered (vii. 24). So was it with the person instanced in

14 *οἴδαμεν γὰρ ὅτι ὁ νόμος πνευματικός ἐστιν· ἐγὼ δὲ σάρκινός εἰμι, πεπραμένος ὑπὸ τὴν ἁμαρτίαν.*

Augustine's Confessions, VIII. v. 'The new will, which began to be in me, whereby I would love thee, O my God, the only certain sweetness, was not yet able to overcome, perfectly, my former will confirmed by long continuance. So, my two wills, the one old, the other new, the one carnal, the other spiritual, conflicted between themselves, and rent my soul by their disagreement. Then did I understand by experience in myself what I had read, how the flesh lusteth against the Spirit, and the Spirit lusteth against the flesh. I was myself on both sides; but, *more in that which I approved in myself*, than in what I condemned in myself. I was not *more in that which I condemned*, because, for the most part, I suffered unwillingly what I did willingly: according to the Apostle's words, 'What I hate, that do I. It is no more I that do it; but sin that dwelleth in me.'"

VER. 14. οἴδαμεν] it is conceded by all. γὰρ] looks back to the affirmation that the law is holy, just, and good, and introduces a new proof of the position. πνευματικός] 1. requires a spiritual and perfect obedience (Calvin); 2. has respect to what is inward and sincere (Beza); 3. is fulfilled only by those who are actuated by the Holy Spirit (Tholuck); 4. is the expression of the Holy Spirit, the absolute πνεῦμα (Meyer, Hodge). The last is preferable, as a single definition; but it is better to combine all four of these views. The idea intended to be suggested by the epithet πνευματικός is that of absolute and unmixed *perfection*, in contrast with the *imperfection* of the regenerate man. The moral law is spiritual, simply and purely. There is no *mixture* in it of the sensual with the spiritual, of the flesh with the spirit, as there is in the character of the believer. Law is nothing but holiness. "The law of the Lord is perfect," Ps. xix. 7. Compare the "perfect will (law) of God," Rom. xii. 2. It is marked by what Owen (Mortification, Ch. xi.) denominates "the holiness, spirituality, fiery severity, inwardness, absoluteness of the law." "The law is perfect, and bindeth every one to full conformity, in the whole man, unto the righteousness thereof, and unto entire obedience for ever; so as to require the utmost perfection of every duty, and to forbid the least degree of every sin. It is spiritual, and so reacheth the understanding, will, affections, and all other powers of the soul; as well as words, works, and gestures" (Westminster Larger Catechism, 99). ἐγὼ δὲ] "But I, on the contrary." The ἐγὼ, here, denotes the writer himself in his present moral condition, as εἰμι shows. He looks into himself as he now is, and finds in the mixed experience of holiness and sin, which he subsequently delineates, a striking contrast to the unmixed holiness of the law. The law is perfect; he is imperfect. In order to the correct exegesis, it is necessary, in the outset, to notice two senses in which ἐγὼ is used, in this section, by St. Paul: 1. *comprehensive*; 2. *limited*. The comprehensive ἐγὼ denotes the entire person of the believer, as actuated by *both* the Holy Spirit, and the remainders of the evil principle of sin. The ἐγὼ in this sense is complex, and contains a mixture of both the spiritual and the carnal, in which, however, *the spiritual predominates*. The limited ἐγὼ, on the other hand, denotes the person of the believer *only as actuated by the Holy Spirit*, omitting and excluding the workings of remaining sin. The instances of this latter signification are only two: viz., ἐγὼ in verses 17 and 20 qualified by οὐκέτι. This limited ἐγὼ is also described, in verse 22, as ὁ ἔσω ἄνθρωπος, and in verses 23 and 25, as ὁ νόμος τοῦ νοός. The comprehensive ἐγὼ includes the limited ἐγὼ *plus* the remnants of the old sinful nature; the limited ἐγὼ includes only the new principle of holiness *minus* these remnants. The former is a complex of grace and sin; the latter is grace simply and only. It is evident, that not all that is predicable of the former ego may be predicated of the latter. In verse 16, St. Paul attributes a sin to the comprehensive ἐγὼ which, in verse 17, he asserts is not committed by the limited ἐγὼ. In verse 20, he repeats the statement. σάρκινός] This is the reading of ℵABCDEFG Griesb., Lachm., Scholz, Tisch. The Receptus reads σαρκικός. In classical usage, σάρκινός is rather physical, than mental, in its signification. "Words with the termination in ινός designate the substance of which anything is made; thus θυϊνος, of thyine wood (Rev. xviii. 12), ὑάλινος, of glass (Rev. iv. 6). One of these is σάρκινός, the only form of the word which classical antiquity recognized (σαρκικός, like the Latin 'carnalis,' having been called out by the ethical necessities of the Church), and in 2 Cor. iii. 3 well rendered 'fleshy:' that is, having flesh for the substance and material of which it is made" (Trench's Synonymes of the New Testament, Second Series, § xxii.). If the classical use is insisted upon, then σαρκικός would be a stronger word than σάρκινός, in this passage: the latter referring rather to the body than to the soul, and finding the seat of the sin that is charged upon the person more in his flesh than in his will. In this case, σάρκινός would, perhaps, allude to the "vile body" by which the believer is hampered (Phil. iii. 2). But the use of the two words by St. Paul in 1 Cor. iii. 1, 3 (a passage that throws much light upon this one) proves that they are interchangeable. The same authorities (ℵABC Griesb., Lachm., Tisch.) read σαρκίνοις in 1 Cor. iii. 1, and σαρκικοί (twice) in 1 Cor. iii. 3. But the very same persons are spoken of, in both places: showing, as Tischendorf (in loco) remarks, that St. Paul employed "duplicem formam promiscue." So, Lange. This epithet σάρκινός (or σαρκικός), which the apostle applies to himself as descriptive of his moral state at the time of his writing, determines the interpretation of the whole section. It is not the equivalent of ψυχικὸς. Paul does not say that he is a "natural man." The ψυχικὸς ἄνθρωπος is unregenerate. See 1 Cor. ii. 14; Jude 19. The epithet "carnal" in this passage does not signify total depravity. It designates a partial and not a total tendency of the ἐγὼ. It is used comparatively. Compared with the *law*, he is carnal. The law is absolutely and totally spiritual (πνευματικός), but he is not absolutely and totally holy. He is still to some extent, and he feels it to be no small extent (verse 24), ruled by σάρξ. But he is not wholly and completely ruled by it. He is inwardly inclined to good (verses 15, 19, 21); is disinclined to, and hates evil (verses 15, 16, 19); "delights in the law of God" (verse 22); and "serves the law of God" (verse 25). The natural man is not thus described in Scripture. That a regenerate man may be called "carnal" is proved by 1 Cor. iii. 1, 3. Here, this epithet is applied to certain believers who, by reason of the weakness of their faith, are denominated "babes in Christ;" who are described as "laborers together with God," as "God's husbandry and God's building" (verse 9), as "the temple of God," in whom "the Spirit of God dwelleth" (verse 16), yet, by reason of "envying and strife and divisions," are also described as "carnal," and "walking as men." πεπραμένος, etc.] this clause explains the meaning of the epithet σάρκινός which St. Paul applies to himself. The carnality which he mourns over is a species of bondage. Compare αἰχμαλωτίζοντα in verse 25. The phrase πέπρακεν εἰς τὰς χεῖρας is found in the Septuagint version of 1 Sam. xxiii. 7. The word πεπραμένος, like σάρκινός, is used *relatively*. It denotes, not the absolute and total bondage of the unregenerate, but the *partial* bondage of the imperfectly sanctified. The succeeding explanation proves this. Similar descriptions of the inward state of the renewed soul are frequent in Scripture. Compare Ps. xxxviii.

1–10; xxxix. 8–11; xl. 12; li. 1–12; lxix. 5; xc. 7, 8; cxix. 96, 120, 176; Isa. vi. 5; Mat. xxvi. 41; Rom. viii. 23; 1 Cor. ix. 26, 27; iii. 1–4; Eph. vi. 12; Phil. iii. 12–14; Heb. xii. 1; 1 John i. 8. The continual prayer and struggle that mark the Christian race and fight, show that although the regenerate believer is not in the total and hopeless slavery of the unregenerate man, he is yet under so much of a bondage as to prevent perfect obedience; to make him "poor in spirit" (Mat. v. 3), "weary and heavy laden" (Mat. xi. 28); and to force from him the cry: "O wretched man, who shall deliver me?" Otherwise, there would be no call for such prayer and struggle. The following are some of the characteristics of this partial bondage of the believer, as compared with the total bondage of the unbeliever. 1. It is accompanied with the hope and expectation that it will one day cease entirely (Rom. vii. 24; viii. 24, 25; Ps. xxxviii. 15; xl. 1–3; Lam. iii. 26). The unbeliever has no such hope or expectation (Eph. ii. 12). 2. It is accompanied with weariness and hatred of the sin that causes the bondage (Rom. vii. 15, 19, 23, 24). The unbeliever, if unconvicted ("alive without the law"), has no feeling upon the subject; if convicted ("the commandment coming") has only the emotions of remorse and fear, which are not hatred of sin, or weariness of it (2 Cor. vii. 10). 3. The believer positively loves holiness, and hates sin; he is inclined to good, and disinclined to evil, as the terms θέλω and μισῶ imply (Rom. vii. 15, 16, 19, 20, 21, 22). The unbeliever hates holiness, and loves sin; is inclined to evil, and disinclined to good (Rom. viii. 7). ὑπὸ] in connection with πεπραμένος refers to the custom of compelling captives to pass under a yoke. Compare αἰχμαλωτίζοντα, in verse 23. Like ταλαίπωρος (ver. 24), it implies a weary consciousness of bondage.

VER. 15 begins the explanation, in detail, of the statement

[15] ὃ γὰρ κατεργάζομαι, οὐ γινώσκω· οὐ γὰρ ὃ θέλω, τοῦτο πράσσω, ἀλλ' ὃ μισῶ, τοῦτο ποιῶ.

that the writer is "carnal, sold under sin." If not explained, the language might be taken in the *absolute* unqualified sense, and he be understood to say that he is a lost man: "in the gall of bitterness, and in the bond of iniquity" (Acts viii. 23). γὰρ] looks back to the assertion in verse 14, and introduces the proof and explanation of it. κατεργάζομαι] the present tense denotes what the writer is now doing. It does not, however, denote *unresisted*, *habitual*, and *uniform* action. St. Paul does mean to teach that he "disallows of" and "hates" every single thing, without exception, that he is now doing; because he subsequently describes himself as "inclined to good" (verse 21), and "serving the law of God" (verse 25). Consequently, κατεργάζομαι denotes *repressed* and *intermittent* action, in distinction from unresisted habitual and uniform action. The apostle acknowledges that often, but not invariably, he commits actual sin of thought, word, and deed. He teaches, also, that a part of his inward experience, but not the whole of it, is the working of remaining concupiscence (ἐπιθυμία). He is conscious of the "lusting of the flesh against the Spirit;" but *also*, of the "lusting of the Spirit against the flesh" (Gal. v. 17). The difference between repressed and intermittent, and habitual and uniform action, is marked in 1 John i. 8, compared with 1 John iii. 6, 9. Upon this important point, we avail ourselves of the views of Owen, whose explanation of the seventh chapter of Romans, in his treatises upon Indwelling Sin and the work of the Holy Spirit, is marked by his usual psychological subtlety, and spiritual insight. "There are in believers," says Owen (Holy Spirit, IV. vi.), "inclinations and dispositions to sin proceeding from the *remainders* of an habitual principle. This the Scripture calls the 'flesh,' 'lust,' 'the sin that dwelleth in us,' 'the body of death;' being what yet remaineth in believers of that vicious corrupted depravation of our nature which came upon us by the loss of the image of God. This still continueth in believers, inclining them unto evil, according to the power and efficacy that is remaining in it, in *various degrees.*" This remaining corruption, or concupiscence, Owen asserts to be of the nature of a habit (habitus), or disposition; yet its workings in the believer are not habitual, in the sense of being *unrepressed*, *uniform*, and *invariable;* because they are resisted and more or less overcome, by grace in the soul. The "lustings of the Spirit against the flesh" (Gal. v. 17) prevent the flesh from having that unintermittent and unvarying operation which it has in the unregenerate. "We must distinguish," says Owen (Indwelling Sin, Chap. vi.), "between the habitual frame of the *heart*, and the natural propensity or habitual inclination of the *law of sin* in the heart. The habitual inclination of the heart is denominated from the principle that bears chief or sovereign rule in it; and therefore in believers it is unto good, unto God, unto holiness, unto obedience. The believer's *heart* is not habitually inclined unto evil by the remainders of indwelling sin, but this *sin in the heart* hath a constant habitual propensity unto evil, in itself considered, or in its own nature." In other words, indwelling sin in the believer is of the nature of a habit or disposition, in distinction from an act; but it is not the characteristic of a believer, as it is of an unbeliever, to habitually indulge and act out this habit or disposition. "Upon the introduction of the new principle of grace and holiness," says Owen (Holy Spirit, IV. vi.), "this habit of sin is weakened, impaired, and so disenabled, as that it cannot nor shall incline unto sin, with that *constancy* and *prevalency* as formerly, nor press ordinarily with the same urgency and violence. Hence in the Scripture it is said to be dethroned by grace, so as that it shall not reign or lord it over us, by hurrying us into the pursuit of its uncontrollable inclinations, Rom. vi. 12. Those who have this spiritual principle of holiness, may be surprised into actual omission of duties, and commission of sins, and a *temporary* indulgence of corrupt affections. But *habitually* they cannot be so. An habitual reserve for anything that is sinful, or morally evil, is eternally inconsistent with this principle of holiness. This spiritual principle of holiness in the believer disposeth the heart unto duties of holiness constantly and evenly. He in whom it is feareth always, or is in the fear of the Lord all the day long. It is true, that the actings of grace in us are sometimes more intense and vigorous than at other times; and we ourselves are sometimes more watchful, and diligently intent on all occasions of acting out grace, whether in solemn duties, or in our general course, than we are at some other times. Moreover, there are especial seasons wherein we meet with greater difficulties and obstructions from our lusts and temptations than ordinary, whereby this holy disposition is intercepted, and impeded. But notwithstanding all these things which are contrary to it, and obstructive of its operations, in itself and in its own nature it doth constantly and evenly incline the soul unto duties of holiness." γινώσκω] Explanations: 1. γινώσκω denotes *love* and *inclination;* and not mere approbation, which may exist without love of holiness or hatred of sin. This is the Hebraistic and Biblical use of the word. It is like יָדַע in Gen. xviii. 19; Ps. i. 6; xxxvi. 10; cxliv. 3; Hosea viii. 4; Amos iii. 2. Compare, also, Mat. vii. 23; John x. 14; 1 Cor. viii. 3; xvi. 18; 2 Tim. ii. 19; 1 Thess. v. 12 (Ellicott in loc.). This signification is adopted by Augustine, Erasmus, Beza, Pareus, Grotius, Rosenmüller, Semler. That this is the correct view, is proved by the fact that οὐ γινώσκω is in the next clause explained by οὐ θέλω and μισῶ; and also by the subsequent description of the writer's moral state, in which positive aversion toward and hatred of evil, together with struggle against it, are delineated. 2. γινώσκω denotes the approbation of *conscience.* This is the classical use of the word. See Liddell and Scott, in voce. Τὰ χρήσθ' ἐπιστάμεθα καὶ γιγνώσκομεν, οὐκ ἐκπονοῦμεν δὲ (Euripides, Medea, 1077). Compare Ovid's "video meliora, proboque; deteriora sequor" (Met. vii. 20, 21). That the writer's feeling toward the moral law is more than the necessary and organic action of conscience, is proved by the employment of συνήδομαι in verse 22, and δουλεύω in verse 25; as well as of θέλω and μισῶ, in other places. He not only "approves" of the law, but he "delights in" it, and "serves" it. St. Paul employs δοκιμάζω and συνίστημι, when he wishes to indicate the approbation of conscience. Compare Rom. ii. 18; iii. 5; xiv. 22; 1 Cor. xvi. 3; 2 Cor. iii. 1; iv. 2; x. 18. 3. γινώσκω means *knowledge*, or *intelligence*, simply. According to this view, St. Paul asserts his ignorance of the sin which he commits. He does not understand the moral significance of it. This explanation of the word is adopted by Chrysostom, De Wette, Meyer, Tholuck, Ruckert, Philippi. It implies that the writer's inward state, described by σάρκινός and πεπραμένος, is one of insensibility; the same as that described in verse 9 by the phrase: "alive without the law." But this is a mental state that passed away, "when the commandment came." If the person were still in this state of spiritual apathy, and ignorance, he could not feel the burden of being "sold under sin," or the spiritual sorrow implied in ταλαίπωρος ἐγὼ (verse 24). In Luke xxiii. 34, where the moral ignorance and unconsciousness of the unconvicted sinner is spoken of, οἴδασι is used. The same ἐγὼ which is to be supplied with κατεργάζομαι, is to be supplied with οὐ γινώσκω. The very same person who commits the sin is disinclined to it, and hates it (verse 15). The ἐγὼ is the comprehensive ἐγὼ, including the "new man" together with remnants of the "old man." Both of these coexist in the unity of a single self-consciousness.

> "I hate my own vain thoughts that rise,
> But love thy law, my God."

St. Paul, as a person in whom there is a renewed nature and the remainders of a sinful one, has within himself the basis for a twofold activity and experience,—that of grace, and that of sin,—and can say "*I* hate what *I* do." And yet he is not a double-minded man: ἀνὴρ δίψυχος (James i. 8). There are not two principles of action within him, of *equal* strength and efficiency. There is only one principle, in the proper sense of the term, and the dying *fragments* of another. Grace is stronger than sin, in the believer. It is the dominant characteristic in him (vi. 17, 18, 22); and with reference to it, he is to be denominated a "saint" (viii. 27; xii. 13; xvi. 15; 1 Cor. vi. 2; Eph. i. 1; Col. i. 2; Heb. vi. 10, et passim), and "perfect" (Mat. xix. 21; 1 Cor. ii. 6; Phil. iii. 15; James i. 4; iii. 2). οὐ γὰρ θέλω, etc.] This clause is explanatory of ὃ κατεργάζομαι, οὐ γινώσκω; and shows that the writer does not wish to be understood as saying that he is wholly depraved and unregenerate. He is right at heart, and in his disposition, notwithstanding his sins, and failures in duty. When he sins, he does not do what he loves, but what he hates. θέλω implies feeling and affection. It denotes the inclination of the will, and not a mere volition, or resolve. It is a bias of the faculty, contrary to that denoted by μισῶ. As the latter does not signify mere volitionary action, neither does the former. The former implies desire, and the latter aversion. For the Biblical signification of θέλω, see Mat. ix. 13; xii. 7; xvii. 4; xxvii. 43; John v. 21, 40; xxi. 18; Rom. xiii. 3; Gal. v. 17; Heb. x. 5, 8; Rev. xxii. 17. In these instances the general disposition or bent of the will is intended. Hence, in Scripture, the activity denoted by θέλημα is often attributed to καρδία. See comment on ii. 5. Whenever a particular decision, or a particular act of choice, in distinction from the bent or inclination, is intended, the term employed is βουλή, or βούλημα. See Luke vii. 30; xxiii. 51; Acts ii. 23; xxvii. 42, 43; Rom. ix. 19; 1 Cor. iv. 5; Eph. i. 11; Heb. vi. 17. This distinction between θέλημα and βουλή is not so carefully and sharply marked in the classical use of the words, as it is in the Biblical.

The term θέλω, then, denotes a state of the will and affections, and not the action of the moral reason and conscience, as Meyer, and others maintain. It is more, also, than the schoolman's *velleitas*, as Tholuck, and others, explain it. This is a mere *wish*, in distinction from a will or positive inclination. The phraseology of St. Paul, in this passage, must not be confounded with that of Plato in the Republic, ix. 589, Protagoras, 345, and Timæus, 86; where he asserts that "no wise man supposes that any one sins willingly; but that all men well know that those who commit base and wicked acts do so involuntarily,"—a sentiment combated by Aristotle (Ethics, iii. 5), and contradictory to Plato's own views as expressed elsewhere; particularly when speaking of the punishment to be inflicted upon sin in the future world (Gorgias, 525). There is also in Epictetus (Enchiridion, ii. 26) a passage singularly resembling this of St. Paul, so far as the words are concerned, but the meaning of which is the same with that of Plato: ὃ μὲν θέλει (i. e., ὁ ἁμαρτάνων) οὐ ποιεῖ, καὶ ὃ μη θέλει ποιεῖ. See also Sophocles, Œdipus Colonus, 270. The reference, in these statements of Plato and Epictetus, is to the selfish suffering and regret experienced by the transgressor after his transgression. He wishes that he had not committed the sin which reason condemns, and for which conscience is distressing him, and thus seems to have sinned against his will. He makes some ineffectual resolutions and attempts to reform, and then ceases the struggle.

This is far from being the same as loving holiness, and hating and *constantly struggling* with sin; which is the description of St. Paul's experience. Regret is not repentance; a wish (velleitas) is not a will (voluntas); volitions are not an inclination. The experience described by Plato and Epictetus is that of the natural man under conviction of sin, *but without love of holiness.* It is the experience of Tarquin after the rape of Lucrece, so powerfully delineated by Shakspeare; of the remorseful but impenitent Danish king, who cannot pray, "though inclination be as sharp as will," because one "cannot be pardoned, and retain the offence:" an experience which is summed up and concentrated in the marvellous sonnet (cxxix.) of the great human Searcher of the human heart:

"The expense of spirit in a waste of shame
  Is lust in action; and till action, lust
Is perjured, murderous, bloody, full of blame,
  Savage, extreme, rude, cruel, not to trust;
Enjoyed no sooner, but despised straight;
  Past reason hunted; and no sooner had,
Past reason hated, as a swallowed bait,
  On purpose laid to make the taker mad;
Mad in pursuit, and in possession so;
  Had, having, and in quest to have, extreme;
A bliss in proof,—and proved, a very woe;
  Before, a joy proposed; behind a dream:
All this the world well knows; yet none knows well
To shun the heaven that leads men to this hell."

In all such instances and experiences as these, the contest with evil, not being founded in a real and spiritual hatred of evil, is not persevering and "unto blood" (Heb. xii. 4), but only "for a while" (Mat. xiii. 21). It is not successful, but a failure. The experience described by St. Paul, on the contrary, is that of one whose struggle is life-long and *victorious*, as the triumphant, "I thank God, through Jesus

[16] *εἰ δε ὃ οὐ θέλω, τοῦτο ποιῶ, σύμφημι τῷ νόμῳ ὅτι καλός·* [17] *νυνὶ δὲ οὐκέτι ἐγὼ κατεργάζομαι αὐτό, ἀλλὰ ἡ ἐνοικοῦσα ἐν ἐμοὶ ἁμαρτία.*

Christ our Lord," implies (verse 25). οὐ πράσσω] is equivalent to οὐ ποιῶ, as the exchange of the words in verse 19 shows. Intermittent, in distinction from habitual and uniform action, is intended. See comment on verse 15. That a person should never, in a single instance, do what he is inclined to do, is psychologically impossible. μισῶ] denotes spiritual and holy detestation: the same emotion in kind with that of God (Lev. xx. 23; Ps. v. 6; x. 3; Prov. vi. 16; viii. 13; Is. lxi. 8; Jer. xliv. 4; Rev. ii. 6); and identical with that enjoined upon believers (Ps. xcvii. 10; Eccl. iii. 8; Amos v. 15; Mat. vi. 24), and exercised by them (Ps. ci. 3; cxix. 113, 128, 163; cxxxix. 21, 22; Prov. viii. 13). ποιῶ] denotes intermittent action. That a person should invariably do what he hates, is as impossible as that he should never, in a single instance, do what he loves.

VER. 16. The apostle continues the argument upon which he entered in verse 14: viz., to show from the experience of the believer, in his struggle with remaining sin, that the law is holy. The fact, stated in verses 14 and 15, that the believer is only partially in bondage to sin, and that when he sins he does something that is contrary to his inclination, and something that he hates, proves that he agrees (σύμφημι) with the law: loving what the law commands, and hating what the law forbids. Assuming then, as he does, that his love and hatred, in the premises, are right and not wrong, it follows that the law is not sin (verse 7). It enjoins what is lovable, and prohibits what is hateful. δέ] is transitive: "now" if, etc. θέλω and ποιῶ] have the same signification as in verse 15, being merely a repetition. σύμφημι] denotes a co-testimony with the law. The law claims to be righteousness and not sin, and the believer, by his love of righteousness and hatred of sin, coincides, or accords with the claim. The reference in this word is more to the conscience, than to the heart and will. In verse 22, where the affections are intended, a stronger term (συνήδομαι) is used.

VER. 17 looks back to verse 15, and aims to show that the sinning there spoken of is not the unresisted, impenitent, and uniform sinning of unregenerate and unforgiven men, but a particular kind of sinning that is accompanied with sorrow, hatred of it, and struggle with it. νυνὶ] is logical, not temporal: "now, since this is the case:" namely, that I *hate* what I do, and do not do what I *love.* δὲ] is adversative. οὐκέτι] the logical use, as in vii. 20; xi. 6. ἐγὼ] is here employed in the *limited* sense, to denote the principle of holiness implanted by regeneration, and this *only.* This is the controlling principle in the believer, and constitutes the true man within the man. Hence, in verse 22, it is denominated the ἔσω ἄνθρωπος. The remainders of the principle of sin are not put into the ἔγω in this limited sense (as they are in the comprehensive sense), but are set off by themselves, and called ἡ ἐνοικοῦσα ἁμαρτία; so that the action of the limited and qualified "I" is different in its nature and quality, from that of the "indwelling sin." The ἐγὼ in this narrow sense is holy, but indwelling sin, of course, is sinful. The former is grace in the soul; the latter is corruption in the soul. Take away from the soul all indwelling sin, and leave only this limited ἐγὼ (which St. Paul asserts is not the author of sin: οὐκέτι ἐγὼ κατεργάζομαι αὐτὸ), and perfect sanctification would be the result. This is done at death, when "the souls of believers are made perfect in holiness, and immediately pass into glory" (Westminster S. C., 37). αὐτὸ] this thing, namely, which I hate (ὃ μισῶ), and to which I am not inclined (ὃ οὐ ϑέλω). ἐνοικοῦσα ἐν ἐμοὶ] sin is a resident alien in the believer, a "squatter," in the provincial sense, and not the true citizen and inhabitant. The figure is taken from a house (οἶκος) into which an intruder has crowded. This representation shows still again, in addition to the preceding explanatory clauses, that the writer is not willing to be understood by his phraseology in verse 14, that he is wholly carnal, and totally in bondage to sin. "There is nothing," says Owen (Indwelling Sin, Ch. vi.), "more marvellous or dreadful in the working of sin, than this its importunity. The soul knows not what to make of it; it dislikes, abhors, abominates the evil it tends unto; it despiseth the thoughts of it, hates them as hell; and yet is by itself imposed on with them, as if it were another person, an express enemy got within him. All this the apostle discovers in Rom. vii. 15–17. 'The things that I do, I hate.' It is not of outward actions, but the inward risings of the mind that he treats. 'I hate them,' saith he, 'I abominate them.' But why, then, will he have anything more to do with them? If he hate them, and abhor himself for them, then let them alone, have no more to do with them, and so end the matter. Alas! saith he, verse 17, 'It is no more I that do it, but sin that dwelleth in me.' I have one within me that is my enemy, that with endless resistless importunity puts these things upon me, even the things that I hate and abominate; I cannot be rid of them, I am weary of myself, I cannot fly from them; 'O wretched man that I am, who shall deliver me?' I do not say that this is the *ordinary* [uniform] condition of believers, but thus it is often, when the law of sin riseth up to war and fighting. It is not thus with them in respect of particular sins, this or that sin, outward sins, sins of life and conversation; but yet in respect of vanity of mind, inward and spiritual distempers, it is often so. Some, I know, pretend to great perfection, but I am resolved to believe the apostle before them all and every one." Compare Howe's Blessedness of the Righteous, Ch. xx. This phraseology of St. Paul, distinguishing the true ego from what does not belong to it, finds a parallel in Shakspeare's Hamlet, Act v., Sc. ii.

> "Was't Hamlet wronged Laertes? Never Hamlet.
> If Hamlet from himself be ta'en away,
> And, when he's not himself, does wrong Laertes,
> Then Hamlet does it not, Hamlet denies it.
> Who does it then? His madness. If't be so,
> Hamlet is of the faction that is wronged;
> His madness is poor Hamlet's enemy."

Though indwelling sin (i. e., the remainders of original sin), is thus distinguished by St. Paul from the principle of holiness, or the limited and true ἐγὼ, it must not be inferred that it is not culpable, and properly sin. This is the Tridentine view (Canones Tridentini, Sessio v.). The Council of Trent decided that concupiscence (ἐπιθυμία), in the unregenerate as well as the regenerate, is not sin in the strict signification (Shedd's History of Doctrine, ii. 147 sq.). This is an error. For, although the remainders of original sin do not constitute a part of the limited ἐγὼ, they do of the *comprehensive* ἐγὼ; and man is responsible for all that is found in his *total* personality. The carnal desires of indwelling sin interpenetrate the entire self-consciousness of the believer, and make a part of that larger "I" which comprises a *twofold* activity and has a *twofold* experience; which, as in verse 15, can say *I* hate what *I* do. The risings of evil desire in the believer, as well as the outward acts in which they are expressed, are as really a part of himself and his self-consciousness, as are his holy desires and the holy acts in which they are expressed. "With the mind, I *myself* serve the law of God; but with the flesh [I *myself* serve] the law of sin" (vii. 25). When he sins, either inwardly or outwardly, he is spontaneously inclined and self-determined. There is no compulsion in the exercise of these internal lusts, or in the perpetration of the external acts. They are a mode of the *will.* They are self-will, and ill-will. While, therefore, *ἡ ἐνοικοῦσα ἁμαρτία* can be distinguished from the limited ἐγὼ, or, in other words, remaining lust from the new principle of holiness implanted by regeneration, the two cannot be *divided* and *separated* from each other, so as to constitute two persons. Hence, when St. Paul, for the purpose of analysis and explanation, has denominated the new principle of spiritual life the ἐγὼ, he does not denominate the remainders of the old principle of sin an ἐγὼ also (they are then, *οὐκέτι* ἐγὼ); because in this case there would be not only a duplication of the activity and of the experience, but of the unity itself of the human soul. There would be two egos. This would be an error in anthropology similar to that of Nestorianism in Christology. This coexistence and interpenetration, in one self-consciousness, of the actings of indwelling sin with those of the principle of spiritual life, or in St. Paul's phraseology of the flesh with the spirit, are feelingly and vividly expressed in the lines of Cowper:

> "My God, how perfect are thy ways!
> But mine polluted are;
> Sin twines itself about my praise,
> And slides into my prayer.
>
> When I would speak what thou hast done
> To save me from my sin,
> I cannot make thy mercies known,
> But self-applause creeps in.
>
> Divine desire, that holy flame
> Thy grace creates in me;
> Alas! impatience is its name
> When it returns to thee.

18 *οἶδα γὰρ ὅτι οὐκ οἰκεῖ ἐν ἐμοί, τουτέστιν ἐν τῇ σαρκί μου, ἀγαθόν. τὸ γὰρ θέλειν παράκειταί μοι, τὸ δὲ κατεργάζεσθαι τὸ καλὸν οὔ·*

This heart, a fountain of vile thoughts,
How does it overflow!
While *self* upon the surface floats,
Still bubbling from below."—WORKS, iii. 11.

While, however, indwelling sin in the regenerate is sin in the strict sense of guilt, and requires to be expiated by the atoning blood of Christ, yet it is not so intense and malignant a form of sin, as is the impenitent and hardened sin of the natural man. It is wearily felt to be bondage; is continually mourned over and struggled with, by the believer. It is sin in its dying and waning state, which is not so intense and determined a mode, as sin in its growing and waxing state. The former is the *minuendo* movement of sin; the latter the *crescendo*.

VER. 18 amplifies and confirms the statement in verse 17. οἶδα] "I know from my own experience," i. e. γὰρ] introduces the explanation and further proof of the statement in the preceding verse. οἰκεῖ] alludes to ἐνοικοῦσα in verse 17. ἐμοί] is the comprehensive ἐγὼ, which includes the limited ἐγὼ of verse 17 (the ἔσω ἄνθρωπος of verse 22), together with the remainders of sin designated by ἡ ἐνοικοῦσα ἁμαρτία in verse 17. These all combined in one unity constitute the total person St. Paul, as he is now at the moment of writing. τουτέστιν] introduces an explanation, to prevent the reader from understanding the writer to say absolutely, and without qualification, that "no good thing dwells" in his total personality. The Holy Spirit "dwells" in him (John xiv. 17; Rom. viii. 9, 11; 1 Cor. iii. 16 compared with verses 1 and 3; 2 Tim. i. 14; 1 John iv. 12); and the new principle of holiness, "the law of the Spirit of life in Christ Jesus," also resides in him (Rom. vi. 13, 17; vii. 6, 22, 25). Taking the term "me" in the wide sense, St. Paul is not willing to say that there is no holiness in him. "Fatetur nihil boni in se habitare: deinde correctionem subjicit, ne sit contumeliosus in dei gratiam, quæ ipsa quoque in eo habitat, sed pars carnis non erat." Calvin in loco. *ἐν τῇ σαρκί*] In order to explain his meaning, the apostle distinguishes the remainders of sin within him from the principle of spiritual life within him, and asserts that it is to the *former* alone that his assertion that "no good thing dwelleth in him" refers. It does not refer to the *ἔσω ἄνθρωπος*, or the limited *ἐγὼ*. This latter is the product of regenerating grace, and, consequently, is holy in its nature. This is "spirit" and not "flesh." This hates sin, and does not commit sin (verses 15, 17). In order that this holy principle may not be involved in the charge of total depravity that is here made, the writer carefully distinguishes it from the indwelling corruption that is intimately associated with it, it is true, but which is a very different thing from it. The *σάρξ* here described as having nothing good in it, is the same as *ἡ ἐνοικοῦσα ἁμαρτία* in verse 17, and *ὁ νόμος ἐν τοῖς μέλεσίν* in verse 22; both of which make a part of the *ἐγὼ* in the comprehensive sense, but no part of the *ἐγὼ* in the limited signification. This *σάρξ* or indwelling sin, it should be noticed, is not strictly, and in the full sense of the term, a *principle*, but only the *remainders* of one. It is true that St. Paul denominates it a "law in the members" (verse 23), and a "law of sin" (verses 23, 25). And theologians speak of indwelling sin, as a "principle," a "disposition," a "sinful nature," etc. But this is for the purpose of teaching that indwelling sin is something more than actual transgression. It is inward lust, deeply seated, and making continual and strong opposition to the principle of holiness. But, the *νόμος ἁμαρτίας* in the believer is not a "law" or "principle" of life and conduct, in the *full* and *strict* sense in which these terms are applicable to the νόμος τοῦ νοός, or ἐσώ ἄνθρωπος (verses 22, 23). A principle or law of action, in the strict sense, is the *dominant* force in the subject of it. In this sense, holiness is the only principle in the regenerate person. The "law of the mind," and not the "law of sin," is the superior and controlling power in him. There cannot be two dominant principles, one of holiness and one of sin, in the same man at the same time. But there may be a principle of holiness and *fragments* of a principle of sin, in one and the same person, at one and the same moment. And these fragments may be denominated a principle, in a *qualified* and *secondary* sense. "There are in believers, inclinations and dispositions to sin proceeding from the *remainders* of an habitual principle. This the Scripture calls the 'flesh,' 'lust,' 'the sin that dwelleth in us,' 'the body of death'" (Owen's Holy Spirit, IV. vi.). "In every regenerate person there are, in a *spiritual* sense, two principles of all his actings; two wills; there is a will of the flesh, and there is a will of the Spirit; a regenerate man is spiritually, and in Scripture expression, two men; a new man and an old. There is an 'I,' and an 'I' at opposition; a will and non-willing; a doing and non-doing; a delighting and non-delighting; all in the same person. Rom. vii. 15, 19, 22. But, there is not a duality of wills in a *physical* sense, as the will is a natural faculty of the soul; but in a *moral* and *analogical* sense, as the word is taken for a habit or principle of good or evil" (Owen's Saints' Perseverance, Ch. xv.). "The two contrary principles of spirit and flesh, of grace and sin, cannot exist in the *highest degree* at the same time, nor be actually *prevalent* or *predominant* in the same instances. That is, sin and grace cannot bear rule in the same heart at the same time, so as that it should be *equally* under the conduct of them both. Nor can they have in the soul contrary inclinations *equally efficacious;* for then would they absolutely obstruct all sorts of operations whatever" (Owen's Holy Spirit, IV. vi.). "There are two laws in us, the law of flesh, or of sin; and the law of the mind, or of grace. But contrary laws cannot obtain *sovereign* power over the same person at the same time. The sovereign power in believers is in the hand of the law of grace; so the apostle declares, Rom. vii. 22: 'I delight in the law of God in the inward man'" (Owen's Indwelling Sin, Ch. vi.). μου] the partitive genitive. No good thing dwells "in the flesh of me:" in that part of the comprehensive "me" which the writer has denominated "indwelling sin," and which is no part of the limited "me." ἀγαθόν] is anarthrous, to denote abstract goodness. There is no holiness in indwelling sin; remaining lust is totally depraved. γὰρ] introduces the proof and explanation of the preceding clause. τὸ θέλειν] supply τὸ καλὸν, suggested from the succeeding clause. The inclination of the regenerate will is intended, as in verses 15 and 16. See comment. παράκειταί] The writer conceives of the entire personality (the comprehensive ἐγὼ) as a locality, in which he looks about to see what there is. He sees a holy disposition "lying alongside" of evil and antagonistic desires. μοι] is the comprehensive ἐγὼ. κατεργάζεσθαι] "to accomplish." The preposition is intensive: effectual and perfect performance is meant. The comprehensive ἐγὼ, as made up of the new man and relics of the old man, is unable to carry out completely, and with no defect or failure of any kind, its regenerate and holy inclination. This appears in two ways: 1. The believer, even when he obeys, which is his general habit, never comes perfectly up to the ideal of the law which is πνευματικός (verse 14). Remaining corruption hinders the working of grace; the flesh lusts against the spirit, "so that ye cannot do [perfectly] the things that ye would" (Gal. v. 17). Hence, the obedience of the believer

[19] οὐ γὰρ ὃ θέλω ποιῶ ἀγαθόν, ἀλλὰ ὃ οὐ θέλω κακόν,
τοῦτο πράσσω. [20] εἰ δὲ ὃ οὐ θέλω, τοῦτο ποιῶ, οὐκέτι

is not so complete and normal as it will be when he is "a just man made perfect" (Heb. xii. 23), and when indwelling sin no longer "lies alongside" of the new nature. "Take an instance in prayer. A man addresseth himself unto that duty; he would not only perform it, but he would perform it in that manner that the nature of the duty, and his own condition, do require. He would 'pray in the Spirit,' fervently, 'with sighs and groans that cannot be uttered;' this he aims at. Now oftentimes he shall find a rebellion, a fighting of the law of sin, in this matter. He shall find difficulty to get anything done, who thought to do all things. I do not say that it is thus *always*, but it is so when sin wars and rebels, which expresseth an especial acting of its power" (Owen's Indwelling Sin, Ch. vi.). 2. The believer sometimes yields to inward corruption, and actually transgresses the law. οὔ] is followed by εὑρίσκω in DEFG Peshito, Vulgate, Receptus. It is wanting in ℵABC Copt., Lachm., Tisch., Tregelles. If rejected, παράκειταί must be supplied with οὔ.

Ver. 19 is only an emphatic reaffirmation of what has been said in verses 15–18. θέλω] signifies love and inclination. See comment on verse 15. ποιῶ] denotes intermittent and imperfect action. The believer frequently, but not invariably, fails altogether to do the good to which he is inclined; and when he does the good to which he is inclined, it is never with an absolute perfection of service such as the "spiritual" law requires. See comment on verse 18. πράσσω] In St. Paul's use, there is no distinction between this word and ποιῶ. The two are interchangeable. In verse 15, πράσσω is connected with holiness (ὃ θέλω); in this verse,

ἐγὼ κατεργάζομαι αὐτό, ἀλλὰ ἡ οἰκοῦσα ἐν ἐμοὶ ἁμαρ-
τία. 21 *εὑρίσκω ἄρα τὸν νόμον τῷ θέλοντι ἐμοὶ ποιεῖν,*

with sin (ὃ οὐ θέλω). In verse 15, ποιῶ is connected with ὃ μισῶ = ὃ οὐ θέλω; and in verse 19, with ὃ θέλω. Compare Gal. v. 17.

VER. 20 is an inference drawn from the proposition in the last clause of verse 19, and is a repetition of the inference drawn in verse 17 from the same proposition in verses 15 and 16. The apostle is particular and emphatic, in his endeavor to discriminate between grace and sin, the spirit and the flesh, in himself, and to prevent what is predicable of the latter from being predicated of the former. See comment on verses 15–18.

VERSES 21–23 contain a conclusion, introduced by ἄρα, drawn from the course of reasoning in verses 14–20. εὑρίσκω] is a common word in reasoning, and implies that some truth has been brought to view by the previous argumentation. τὸν νόμον] the written law, but as including the unwritten. Two constructions are possible: 1. νόμον is the object of θέλοντι ποιεῖν, having τὸ καλόν in apposition with it, as exegetical. Compare 2 Tim. iv. 7. (Hornbergius, Knapp, Tholuck, Olshausen, Fritzsche). 2. It is the object of εὑρίσκω, and is taken in the sense of a "general rule," or a "common fact" (Luther, Calvin, Beza, Grotius, De Wette, Philippi, Hodge, Stuart). The first construction is preferable, because: 1. It is improbable that the writer, within so brief a space, would employ the same word in *three* different senses: viz., a rule of conduct; an inward inclination, or disposition; and a common fact. This would be the only instance in the New Testament of the latter signification. 2. Because, by this construction τὸ καλόν constitutes a regular antithesis to τὸ κακὸν in the next clause, and

τὸ καλόν, ὅτι ἐμοὶ τὸ κακὸν παράκειται· [22] συνήδομαι γὰρ τῷ νόμῳ τοῦ θεοῦ κατὰ τὸν ἔσω ἄνθρωπον,

also reminds the reader of the epithets ἁγία, δικαία, and ἀγαθή (verse 12), which St. Paul has previously shown to belong eminently to ὁ νόμος. παράκειται] For the figure, see comment on verse 18. In verse 18, the principle of holiness "lies alongside" of the remaining corruption; here, the remaining corruption "lies alongside" of the principle of holiness.

VER. 22. συνήδομαι] is emphatic by position. It denotes a feeling of the heart, positive enjoyment. Plato (Republic, v. 462) uses it in this sense: "When any one of the citizens experiences any good or evil, the whole state will make his case their own, and either rejoice (ξυνησθήσεται), or sorrow with him." So, also, Euripides (Medea, 136): οὐδέ συνήδομαι γύναι, ἄλγεσι δῶματος. The preposition is intensive (Wahl and Bretschneider). ἔσω ἄνθρωπον] is identical with the limited ἐγὼ of verses 17 and 20, and ὁ νόμος τοῦ νοός in verse 23, and ὁ νους (put for ὁ νόμος τοῦ νοός), in verse 25. It is described in the context as "hating" evil; as "delighting in" good; and as "serving" the law of God (vii. 15, 22, 25). It is the "spirit," as the contrary of the "flesh" (Mat. xxvi. 41; Gal. v. 17); "the law of the spirit of life" (Rom. viii. 1); the "spiritual mind" (Rom. viii. 6); the "new creature" (2 Cor. v. 17); the "new man" (Eph. iv. 24; Col. iii. 10); the "new spirit" (Ezek. xi. 19); the "new heart" (Ezek. xviii. 31); the "heart of flesh" (Ezek. xi. 19); the "clean heart" (Ps. li. 10); the "right spirit" (Ps. li. 10); and the "good treasure of the heart" (Mat. xii. 35). "Interior homo est novus seu regeneratus, mens illuminata, voluntas renovata." Pareus, in loco. The ἔσω ἄνθρωπος is not the mere voice of reason and conscience. Conscience does not delight in holiness (συνήδομαι, verse 22); it only approves of it (σύμφημι, verse 16). The approbation of the conscience may coexist with the hatred of the heart. For the nature of conscience, see i. 32; iii. 3, 13, 15, 22, 23; James ii. 19. Such terms as θέλω and μισῶ are inapplicable to the conscience. Reason and conscience belong to the understanding, and not to the will; they are cognitive, not voluntary; perceptive, not affectionate; legislative, not executive.

Neither is the ἔσω ἄνθρωπος that slight remainder of holiness, that faint *clinamen* to good, which the Semi-Pelagian anthropology attributes to the unregenerate man, constituting a point of contact for the Holy Spirit, and a factor in the act of regeneration. This view is taken by Meyer and others, who reject, with Semi-Pelagianism, the Augustinian doctrine of total depravity, and adopt the synergistic theory of regeneration. The objection to this view is, that this faint clinamen is, by the acknowledgment of the advocates of the view themselves, an ineffectual power. It is not efficient and successful in the conflict with sin. It is *velleitas*, and not *voluntas*. See the statements of Faustus and Cassian (Shedd's History of Doctrine, II. 104–108). But St. Paul's description of the ἔσω ἄνθρωπος makes it to be a dominant and controlling principle, able to struggle with and triumph over the powerful remnants of corruption (vii. 25). It is not a weak and vacillating aspiration, but a strong and abiding disposition. The ἔσω ἄνθρωπος is the human spirit regenerated and inhabited by the Holy Spirit. It is not the merely human, but the human and divine in synthesis.

Neither is the ἔσω ἄνθρωπος exactly identical with the ἔσωθεν ἄνθρωπος of 2 Cor. iv. 16, though having much in common with it. This latter is antithetic to the ἔξω ἄνθρωπος, and denotes the soul *alone*, as distinguished from the body: "our intellectual and moral nature, in distinction from our cor-

23 βλέπω δὲ ἕτερον νόμον ἐν τοῖς μέλεσίν μου ἀντιστρατευόμενον τῷ νόμῳ τοῦ νοός μου καὶ αἰχμαλωτίζοντά με ἐν τῷ νόμῳ τῆς ἁμαρτίας τῷ ὄντι ἐν τοῖς μέλεσίν μου.

poreal" (Meyer); "man's higher nature, his soul as the subject of the divine life" (Hodge). Compare Milton's:

> "This attracts the soul, governs the inner man, the nobler part."
> —PARADISE REGAINED, ii. 476.

The ἔσω ἄνθρωπος, as standing for the regenerate man, includes the physical part together with the spiritual; because the new life affects the body as well as the soul. It is, therefore, more comprehensive than the ἔσωθεν ἄνθρωπος of 2 Cor. iv. 16.

VER. 23. βλέπω] continues the figure contained in παράκειται, in verse 18. See comment. ἕτερον] another *species;* numerical difference would be indicated by ἄλλον. An inclination, or propensity, different in kind from that denoted by συνήδομαι τῷ νόμῳ (the characteristic of the ἔσω ἄνθρωπος), is meant. It is the disposition described in viii. 7, as "enmity towards God," and "insubmission to the law of God." νόμον] is here used in the signification, not of an outward statute, but of an inward actuating principle. Law, either material or mental, has two phases. 1. Viewed objectively, as proceeding from the lawgiver, it is a command. 2. Viewed subjectively, as inhering in the subject upon which it is imposed, it is an inward impulse or principle of action. The laws of matter, in their objective phase, are the rules of material motion prescribed by the Creator, as expressed mathematically in the formulæ of physical science; and in their subjective phase, they are the forces themselves of matter, inhering in and moving the material universe. A force of nature is a law of nature in concrete action. In like manner, the moral law may be viewed objectively, as the command of God expressed in the decalogue and in conscience; or subjectively, as the principle of action in the creature's will. In a holy angel, the objective law of God is also a subjective disposition. The angelic will is one with the holy commandment. The angel is not conscious of any difference between his inclination, and the rule of action prescribed by his Maker. Law, in the sphere of sinless perfection, as it is in that of material nature, is one with life and actuating force. The objective and the subjective are one and the same. In the case of fallen man or angel, there is no longer this identity of the objective law with the subjective inclination. The two are brought into antagonism by sin, and the law "ordained to life is found to be unto death" (vii. 10). In regeneration, this original relation between law and will is restored. The moral law is caused once more to be an inward and actuating principle; "written not in tables of stone, but in fleshy tables of the heart" (2 Cor. iii. 3; Jer. xxxi. 33; Ps. xxxvii. 31). There being these two phases or aspects of law, it is easy to see how the same word νόμος comes to be used by St. Paul, sometimes to denote the external command, and sometimes the internal disposition; sometimes God's statute, and sometimes man's inclination. "A law," says Owen (Indwelling Sin, Ch. i.), "is taken either properly, for a directive rule, or improperly, for an operative effective principle which seems to have the force of a law." Similarly, Fritzsche (in loco) remarks that ἁμαρτία personified is said *dare legem.* This subjective signification is seen in the classical use of νόμος to denote a "custom," or "usage:" i.e., a course of action. Schmidt (Synonymik der Griechen Sprache, I. 210) remarks that the older writers, like Homer and Sophocles, employ θεσμός to designate the divine law, and νόμος to denote human statutes. Liddell and Scott say that Draco's laws were entitled θεσμοί, because each began with θεσμός, while those of Solon were denominated νόμοι. The νόμος εν μέλεσίν, then, is identical with ἡ οἰκοῦσα ἁμαρτία. ἐν τοῖς μέλεσίν] describes the quality and nature of this "other" law, or principle of action. It should be noticed that St. Paul does not say τῶν μελῶν, but ἐν μέλεσίν. This "law of sin" is not the true and proper principle of action for the members. It is an intruder that ought not to be there. See the explanation of ἐνοικοῦσα, in verse 17. Indwelling sin is not the original and created impulse *of* the members, but something that has subsequently come *into* them, and resides *in* them. μέλεσίν includes the mental faculties, as well as the bodily organs. See comment on vi. 13, 19. It is equivalent to σαρκί μου, in verse 18. The "law," or principle, of indwelling sin resides in all the faculties of both soul and body. Its workings or "motions" (παθήματα, verse 5) are seen in the imagination, the intellect, the feelings of the heart, and the determinations of the will, as well as in the inordinate cravings of the body. These are all of them "members," that is to say, organs and instruments of the human agent, in and by which remaining corruption works in a believer. ἀντιστρατευόμενον] denotes an unceasing but not necessarily successful warfare: a campaign. Compare 1 Pet. ii. 11; James iv. 1. "Ἀντιστρατεύεσθαι is to rebel against a superior; στρατεύεσθαι is to assault or war for a superiority" (Owen's Indwelling Sin, Ch. vi.). νόμῳ] is antithetic to νόμον, and like that is employed in the subjective sense of an actuating principle. The use of the article with νόμῳ, and its omission with νόμον, indicates the superior dignity and strength of the "law of the mind." νοός] In the classics, the word denotes the mind either as perceiving, or as feeling, or as purposing. Sometimes it is put for the understanding, and sometimes for the heart; sometimes for reason and judgment, and sometimes for mood and inclination. See Liddell and Scott in voce. The Biblical use is equally varied. In the New Testament, *νοῦς* is nearly the same as *πνεῦμα*. The *νόμος τοῦ νοός* is denominated *ὁ νόμος τοῦ πνεύματος* (viii. 2), and *τὸ φρόνημα τοῦ πνεύματος* (viii. 6). One and the same principle of spiritual life, the contrary of the "law of sin," is designated by all three phrases. The following particulars are to be noted. 1. Like *πνεῦμα*, *νοῦς* may denote the faculty of rational perception, the *reason:* Luke xxiv. 45; 1 Cor. xiv. 15; Phil. iv. 7; Titus i. 15; Rev. xiii. 17, compared with 1 Cor. xiv. 2; ii. 11; Luke i. 80. 2. Like *πνεῦμα*, *νοῦς* may denote the moral temper and disposition, the *will:* 1 Cor. ii. 16; i. 10; Eph. iv. 23; Coloss. ii. 18, compared with Mat. v. 3; Rom. viii. 15; 1 Cor. ii. 12; iv. 21; Gal. vi. 1; Eph. i. 17; iv. 23. 3. Like *πνεῦμα*, *νοῦς* may be infected with sin: Rom. i. 28; xii. 2; Eph. iv. 17; 2 Tim. iii. 8; Tit. i. 15, compared with Mark i. 23; 1 Thess. v. 23. 4. In St. Paul's classification in 1 Thess. v. 23, *πνεῦμα*, or *νοῦς*, is the highest part of the human constitution. 5. In the New Testament, *πνεῦμα* denotes either the Divine Spirit (Mat. i. 18; John iv. 24; Rom. viii. 9), or the human spirit (Luke xxiii. 46; Rom. i. 9); but *νοῦς* is used only of the human spirit. There being these various significations, the meaning of *νοῦς* must be determined by the context. The connection of thought shows that as used in this place, 1. It is *rational*, because the perception of the moral law is implied. 2. It is *voluntary*, because there is a disposition (*νόμος*) in the *νοῦς*. 3. It is *spiritual* and *holy*, because it is the contrary of *σάρξ* and *ἁμαρτία* (verses 17, 18, 23), is identical with *ὁ ἔσω ἄνθρωπος* and the limited *ἐγὼ* of verses 17 and 20, and by means of it, St. Paul "serves the law of God" (verse 25). Consequently, *νοῦς* here denotes the human understanding and will in *synthesis*, and as *regenerate.* The understanding is enlightened, and the will is enlivened by the Holy Spirit, who dwells in the *νοῦς*, thus regenerated, as the source and support of its divine life. It is not mere reason, or the "higher nature" in man. (The "better self," of Meyer, and others.) This may be, and in the unregenerate is, fallen and depraved. But it is this higher nature as renewed and sanctified by the Holy Ghost. "*Interior homo* non anima simpliciter dicitur, sed spiritualis ejus pars quæ a deo regenerata est." Calvin ad Rom. vii. 22. This is the governing power in St. Paul, as he describes himself; though it is constantly beset and impeded in its action, by the "law of sin," or remainders of the old principle of evil. The regenerated νοῦς has the spiritual discernment (1 Cor. ii. 14); but this discernment is more or less obscured and dimmed by the remnants of the darkened understanding (Eph. iv. 18). It has the holy inclination and affections, but these are more or less opposed and blunted by the relics of the old inclination and affections. αἰχμαλωτίζοντά] the spear (αἰχμή) is the instrument with which a captive is taken. The captivity is the same as that denoted by πεπραμένος in verse 14: relative and temporal; not absolute, endless, and hopeless. ἐν] denotes the instrument. This is the reading of ℵBDEFG Vulg., Lachm., Tisch., Tregelles. It is omitted ACL Peshito, Receptus.

VER. 24. ταλαίπωρος] from τλαιεῖν πεῖραν: to endure trial. It is the nominative of address, for the vocative (Winer, p. 182). The word designates the same weary and burdened feeling that is expressed by πεπραμένος, in verse 14, and is delineated in verses 15–23. It is a strong term. Compare Rev. iii. 17; Rom. iii. 16. But it does not, in this place, denote hopelessness or despair, as is shown by verse 25. The conflict is long and severe, so that the believer is "weary and heavy-laden." With Isaiah, he cries: "Woe is me! for I am undone; because I am a man of unclean lips." (Isa. vi. 5). With David, he exclaims: "Mine iniquities are gone over mine head; my wounds stink and are corrupt;

[24] *ταλαίπωρος ἐγὼ ἄνθρωπος· τίς με ῥύσεται ἐκ τοῦ σώματος τοῦ θανάτου τούτου;* [25] *χάρις τῷ θεῷ διὰ*

thine arrows stick fast in me; there is no rest in my bones, because of my sin" (Ps. xxxviii. 2–5). But neither Isaiah, nor David, nor St. Paul despaired of ultimate victory over indwelling corruption. τίς ῥύσεται] the future form expresses the need of help, together with the *expectation of obtaining it.* Compare Ps. xxxviii. 15–22. It is not the wail of a lost and condemned soul; or the appealing cry of the natural man under conviction but as yet without evangelical hope (Eph. ii. 12). St. Paul cries, Who shall deliver me? "non quod desperet, ignoret, dubitet; sed ut desiderium suum indicet, et suspiriis perpetuis opus esse docet." Pareus in loco. "He asks not by whom he was to be delivered, as one in doubt, like unbelievers; but it is the voice of one panting and almost fainting, because he does not find immediate help, as he longs for." Calvin in loco. σώματος τοῦ θανάτου] 1. the figurative signification: body, in the sense of a sum total; mortifera peccati massa (Calvin). Compare vi. 6. 2. the literal signification: the body as the subject and seat of physical death (Meyer). The first is preferable. The apostle desired something more than deliverance from his dying body. τούτου] this particular death which is the wages of sin, and which is a combination of physical and spiritual death. See comment on vi. 23. Erasmus, Beza, Calvin, Philippi, Olshausen make it to agree, by Hebraism, with σώματος.

VER. 25. χάρις] (sc. εἴη) is the reading of B. Æth., Copt., Lachm., Tisch., Tregelles. The Receptus, with A Peshito, reads εὐχαριστῶ. This is the utterance of the regenerate, and not of the natural man. St. Paul expresses his own consciousness in immediate connection with the preceding ac-

Ἰησοῦ Χριστοῦ τοῦ κυρίου ἡμῶν. ἄρα οὖν αὐτὸς ἐγὼ τῷ μὲν νοῒ δουλεύω νόμῳ θεοῦ, τῇ δὲ σαρκὶ νόμῳ ἁμαρτίας.

count of his experience, all in the same present tense. The consciousness is one and continuous, from verse 14 to verse 25 inclusive. The struggle with indwelling sin is accompanied with the conviction of a victorious issue. It is violent exegesis, to suppose that an epochal event like that of the new birth comes between verse 24 and verse 25; breaking the self-consciousness into two halves, one of which is that of the lost man, and the other that of the saved. This is the view of Meyer, who remarks that "there is no change of person, but only of scene. The as yet unredeemed man sighs out his misery *out* of Christ; now he is *in* Christ, and gives thanks for the happiness that has come to him in *answer* to his cry for deliverance." But, τίς ῥύσεται is not the form of a prayer for salvation from perdition. This would require the imperative mode (ἱλάσθητί μοι), and the direct address of the vocative. Compare Luke xviii. 13. διὰ Χριστοῦ] Christ is both the author of the deliverance, and the mediator through whom thanks to God for it are presented. ἄρα οὖν] introduces an inference from the reasoning that began with verse 14, and ends with ἡμῶν in verse 25. This reasoning shows that the writer is a person who obeys the law of God in the main and principally, but who also more or less yields to indwelling sin. αὐτὸς ἐγὼ] "*I myself:*" both the obedience and the disobedience are personal action. The ἐγὼ is comprehensive, including both the renewed nature, and the remainders of the old. The νοῦς that serves the law of God, and the σάρξ that serves the law of sin, constitute the αὐτὸς ἐγὼ. νοῒ] is put for τῷ νόμῳ τοῦ νοός in verse 23. See the comment. δουλεύω] denotes an activity that is habitual, and central. It is subjection. See the explanation of δουλεύω and δοῦλος, in vi. 16–20. At the same time, though in kind this activity is spiritual and holy, yet in degree it is not marked by the absolute perfection of the spiritual law (verse 14), by reason of the impeding and vitiating influence of ἡ ἐνοικοῦσα ἁμαρτία (verse 17). See comment on verse 18. The fact that St. Paul mentions his obedience of the law of God first in the order, shows that he regards this as the prominent fact in his present experience and moral state. νόμῳ] is objective: the divine command, primarily as written, but inclusive of the unwritten. σαρκὶ] is the same as ἡ ἐνοικοῦσα ἁμαρτία in verses 17, 20; as σαρκί in verse 18; and as νόμος ἐν μέλεσίν and νόμος τῆς ἁμαρτίας in verse 23. With the remainders of original sin (= indwelling sin), the apostle yields to the "law of sin." The verb δουλεύω must be supplied with σαρκὶ. But δουλεύω in this connection, cannot have so strong a meaning as in the preceding clause in connection with νόμῳ θεοῦ. St. Paul does not serve sin so much as he serves holiness. His service of sin is indeed a subjection and a bondage, so that he feels himself to be "sold under sin;" but it is not so radical and central a service as that by which he serves God. The latter service is accompanied with love, peace, and joy; the former with aversion, unrest, and unhappiness. St. Paul loves Christ while he serves him; but hates Satan while he serves him. He is blessed in the first service; he is wretched in the last. Respecting the former, he says γινώσκω, θέλω, συνήδομαι, χάρις τῷ θεῷ; respecting the latter, he says μισῶ, οὐ θέλω, πεπραμένος εἰμι, ταλαίπορος ἄνθρωπος. νόμῳ] is subjective in its signification: an actuating principle. Sin, unlike holiness, can be a "law" in the *objective* use of the term. There cannot be an external statute, given by a lawgiver, commanding a man to sin. Sin may be an inward principle of action, but not an outward commandment. Holiness is both. Hence there is a rhetorical contradiction in this phraseology of St. Paul, that is unavoidable from the nature of the case. For when the apostle "serves the law of sin, with the flesh," he serves indwelling sin, with indwelling sin. There is no external statute obeyed by the inward principle. But it is not so, in the other case. When St. Paul "serves the law of God, with the mind," he obeys an objective law with a subjective principle.

Recapitulating, then, the following are the reasons for referring Rom. vii. 14–25 to the regenerate. 1. The present tense is uninterruptedly employed: aorists, imperfects, and pluperfects having been used in verses 7–14. 2. The plan of the Epistle favors this view. The apostle first shows that the law cannot *justify* the natural man, and then proceeds to show that it cannot *sanctify* him. This latter is evinced, by considering the relation of the law, first, to original sin in the unregenerate (vii. 7–14); secondly, to indwelling sin in the regenerate (vii. 14–25). The law, in neither instance, can eliminate the depravity. 3. This view accords with the representations of scripture, which attribute remaining corruption, and a struggle therewith, to the regenerate. Compare Isa. vi. 5; lvii. 17, 18; Ps. xix. 12, 13; xxxviii. 1–8; xxxix. 8, 11; xl. 12; li. 2, 6, 10; lxxvii. 3; lxxxviii. 7; cxix. 120; cxxxix. 23, 24; Rom. viii. 23, 26; Gal. vi. 5. 4. The wearisome and wearing conflict described, is inconsistent with the Scripture representations of the natural man, as indifferent and at ease in sin. Compare Ps. lxxiii. 4–12; cxix. 70; Mat. xiii. 13–15; Rom. iii. 9–18; vii. 8, 9.

Meyer, at the close of his exegesis of this paragraph (in which he refers it to the unregenerate) remarks: "The interpretation of verses 14–25 is of decisive importance, in respect to the church doctrine of original sin. If Paul is speaking in verse 14 sq. of the *natural* man, and not of the regenerate, then he predicates of the character of the natural man what the church dogma decidedly denies to it." Meyer concedes that the exegesis that refers this paragraph to the unbeliever, is incompatible with the doctrine of total depravity. It supposes an element of holiness, slight and weak yet real, still remaining in man after the fall, which accounts for the struggle with sin that is ascribed, by this interpretation, to the unregenerate.

It has been objected to the interpretation which finds the Christian experience in this paragraph, that its influence upon personal piety is injurious. But the searching scrutiny into indwelling sin, together with the doctrine that *it is guilt*, and *must be resisted continually and unto blood*, is adapted in the highest degree to promote humbleness of mind, great watchfulness and self-distrust, and reliance upon the Redeemer. Certainly nothing can be more demoralizing, than the denial that inward lust is sin, and the assertion that until it is acted out it is innocent.

CHAPTER VIII

St. Paul, in this chapter, continues to discuss the connection between justification and progressive sanctification. There is no difference between the experience described in Rom. viii., and that delineated in vii. 14–25. The same conflict between grace and indwelling sin is found in both chapters. The person in the seventh chapter who is "sold under sin" (vii. 14), and "serves with the flesh the law of sin" (vii. 25), and cries, "O wretched man who shall deliver me" (vii. 24), and yet "thanks God through Jesus Christ" for his deliverance, and "serves with the mind the law of God" (vii. 25), belongs to that class in the eighth chapter, who have been "made free from the law of sin and death, by the law of the Spirit of life" (viii. 2), and yet are exhorted "not to live after the flesh" (viii. 12), and to "mortify the deeds of the body" (viii. 13); who "have received the spirit of adoption, crying Abba Father" (viii. 15), and yet "groan within themselves, waiting for the adoption, to wit, the redemption of the body" (viii. 23), and "with patience wait for" sinless perfection and heavenly blessedness (viii. 25). Says Philippi, on Rom. vii. 13: "In the two passages, Rom. vii. 14–25, viii. 1–11, one immediately following the other, are pictured the two aspects, ever appearing in mutual connection, of one and the same spiritual status; so that the regenerate man, according as his glance is directed to the one or the other aspect of his nature, is able to affirm of himself, as well what is said in vii. 23, 24, as what is said in viii. 2. Hence, also, he raises from his heart, with equal

1 *Οὐδὲν ἄρα νῦν κατάκριμα τοῖς ἐν Χριστῷ Ἰησοῦ·*
2 *ὁ γὰρ νόμος τοῦ πνεύματος τῆς ζωῆς ἐν Χριστῷ Ἰησοῦ
ἠλευθέρωσέν με ἀπὸ τοῦ νόμου τῆς ἁμαρτίας καὶ τοῦ θα-*

sincerity and truth, the twofold cry, 'Wretched man,' and 'I thank God.'"

Ver. 1. οὐδὲν] is highly emphatic, by its position: "none at all, of any kind." ἄρα] is not a deduction from the single verse vii. 25 (Luther, Meyer, De Wette), but from the whole previous discussion of the nature and effects of the δικαιοσύνη θεοῦ (iii. 21–vii. 25). The last verse of the seventh chapter relates only to progressive sanctification, and to connect deliverance from condemnation with sanctification merely, would be extremely anti-Pauline. The apostle has in mind his previous account of the expiatory work of Christ, as is proved by his explanation of his meaning, in verse 3. νῦν] in this justified condition, i. e. κατάκριμα] a sentence of condemnation. See comment on v. 16. ἐν Χριστῷ] the preposition denotes the inward and spiritual relation of the believer to Christ. Compare viii. 9, 10. The clause μὴ κατὰ σάρκα περιπατοῦσιν ἀλλὰ κατὰ πνεῦμα is omitted by ℵBCDF Sahid., Copt., Æth., Griesbach, Mill, Lachm., Tisch., Tregelles. It is supported by AE Peshito (in part), Receptus. If retained, it is epexegetical of ἐν Χριστῷ: those who are "in Christ" conduct in this manner. It does not mention the ground of the freedom from condemnation, but a characteristic of those who have been freed, upon the ground of Christ's ἱλαστήριον (iii. 25). "Non assignari a Paulo causam, sed modum, quo solvimur a reatu." Calvin in loco.

Ver. 2. γὰρ] introduces the statement of the reasons why there is no condemnation to a believer. There are two of them: sanctification, mentioned in verse 2; and justification, mentioned in verse 3. The two are combined, because it has been the object of St. Paul, in chapters vi. and vii., to prove that justification is not antinomian, but necessarily connected with sanctification. Pareus and Venema consider justification to be the subject of both verses. *νόμος*] has here its subjective signification of an actuating principle; and *ὁ νόμος τού πνεύματος τῆς ζωῆς* is the same as *ὁ νόμος τοῦ νοός* (vii. 23), and *ὁ ἔσω ἄνθρωπος* (vii. 22), the limited *ἐγὼ* (vii. 17, 20), and *τὸ φρόνημα τοῦ πνεύματος* (viii. 5). See the comment upon these passages. It designates the principle of holiness, the "new man." *πνεύματος τῆς ζωῆς*] the genitive of authorship: the Holy Spirit is the author of this *νόμος; πνεῦμα* without the predicate *τῆς ζωῆς* would denote merely the human *πνεῦμα;* with it, the third person in the trinity is meant. Compare *πνεῦμα ἁγιωσύνης*, in i. 4, and comment. The Holy Spirit is the source and author of spiritual life, and by his efficiency originates the "law," or principle, here spoken of. *ἐν Χριστῷ*] to be connected with *ζωῆς* (Luther, Beza); with *νόμος* (Semler); with *νόμος τοῦ πνεύματος τῆς ζωῆς* (Calvin); with *ἠλευθέρωσέν με* (Theodoret, Erasmus, Rückert, Tholuck, Olshausen, De Wette, Fritzsche, Meyer). The last is preferable. It is only as united to Christ, and in him, that such an inward and powerful law of action, and such spiritual freedom, is possible. *ἠλευθέρωσέν*] Compare vi. 18, 22, and the comment. Sinless perfection is not meant; there are remnants of corruption. But there is freedom in the sense that sin shall not have "dominion," or "lordship." The "law of the Spirit of life," in the believer, has overcome the "law of sin and death." The "new man" has bound the "strong man." The aorist signification is to be observed; referring to the time and act of regeneration, when the freedom was begun and established. *με*] is the reading of ACDEL Vulg., Sahidic, Receptus, Lachm.; and agrees better with the "I" so constantly employed in the preceding chapter; ℵBF Peshito, Tisch. read *σε*. *νόμου τῆς ἁμαρτίας καὶ* τοῦ θανάτου] νόμος is subjective in signification. The inward principle of sin is meant; but *original* in distinction from *indwelling* sin: "sin in the unregenerate, as distinguished from sin in the regenerate" (Pareus in loco). The "law of sin and death" is not the equivalent of the "law in the members," or the "law of sin in the members," spoken of in vii. 23. It is more than this. It is the παλαιὸς ἄνθρωπος (vi. 6); the principle of sin and death originated in Adam, and inherited from him. This has been slain, in the believer. The implanting of the new principle of divine life, in regeneration, had freed St. Paul from "the law of sin and death," but not from "the law in the members." With the latter, he was still struggling in the manner described in vii. 14–25. But from the former he had been delivered. The curse and guilt of original sin was no longer resting upon him; and the domination of original sin as a *controlling* principle of action was destroyed. Only the dying remainders of it were left to molest and weary him. These made his life a severe race and fight, but not a defeat and failure. The difference between original and indwelling sin, or between the "law of sin and death" and the "law in the members," is like that between a serpent whole and uninjured, and a serpent cut into sections. The former is vital in the full sense, and increasing in the intensity and malignity of its life. The latter is virtually dead, though the fragments exhibit for a long time, it may be, a lingering and varying activity.

VER. 3. γὰρ] introduces the second reason why there is no condemnation, making prominent the piacular work of Christ, —verse 2 having referred to the work of the Holy Spirit in regeneration. τὸ ἀδύνατον] 1. To be governed by διὰ, or κατὰ, understood (Beza). 2. The object of ἐποίησε supplied before ὁ θεὸς (Erasm., Luther). 3. A parenthetical nominative-clause, in apposition with the proposition beginning with ὁ

νάτου. 3 τὸ γὰρ ἀδύνατον τοῦ νόμου, ἐν ᾧ ἠσθένει διὰ τῆς σαρκός, ὁ θεὸς τὸν ἑαυτοῦ υἱὸν πέμψας ἐν ὁμοιώματι σαρκὸς ἁμαρτίας καὶ περὶ ἁμαρτίας κατέκρινεν τὴν ἁμαρ-

θεὸς and ending with πνεῦμα in verse 4 (De Wette, Fritzsche, Meyer). The last is preferable. The thing that was impossible for the law to do ("quod erat impossibile legi," Vulgate) was, to condemn sin, and *also* save the sinner. Simple condemnation of sin was no impossibility to the law, but its proper office. νόμου] is objective in signification, and designates the written law, yet inclusive of the unwritten. ἐν ᾧ] "for the reason that:" Rom. ii. 1; Heb. ii. 18; vi. 17; 2 Pet. ii. 12. ἠσθένει] denotes utter impotence, as in v. 6. The law was powerless to perform the *double* function of condemning sin, and saving the sinner. διὰ] assigns the reason of the impotence: the law is not weak per se, but through man's sin. Compare vii. 7 sq. σαρκός] sinful human nature. Compare vii. 5. ὁ θεὸς] God the Father, as the context shows. The sending of the Son is the official work of the first trinitarian person. Luke ii. 49; xxii. 49; John v. 36, 37; xviii. 11; xx. 21. ἑαυτοῦ] "his own:" equivalent to the μονογενής of John i. 14, 18; iii. 16, 18; Heb. xi. 17; 1 John iv. 9; and the ἴδιος of John v. 18; Rom. viii. 32. These three epithets distinguish the eternal sonship of the second trinitarian person, from the adoptive sonship of believers, spoken of in viii. 14–17, et alia. "The pre-existence and metaphysical sonship of Christ are implied" (Meyer). ὁμοιώματι] See comment on v. 14; vi. 5. The reference is to that "form of a servant" (Phil. ii. 7; Heb. ii. 14; iv. 15) in which the "own son" of God was sent; implying that this was not the first and original form. The original form was ἡ μορφὴ θεοῦ, Phil. ii. 6. σαρκὸς] denotes, here, complete human nature, both physical and mental, consisting of both body and soul. Compare Mat. xxiv. 22; Luke iii. 6; John i. 14; iii. 6; vi.

51; Rom. i. 3; ix. 5; Coloss. i. 22; 1 Tim. iii. 16; Heb. ii. 14. ἁμαρτίας] the genitive of quality, showing that the human nature spoken of is a sinful and corrupt human nature, if contemplated *in itself* and *apart from* the miraculous conception by the Holy Ghost. The qualifying epithet ἁμαρτίας describes human nature simply as it descends from Adam. As such, it is a sinful nature. St. Paul is contemplating it from *this point of view*, only, when he employs this epithet. It does not follow that when a portion of this sinful and corrupt human nature is *assumed into union* with the Eternal Logos, it is still sinful and corrupt. In and by the miraculous conception, it is perfectly sanctified, so that though it is "sinful flesh," or corrupt human nature, in Mary the mother, it is a "holy thing," or perfect human nature, in Jesus the child. Compare Luke i. 35; 2 Cor. v. 21; Heb. iv. 15; x. 5; 1 Pet. ii. 22. The apostle desires to show the great condescension of the Eternal Son in his assumption of human nature. The Logos does not take into personal union with himself a human nature created *ex nihilo* for this particular purpose, and which, consequently, could not be a σάρξ ἁμαρτίας, but he assumed into union with himself a human nature that descended by ordinary generation from Adam down to the Virgin Mary (Luke iii. 38; Heb. ii. 14), and which in *this* connection and relation was "sinful flesh." Before, however, it could become a constituent part of the God-man, it must be entirely purged from the effects of the fall. The Logos thus humbled himself to the very lowest degree that was compatible with his own personal sinlessness. He could not unite himself to a nature that was sinful at the instant of the union, but he did unite himself with a nature that once had been sinful, and required to be "prepared" for such a union (Heb. x. 5). See Pearson, On the Creed, Art. III.; Owen, Holy Spirit, II. iv.; Turretin, XIII. xi. 10; Wollebius, i. 16; De Moore, xix., § 14;

Van Mastricht, IV. x. 5, 6; Calvin, II. xiii.; Formula Concordiæ, De peccato originis. De Wette explains ἁμαρτίας by Christ's temptability; but Christ's temptability was a sinless susceptibility (Heb. v. 15). Pareus, and others, lay emphasis upon ὁμοιώματι, and explain accordingly: "Assumsit carnem veram, non peccatricem, sed peccatrici *simile*." περὶ ἁμαρτίας] 1. to be connected with πέμψας; καὶ being omitted (De Wette, Meyer); 2. to be connected with κατέκρινεν (Chrys., Theod., Luther, Bengel). The latter is the necessary connection, if καὶ is retained, which is the reading of all the mss. Origen, Calvin, Melanchthon, Baur, Stuart, Hodge take ἁμαρτίας in the sense of a sin-offering. But this cannot be the signification of the following τὴν ἁμαρτίαν, which is the equivalent. The literal signification of both περὶ and ἁμαρτία is preferable: "in respect to sin." Compare Gal. i. 4; Heb. x. 6, 8, 18; xiii. 11. The action designated by κατέκρινεν indicates what particular element in sin is referred to: viz., the element of guilt. κατέκρινεν] denotes a judicial condemnation and infliction. Compare Mat. xx. 18; Luke xi. 31, 32; 1 Cor. xi. 32; Rom. v. 16, 17; viii. 1. Christ's suffering was a substituted penalty, by means of which sin was "condemned," *i. e.*, vicariously punished. τὴν ἁμαρτίαν] the article denotes the well-known sin that came into the world, as described in v. 12, et passim. σαρκί] is connected with κατέκρινε, and designates the human nature of Christ. In and by means of his humanity, Christ endured that judicial infliction which God the Father visited upon "his own" Son, for the purpose of expiating human guilt. It must be noticed that σαρκί here is not qualified by ἁμαρτίας, as in the previous case; because the human nature is now viewed as a constituent part of the person of the God-man. It is pure and immaculate σάρξ.

VER. 4. ἵνα] introduces the purpose of the action in verse

τίαν ἐν τῇ σαρκί, ⁴ ἵνα τὸ δικαίωμα τοῦ νόμου πληρωθῇ ἐν ἡμῖν τοῖς μὴ κατὰ σάρκα περιπατοῦσιν ἀλλὰ κατὰ πνεῦμα.

3. The condemnation of sin, by means of the atoning death of Christ, is in order to the fulfilment of the law, so that there shall be no κατάκριμα τοῖς ἐν Χριστῷ (verse 1). δικαίωμα] the requirement of the law: all that the law commands to be done. Luke i. 6; Rom. 1. 32; ii. 26; Heb. ix. 1. The singular number denotes the totality of the requisition. This includes 1. obedience of the precept of the law; 2. endurance of the penalty of the law, in case of disobedience of the precept. An unfallen creature is obligated only by the first requirement; a fallen creature lies under the double obligation. He owes perfect obedience for the future, and atonement for the past. πληρωθῇ] denotes complete performance. Mat. iii. 15; v. 17; John xiii. 18; Rom. xiii. 8; Gal. v. 14; Coloss. ii. 10. This perfect execution of all that the law requires from a fallen man is a *vicarious*, and not a personal performance. The believer does not atone for his past sin; neither does he perfectly obey in heart and life. Jesus Christ does both for him. The passive form, πληρωθῇ, implies this. In this vicarious manner, the whole requirement of the law, regarding both precept and penalty, is fulfilled. St. Paul has explained this vicarious agency of Christ in Rom. iii. 21–28; iv. 3–8, 22–25. He there teaches, that Christ's work is *imputed*, or reckoned, to the believer. See comment. ἐν ἡμῖν] *in* us, not *by* us; showing that God is the agent, and man the recipient, in justification. Man does not assist in the remission of sins. τοῖς μὴ κατὰ, etc.] "as those who," etc.: quippe qui. This clause is not appended to indicate the *cause* of the justification, but the necessary effect of it. Those to whom Christ's work is imputed (iv. 24), and in whom the requirement of the law is thereby completely fulfilled (viii. 4), and to whom there is consequently no con-

demnation (viii. 1), are a class of persons who are characterized by a pious life, though not a sinless and perfect one. The imputed righteousness or justification, spoken of in verses 3 and 4, is accompanied with the inherent righteousness or sanctification, spoken of in verse 2. The former does not exist without the latter. St. Paul conjoins them, and mentions both, in proof that the believer is not in a state of condemnation. Whoever is regenerate and forgiven is not under the curse of the law. *σάρκα*] is the contrary of the following *πνεῦμα*, and denotes the principle of sin in the unregenerate; and is equivalent to "the law of sin and death," in viii. 2. It is anarthrous, to denote the species. *περιπατοῦσιν*] denotes the general conduct; the figure is taken from the habitual movements of the body. Believers do not, like unbelievers, invariably yield to the principle of sin. *πνεῦμα*] is anarthrous to denote the species. It designates: 1. The Holy Spirit (Meyer, Hodge, Alford). 2. The principle of holiness in the regenerate (Chrysost., Bengel, Rückert, Philippi, Harless). The latter view is preferable, 1. because of the antithesis with *σάρκα*: regenerate human nature is contrasted with unregenerate; 2. because *πνεῦμα*, here, is the same as *ὁ νόμος τοῦ πνεύματος*, just as *σάρξ* is the same as *ὁ νόμος τῆς ἁμαρτίας καὶ τοῦ θανάτου*, in viii. 2; 3. because this *πνεῦμα* is described, subsequently, as *φρόνημα*: a human inclination, or disposition (viii. 5, 6).

VER. 5. *γὰρ*] introduces the first reason why believers "walk not after the flesh, but after the spirit:" viz., because every man walks according to his inward inclination or disposition. A second reason is given in verse 6. *οἱ ὄντες*] is substituted for *οἱ περιπατοῦσιν* (verse 4), and is stronger than that: "they who *exist* only for the flesh." *κατὰ σάρκα*] See comment on verse 4. *φρονοῦσιν*] (from *φρήν*) is the emphatic word in the clause. It denotes, here, the

5 οἱ γὰρ κατὰ σάρκα ὄντες τὰ τῆς σαρκὸς φρονοῦσιν, οἱ δὲ
κατὰ πνεῦμα τὰ τοῦ πνεύματος· 6 τὸ γὰρ φρόνημα τῆς
σαρκὸς θάνατος, τὸ δὲ φρόνημα τοῦ πνεύματος ζωὴ καὶ

action of both the understanding and will, with a predominant reference to the latter. Compare Mat. xvi. 23; Phil. iii. 19; Coloss. iii. 2. See, also, Beaumont and Fletcher's Noble Gentlemen, iii. 1: "For I am *minded* to impart my love, to these good people and my friends." Also Mat. xxii. 37: "Thou shalt love the Lord thy God with all thy *mind*." They who live (ὄντες) and act (περιπατοῦσιν) in conformity with the "law of sin and death," show that they are *inclined* to sin. The conduct flows from an inward disposition. πνεῦμα (supply ὄντες); and πνεύματος (supply φρονοῦσιν)] have the same meaning as in verse 4. They who live and act in conformity with the "law of the spirit of life," thereby show that they are *inclined* to holiness. The daily life and conduct, in each instance, is in accordance with the particular inward and dominant principle (νόμος) that is in the man. Consequently, believers live a devout life, because they have a renewed nature.

VER. 6. γὰρ] introduces the second reason why believers "walk not after the flesh, but after the spirit:" viz., because the "flesh," or the unregenerate nature, issues in death, and the "spirit," or the regenerate nature, issues in life. φρόνημα] has the same signification with φρονοῦσιν in verse 5. The "will," or inclination, "of the flesh" designates, not indwelling sin in the regenerate, but original sin in the unregenerate. It is the principle of evil in its full strength and domination. It is the same as ἡ ἁμαρτία and ἡ ἐπιθυμία in vii. 7, 8; as ὁ νόμος τῆς ἁμαρτίας καὶ τοῦ θανάτου in viii. 2; and ἡ σάρξ in vii. 5; viii. 3. See comment on viii. 2. θάνατος] See comment on i. 31; v. 12, 21. τὸ φρόν-

εἰρήνη. 7 διότι τὸ φρόνημα τῆς σαρκος ἔχθρα εἰς θεόν· τῷ γὰρ νόμῳ τοῦ θεοῦ οὐχ ὑποτάσσεται, οὐδὲ γὰρ δύναται.

ημα τοῦ πνεύματος] is the equivalent of the verbal form τὰ τοῦ πνεύματος φρονοῦσιν in viii. 5; and is identical with πνεῦμα in viii. 4; with ὁ νόμος τοῦ πνεύματος τῆς ζωῆς in viii. 1; with νοῒ in vii. 25; with ὁ νόμος τοῦ νοός in vii. 23; with ὁ ἔσω ἄνθροπος in vii. 22; and with the limited ἐγὼ in vii. 17, 20. The "will," or inclination, "of the spirit," is the principle of holiness implanted in the believer by the Holy Spirit. ζωὴ] See comment on ii. 7; v. 21. εἰρήνη] See comment on ii. 10; v. 1. This feeling is the effect of the justification and sanctification that have been described as coexisting in the believer.

Ver. 7. διότι] (Rom. i. 19) introduces the reason why the "carnal mind," or "will of the flesh," is death. ἔχθρα] hostility to God, who is the only source of blessedness. This is one of the tersest definitions of sin. γὰρ] introduces the explanation of ἔχθρα. οὐχ ὑποτάσσεται] unsubmission to the law is the sign of enmity towards the Lawgiver. The restless struggle of self-will against righteous authority, is the root of all misery in the universe of God. οὐδὲ δύναται] there is no power in the "will of the flesh," or the principle of sin, to subject itself to the divine law. Satan cannot cast out Satan. Compare Mat. vii. 18; xii. 26; John vi. 44, 65; viii. 34; xv. 5; 1 Cor. ii. 14; 2 Cor. iii. 5. See comment on vi. 16–20. γὰρ] introduces the reason why the carnal inclination is not subject to the law of God: viz., because there is an impossibility that it should be, from the very nature of such an inclination. *Self*-will, by the very idea and definition of it, cannot obey *another's* will. So long as such a νόμος, or actuating principle, as the "carnal mind," remains in the voluntary faculty, it is impossible that this faculty

[8] οἱ δὲ ἐν σαρκὶ ὄντες θεῷ ἀρέσαι οὐ δύνανται. [9] ὑμεῖς δὲ οὐκ ἐστὲ ἐν σαρκὶ ἀλλὰ ἐν πνεύματι, εἴπερ πνεῦμα θεοῦ οἰκεῖ ἐν ὑμῖν. εἰ δέ τις πνεῦμα Χριστοῦ οὐκ ἔχει, οὗτος

should submissively obey the moral law. If it be then asked, if the will as a *faculty* can free itself from this νόμος, or inclination, the answer is in the negative, both from Scripture and the consciousness of man. The expulsion of the sinful inclination, and the origination of the holy inclination, in the human will, is a revolution in the faculty which is accomplished only in its regeneration by the Holy Spirit. Self-recovery is not possible to the human will, though self-ruin is (Hosea xiii. 9).

VER. 8 repeats the sentiment of the preceding verse, in a concrete form. Verse 7 affirms that the carnal mind is inimical to God, and unable to be submissive to Him; verse 8 affirms that carnally minded persons cannot please God. δὲ] 1. is transitive; "now" (De Wette, Philippi, Meyer, Lange); 2. is equivalent to οὖν (Beza, Calvin, Eng. Ver., Rückert, Hodge). The first is preferable, as this verse is not a deduction from the preceding, but only a repetition of it. ἐν σαρκὶ] is equivalent to κατὰ σάρκα in verse 5; with the difference, that the latter denotes the tendency, the former the sphere in which. ἀρέσαι] Compare 1 Thess. ii. 15.

VER. 9 applies, in a negative form, to Christian believers, the foregoing statement respecting the impossibility that one who has the carnal mind can serve and please God. ἐν σαρκὶ] See comment on verse 8. ἐν πνεύματι] the contrary of ἐν σαρκί. See comment on verses 4–6. εἴπερ] 1. "since" (Chrysost., Olshausen, et alii); 2. "if so be" (Calvin, Meyer). Either sense is possible. Compare Rom. iii. 30, 1 Cor. viii. 5, 2 Thess. i. 6, with 1 Cor. xv. 15. Either sense is possible is this verse, as it is in Rom. viii. 17; 1 Pet. ii. 3. The first signification is favored by Rom. vi. 17–22; vii. 4–6; viii. 1–4. In these passages, St. Paul does not speak doubtfully, but affirms that they to whom he is writing have been freed from the principle of sin, and are enslaved to righteousness, and are no longer ἐν σαρκί. The second signification is favored by the following clause: εἰ δὲ, etc.; which implies the possibility of self-deception, and urges to self-examination. πνεῦμα θεοῦ] the Holy Spirit, who is the author of the renewed human πνεῦμα, which has been described in the preceding context. The two are mentioned together in viii. 16. οἰκεῖ] denotes *constant* residence and influence: the immediate operation of the third trinitarian person upon the human soul, implying the action of spirit upon spirit. Compare John xiv. 16, 17, 23; xv. 26; xvi. 7, 13, 14; Rom. viii. 15, 16, 23, 26, 27; 1 Cor. ii. 10, 11; iii. 16; vi. 17, 19; 2 Tim. i. 14. πνεῦμα Χριστοῦ] is identical with πνεῦμα θεοῦ in the preceding clause. This is a proof text not only for the deity of Christ, but for the doctrine of the procession of the Holy Spirit from both Father and Son. As bearing upon Arianizing views, we cite the exegesis of Meyer (in loco): "πνεῦμα Χριστοῦ (compare Phil. i. 19; 1 Pet. i. 11) is no other than the Holy Spirit, the Spirit of God. He is denominated the Spirit of Christ, because the exalted Christ imparts himself in and with the Paraclete (John xiv.); and because, whoever has not this Spirit, is not a member of Christ: οὐκ ἔστιν αὐτοῦ (i. e., Χριστοῦ). Köllner's distinction between the Spirit of *God* as the highest πνεῦμα—the source of all finite πνεῦμα—and the Spirit of *Christ*, as a lower and manifested πνεῦμα, is not necessitated by Rom. viii. 10, 11, and is decidedly forbidden by Gal. iv. 6 compared with Rom. viii. 14–16." αὐτοῦ the genitive, here, is pregnant: comprehending the several conceptions of ownership, authorship, and membership. Compare 1 Cor. i. 12; iii. 23; vi. 15; vii. 22; xv. 23; 2 Cor. x. 7; Gal. iii. 29; v. 24.

οὐκ ἔστιν αὐτοῦ. [10] *εἰ δὲ Χριστὸς ἐν ὑμῖν, τὸ μὲν σῶμα νεκρὸν διὰ ἁμαρτίαν, τὸ δὲ πνεῦμα ζωὴ διὰ δικαιοσύνην.*

Ver. 10 is adversative to the last clause of the preceding verse. εἰ δὲ] "But if, on the contrary." Χριστὸς] is identical with πνεῦμα Χριστοῦ (ver. 9), which is the equivalent of πνεῦμα θεοῦ (ver. 9). Compare 2 Cor. xiii. 5; Coloss. i. 27. The mystical (mysterious) union of the believer with the Redeemer is meant. σῶμα] the material body, in distinction from the renewed immaterial soul, or spirit (πνεῦμα). νεκρὸν] denotes physical death; the penalty of sin so far as the body is concerned. Though not actually dead, it is destined to die: "mortuum pro moriturum" (Bengel). Compare θνητὰ σώματα, v. 11. Physical death still happens to the believer, though the "sting," or retributive element in it, is extracted by the comforting presence of God in articulo mortis (Aug., Calvin, Pareus, Beza, Vitringa, Bengel, Tholuck, Rückert, Usteri, Fritzsche, Meyer, Wordsworth, Hodge). διὰ ἁμαρτίαν] sin is the cause and reason of death, v. 12. πνεῦμα] not the Holy Spirit (Chrysost., Theophyl., Calvin, Grotius); nor the human πνεῦμα, in distinction from, and *excluding* the human ψυχή: the higher nature of man comprising reason, will, and conscience, in their natural condition (Meyer); but the *regenerate* human πνεῦμα as opposed to the σῶμα *only* (Theodoret, De Wette, Philippi, Hodge). The regenerate πνεῦμα comprises both the πνεῦμα and the ψυχή, of St. Paul's catalogue in 1 Thess. v. 23. In regeneration, the Holy Spirit, the divine πνεῦμα, renovates both the human πνεῦμα, and the human ψυχή; so that the two are a regenerate unity. In 1 Pet. ii. 11, ψυχή is put for this unity. All the powers of man, both higher and lower, are renewed and sanctified in the new birth. Hence, the term ψυχή, in the New Testament, is most commonly used in the wide signification, to denote the synthesis of πνεῦμα and ψυχή, as the opposite of σῶμα. Compare Mat. x. 28; Mark xiv. 34; Luke i. 46; John xii. 27; Acts ii. 43; Rom. ii. 9; xiii. 1; 1 Cor. xv. 45, et passim. The only instances in which πνεῦμα and ψυχή are discriminated from each other, and employed in the restricted signification, are Phil. i. 27; 1 Thess. v. 23; Heb. iv. 12. When this distinction is made, the purpose seems to be, to mark off the higher from the lower mental powers; similarly as, in the Kantian philosophy, the "understanding" is distinguished from the "reason," though both alike belong to that unity which constitutes the soul in distinction from the body. And as the terms "understanding," and "reason" are employed interchangeably to denote this unity, so the terms ψυχή and πνεῦμα are employed in the New Testament interchangeably to designate it. Compare Mat. xxvii. 50; Luke i. 47. In common English usage, the human "soul" is the equivalent of the human "spirit;" while yet there are cases in which the connection of thought requires a distinction to be made between them. Ψυχή is used with more latitude than πνεῦμα; the latter never denotes the mere animal life, the former sometimes does (Mat. ii. 20). When both ψυχή and πνεῦμα are viewed as a unity, and as actuated by the "law of sin and death," this unity is denominated σάρξ. This is the unregenerate man, or the "old man." When, on the contrary, they are actuated by the "law of the Spirit of life," the unity is denominated πνεῦμα as the contrary of σάρξ. This is the regenerate man, or the "new man." And this is the use of πνεῦμα here. The human body (σῶμα) is mortal and destined to death; but the regenerate human soul, or spirit (πνεῦμα), is alive, and shall never die. Compare John vi. 50, 51; xi. 26. ζωὴ] is stronger than ζὸν. See comment on ii. 7; v. 21; viii. 6. διὰ δικαιοσύνην] the ground or reason why "the spirit is life." 1. The imputed righteousness, described in iii. 21, 24; iv. 5, 6, et alia (The elder Protestant dogmatists, generally, Reiche,

11 εἰ δὲ τὸ πνεῦμα τοῦ ἐγείραντος τὸν Ἰησοῦν ἐκ νεκρῶν οἰκεῖ ἐν ὑμῖν, ὁ ἐγείρας Χριστὸν Ἰησοῦν ἐκ νεκρῶν ζωο-

Fritzsche, Meyer). "As διὰ ἁμαρτίαν refers not to individual sins, but to the ἐφ' ᾧ πάντες ἥμαρτον in v. 12, so διὰ δικαιοσύνην refers not to individual but to imputed righteousness" (Meyer in loco). This view is favored by διὰ with the accusative. 2. The subjective and inherent righteousness described as the "law of the mind," the "inner man," the "law of the Spirit of life" (Erasmus, Grotius, De Wette, Tholuck, Philippi, Hodge). It is preferable to combine both, since St. Paul has previously mentioned both justification and sanctification as the reason why there is "no condemnation to them that are in Christ Jesus (viii. 1–4). It is still his object to show that the two are inseparably connected, in answer to the charge of antinomianism in vi. 1 sq., 15 sq.; and vii. 7. The renewed soul has eternal life because it is justified and sanctified.

VER. 11. This verse teaches that that remnant of evil which still overhangs the body shall be finally removed. The power of physical death over the σῶμα is to be destroyed by the power of the resurrection. τὸ πνεῦμα] the Holy Spirit = τὸ πνεῦμα τῆς ζωῆς (ver. 1) = πνεῦμα θεοῦ = πνεῦμα Χριστοῦ (ver. 9). The interchange shows that the indwelling of the Holy Spirit is essentially the same as the indwelling of Christ. These two trinitarian persons are one and the same essence subsisting in two different modes. Consequently, an official or personal work of one does not exclude the other from a participation in it. The entire divine essence acts, whenever a particular divine person acts; but this essence is all in each person. τοῦ ἐγείραντος] i. e., τοῦ θεοῦ ἐγείραντος. Compare Acts ii. 24, 32; iii. 15, 26; iv. 10; v. 30; xxvi. 8; 1 Cor. vi. 14; 2 Cor. iv. 14. οἰκεῖ] See comment

ποιήσει καὶ τὰ θνητὰ σώματα ὑμῶν διὰ τοῦ ἐνοικοῦντος αὐτοῦ πνεύματος ἐν ὑμῖν.

on verse 9. Χριστὸν Ἰησοῦν] is the reading of ℵADE Peshito, Vulgate, Copt., Æth., Tisch. Jesus is the personal, and Christ the official name. The first is the more tender and affectionate designation: "Jesus, lover of my soul," etc. "Appellatio *Jesu* spectat ad ipsum; *Christi* refertur ad nos" (Bengel). Christ, rather than Jesus, is the name of the God-man as the head of the Church, and the archetype of the resurrection. Hence the change from Jesus to Christ Jesus in the sentence. ζωοποιήσει] is in the place of ἐγειρεῖ, for the sake of the correlation with ζωή in verse 10. Some commentators (Calvin and others) suppose a twofold reference, to the quickening of both soul and body. But the subject of regeneration and sanctification has already been discussed; so that only the resurrection is intended. θνητὰ] refers to νεκρὸν in verse 10. The body is mortal, "because of sin." διὰ τοῦ ἐνοικοῦντος αὐτοῦ πνεύματος] Compare 2 Tim. i. 14. This reading is supported by ℵAC Copt., Æth., Rec., Lachm. (1st ed.), De Wette, Tholuck, Tisch. The reading διὰ τὸ ἐνοικοῦν αὐτοῦ πνεῦμα is supported by BDEL Peshito, Vulg., Erasmus, Griesbach, Mill, Bengel, Lachm. (2d ed.), Fritzsche, Meyer, Philippi, Tregelles. The weight of authority, so far as the uncials and early versions are concerned, is on the whole in favor of the Receptus reading. The charge and countercharge of an alteration of the reading, made by the Macedonians and the orthodox, only shows that there was a difference in the manuscripts in the year 381. The genitive reading is favored by the preceding context, in which the Holy Spirit has been described as the author and source of life: τὸ πνεῦμα τῆς ζωῆς (ver. 2). St. Paul connects the resurrection of the body with the regeneration of the soul. Soul and body constitute one human person, so that the renova-

12 Ἄρα οὖν, ἀδελφοί, ὀφειλέται ἐσμὲν οὐ τῇ σαρκὶ τοῦ
κατὰ σάρκα ζῆν. 13 εἰ γὰρ κατὰ σάρκα ζῆτε, μέλλετε
ἀποθνήσκειν. εἰ δὲ πνεύματι τὰς πράξεις τοῦ σώματος

tion of the former naturally carries with it that of the latter. And the author of the former is naturally the author of the latter. Regeneration and resurrection are two parts of one entire purpose and process of redemption. If God has accomplished the first, he certainly will the last. αὐτοῦ] is highly emphatic, by its collocation between the substantive and its participle.

VER. 12 contains an inference, introduced by ἄρα οὖν, from verses 10 and 11. The "glorious" (1 Cor. xv. 43) resurrection of the "celestial" (1 Cor. xv. 40) body, which results from the indwelling of the Holy Spirit in the soul, is a motive to live a devout and pious life. ὀφειλέται] there is no obligation to sin; the relation of debtor obtains only toward righteousness. σαρκὶ] the same as the following σάρκα. τοῦ ζῆν] the genitive either of design or result. κατὰ σάρκα] See comment on viii. 4, 5. St. Paul does not supply the apodosis, viz.: ἀλλὰ τῷ πνεύματι, τοῦ κατὰ πνεῦμα ζῆν; either because it is self-evident, or because of the rapidity of his thought.

VER. 13 mentions the reason, introduced by γὰρ, for the statement in verse 12. κατὰ σάρκα ζῆτε] = κατὰ σάρκα ὄντες (ver. 5) = κατὰ σάρκα περιπατοῦντες (ver. 4). A life and conduct flowing from a corrupt nature is meant. μέλλετε] denotes the certainty resulting from the divine decision, and not mere futurition: μέλλειν signifies, "certum et constitutum esse, secundum vim fati." Ellendt Lex. Soph., ii. 72. "Ye are destined to die." Compare iv. 24. ἀποθνήσκειν] the contrary of the following ζήσεσθε: eternal death (Meyer). It is comprehensive of all the penal evil that is inflicted upon sin. See the explanation of θάνατος in v. 12. That eternal death is compatible with the resurrection of the body, is proved by Mat. x. 28; John v. 28, 29; Acts xxiv. 15; Daniel xii. 2. The reanimation of a human body to "the resurrection of damnation," is a part of the penalty of sin. πνεύματι] 1. the Holy Spirit (Meyer); 2. the regenerate human spirit (Theodoret, Philippi). We adopt the second view, in consonance with the interpretation of πνεῦμα given in verses 4, 5, 6, 9, 10. See comment on verses 4 and 6. St. Paul still has in view the conflict in the believer between the new nature and the remainders of the old; and is presenting motives for walking according to the former, and not the latter. In this connection and antithesis, consequently, πνεῦμα denotes regenerate human nature: πνεῦμα is put for νόμος τοῦ πνεύματος, as νοῦς is put for νόμος τοῦ νοός in vii. 23, 25. If the believer, by means of the principle of holiness, or "the law of the Spirit of life," mortifies the remainders of the principle of sin, or "the law in the members," he shall live. "Not to be daily employing the spirit and new nature for the mortifying of sin, is to neglect that excellent succor which God hath given us against our greatest enemy. If we neglect to make use of what we have received, God may justly hold his hand from giving us more. Not to be daily mortifying sin, is to sin against the grace of God, who hath furnished us with a principle of doing it." Owen, Mortification, Ch. ii. See Gal. v. 16–25, where the same antithesis between the human σάρξ and the human πνεῦμα appears, and the "lusts" of each are mentioned as antagonizing each other. A "lust of the spirit" is not a lust of the third trinitarian person; but of the regenerated human spirit, in whom the Holy Spirit dwells. The proper seat of the spiritual "lust," or holy desire, is the human person, and not the divine. The latter is the author and cause of it, but not the subject of it. πράξεις] the habits and practices. Compare Luke xxiii. 51; Acts xix. 18; Coloss. iii. 9. The πράξεις τοῦ σώματος are the same as τὰ ἔργα τῆς σαρκὸς (Gal. v. 19), and τὰ παθήματα τῆς σαρκὸς (Gal. v. 24). σώματος] is the reading of ℵABCL Peshito, Sahid., Copt., Æth., Rec., Lachm., Tisch. The reading σάρκος is found in DEF Vulg. Σώματος is here put for σάρκος (Pareus, Owen, De Wette, Reiche, Alford). "Actiones corporis sunt motus et opera carnis peccatricis." Pareus in loco. This view is opposed by Meyer, and others. But that the two terms, though not identical, may be used as equivalents, is proved by Mat. xxvi. 26; John vi. 51; Acts ii. 31; Rom. xi. 28; 1 Cor. xv. 39; Eph. ii. 11; v. 29; Coloss. ii. 1, 5; Heb. ix. 13; Jude 8. In 2 Cor. iv. 10, 11, the one is exchanged for the other. That the antithesis requires an equivalent to σάρκος is plain; because, to mortify the body is the same as not to live after the flesh. The writer implies that the one death is identical with the other. The "body" may well stand for the "flesh," although it is not so comprehensive a term, because it is the visible organ through which the principle of sin manifests itself. Compare vi. 12, 13, 19; vii. 5, 23, where the "mortal body," with its "members," is put for the entire man as corrupt. See comment in locis. θανατοῦτε] the sinful habits and practices of the body are killed in the believer, by suppressing their outward manifestation, because of the principle of divine life within him. Here is one of the differences between the renewed and the unrenewed man. The unregenerate might suppress the outward manifestation of sin, and yet no inward death of sin would result, because there is no "law of the Spirit of life,"—no πνεῦμα, as the contrary of σάρξ,—within him, to fight with and slay the "law of sin and death" (viii. 2). There is only one principle in the unregenerate, and this is the principle of sin. Merely to repress its manifestations, would not result in its extirpation. "Mortification is not the business of unregenerate men; conversion is their work. The conversion of the whole soul, not the mortification of

θανατοῦτε, ζήσεσθε. 14 *ὅσοι γὰρ πνεύματι θεοῦ ἄγονται, οὗτοί υἱοί εἰσιν θεοῦ.*

this or that particular lust." Owen, On Mortification, Ch. vii. The Christian duty to mortify indwelling sin is urged in Gal. v. 24; Coloss. iii. 5. See Owen, On the Mortification of Sin in Believers; and Holy Spirit, IV. viii. ζήσεσθε] eternal life is meant. See comment on vi. 22, 23.

VER. 14. γὰρ] introduces the reason why those shall "live" who mortify the deeds of the body. πνεύματι θεοῦ] is the Holy Spirit. The regenerate πνεῦμα (= νόμος τοῦ πνεύματος), or the principle of divine life, is neither self-originated, nor self-sustained. The "new man," or "inward man," or "law of the mind," or "law of the Spirit of life," or "spiritual mind," is the product of God the Holy Ghost regenerating and indwelling. In this eighth chapter we find the Holy Spirit, in distinction from the regenerate human spirit, mentioned ten times: viz.: "Spirit of life" (ver. 1); "Spirit of God" (ver. 9, 14); "Spirit of Christ" (ver. 9); "Spirit that raised Christ" (ver. 11); "Spirit that indwells" (ver. 11); "Spirit that witnesses" (ver. 16); "Spirit having first fruits" (ver. 25); "Spirit that helps" (ver. 26); "Spirit that intercedes" (ver. 26). ἄγονται] Compare John vi. 44, where the same agency is designated as "drawing." These words imply that the Divine agency is prior, in the order, to the human. οὗτοί] is emphatic by position, and the emphasis is excluding: "these, and no others." υἱοί] Christian sonship is intended: denoting 1. Similarity of disposition, Mat. v. 9, 45; Gal. iii. 7. 2. An object of peculiar affection, Rom. ix. 26; 2 Cor. vi. 18. 3. One entitled to peculiar privileges, Deut. xiv. 1; Hosea i. 10; Rom. ix. 4; 1 John iii. 2. These particulars discriminate *Christian* sonship, which is founded upon adoption, from *natural* sonship, which is based upon

15 οὐ γὰρ ἐλάβετε πνεύμα δουλείας πάλιν εἰς φόβον, ἀλλὰ ἐλάβετε πνεῦμα υἱοθεσίας, ἐν ᾧ κράζομεν Ἀββᾶ ὁ πατήρ.

creation and is applicable to all men indiscriminately, either as subjects of the divine government, or as related to each other. Natural sonship, in its various modes and forms, is mentioned in Gen. iv. 20, 21; v. 3; Job xxxviii. 28; Malachi ii. 10; Luke xvi. 25; Acts xvii. 28; James i. 17.

VER. 15 contains a proof of the statement in verse 14, derived from the experience of the persons addressed. ἐλάβετε] the aorist signification is to be retained: "ye did not receive," when ye received the Holy Spirit, i. e. πνεῦμα] is subjective, denoting a temper or disposition of the πνεῦμα. Compare Rom. xi. 8; 1 Cor. ii. 12; iv. 21; 2 Tim. i. 7. Similarly, the English word "mind" may denote the immaterial substance, objectively; or the mood and temper of it, subjectively. The article is omitted, because a particular kind of disposition is meant. δουλείας] the genitive of description. The temper, in question, is servile: that of a trembling slave before a hated taskmaster. πάλιν] previous to the reception of the Holy Spirit, in their regeneration, they had possessed the spirit of bondage. They were then not under grace, but under law (vi. 14); and "the law worketh wrath" (iv. 15). The legal spirit has nothing genial or spontaneous in it: no enjoyment. This wretched spirit, or frame of mind, was not introduced a second time, by the reception of the Holy Ghost. εἰς] denotes the tendency and result of the spirit of bondage. φόβον] fear is the principal impression made by the moral law, upon the unbeliever. "The law can do nothing but restrain by the threat and dread of death; for it promises no good except under condition of perfect obedience, and denounces death for a single transgression." Calvin in loco. ἐλάβετε] is repeated for the sake of impressiveness. Compare 1 Cor. ii. 6, 7; Phil. iv. 17. πνεῦμα] has the same subjective signification as in the preceding clause. υἱοθεσίας] the genitive of description. It is not put simply for υἱότης, "sonship" (Chrys., Theod.); because it is the object of the writer to indicate the peculiar nature of the sonship. The sonship in question is not the *natural* sonship which results from generation, as in the instance of the eternal and only begotten Son, or from creation, as in the instance of men and angels; but it is the *adoptive* sonship, which results from a gracious act of God constituting and establishing it. Meyer remarks that υἱοθεσία is the proper term for adoption, and cites Plato, Legum, xi. 929, where υἱὸν θέσθαι and θετὸν υἱόν ποιήσασθαι are the phrases employed. See comment on πατέρα τέθεικά σε, in Rom. iv. 17. ἐν ᾧ] the element in which, and the power by which. κράζομεν] the term for fervent supplicatory prayer. Gal. iv. 6. ἀββᾶ] is the Greek form of the Syriac אַבָּא, for the Hebrew אָב. Compare Mark xiv. 36; Gal. iv. 6. Wolfius (in loco) quotes a passage from the Talmud, showing that bond servants were not allowed by the Jews to call their master אַבָּא, this being an appellation which only children might use. πατήρ] 1. an explanation of the Syriac word, for Greek readers (Rückert, Reiche, Hodge, and others). This does not seem natural, in such an ardent train of thought; 2. a repetition of the name, characteristic of the fond familiarity of a child (Chrys., Theodore Mops., Grotius, Alford); 3. the two terms express the fatherhood of God, for both Jews and Gentiles (Aug., Anselm, Calvin); 4. ἀββᾶ has become a proper name, understood and employed by Greek-speaking Christians, with which their own ὁ πατήρ is joined in the ardor of petition (De Wette, Philippi, Meyer). The last view is preferable; for this is what occurs in every instance in which the Scriptures are translated into any language. Compare the terms Jehovah, Christ, etc.

16 αὐτὸ τὸ πνεῦμα συμμαρτυρεῖ τῷ πνεύματι ἡμῶν ὅτι ἐσμὲν τέκνα θεοῦ. 17 εἰ δὲ τέκνα, καὶ κληρονόμοι· κληρονόμοι μὲν

VER. 16. A fuller explanation of ἐν ᾧ κράζομεν, etc. αὐτὸ] "himself." Compare Luke xxiv. 15; John xvi. 27. τὸ πνεῦμα] the Holy Ghost. συμμαρτυρεῖ] the force of the preposition is to be retained. There are two persons actually concerned: the believer, and the third trinitarian person. The latter *co*-witnesses with the former, and confirms the testimony of the believer's consciousness. It is as if, when the believer says: "I am a child of God," the Holy Spirit made answer: "Thou art indeed a child." In this reference, Pareus quotes John viii. 17: "The testimony of two men is true." Yet all this occurs in the unity of a single self-consciousness. The human spirit is not conscious of the Divine Spirit, as of an agent other than and distinct from itself. This is enthusiasm, in the bad sense. The Holy Ghost is indeed an agent distinct from and other than the human soul; but there is no report to this effect, in the immediate consciousness here described. The believer would not have known that there is another person than himself concerned in this confident personal assurance of adoption, had it not been taught to him. His own mind makes no report of two agents, or persons. The witness of the Spirit is not a doctrine of psychology, but of revelation. At the same time, that it is not a doctrine repellant to human reason, is shown by the δαιμῶν of Socrates. The assurance of faith is the highest degree of saving faith. The former is described in 2 Tim. i. 12; iv. 7, 8; the latter, in Mark ix. 24. The first is the "blade;" the last, the "full corn in the ear." πνεύματι ἡμῶν] the regenerate human spirit, as in verses 4, 5, 6, 9, 10, 13. τέκνα] a tenderer term than υἱοί, Gal. iv. 28.

VER. 17. A deduction of consequences, from verse 16.

θεοῦ, συνκληρονόμοι δὲ Χριστοῦ, εἴπερ συνπάσχομεν ἵνα καὶ συνδοξασθῶμεν.

18 *Λογίζομαι γὰρ ὅτι οὐκ ἄξια τὰ παθήματα τοῦ νῦν*

Heirship follows from sonship. θεοῦ] God is regarded not as the deceased testator, but the living dispenser of his wealth. Compare Luke xv. 12. συνκληρόνομοι δὲ] a more specific description of the children; Christ being their elder brother (verse 29), they have a share in the kingdom of God with him. According to the Roman law, the inheritance of the first-born is no greater than that of the other children; according to the Hebrew law, it was double. Some commentators (Fritzsche, Tholuck) suppose St. Paul to have the Roman law particularly in his eye; but this would be utterly incongruous with St. Paul's feeling, and that of every true disciple, toward the Lord. Compare 1 Cor. xv. 8, 9. Fellowship in the inheritance, and not equality in it, is the chief thing. εἴπερ] See comment on verse 9. συνπάσχομεν] suffering on account of the gospel is fellow-suffering with Christ. Mat. xx. 22; 1 Pet. iv. 13. ἵνα] the predetermined purpose of God.

The paragraph ver. 18–31 contains three reasons for enduring suffering with Christ: 1. the present suffering is far outweighed by the future blessedness (ver. 18–25); 2. the Holy Spirit helps the believer to endure (ver. 26, 27); 3. everything, be it joy or sorrow, inures to the ultimate good of the children of God (ver. 28–31).

Ver. 18. λογίζομαι] denotes, here, a confident judgment, as in ii. 3; iii. 28. γὰρ] introduces the succeeding reason for endurance. οὐκ ἄξια] not of sufficient weight or consequence: "worth" has no reference to merit (Papal exegetes), but is employed as in the English phrase, "worth while." τοῦ νῦν καιροῦ] is like ὁ νῦν αἰών in Mat. xii. 32: a tem-

καιροῦ πρὸς τὴν μέλλουσαν δόξαν ἀποκαλυφθῆναι εἰς ἡμᾶς. [19] ἡ γὰρ ἀποκαραδοκία τῆς κτίσεως τὴν ἀποκάλ-

porary duration. πρὸς] "in comparison with": οὐδενὸς ἄξιός ἐστι πρὸς τὴν ἀλήθειαν, Plato, Gorgias, 371. μέλλουσαν] is emphatic by position. δόξαν] has here, principally, an objective meaning: the divine glory that accompanies the final advent of Christ. Compare 1 Tim. vi. 14, 15; 2 Tim. iv. 8; Titus ii. 13; 1 Thess. iii. 13; 2 Thess. i. 10; ii. 1–4; James v. 7, 8; 2 Pet. iii. 4; iii. 12. The splendor of this future triumph of Christ and his church, will far outweigh their present despised and suffering condition. εἰς] not "in" (Eng. Ver.), but "unto." Though there is an inward revelation associated with the outer, yet the latter is chiefly in mind, as the context shows.

VER. 19. γὰρ] introduces the proof that there is to be a glorious appearing of the Redeemer. ἀποκαραδοκία] καραδοκεῖν signifies to look for something with uplifted head: ἀπο is intensive. The earnestness with which the "creature" expects the future epiphany is proof that it will certainly occur; otherwise, the longing would be a mockery. The argument is derived from the connection between any fixed form of human consciousness, and its correlative object. The craving of hunger demonstrates that there is food somewhere; of thirst, that there is water somewhere. A world of cravings and expectations, without their correlates, would be an irrational one. In like manner, to suppose that the "creature" should steadily and unceasingly long after a mere phantasm and fiction, is absurd. κτίσεως] denotes: 1. the creative act, Rom. i. 20; 2. the created thing, Mark x. 6; xiii. 19; Coloss. i. 15; 2 Pet. iii. 4; Mark xvi. 15; Coloss. i. 23. In this place, it has the second signification. The various explanations of the meaning of κτίσις, here, are reducible to the following: 1. The material creation, animate and inanimate, organic and inorganic (Irenæus, Jerome, Ambrose, Chrysost., Theophylact, Luther, Calvin, Beza, Grotius, Pareus, Calovius, F. Turretin, Wolfius, De Wette, Fritzsche, Tholuck, Neander, Meyer, Philippi, Haldane, Chalmers, Alford, Hodge); 2. The rational creation: mankind generally, exclusive of believers (Augustine: Expos. ad Rom., 53, who fears Manichæism, if material nature be regarded as "groaning," Locke, Lightfoot, Semler, Baumgarten-Crusius, Stuart); 3. The whole creation, material and rational, as unredeemed and craving redemption (Origen, Theodoret, Rosenmuller, Olshausen, Lange, Schaff, Forbes); 4. Redeemed men: the entire paragraph referring only to the church. Those who have "the first fruits of the Spirit" are the apostles, in distinction from the body of Christians (Ittig, Deyling, Lampe). Wolfius, though adopting the first view, regards this last explanation as next in value. The first view is favored by both the nearer and the remoter context. St. Paul has spoken of the glorious resurrection of the body (ver. 11). Hence, it is natural that he should speak of that external world in which the body dwells. He has also spoken of the glorious advent of Christ, at the end of this material world (ver. 18). It is natural that he should speak of the alteration in this material world which is to occur, according to many scripture passages, at that time. As the body of the believer was made subject to death on account of sin, but is to be raised in glory; so, that outward world in which the believer's body resides was cursed (Gen. iii. 17–19), but is to be repristinated as a suitable dwelling-place for it. There being this connection and correlation between the believer's body and the visible world, it is not unnatural that a yearning for this rehabilitation should be metaphorically ascribed to the latter. As the believer longs for the "redemption of his body," so that creation in whose environment he is to dwell longs for deliverance from the "bondage of corruption." In determining the scope of κτίσις, voluntary creatures, men and angels, are excluded by οὐχ ἑκοῦσα, in verse 20; unregenerate men are excluded by ἀποκαραδοκία, in verse 19: the natural man does not earnestly expect the "manifestation of the sons of God;" and Christians are excluded by verse 23. Origen's explanation of κτίσις as the whole created universe of mind and matter, presents a combination so heterogeneous that it would be impossible to attribute a longing to it in one and the same sense. Matter inanimate and animate, angels good and evil, and men believing and unbelieving, cannot have a common aspiration. Hence, κτίσις is best referred to the irrational creation, and the "earnest expectation" is tropical, and not literal. Material nature is metaphorically in sympathy with redeemed man, and shall be restored with him. "Simplicius est, generatim de universa mundi machina, et rebus creatis, etiam brutis et inanimis, accipere κτίσις, puta astris, elementis, animalibus, terræ fructibus, et quæcunque usibus hominis primitus fuerint a deo destinata." Pareus in loco. Compare viii. 39, where the material terms ὕψωμα and βάθος are associated with κτίσις. ἀποκάλυψιν] the completion of the work of redemption, in the perfect sanctification of the believer's soul, and the glorious resurrection of his body. The first occurs at death, and the last at the advent of Christ spoken of in verse 18. It is "the shining forth" of the righteous (Mat. xiii. 43). Compare 1 John iii. 1, 2; Rev. xxii. 4; Dan. xii. 3. ἀπεκδέχεται] denotes long-continued waiting. Such personification of material nature is common in Scripture. Compare Deut. xxxii. 1; Job xii. 7, 9; Ps. xix. 1 sq.; lxviii. 8, 16; xcvi. 11, 12; cxlviii. 3–10; Isa. i. 2; xiv. 8; lv. 12.

VER. 20, with verse 21, assigns the reason, introduced by γὰρ, for the "expectation" mentioned in verse 19. μα-

υψιν τῶν υἱῶν τοῦ θεοῦ ἀπεκδέχεται. 20 τῇ γὰρ ματαιό-
τητι ἡ κτίσις ὑπετάγη, οὐχ ἑκοῦσα, ἀλλὰ διὰ τὸν ὑπο-

ταιότητι] is emphatic by position: the term denotes, primarily, weakness, helplessness, frailty of a physical kind. The Septuagint translates הֶבֶל (= Abel, Gen. iv. 2) by ματαιότης, in Eccl. i. 2, 14; ii. 1, 11, 15 et alia. The reference in such passages is, to the perishable, transitory, and unsatisfying nature of visible and earthly things. In Ps. iv. 3 (compare Acts xiv. 15), ματαιότης denotes an idol, which is a nonentity (1 Cor. viii. 4; Isa. xli. 24, 29). In the New Testament, the word is most commonly employed in a moral and spiritual sense. Rom. i. 21; 1 Cor. xv. 17; Eph. iv. 17; Tit. iii. 9; James i. 26; 1 Pet. i. 18; 2 Pet. ii. 18. In this place, it denotes the tendency to deterioration and dissolution characteristic of material nature: its equivalent, φθορά, in verse 21, proves this. The material creation, in the midst of which the "sons of God" are now placed, has no permanency. The instant anything begins to exist here upon earth, it begins to die. Such an environment is unsuited to the sinless spirit and the celestial body of the risen believer. The "justified man made perfect" (Heb. xii. 23) would be out of place, in an outward world of decay and death. ὑπετάγη] is passive, not middle. God is the efficient. The aorist refers to a well-known historical fact, viz.: the "curse" mentioned in Gen. iii. 14–19. The voluntary disobedience of man brought evil upon the involuntary (οὐχ ἑκοῦσα) physical creation with which he was connected. According to the Biblical representation, physical nature, *so far as it is connected with man and with sin*, differs, in important respects, from what it is by creation, and prior to the origin of sin. The human body is now mortal; by creation, and before apostasy, it was not (Gen. iii. 22–24; Rev. xxii. 14). The natural and material world for the unfallen Adam, was an Eden; for the fallen Adam, a cursed and thistle-bearing earth (Gen. ii. 8, 9; iii. 17–19, 24). As Scripture is silent upon details, it is impossible to define particularly. But it must be observed, that the statements in Genesis and in the Epistle to the Romans, respecting the curse upon physical nature, relate only to the *human* world, and the sin of *man*. There is nothing in these portions of revelation that necessitates the assertion that the curse upon physical nature extends throughout universal space. So far as material nature is connected with man, and his transgression, it is "cursed" for his sake. Nature as connected with the fallen angels is also cursed. But nature as connected with those myriads of holy and blessed spirits who constitute the vast majority of God's rational creatures, is not cursed, but effulgent and glorious. "The Scriptures everywhere make prominent the coherence and correspondence between the spiritual and natural world. There must be a heaven, because there are heavenly beings: because there is a God, and because there are angels and saints. There must be a hell, because there are devils. Thus, paradise corresponded with Adam in his state of innocence; the cursed ground with fallen man; the promised land, as the type of the future paradise, with the typical people of God; a darkening and desolation of the land, with every moral and religious decline of the people (Deut. xxviii. 15; Isa. xxiv. 17; Joel ii.); an exaltation of nature, with every spiritual period of salvation (Deut. xxviii. 8; Ps. lxxii.; Isa. xxxv.; Hosea ii. 21); the darkening of the sun, and the earthquake, at the death of Christ; the conflagration of the world, in connection with the day of judgment (2 Pet. iii. 10; Rev. xvi.); the renovation of the world, in connection with the triumph of Christ and his church (Isa. xi.; lx.; Rev. xx.–xxii.)." Lange on Rom. viii. 18–27. οὐχ, ἑκοῦσα] "non volens: id est, contra naturalem propensitatem." Pareus in loco. Nature instinctively recoils from

τάξαντα, ἐπ' ἐλπίδι 21 *ὅτι καὶ αὐτὴ ἡ κτίσις ἐλευθερωθή-*
σεται ἀπὸ τῆς δουλείας τῆς φθορᾶς εἰς τὴν ἐλευθερίαν

weakness, pain, and death: "invita et repugnante natura." Calvin. διὰ] 1. is here equivalent to "through," having a prevailing reference to the efficient cause. Compare John vi. 57. In this case, the preposition combines the meaning of "on account of," with that of "by means of." According to this explanation, the unwillingness, or repugnance of nature is overcome by God's direct efficiency. 2. διὰ has its usual signification with the accusative: "on account of" (Eng. Ver., "by reason of"). According to this explanation, the "creature" represses its unwillingness and repugnance, and submits to "vanity," because God inspires it with the hope of final deliverance from it. The common use of διὰ with the accusative favors the latter interpretation. Winer (p. 399, Note) remarks, that, "probably, Paul intentionally avoided saying διὰ τοῦ ὑποταξάντος, because Adam's sin was the special and direct cause of the ματαιότης." ἐφ' ἐλπίδι] *upon* (not *in*, which would require ἐν) hope, as the ground. Compare iv. 18. These words may be connected with ὑποτάξαντα (Vulgate, Luther, Calvin, Olshausen); or with ὑπετάγη (Meyer). The latter construction makes the hope more prominent, as the motive for overcoming the unwillingness and submitting to "vanity." There are two subjections: one to the curse, and the other to the hope that the curse will be removed. Hope is not actual fruition (ver. 24), and calls for patience.

VER. 21. ὅτι] is the reading of ABCEL Receptus, Lachm. (διότι is that of ℵDF Tisch.): not, "because" (Eng. Ver.), but, "that." The particle denotes what the hope is; as in Phil. i. 20. καὶ] the irrational creation, *also*, as well as the church. αὐτὴ] the creation *itself*, as well as the soul of man.

ἐλευθερωθήσεται] this deliverance of material nature from the curse connected with Adam's sin is frequently mentioned in Scripture. It is the παλιγγενεσία of Mat. xix. 28; and the ἀποκατάστασις πάντων of Acts iii. 21. See Isa. xi. 6–9; xxxv. 1–10; Heb. xii. 26–28; 2 Pet. iii. 10–13; Rev. xxi., xxii. φθορᾶς] the genitive of apposition: the bondage which is a corruption (Tholuck, Meyer, Philippi). The δουλεία τῆς φθορᾶς is the equivalent of the ματαιότης. If freed from the former, the creature is not subject to the latter. φθορὰ denotes either physical corruption, putrefaction, and thus death and destruction (1 Cor. xv. 42, 50; 2 Pet. ii. 12); or moral and spiritual corruption, and death (Gal. vi. 8; 2 Pet. i. 4; ii. 19). The first is the meaning here, in accordance with the nature of the subject. When external nature is renovated and prepared for a residence of the redeemed, fragility and vanity, decay and death will no longer characterize it. δόξης] the genitive of apposition. The creation is introduced (by participation in it) into that liberty which is the glory of the children of God. The restoration of material nature is a condition similar, in its own lower sphere, to the restoration of man's spiritual nature, in its higher sphere. St. Paul here teaches, not the annihilation of this visible world, but its transformation.

VER. 22 presents a proof, introduced by γὰρ, that there is such a subjection to vanity, and such a bondage, in the external world around man, as has been described in verses 19–21. On the general subject of the groaning of the creation, see Lange in loco, pp. 286–288. οἴδαμεν] is universal: every one knows; "we are sure" (ii. 2, Eng. Ver.). It is a fact of common observation and belief. Compare Mat. xxii. 16; Rom. iii. 19; vii. 14; 1 John iii. 15. The apostle refers to that general human conviction that nature is not now in its normal and ideal state, which expresses itself in the legends

τῆς δόξης τῶν τέκνων τοῦ θεοῦ. [22] οἴδαμεν γὰρ ὅτι πᾶσα ἡ κτίσις συστενάζει καὶ συνωδίνει ἄχρι τοῦ νῦν· [23] οὐ

respecting a former golden age, and the reign of Saturn (Ovid, Fasti, iv. 197; Virgil, Bucolica, iv. 6); in the speculations of Plato concerning a pre-existence of the human soul, in an environment of beauty and perfection suited to it (Phædo, 73–80); in that minor undertone which characterizes the deepest and most sympathetic strains in modern music and poetry; and lastly, in the common utterance of ordinary untutored human nature, when, weary of earth and time, it "would not live always." πᾶσα ἡ κτίσις] all material nature, excluding the church, as verse 23 shows. συστενάζει καὶ συνωδίνει] the figure is that of a woman in labor: "the pains of birth, not of death" (Calvin). The preposition denotes either, that all the parts and elements of the immaterial creation suffer conjointly; or, in sympathy with the children of God (Calvin). ἄχρι τοῦ νῦν] from the apostasy, to the present moment. This bondage and travail of material nature has found a lofty and impressive utterance in Wordsworth's Ode on The Intimations of Immortality.

"There was a time when meadow, grove, and stream,
The earth, and every common sight,
To me did seem
Apparelled in celestial light,
The glory and freshness of a dream.
It is not now as it hath been of yore:
Turn whereso'er I may,
By night or day,
The things which I have seen, I now can see no more.
Waters on a starry night
Are beautiful and fair;
The sunshine is a glorious birth;
But yet I know, where'er I go,
That there hath passed away a glory from the earth."

μόνον δέ, ἀλλὰ καὶ· αὐτοὶ τὴν ἀπαρχὴν τοῦ πνεύματος ἔχοντες, ἡμεῖς καὶ αὐτοὶ ἐν ἑαυτοῖς στενάζομεν υἱοθεσίαν

In respect to the teachings of this paragraph, the following points (says Pareus in loco) are certain. "1. The creation is made subject to vanity (viii. 20); 2. is to be delivered (ver. 21); 3. angels and redeemed men dwell together in heaven (Mat. xviii. 10); 4. the redeemed are in glory with Christ, where the throne and house of God are (John xvii. 24); 5. the visible heavens and earth are to be burned up (2 Pet. iii. 10); 6. new visible heavens and earth are to be prepared (2 Pet. iii. 13). It is uncertain, but probable, that all creatures not required in the new heavens and earth will be destroyed: viz., animals, and plants, etc. How the elements are to be purified is unknown; and so, likewise, is the locality, quantity, and quality of the new heavens and earth."

VER. 23 contains a second proof of the proposition in verse 18, derived from the *believer's* bondage and hope. Nature is in bondage, yet with expectation of deliverance; and so is even the church of Christ itself. *οὐ μόνον δέ*] supply *πᾶσα ἡ κτίσις συστενάζει*. *αὐτοὶ*] Paul and his Christian readers, and thus inclusive of the church universal. *ἀπαρχὴν*] the first sheaves of grain were a pledge of the entire harvest. The "first fruits of the Holy Spirit," alluded to, are the regenerated human nature, which has been denominated the "inner man," the "law of the mind," the "spiritual mind," the "law of the Spirit of life." The reference is not to any superiority of that generation of Christians over all others; but to the relation which the divine life in its beginnings sustains to its ultimate result in heaven (Eph. i. 14). *πνεύματος*] The Holy Spirit: partitive genitive (xvi. 5; 1 Cor. xv. 20; James i. 18). *καὶ αὐτοὶ*] repeated for empha-

ἀπεκδεχόμενοι, τὴν ἀπολύτρωσιν τοῦ σώματος ἡμῶν.
24 τῇ γὰρ ἐλπίδι ἐσώθημεν· ἐλπὶς δὲ βλεπομένη οὐκ ἔστιν

sis. στενάζομεν] the Apostle has already uttered this groan in the exclamation: "O wretched man, Who shall deliver me" (vii. 24); and has analyzed this phase of the believer's experience, in vii. 14–25. This verse proves that the experience in chapter viii. is the same in kind with that in chapter vii. 14–25. υἱοθεσίαν] as believers, they already were adopted (ver. 15), but their redemption was incomplete. They had not attained to sinless perfection; their body was still the "vile body" (Phil. iii. 21); and the outer world around them was under the curse. This imperfection and incompleteness was not to be removed, until the glorious advent of Christ (ver. 18), and the "manifestation of the sons of God" (ver. 19). ἀπολύτρωσιν τοῦ σώματος] explains υἱοθεσίαν. It is the deliverance of the body from its corruptible and mortal condition (the consequence of sin), and its transformation into the incorruptible and glorious body spoken of in 1 Cor. xv. 51 sq.; 2 Cor. v. 1–4; Phil. iii. 21.

Ver. 24 gives a reason, introduced by γὰρ, for "waiting for the redemption of the body." ἐλπίδι] "with hope" (not "by hope:" Eng. Ver.): the dative of manner (Bengel, Meyer); and not hope put for faith (Chrysost., De Wette). Hope is the accompaniment of Christianity. Paganism is hopeless. Compare the pagan utterances: "Hope is the dream of one awakened;" and, "fœdus mundum intravi, anxius vixi, perturbatus morior." ἐσώθημεν] the aorist refers to the time of regeneration, and the act of faith. βλεπομένη] whose object is before the eyes. καὶ] denotes the addition of hope to actual vision, which would be superfluous.

Ver. 25. δι' ὑπομονῆς] "patiently:" "διὰ when applied to the

ἐλπίς. ὃ γὰρ βλέπει τις, τί καὶ ἐλπίζει; 25 εἰ δὲ ὃ οὐ
βλέπομεν ἐλπίζομεν, δι' ὑπομονῆς ἀπεκδεχόμεθα.
26 *Ὡσαύτως δὲ καὶ τὸ πνεῦμα συναντιλαμβάνεται τῇ*
ἀσθενειᾳ ἡμῶν. τὸ γὰρ τί προσευξώμεθα καθὸ δεῖ οὐκ
οἴδαμεν, ἀλλ' αὐτὸ τὸ πνεῦμα ὑπερεντυγχάνει στεναγμοῖς

mental states in which something is done, may be referred to the notion of instrumentality. Hence, with its substantive it is a circumlocution for an adverb, or adjective" (Winer, 379). ὑπομονῆς] See comment on ii. 7; v. 3, 4. ἀπεκδεχόμεθα] the present tense indicates an action going on.

VER. 26. St. Paul now passes to the second reason for enduring suffering for and with Christ (ver. 18). ὡσαύτως] introduces the reason. τὸ πνεῦμα] the Holy Spirit: compare verses 16 and 23. καὶ] in addition to the expectation previously mentioned. συναντιλαμβάνεται] Compare Luke x. 40. The Holy Spirit co-operates with the regenerate will, and ensures success. ἀσθενείᾳ] that weakness of the soul which is felt in the struggle with indwelling sin, and expresses itself in the cry for help (vii. 24), and the groaning (viii. 23). προσευξώμεθα] prayer is the particular, in which the believer is helped. The Divine Spirit is a "Spirit of supplications," Zech. xii. 10. καθό δεῖ] the emphasis must be laid upon these words. They denote, not the matter of the prayer, but the manner of it. The believer knows what (τί) he should pray for: viz., the forgiveness of sins, etc.; but he does not know how to pray for this with the earnestness and perseverance that are requisite (καθό δεῖ). The aorist subjunctive, which is best supported by the mss., is equivalent to a subjective future. ὑπερεντυγχάνει] is followed by ὑπὲρ ἡμῶν in CKL Vulgate, Peshito, Copt., Receptus. This is omitted in ℵABD Lachm., Tisch., Tregelles. It is implied in the preposition with the verb. The action denoted by ὑπερεντυχάνει is not

ἀλαλήτοις· 27 ὁ δὲ ἐρευνῶν τὰς καρδίας οἶδεν τί τὸ φρόνημα τοῦ πνεύματος, ὅτι κατὰ θεὸν ἐντυγχάνει ὑπὲρ

performed in heaven (Fritzsche); but in the believer's heart, as the following verse shows (Augustine, Philippi). Christ, in his priestly office, is the intercessor in heaven, for his people (Heb. vii. 25; ix. 24); but the Holy Spirit is ἄλλον παράκλητον (John xiv. 16) who intercedes within their souls. There is no distinction in consciousness, between the workings of the regenerate spirit and the Holy Spirit. Yet, it is the creature and not the Creator who supplicates for blessings. The Holy Ghost is not the subject that is needy and asks for spiritual good. At the same time, the communion between the Holy Spirit and the believer is so intimate, and the human soul is so utterly helpless and dependent, that the believer's prayer under the Spirit's actuation is here denominated the "groaning of the Holy Spirit." This is to be understood in the Christian, and not the pantheistic sense. See comment on viii. 16. στεναγμοῖς] with allusion to στενάζομεν in verse 23. The groans arising from a sense of indwelling sin result in groans in prayer for deliverance from it. ἀλαλήτοις] transcending the power of words to fully express them: not unuttered, or dumb (Grotius, Fritzsche), but unutterable. There is some expression, but not an adequate one. Compare 2 Cor. ix. 15; 1 Pet. i. 8.

Ver. 27. δὲ] is adversative: although the intercession is unutterable, *yet* God knows, etc. ὁ ἐρευνῶν] God is the Searcher of hearts (1 Sam. xvi. 7; Prov. xv. 11). φρόνημα] the inclination, or disposition: "intentio Spiritus" (Pareus). See comment on viii. 6, 7. Compare also 1 Cor. ii. 11. φρόνημα is related to καρδίας. God, by searching into the state of the believer's heart, perceives what is the mind of the Holy Spirit, because the Holy Spirit has produced this state

ἁγίων. [28] οἴδαμεν δὲ ὅτι τοῖς ἀγαπῶσιν τὸν θεὸν πάντα συνεργεῖ εἰς ἀγαθόν, τοῖς κατὰ πρόθεσιν κλητοῖς οὖσιν.

of heart. The effect is the index of the cause. God sees his own image in his child. ὅτι] not, "because" (Tholuck, De Wette, Philippi), for God would know, even if the intercession were not κατὰ θεὸν; but, "that," as explanatory (Grotius, Reiche, Fritzsche, Meyer). In order to render ὅτι, "because," οἶδεν must have the meaning of "approve." κατὰ θεὸν] the intercession is in accordance with the divine nature and will. St. Paul says κατὰ θεόν, rather than κατὰ αὐτόν, for the sake of emphasis. Compare 2 Cor. vii. 9, 10. The connection of thought in verses 26 and 27 is this: The believer, through the intercession of the Holy Spirit, has holy desires that are so deep and intense that he cannot give full expression to them. The prayer is a groaning too deep for words. But, though thus unutterable, it is yet perfectly comprehended by God, the Searcher of Hearts. God knows the mind of the Holy Ghost, who has prompted this unspeakable longing in the believer's heart, and knows that this mind is "according to the will of God." The prayer, therefore, though inadequately expressed, will be heard and answered, because, "if we ask anything according to his will, he heareth us" (1 John v. 14).

VER. 28 mentions the third reason (introduced by δὲ, transitive: "now") for enduring suffering for Christ. οἴδαμεν] the universal experience of the church, not of the world. τοῖς] dative of advantage. ἀγαπῶσιν] a designation for believers, 1 Cor. ii. 9; Eph. vi. 24; James i. 12. πάντα] all events, afflictions included (v. 35). συνεργεῖ] is followed by ὁ θεός, as the subject, in AB Lachm.; but this is rejected by most editors. ἀγαθόν] anarthrous, to denote good generally. τοῖς κατὰ] "as for those who:" giving the reason of the action in

29 ὅτι οὓς προέγνω, καὶ προώρισεν συμμόρφους τῆς εἰκόνος τοῦ υἱοῦ αὐτοῦ, εἰς τὸ εἶναι αὐτὸν προτότοκον ἐν πολ-

συνεργεῖ. πρόθεσιν] the divine purpose to save individual persons. Rom. ix. 11; Eph. i. 11; 2 Tim. i. 9. The patristic exegesis varies here, according as the Greek or the Latin (Augustinian) anthropology is adopted by the exegete. Clement of Alexandria, Origen, Cyril Jerus., Chrysost., Theodoret, Theophylact, explain πρόθεσιν as the believer's purpose. Ambrose, Augustine, and Jerome as the divine purpose. κλητοῖς] the call is effectual (ver. 30).

VER. 29, and 30, explain what is involved in κατὰ πρόθεσιν κλητοῖς. προέγνω] is found only in this place, and in xi. 2; 1 Pet. i. 20; Acts xxvi. 5; 2 Pet. iii. 17. In the third of these passages, it signifies a man's previous acquaintance with another man; and in the fourth, his previous knowledge of a certain thing. In the other three instances, the word denotes an act of God. In 1 Pet. i. 20, it is applied to Christ, as having been "foreordained (προεγνωσμένου) before the foundation of the world." In xi. 2, it is said that "God hath not cast away his people whom he foreknew (προέγνω);" and the context shows that it means the same as elected (xi. 5). The noun πρόγνωσις is found in Acts ii. 23; 1 Pet. i. 2, and in both instances denotes the divine purpose, or decree. Calvin (in loco) thus defines προέγνω: "Not foreknowledge as bare prescience, but the *adoption* by which God had always, from eternity, distinguished his children from the reprobated." In classical usage, προγιγνώσκω would signify mere prescience (though in later Greek, γιγνώσκω, like scisco, sometimes signifies to determine, or decree); but in the New Testament usage, it is employed in the sense of the Hebrew יָדַע, to denote love and favor of some kind or other. See the explanation of γινώσκω, in vii. 15. Says Pareus (in loco),

"προέγνω Hebraismo significat, quos ab æterno ex perdita massa humana misericorditer in Christo pro suis deus cognovit, dilexit, elegit: Hebræis, enim, יָדַע *cognoscere* est, *amare*, *curam agere*. Etiam maritalem concubitum vocant *cognitionem*, quia est intimi amoris conjugalis opus est (Gen. iv. 1). Sic, de deo dicitur, 'novit (ἔγνω) dominus qui sunt sui' (2 Tim. ii. 19). Πρόγνωσις, ergo, non notitiam præscientiæ, qua omnia ab æterno, bona et mala, deus præscivit; sed notitiam *amoris*, *electionis*, *curæ*, qua, quos voluit, gratuito electionis favore in Christo, dignatus est." Accordingly, to "foreknow," in the Hebraistic use, is more than simple prescience, and something more, also, than simply to "fix the eye upon," or to "select." It is this latter, but with the additional notion of a benignant and kindly feeling toward the object. See comment on ix. 13. This latter feeling (denominated "love," in Rom. ix. 13; 1 John iv. 10, 19; Eph. v. 25; Gal. ii. 20; Jer. xxxi. 3, et alia), it must be observed, does not have its ground or cause in any morally loveable quality in the object. The object is a sinner, and an enemy of God (v. 8, 10; viii. 7). God's *electing* love is his compassion, and not his complacent delight in spiritual excellence and holiness. It is prior to all holiness, and all excellence, being the cause of it (viii. 29; xi. 2; 1 Pet. i. 2; 2 Tim. i. 9). The ground of it is in himself alone. His election is "according to his good pleasure," Eph. i. 9; and "after the counsel of his own will," Eph. i. 11. The chosen people of God were informed explicitly, and with repeated emphasis, that the cause of their election was not their own righteousness or merit. "Understand, therefore, that the Lord thy God giveth thee not this good land to possess it for thy righteousness; for thou art a stiffnecked people," Deut. ix. 4–8. It is at this point, that the two generic explanations (predestinarian, and anti-predestinarian) of προέγνω take their start. The Augustinian and Calvinistic explanation asserts that the divine act of election does not have its motive and reason in any spiritual excellence, either present and seen, or future and foreseen, in the elected person; but solely in the divine self-determination (Mat. xi. 26). The Semi-Pelagian and Arminian explanation asserts what the other denies. Many Lutheran exegetes, also, are anti-predestinarian. Meyer (in loco) remarks: "Richtig, da der Glaube der subjective Heilsgrund ist, Calov, und unsere älteren Dogmatiker: quos *credituros* prævidit vel *suscepturos vocationem.*" Concerning the dogmatic Lutheranism of the Formula Concordiæ, however, Müller (On Sin, ii. 229) remarks that the statements in this symbol "respecting the nature and depth of human depravity, obviously sanction the doctrine of unconditional predestination." The Arminian interpretation, that God elects those whom he foreknows will believe and repent, would require some such clause as συμμόρφους τῆς εἰκόνος to be connected with προέγνω. The fact that it stands isolated, and without a qualifying adjunct, is significant. προώρισεν] to destine, or appoint beforehand. There is all the certainty implied in the pagan fate, but referred to a wise and intelligent person, Acts iv. 28; Eph. i. 5, 11. συμμόρφους] having the same μόρφη with the glorified Redeemer (Phil. iii. 21; 1 John iii. 2), with allusion to the ἀποκάλυψιν of verse 19, and the ἀπολύτρωσιν of verse 23. It does not include a participation in Christ's sufferings (Calvin); because it is the exaltation (δόξαν, ver. 18) of the Redeemer that is referred to. εἰκόνος] both spiritual (1 Cor. xi. 7; Coloss. i. 15), and corporeal (1 Cor. xv. 49): the sinless spirit, and the celestial body. εἰς τὸ εἶναι] is exegetical of συμμόρφους: the end, and not the result. Believers are predestinated to this perfect conformity with Christ, in order that he may be glorified as the head and first-born of the redeemed. προτότοκον ἐν πολλοῖς] the preposition, with the dative, denotes that Christ is one of the number. Compare

λοῖς ἀδελφοῖς· [30] οὓς δὲ προώρισεν, τούτους καὶ ἐκάλεσεν· καὶ οὓς ἐκάλεσεν, τούτους καὶ ἐδικαίωσεν· οὓς δὲ ἐδικαίωσεν, τούτους καὶ ἐδόξασεν.

[31] Τί οὖν ἐροῦμεν πρὸς ταῦτα; εἰ ὁ θεὸς ὑπὲρ ἡμῶν,

Coloss. i. 18. In Coloss. i. 15 (πρωτότοκος πάσης κτίσεως), the preposition is not employed, because, as verses 16 and 17 show, Christ is not a part of the creation. He is prior to all creation. The preposition in composition governs the following genitive: "begotten before every creature." Compare πρωτός μου, in John i. 30. ἀδελφοῖς] sons of God by adoption, in distinction from ὁ μονογενὴς υἱὸς (John i. 18).

VER. 30. ἐκάλεσεν] like κλητοῖς in ver. 28. Compare 1 Cor. i. 9, 24; Eph. i. 18; 2 Tim. i. 9. It is not the external call (Mat. xx. 16; xxii. 14), but the internal and effectual; because, the "called," here, are the "justified." There are four elements in the effectual call: 1. conviction of conscience; 2. illumination of the understanding; 3. renewal of the will; 4. faith in Christ. Westminster S. C., 31. ἐδικαίωσεν] See comment on Rom. ii. 13; iii. 4. ἐδόξασεν] The future glorification of the believer is designated by the aorist, as his justification, calling, predestination, and election have been; because all of these divine acts are eternal, and therefore simultaneous for the divine mind. All are equally certain.

Verses 31–39 are an inference more immediately from verses 28–30. But, as St. Paul has come to the winding up of that part of the Epistle which relates to the necessity, nature, and effects of gratuitous justification, this inference has also a remoter reference to the whole course of reasoning upon this subject. Respecting the tone and style, Erasmus asks: "Quid unquam Cicero dixit grandiloquentius?"

VER. 31. οὖν] as an inference from the foregoing, i. e. πρὸς] "in respect to." ταῦτα] the statements immediately,

τίς καθ' ἡμῶν; 32 ὅς γε τοῦ ἰδίου υἱοῦ οὐκ ἐφείσατο, ἀλλὰ
ὑπὲρ ἡμῶν πάντων παρέδωκεν αὐτόν, πῶς οὐχὶ καὶ σὺν
αὐτῷ τὰ πάντα ἡμῖν χαρίσεται; 33 τίς ἐγκαλέσει κατὰ
ἐκλεκτῶν θεοῦ; θεὸς ὁ δικαιῶν· 34 τίς ὁ κατακρινῶν;

and more remotely made respecting justification by faith in Christ. θεὸς] sc. ἐστιν.

Ver. 32 answers the foregoing question. γε] "surely." ἰδίου] see comment on ἑαυτου, in viii. 3. ἐφείσατο] the reference is to the judicial suffering which the Son of God endured. He was not spared the expiating agony which he volunteered to endure. The cup was not taken from his lips, until he had drank it, Mat. xxvi. 39. Compare 2 Pet. ii. 4. ὑπὲρ] is equivalent to ἀντί, by reason of its connection with παρέδωκεν. Compare 2 Cor. v. 20, 21; Philemon 13. See comment on Rom. v. 6. παρέδωκεν] viz.: as an ἱλαστήριον. πῶς οὐχὶ] "how shall he not still more:" the argument from the greater to the less. πάντα] everything requisite to eternal life and blessedness. χαρίσεται] denotes the action of the same χάρις that delivered up Christ as an oblation for sin.

Verses 33 and 34 prove that all things shall be graciously given to believers, from the fact: 1. that God the Father will interpose no obstacle; 2. that Christ will not. ἐγκαλέσει] to summon a person before a judicial bar, and bring a charge against him. ἐκλεκτῶν] the κλητοι of verses 28, 31. θεὸς ὁ δικαιῶν] there are two modes of punctuation. 1. This clause is the interrogative answer to τις ἐγκαλέσει, and Χριστὸς ὁ ἀποθανών . . . ἡμῶν is the same to τίς ὁ κατακρίνων (Aug., Olsh., De Wette, Alford, Griesb., Lachm.); 2. The two above-mentioned clauses are direct answers to the two questions (Luther, Beza, Calvin, Grotius, Wolfius, Tholuck, Fritzsche, Philippi, Lange, Stuart, Hodge, Eng. Ver., Tisch.). κατακρινῶν] to pass a condemning sentence, ii. 1; xiv. 23. Ἰησοῦς] is sup-

Χριστὸς Ἰησοῦς ὁ ἀποθανών, μᾶλλον δὲ ἐγερθείς, ὅς ἐστιν ἐν δεξιᾷ τοῦ θεοῦ, ὅς καὶ ἐντυγχάνει ὑπὲρ ἡμῶν. 35 *τίς ἡμᾶς χωρίσει ἀπὸ τῆς ἀγάπης τοῦ Χριστοῦ; θλῖψις ἢ στενοχωρία ἢ διωγμὸς ἢ λιμὸς ἢ γυμνότης ἢ κίνδυνος ἢ μάχαιρα;*

ported by ℵACFL Vulg., Copt., Æth., Lachm. (bracketed), Tisch.); is omitted by BD Tregelles. The connection favors the formality of the full name of Christ, as the Judge of quick and dead. ἀποθανῶν] as the ἱλαστήριον, i. e. μᾶλλον δὲ] "nay more." ἐγερθείς] the resurrection is the evidence of the sufficiency and acceptance of his sacrifice (iv. 25). This fact, together with the session upon the right hand of God, and the intercession, prove Christ's power to save his people from condemnation. ὅς] is the reading of ℵABC Peshito, Æth., Copt., Lachm., Tisch., Tregelles; καὶ is added by DEL Vulg., Recept. ἐν δεξιᾷ] denotes universal dominion with the Father, Ps. cx. 1; Eph. i. 20; Heb. i. 3; Rev. iii. 21. ἐντυγχάνει] the intercession whereby he presents the merits of his work in ἀποθανών, Heb. vii. 25; ix. 24; 1 John ii. 2.

VER. 35. τίς] not τί (as would be more natural), because of the preceding τίς. χωρίσει] looks back to the παθήματα of ver. 18. The tribulation and sorrow of this life lead the believer to think that he is forsaken of his Redeemer, and particularly that he is not beloved by him. Χριστοῦ] is subjective (most commentators). Verse 37 proves this to be the correct view. It is Christ's perfect and almighty love toward the believer, and not the believer's imperfect and feeble love toward Christ, that supports under the distress and persecution of the present time. If this were lost, all is lost; even the believer's own love for Christ. διωγμὸς, etc.] the kinds of suffering mentioned are, naturally, such as characterized the early Church, and the martyr-age. But if the Redeemer's love is unchanging in the extraordinary circumstances of his people,

36 καθὼς γέγραπται ὅτι ἕνεκεν σοῦ θανατούμεθα ὅλην τὴν
ἡμέραν, ἐλογίσθημεν ὡς πρόβατα σφαγῆς. 37 ἀλλ' ἐν τούτοις πᾶσιν ὑπερνικῶμεν διὰ τοῦ ἀγαπήσαντος ἡμᾶς. 38 πέπεισμαι γὰρ ὅτι οὔτε θάνατος οὔτε ζωή, οὔτε ἄγγελοι

it certainly will be in the ordinary. If he walks with his disciples on the sea, he surely will on the land.

VER. 36. καθὼς] such trials as have been mentioned are to be expected: the Old Testament saints suffered in the same manner. γέγραπται] in Ps. xliv. 22, according to the Septuagint version. ὅτι] is recitative, marking the quotation. ὅλην] not "daily," but at any time in the day: "all the day long" (Eng. Ver.). σφαγῆς] not the sacrificial slaughter (Theophylact), but that of the market. The Roman regarded the Christian as a cheap and common victim.

VER. 37. ἀλλ'] "no, we shall not be separated, *but*," etc. τούτοις] those mentioned in verses 35, 36. ἀγαπήσαντος] 1. God the Father (Chrys., Grotius, Bengel, Olsh.); 2. Christ (Rückert, De Wette, Philippi, Tholuck, Meyer). The latter is preferable, because of verse 35. Compare Gal. ii. 20; Phil. iv. 13. Both persons are combined in verse 39.

VER. 38. St. Paul strengthens the affirmation of verse 37, by the expression of his own personal conviction. θάνατος and ζωή] are general: covering all the circumstances in which a man can be placed. He must either live, or die. Verse 36 naturally leads to the mention of death, first. The reverse order is found in 1 Cor. iii. 22. ἄγγελοι] angels generally, good and bad. Compare Gal. i. 8. ἀρχαι] the arrangement of words in the text is supported by ℵABCDEF Copt., Æth., Griesb., Lachm., Tisch., Meyer, Alford, Tregelles. The Receptus, L Peshito, place οὔτε δυνάμεις before οὔτε ἐνεστῶτα. In the first arrangement, ἀρχαί is best referred to ἄγγελοι, de-

οὔτε ἀρχαί, οὔτε ἐνεστῶτα οὔτε μέλλοντα, οὔτε δυνάμεις
39 *οὔτε ὕψωμα οὔτε βάθος οὔτε τις κτίσις ἑτέρα δυνήσεται ἡμᾶς χωρίσαι ἀπὸ τῆς ἀγάπης τοῦ θεοῦ τῆς ἐν Χριστῷ Ἰησοῦ τῷ κυρίῳ ἡμῶν.*

noting angelic hierarchies, good and evil; and δυνάμεις to earthly principalities, kings and governments. In the last arrangement, both words are best referred to ἄγγελοι: ἀρχαί designating good angels, and δυνάμεις, evil. Compare Eph. i. 21; Coloss. i. 15. ἐνεστῶτα] present, and immediately impending events. μέλλοντα] events in the nearer or remoter future. Not the glorious and joyful events of the future (verses 18, 19) are intended; but such tribulations as are specified in verse 35.

Ver. 39. οὔτε ὕψωμα οὔτε βάθος] not heaven and hell (Theodoret, Bengel); or heaven and earth (Theophylact, Fritzsche); but space generally (Meyer). ἑτέρα] implies that all the objects that have been enumerated are created things. ἀγάπης θεοῦ] is the same as ἀγάπη Χριστοῦ (ver. 35). Compare v. 8. ἐν Χριστῷ] Christ is both the medium, and the mediator of God's love toward the believer.

CHAPTER IX

§ 4. *The application of gratuitous justification.* Rom. ix.–xi.

MEYER, Philippi, and others, regard chapters ix.–xi. as only an appendix to the preceding eight; being influenced by an anti-predestinarian bias. But these chapters unquestionably enunciate doctrines that constitute an integral part of the Christian system as conceived and stated by St. Paul; and therefore constitute the fourth and last division in the dogmatic part of the Epistle, in which the writer considers the mode in which the righteousness of God actually becomes the personal possession of the individual. The previous discussion has shown that the proximate and instrumental cause is faith. But the complete comprehension of the subject requires an *ultimate* and *efficient* cause. The question arises whether faith is a self-originated act of the human will, or whether it is wrought in the will by God. The apostle affirms the latter, and teaches that the ultimate reason why the individual believes, is that God elects him to faith, and produces it within him. The doctrine of redemption is thus made to rest upon that of the divine sovereignty in the bestowment of regenerating grace. Were faith in Christ's work to be determined solely and ultimately by the human will, the result of that work would be a failure; since man, uninfluenced by grace, uniformly rejects it. St. Paul goes even further than this, and asserts that owing to the bondage of the will, it must be a failure, viii. 7, 23; ix. 16.

The apostle has already touched upon the doctrine of election in viii. 28–33. He now enters upon the full examination

1 Ἀλήθειαν λέγω ἐν Χριστῷ, οὐ ψεύδομαι, συμμαρτυρούσης μοι τῆς συνειδήσεώς μου ἐν πνεύματι ἁγίῳ, 2 ὅτι

of it, together with the correlated doctrine of reprobation, by first lamenting that a part of the Jews had not obtained the benefits of gratuitous justification (ix. 1–5). He then justifies God, in regard to this fact, by proving, both from Scripture and from reason, that God is under no obligation to work faith in the resisting and disbelieving man, and that the bestowment of grace is optional. Election and reprobation are acts of sovereignty, in which God is perfectly free (ix. 6–29). St. Paul then proves, in respect to the doctrine of reprobation, that the Jews, by their strenuous rejection of the righteousness of God and their zealous pursuit of self-righteousness, are the guilty cause of their own perdition. God does not produce their unbelief and self-righteousness, but merely leaves them in it. He does not stimulate them to pursue after justification by the works of the law, but only permits them to do as they please (ix. 30–x. 21). After this statement and defence of the doctrine of election and reprobation, St. Paul assigns as one reason for the preterition of a portion of the Jews, that the gospel might pass to the Gentiles, and then prophetically announces the final election of the body of the Jewish people, in connection with the final triumph of Christianity in the world (xi. 1–36). He thus closes the discussion of a topic in itself depressing, with the consolatory prediction of a hopeful future for the Jew. Says Coleridge (Table Talk, Aug. 14, 1833), "When I read the ninth, tenth, and eleventh chapters of the Epistle to the Romans to that fine old man, Mr. ——, at Highgate, he shed tears. Any Jew of sensibility must be deeply impressed by them."

Ver. 1. **ἐν Χριστῷ**] in his communion with Christ: the sphere and element in which he says what follows. This

λύπη μοι ἔστιν μεγάλη καὶ ἀδιάλειπτος ὀδύνη τῇ καρδίᾳ
μου· 3 ηὐχόμην γὰρ ἀνάθεμα εἶναι αὐτὸς ἐγὼ ἀπὸ τοῦ

would be, for St. Paul, the highest conceivable evidence of veracity and sincerity. He could not possibly speak a lie "in Christ." οὐ ψεύδομαι] the negative form after the positive renders the affirmation more solemn and impressive. Compare Isa. xxxviii. 1; John i. 20; 1 Tim. ii. 7. συνμαρτυρούσης] the participle assigns a reason: "since it witnesses." Compare ii. 15; viii. 16. ἐν πνεύματι] belongs with συνμαρτυρούσης: St. Paul's conscience is under the actuation of the Holy Spirit.

VER. 2. λύπη] the cause of this grief: viz., the fact that the Jews are not enjoying the benefits of that method of justification which has been described, the apostle does not mention directly, but leaves it to be inferred from what follows. "His great grief relates not only to the fall of his people, which had already occurred, but to the apostle's tragical position toward his brethren according to the flesh, and to his trying prophetic call now to disclose publicly the whole reprobating judgment pronounced on Israel, with its incalculably sad consequences." Lange in loco.

VER. 3. ηυχόμην] the rendering of the English Version is accurate: "I could wish." "Imperfects of this kind imply a wish to do a thing, or that a thing should be done, if it were possible (si posset), or allowable (si liceret)." Fritzsche in loco. Winer (p. 283) remarks that ηὔχομην, in this passage, is like ἐβουλόμην in Acts xxv. 22, which "is to be explained by 'I could wish.' There is expressed here, not a desire which has been active at some former time merely (under different circumstances), volebam, but a wish still felt by the speaker. This, however, is not stated directly, in the present tense (volo); for this can be done only when the performance is viewed as dependent solely on the will of the speaker; nor by means of ἐβουλόμην with ἄν, for this would imply the qualification, 'but I will not;' nor yet by the much weaker βουλοίμην ἄν, velim, 'I should wish;' but definitely: 'I was wishing,' or 'I wished,' that is, if it were proper, if it were permissible." So, also, Ellicott on ἤθελον, in Galatians iv. 20: "The imperfect here must be referred to a suppressed conditional clause: vellem, sc. si possem, si liceret; but must be distinguished from the imperfect with ἄν, which involves the qualification, 'but I will not,' which is not here intended." Similarly Meyer (in loco): "He would wish, if the wish could be realized for the benefit of the Israelites." This is also the view of Chrys., Photius, Theophylact, Luther, Pareus, Calvin, Beza, Lightfoot, Witsius, Wolfius, Whitby, Stuart, Hodge. The Vulgate and Luther explain by the simple imperfect: "I wished," or, "was wishing" (optabam). The meaning in this case would be, either, 1. When a Jew, I wished to keep the Jews from Christ; or, 2. When a Christian, I actually wished to be accursed. ἀνάθεμα] is the Septuagint rendering of חֵרֶם, a votive offering dedicated to God without ransom (Lev. xxvii. 28, 29). And since such offerings were mostly piacular, relating to sin and guilt, the חֵרֶם, generally, was an offering devoted to death and destruction, as the expression of the divine displeasure (Zech. xiv. 11). In this way, ἀνάθεμα denotes an object given up to the divine wrath: an accursed thing. Compare 1 Cor. xvi. 22. This explanation is accepted by the great majority of commentators. Another explanation makes ἀνάθεμα to mean excommunication ("from Christ," signifies, from his church) (Grotius, Hammond, and some Lutheran exegetes). Wieseler, in his thorough exegesis of Gal. i. 8, 9, has shown the untenableness of this view. Still another view explains ἀνάθεμα as denoting an ignominious death, of one apparently separated from Christ (Jerome, Locke, Limborch, Doddridge).

Adopting the first-mentioned explanation of ἀνάθεμα, the meaning of St. Paul in this passage is, that if it were possible, and permitted by God, and would secure the eternal salvation of his "brethren and kinsmen according to the flesh," he would be willing to be made a *vicarious sacrifice* for them, like the typical lamb of the old economy, and the Lamb of God, of the new. In this utterance of self-sacrificing love for his kinsmen, the apostle evinces that the same mind is in him that was also in Christ Jesus (1 Cor. ii. 16; Phil. ii. 5–8). The Redeemer was willing, and in his case it was possible and permissible, to endure, objectively, the pains and penalty of sin without the subjective consciousness of sin; to come under the *reatus peccati*, without the *culpa peccati.* St. Paul affirms solemnly, and as a man in Christ, that if it were possible and permissible, and the blessing which he desires for his people could come from it, he would do the same thing. Thinking merely of pain as positively inflicted ab extra, and as distinct from the sense of personal culpability and shame, he would endure any degree and amount of pain positively inflicted, if thereby his brethren could be brought to believe in Christ. He would undergo the pangs of perdition, if they could be separated from its personal sinfulness. "Anathema fieri cupit non a Christi charitate et amicitia, sed tantum a Christi felicitate et fructu amicitiæ. Optat non fieri Christi hostis, sed non frui Christi conspectu et beatitudine æterna ut hæc fratribus contingat. Vult perire non ut Christi inimicus, sed ut fratrum servator. Sicut et Christus pro nobis factus חֵרֶם, *execratio a deo*, non ut hostis dei, sed ut noster redemptor." Pareus in loco. This same spirit is exhibited by Moses, toward his brethren, in Ex. xxxii. 32. αὐτὸς ἐγὼ] in distinction from the mass of his kinsmen, who are *actually*, and not vicariously, an ἀνάθεμα. ἀπὸ Χριστοῦ] separate, and away from Christ. This clause must be interpreted in harmony with the explanation of ἀνάθεμα. One who is devoted to death, or "accursed," because of his own personal sin, is separated from God, absolutely, and in every sense. He has no filial relation to God, while he is suffering. Such was the status of the unbelieving Jews; and such is the status of the lost. But one who is devoted to death for another's sin, or *vicariously* "accursed," is separate from God only relatively, and partially. He may still be in blessed relations with God. Our Lord was not absolutely separated, and eternally cast away from God, as are Satan and his angels. His desertion by the Father was only temporary; and though while it lasted it was a total eclipse of the Father's face, and an hour of inconceivable and infinite agony, yet it was not accompanied, as in the instance of the damned, with the consciousness of personal worthlessness and guilt, and the sense of God's abhorrence and hatred of workers of iniquity (Ps. v. 5). Even in the hour when Christ was submitting to the stroke of justice from his Father's hand (Zech. xiii. 7), in accordance with the covenant and understanding between the two divine persons, he knew that he was still and ever the Father's "dear son," "well-beloved," and "only-begotten." When, therefore, St. Paul "could wish" that he were "accursed from Christ," he does not mean that he would be willing, if thereby he could save others from sin and hell, to live himself forever in sin and hell, in rebellion against God. His willingness is like that of his Redeemer: a willingness to endure suffering, but not to commit sin, or to be personally sinful. Calvin's explanation (in loco) is unguarded, from overlooking the element of *vicariousness*, in the "curse" which St. Paul was willing to submit to. "The clause 'from Christ' signifies a separation. And what is it to be separated from Christ, but to be *excluded from the hope of salvation?* It was, then, a proof of the most ardent love, that Paul hesitated not to wish for himself that *con-*

Χριστοῦ ὑπὲρ τῶν ἀδελφῶν μου, τῶν συγγενῶν μου κατὰ σάρκα, 4 *οἵτινές εἰσιν Ἰσραηλεῖται, ὧν ἡ υἱοθεσία καὶ ἡ δόξα καὶ αἱ διαθῆκαι καὶ ἡ νομοθεσία καὶ ἡ λατρεία καὶ αἱ ἐπαγγελίαι,* 5 *ὧν οἱ πατέρες, καὶ ἐξ ὧν ὁ Χριστὸς τὸ*

demnation which he saw impending over the Jews, in order to deliver them." ὑπὲρ] takes its signification from ἀνάθεμα. If that has been correctly interpreted, ὑπὲρ, here, includes both the idea of substitution and advantage. See comment on v. 6.

VER. 4. οἵτινές] denotes the class. Ἰσραηλεῖται] the name of honor: Gen. xxxii. 28; John i. 48; Phil. iii. 5. υἱοθεσία] the national and theocratic sonship (Ex. iv. 22; Deut. xiv. 1), not the spiritual and Christian (Ezek. xxxvi. 26; Rom. viii. 14); the latter implies personal faith, and individual reconciliation through the Messiah. Compare ix. 6–8. καὶ] is repeated five times, for the sake of deep emphasis. δόξα] a general term for the Old Testament theophanies, particularly those connected with the tabernacle and temple. Compare Ex. xxiv. 16; xl. 34; 1 Kings viii. 10; Ezek. i. 28. διαθῆκαι] those with Abraham, and the succeeding patriarchs, Gal. iii. 16, 17; Eph. ii. 12. BDEFG Vulg., Æth., Lachm. read ἡ διαθήκη. νομοθεσία] the Sinaitic legislation, moral and ceremonial. λατρεία] the Jewish tabernacle and temple worship. ἐπαγγελίαι] the Messianic promises and prophecies.

VER. 5. πατέρες] Abraham, Isaac, and Jacob, Ex. iii. 13, 15; iv. 5; Acts iii. 13; vii. 32. τὸ κατὰ σάρκα] is in apposition with Χριστὸς, which is the subject of ἐγένετο understood. The total human nature of Christ is designated by the clause. See comment on i. 3. ὁ ὢν ἐπὶ, etc.] "The common explanation, according to which this clause is referred to Christ is,

κατὰ σάρκα, ὁ ὢν ἐπὶ πάντων θεὸς εὐλογητὸς εἰς τοὺς αἰῶνας, ἀμήν.

in grammatical respects, the most natural, since ὁ ὢν = ὅς ἔστιν (John i. 18; xii. 17; 2 Cor. xi. 31), and τὸ κατὰ σάρκα naturally suggests an antithetic clause in which a higher characteristic of Christ is mentioned" (De Wette, in loco). De Wette, however, hesitatingly suggests that the grammar should be overruled, "because such a high title is nowhere else given to Christ, except, perhaps, Tit. i. 3; ii. 13." Meyer (in loco) asserts that Christ is never described in the New Testament as God over all. This is an error. See Eph. i. 20–22; Phil. ii. 10; Rev. xv. 3; xix. 16. Meyer concedes that the Christology of Paul is the same as that of John. But, John i. 1, 3, attributes identity of essence and creative power to the Logos, and this constitutes him θεὸς ἐπὶ πάντων. The filial subordination of the Son of God, in the trinitarian relations, is compatible with his supremacy and dominion over the created universe. The sphere of the divine essence, and that of finite substance created ex nihilo, are totally diverse. Supremacy in reference to the latter does not imply supremacy in reference to the former. The clause is referred to Christ, by Irenæus, Tertullian, Hippolytus, Origen, Cyprian, Epiphanius, Athanasius, Chrysostom, Basil, Theodore Mops., Augustine, Jerome, Theodoret, Ambrose, Hilary, Luther, Erasmus (Paraphr.), Calvin, Beza, Michaelis, Wolf, Flatt, Klee, Usteri, Olshausen, Tholuck, Ruckert, Philippi, Hahn, Thomasius, Ebrard, Delitzsch, Stuart, Hodge, Alford, Wordsworth. Erasmus, in his Annotations, proposed a colon after σάρκα, and thereby the conversion of the clause into a doxology. The doctrine of the divinity of Christ, he remarks, would not be trenched upon by this arrangement, since the Logos is included in the Godhead. He found this punctuation in two manuscripts of the eleventh and twelfth centuries. The uncials ℵAB have no punctuation; CL 5. 47, punctuate after σάρκα; 71, after πάντων; 17, after θεὸς (Tisch., in loco). The punctuation suggested by Erasmus did not go into the Receptus; but Wetstein, Semler, Lachmann, Fritzsche, Baur, Meyer, and Tischendorf have adopted it. Considering the great preponderance of authority, as well as of grammar and context, against it, its adoption evidently rests upon subjective considerations. The reasons for the historical interpretation are the following: 1. The antithesis to κατὰ σάρκα requires it; an antithesis previously employed in the Epistle (i. 3, 4). 2. It is supported by similar constructions in Paul's writings: Rom. i. 25; 2 Cor. xi. 31; Gal. i. 5. 3. If it were a doxology to God, and not a predicate of Christ the antecedent, it would, at best, be very harsh and abrupt, and would certainly require the introductory particle δὲ; see 1 Tim. i. 17. 4. If it were a simple unrelated doxology, εὐλογητὸς would precede θεὸς; see Mat. xxi. 9; Luke i. 68; 2 Cor. i. 3; Eph. i. 3; 1 Pet. i. 3, and the Old Testament בָּרוּךְ יְהוָֹה. 5. It is supported by the actual doxologies to Christ. Compare Heb. xiii. 21; 2 Tim. iv. 18; 1 Pet. iv. 11; 2 Pet. iii. 18; and by such texts as John i. 1; Phil. i. 10; Tit. i. 3; ii. 13; Rev. xv. 3; xix. 16. Meyer (in loco) attempts to escape the force of the texts in Hebrews, 2 Timothy, and 2 Peter, by the assertion that these are post-apostolic writings. Erasmus also suggested a second punctuation, which he did not favor, found in a codex of the eleventh or twelfth century, namely, a period after ἐπὶ πάντων, whereby Christ would be described as over all (either men or Jews); the remainder of the clause being regarded as a doxology to God. This is adopted by Locke, Clarke, Wetstein, Baumgarten-Crusius. πάντων] is neuter.

Ver. 6 is the beginning of the theodicy, in reference to the fact that the Jews have not obtained the benefits of gra-

6 *οὐχ οἷον δὲ ὅτι ἐκπέπτωκεν ὁ λόγος τοῦ θεοῦ. οὐ γὰρ πάντες οἱ ἐξ Ἰσραήλ, οὗτοι Ἰσραήλ·* 7 *οὐδ' ὅτι εἰσὶν σπέρμα Ἀβραάμ, πάντες τέκνα, ἀλλ' Ἐν Ἰσαὰκ κληθήσεταί*

tuitous justification. οὐχ οἷον δὲ ὅτι] = οὐ τοῖον δὲ λέγω, οἷον ὅτι (Beza, Fritzsche, Winer, Buttmann, Meyer). ἐκπέπτωκεν] to "fall out its place," or utterly fail. λόγος] the promise of salvation through the Messiah, given to Abraham and his seed. The apostle's expression of grief concerning the Jewish nation (ver. 2), might lead to the inference that God's covenant with their fathers was a *total* failure. This is not so, he says. ἐξ Ἰσραήλ] lineal descendants of Jacob. Ἰσραήλ] spiritual descendants of Jacob (ii. 28, 29; Gal. iii. 7). "Not the natural but the spiritual seed of Abraham is destined to inherit the promise" (Philippi, on Rom. xi.). "The promise was given to Abraham and his seed in such a manner, that the inheritance did not belong to every individual one of his seed without distinction; it hence follows, that the defection of some does not prove that the covenant does not remain firm and valid" (Calvin, in loco).

VER. 7 continues the explanation. εἰσὶν] sc. οἱ ἐξ Ἰσραήλ. τέκνα] sc. Ἀβραάμ. ἀλλ'] is not followed by γέγραπται, because the dictum in Gen. xxi. 12 is well known. Compare Gal. iii. 11. Ἰσαὰκ] the individual, as a *type*, as opposed to Ishmael the individual, as a *type*. St. Paul does not mean that all of the lineal descendants of Isaac, without exception, are spiritually elected, and that all of the lineal descendants of Ishmael, without exception, are spiritually rejected. Isaac represents the spiritually elect, and Ishmael the spiritually reprobate. κληθήσεταί] 1. to be chosen, Isa. xlviii. 12; xlix. 1 (Calvin, and most interpreters); 2. to be named (in accordance with יִקָּרֵא in Gen. xxi. 12) (Meyer); 3. to be, or to be created (Tholuck). The first agrees best with viii. 28, 30, 33,

σοι σπέρμα· [8] τουτέστιν, οὐ τὰ τέκνα τῆς σαρκός ταῦτα τέκνα τοῦ θεοῦ, ἀλλὰ τὰ τέκνα τῆς ἐπαγγελίας λογίζεται

and the succeeding context in this chapter. "In order that the children of the promise may be the seed of Abraham, they are called in Isaac, that is, are gathered together in Christ by the call of grace." Augustine, City of God, xvi. 32.

VER. 8 explains verse 7. Compare Gal. iv. 22–31. The promise of everlasting blessedness through the Messiah had reference to a spiritual and not to a carnal descent from Abraham. "For the promise, that he should be the heir of the world, was not to Abraham, or to his seed, through the law, but through the righteousness of faith" (Rom. iv. 13). "They which are of faith, the same are the children of Abraham" (Gal. iii. 7). Christ (Mat. viii. 12) asserts that some of "the children of the kingdom" by lineal descent, shall "be cast out into outer darkness." σαρκός] carnal descent. θεοῦ] spiritual descent. ἐπαγγελίας] the genitive of cause: they who are the spiritual offspring and product of the promise made to Abraham, with allusion to Isaac's supernatural birth. Compare John i. 13; Gal. iii. 29; iv. 28. An impenitent and unbelieving Jew (the "Jew outwardly," ii. 28) was not a child of the promise. Ishmael stands for this class. λογίζεται] by God, i. e. σπέρμα] spiritual seed, i. e. "Two things," says Calvin (in loco), "are to be considered, in reference to the selection by God of the posterity of Abraham, as a peculiar people. The first is, that the promise of blessing through the Messiah has a relation to all who can trace their natural descent from him. It is offered to all, without exception, and for this reason they are all denominated the heirs of the covenant made with Abraham, and the children of promise. It was God's will that his covenant with Abraham should be sealed, by the rite of circumcision, with

εἰς σπέρμα. [9] ἐπαγγελίας γὰρ ὁ λόγος οὗτος, Κατὰ τὸν καιρὸν τοῦτον ἐλεύσομαι καὶ ἔσται τῇ Σάρρᾳ υἱός. [10] οὐ

Ishmael and Esau, as well as with Isaac and Jacob; which shows that the former were not wholly excluded from him. Accordingly, all the lineal descendants of Abraham are denominated by St. Peter (Acts iii. 25) the children of the covenant, though they were unbelieving; and St. Paul, in this chapter (verse 4) says of unbelieving Jews: 'whose are the covenants.' The second point to be considered is, that this covenant, though thus offered, was rejected by great numbers of the lineal descendants of Abraham. Such Jews, though they are 'of Israel,' they are not 'Israel;' though they are the 'seed of Abraham,' they are not the 'children of the promise.' When, therefore, the whole Jewish people are indiscriminately denominated the heritage and peculiar people of God, it is meant that they have been selected from other nations, the offer of salvation through the Messiah has been made to them, and confirmed by the symbol of circumcision. But, inasmuch as many reject this outward adoption, and thus enjoy none of its benefits, there arises another difference with regard to the fulfilment of the promise. The general and national election of the people of Israel not resulting in faith and salvation, is no hinderance that God should not choose from among them those whom he pleases to make the subjects of his special grace. This is a second election, which is confined to a part, only, of the nation."

Ver. 9. A proof, from the history of Abraham, that only the spiritual children are the children intended in the promise to him. ἐπαγγελίας] is emphatic: "a word of *promise*, is the following word." The citation is condensed freely from the Septuagint version of Gen. xviii. 10, 14. κατὰ τὸν καιρὸν]

μόνον δέ, ἀλλὰ καὶ Ῥεβέκκα ἐξ ἑνὸς κοίτην ἔχουσα, Ἰσαὰκ τοῦ πατρὸς ἡμῶν·

1. When this time returns next year: כָּעֵת חַיָּה: according to the living time; tempore vivente, vel redeunte (Gesenius, Meyer, Tholuck, Hodge); 2. "according to the time of life" (Eng. Ver.): the time of child-bearing, between conception and birth. Compare Gen. xvii. 21; xxi. 2; 2 Kings iv. 16, 17. The usual course of nature would be followed, though the conception would be miraculous. The child would be nourished the usual time in the womb (Hammond). Ishmael was already born when God made this promise that Sarah should have a son. The blessing of the Abrahamic covenant, therefore, did not refer to those of whom Ishmael was the type. As Ishmael, who was born according to the common course of nature, and without a special divine promise, was not that "seed of Abraham" to which God had bound himself by the promise to Abraham, but Isaac, who was born supernaturally, and according to a special promise, was this seed, so not all Jews who are merely lineal descendants of Abraham are the "seed" intended in the original covenant between God and Abraham, but only such Jews (together with such Gentiles) as have the faith of Abraham, are this seed.

VER. 10. A second, and even more striking proof of the doctrine of election, taken from the history of Jacob. Ishmael was illegitimate; but Esau and Jacob were twins, and legitimate children. Yet God rejects the former and elder, and elects the latter and younger. *οὐ μόνον δέ*] 1. supply *τοῦτο* (Erasmus, De Wette, Tholuck); 2. supply *Σάρρα λόγον ἐπαγγελίας εἶχεν*, or, *ἐπαγγελμένη ἦν* (Fritzsche, Meyer). *Ῥεβέκκα*] sc. *λόγον ἐπαγγελίας εἶχεν*, or, *ἐπαγγελμένη ἦν*. *ἑνὸς*] denotes an individual, simply, who is then named. *κοίτην*] sexual

11 μήπω γὰρ γεννηθέντων μηδὲ πραξάντων τι ἀγαθὸν ἢ φαῦλον, ἵνα ἡ κατ' ἐκλογὴν πρόθεσις τοῦ θεοῦ μένῃ, οὐκ ἐξ

intercourse. Compare xiii. 13. It is Septuagint usage. Classical writers employ εὐνή and λέχος. The fact is mentioned to show that carnal descent does not determine spiritual relationships. ἡμῶν] St. Paul is now speaking to Jews.

Ver. 11. μήπω] the subjective negative is employed, and not οὔπω, because the fact mentioned is regarded as bearing upon the divine decision in the case. γεννηθέντων] the birth is the consequence of the κοίτην. This word does not signify creation ex nihilo. The children, though not yet born, were nevertheless in existence. The divine decision did not relate to nonentities; as in the supralapsarian theory. These two human individuals had both a physical and a psychical existence in the mother's womb. Compare Heb. vii. 10; Ps. cxxxix. 13–16; Job x. 10. As descendants, also, of Adam, they also existed in him. πραξάντων] actual individual transgression is meant. St. Paul does not exclude sin altogether, so as to imply innocence; because one of these individuals was elected to salvation, and salvation presupposes sin and condemnation. There was original sin, though no actual transgression. Esau and Jacob are included in the πάντες which is the subject of ἥμαρτον, in v. 12. "When the apostle says that neither of the children had then done any good or evil, what he took for granted must be added,—that they were both the children of Adam, by nature sinful, and endued with no particle of righteousness" (Calvin, in loco). "As regards original sin, both children were alike, and as regards actual sin, neither had any." Augustine's City of God, xvi. 5. κατ' ἐκλογὴν] is modal, here: the electing purpose: "propositum dei ad electionem spectans" (Wolfius, in loco). The divine purpose to bestow regenerating grace does not include all men indis-

ἔργων ἀλλ᾽ ἐκ τοῦ καλοῦντος, [12] ἐρρέθη αὐτῇ ὅτι ὁ μείζων δουλεύσει τῷ ἐλάσσονι,

criminately, but makes a selection from among them. μένῃ] denotes the fixedness and immutability of the divine purpose. Compare John xii. 34; 2 Cor. ix. 9. οὐκ ἐξ ἔργων . . . . καλοῦντος] belongs with μένῃ, as an explanatory clause. Compare Rom. iii. 20; iv. 2. The divine purpose in electing one, and rejecting another, is not founded upon the conduct of man, but upon the divine self-determination. There is an internal reason for this self-determination, that is not known to man; so that the purpose of election, or of rejection, as the case may be, is not mere caprice, or a decision without any reason whatever. But there is no reason external to God, for this purpose, derived from human character and conduct. St. Paul expressly asserts that Jacob was not elected for anything that he had done, good or evil; and that Esau was not rejected for anything that he had done, good or evil. Jacob, in Rebecca's womb, had done nothing that was a reason why he should be selected, rather than Esau, to be the theocratic head of the chosen people; and Esau had done nothing that was a reason why he should be rejected rather than Jacob. Jacob and Esau, like Isaac and Ishmael, are *types* of the two classes that have been spoken of: viz.: the "children of the promise," and the "children of the flesh" (ver. 8). The theocratic election of Isaac and Jacob illustrates the spiritual election of individuals; and the theocratic reprobation of Ishmael and Esau illustrates the spiritual reprobation of individuals. καλοῦντος] the electing purpose depends wholly upon God who calls. See comment on viii. 30.

VER. 12. ἐρρέθη] in Gen. xxv. 23. The citation is from the Septuagint. The immediate reference was to the right of primogeniture, yet as typical of the spiritual birthright of

13 καθὼς γέγραπται Τὸν Ἰακὼβ ἠγάπησα, τὸν δὲ Ἠσαῦ ἐμίσησα.

"the children of the promise" who "are counted for the seed" (ver. 8). So far as the fulfilment of the prophecy that the elder should serve the younger is concerned, it was fulfilled in the final incorporation of the Edomites, the descendants of Esau, into the Jewish state, under the Maccabees, after several conquests and revolts. Idumea was first conquered by David (2 Sam. viii. 14); it revolted in the reign of Joram (2 Kings viii. 20); was again subjugated by Amaziah and Uzziah (2 Kings xiv. 7, 22); revolted again under Ahaz (2 Chron. xxviii. 17), and continued independent, until John Hyrcanus subdued it for the last time.

Ver. 13. γέγραπται] in Malachi i. 2, 3: freely cited from the Septuagint. ἠγάπησα] here denotes compassion, not approval or complacency. God pities a sinner, but is displeased with him. ἐμίσησα] the word "hate" is here used in the Hebrew sense, of "loving less," or "showing less favor towards." (Grotius, Calvin, Pareus, Tholuck, Flatt, Stuart, Hodge, Schaff). It is employed comparatively, and not positively, Gen. xxix. 30, 31, 33; Mat. vi. 24; Luke xiv. 26; John xii. 25. In the classical and usual sense, God, as holy, hated *both* Jacob and Esau, because both were the sinful children of Adam, and were alike "children of wrath," Eph. ii. 3. Had the divine purpose been determined by this species of hatred, Jacob would not have been elected any more than Esau. But, since the election and rejection were not founded on any moral trait or conduct of Jacob and Esau, either holy or sinful, the love and hatred here alluded to cannot be God's feeling toward holiness and sin. The "love," here, is the exercise of compassion, and the "hatred" is the non-exercise of compassion. "*Odisse* est non diligere, et bonum vitæ æternæ alicui non velle. *Reprobare*, est non elegere, et bonum æternæ vitæ alicui non velle." Pareus, in loco. Compare Mat. xi. 25, where "to hide" means "not to reveal." It is the negative, and not the positive agency of God. Calvin (in loco) thus explains ἠγάπησα and ἐμίσησα: "I chose the one, and rejected the other; and I was thus led by my mercy alone, and by no worthiness as to works." This showing of compassion, and refraining from showing it, related primarily to the birthright and its privileges: to the theocratic election and reprobation. But as Jacob and Esau were typical persons, the same definition of the terms "love" and "hate" applies to the spiritual election and reprobation of individuals, in the two classes represented by them. When God "loves" a man with *electing* love, he manifests and extends compassion toward him; and at the same time he hates his iniquity. And when God "hates" a man with *reprobating* hatred, he does not manifest and extend his compassion toward him; and at the same time he hates his iniquity. The question arises whether the theocratic corresponded with the individual election and reprobation, in the cases of Jacob and Esau themselves. The fact that each was a typical person favors the affirmative; because the symbol is most naturally homogeneous with that which it symbolizes. It would be unnatural to set forth a spiritually elect person as the type of the reprobated class, and *vice versa.* And the history of Esau shows that his sinful self-will was not overcome by the electing compassion of God. Esau renounced the religion of Abraham, Isaac, and Jacob, in which he had been educated, and to which he might still have adhered, even though he had, by the divine will, lost his primogeniture, and lapsed into idolatry with his descendants. He falls, therefore, into the same class with the apostate Jews, and though "of Israel," was yet not "Israel" (ver. 6).

[14] *Τί οὖν ἐροῦμεν; μὴ ἀδικία παρὰ τῷ θεῷ; μὴ γένοιτο.*
[15] *τῷ Μωυσεῖ γὰρ λέγει Ἐλεήσω ὃν ἂν ἐλεῶ, καὶ οἰκτειρήσω*

Ver. 14 begins an apologetic paragraph, in which the doctrine of election and reprobation is defended. The objection is raised that in such a discrimination as that between Jacob and Esau, God acts unjustly. μὴ ἀδικία] the subjective form of the question implies doubt. Compare iii. 3. παρὰ] in relation to attributes and qualities, is equivalent to "in" (Matthiæ, cited by Meyer). Perhaps it means "before," "in the presence of" God, as a judge (Winer, 395). The charge of injustice evinces, as Calvin (in loco) remarks, that election, in St. Paul's view, is not determined by the greater merit, and reprobation by the greater demerit of the subjects respectively. Had this been the case, there would have been no color of reason for objecting to the doctrine as unjust.

Ver. 15. The scriptural argument is first employed. God, in the Old Testament revelation, has asserted that he will elect and reprobate, according to his own self-determination; and the implication is, that God cannot be doing unjustly in a thing which he has *said* he will do. The argument runs back, ultimately, into the idea and definition of God. The absolutely perfect Being can do no wrong. See comment on iii. 4. The citation is from Ex. xxxiii. 19, according to the Septuagint. ἐλεήσω] denotes mercy. οἰκτειρήσω] denotes compassion. The latter, says Tittmann, is the feeling in view of the suffering; the former is the desire to relieve it. Meyer asserts that the difference between the two words is only of degree: the latter being the stronger term. The distinction between the existence of a feeling and its expression must be observed, here. Mercy or compassion is a necessary feeling in the divine nature; but its *manifestation* toward

persons is optional and sovereign. God may have precisely the same compassionate sentiment toward two sinful and miserable men, considered simply as sinful and miserable, and yet for an internal reason, known only to himself, may refrain from giving it expression toward one of them. This is taught in the words: "I will have compassion upon whom I please to have compassion." Says Charnocke (Goodness of God), "God is necessarily good [compassionate], in regard to his nature, but freely good in regard to the effluxes of it to this or that particular subject he pitcheth upon. He is not necessarily communicative of his goodness as the sun is of his light, that chooseth not its objects, but enlightens all indifferently. This were to make God of no more understanding than the sun, to shine not where it pleaseth, but where it must. God is an understanding agent, and hath a sovereign right to choose his own subjects; it would not be a supreme goodness, if it were not a voluntary goodness. He is absolutely free to dispense his goodness in what methods and measures he pleaseth, according to the free determinations of his own will, guided by the wisdom of his mind, and regulated by the holiness of his nature. He is not to 'give an account of any of his matters' (Job xxxiii. 13); he will have mercy on whom he will have mercy, and he will have compassion on whom he will have compassion; and he will be good to whom he will be good." The key to the doctrine of election and reprobation is in Christ's parable of the laborers (Mat. xx. 1–16). It is "lawful" for God "to do what he will, with his own" unobligated mercy.

VER. 16 is an inference, introduced by ἄρα οὖν, from the words of God in verse 15. It is of a general nature, enunciating a fact in the divine economy of grace. The exercise of grace does not depend upon the will of the person who receives it, but of the person who bestows it; as almsgiving

ὃν ἂν οἰκτείρω. [16] ἄρα οὖν οὐ τοῦ θέλοντος οὐδὲ τοῦ τρέχοντος, ἀλλὰ τοῦ ἐλεῶντος θεοῦ. [17] λέγει γὰρ ἡ γραφὴ τῷ Φαραώ, ὅτι εἰς αὐτὸ τοῦτο ἐξήγειρά σε, ὅπως ἐνδείξωμαι ἐν

is determined not by the volition of the beggar, but of the patron. θέλοντος] sc. ἔστιν ἔλεος: the genitive denotes dependence, together with the notion of possession, like the Latin *penes.* Mercy is not under the control of the needy and helpless person who is endeavoring to obtain mercy. θέλοντος denotes the internal activity, as opposed to τρέχοντος, which designates the intense action of the outward powers. The latter word is borrowed, as is frequent in the Pauline rhetoric, from the games. Compare 1 Cor. ix. 24. Some refer it to Esau's unsuccessful hunt, to procure the venison for his father.

Ver. 17. A confirmation, introduced by γὰρ, of the statement in verse 16: freely cited from the Septuagint version of Ex. ix. 16. ὅτι] is recitative. αὐτὸ τοῦτο] this very thing, specifically. ἐξήγειρά] the word in the original Hebrew, is the Hiphil of עָמַד : to cause to stand, or, to place, which the Septuagint translates by διετηρήθης. St. Paul's rendering is the more exact, of the two. 1. I have raised thee up, and set thee upon the stage of action. Compare Mat. xi. 11; xxiv. 11; John vii. 52 (Theophylact, Calvin, Beza, Bengel, Rückert, Olshausen, Tholuck, Philippi, Meyer, Schaff). 2. I have preserved thee alive (Grotius, Wolfius, Rosenmuller). 3. I have made thee king (Flatt, Benecke). 4. I have excited thee to resist: with reference to σκληρύνει, ver. 18 (Augustine, Anselm, Venema, De Wette, Fritzsche, Haldane, Hodge, Stuart). The first is preferable. Pharaoh's place in history, and his whole course of action was assigned to him by the decree and providence of God. It was not a matter of chance, but a part of the divine plan, with reference to a

σοὶ τὴν δύναμίν μου καὶ ὅπως διαγγελῇ τὸ ὄνομά μου ἐν πάσῃ τῇ γῇ. [18] ἄρα οὖν ὃν θέλει ἐλεεῖ, ὃν δὲ θέλει σκλη-

particular end, which is mentioned in the context. Neither עָמַד nor ἐξήγειρεῖν signify creative efficiency. For the nature of the divine agency in the case, see the explanation of σκληρύνει, in verse 18. ἐνδείξωμαι] viz.: by Pharaoh's defeat and destruction, which was a striking manifestation of the divine omnipotence. διαγγελῇ] denotes a proclamation far and wide, Luke ix. 60. ὄνομά] the name of that God who has shown such might. πάσῃ γῇ] at first, only that part of the world in which the events occurred, and were known; but finally, the whole world, where they are universally known.

VER. 18. A conclusion of the apostle, introduced by ἄρα οὖν, from both of the divine affirmations: that to Moses, and that to Pharaoh. ὃν] in both instances denotes an actually existing individual, and not an ideal one: a real object upon whom the action designated by ἐλεεῖ and σκληρύνει terminates. God never elects or rejects a nonentity. It, also, in both instances, denotes a sinful individual; otherwise, he would not be an object of the merciful action in one case, and of the "hardening" action in the other. God never forgives and never "hardens" a holy being. This pronoun is fatal to the supralapsarian theory, which, in the order of decrees, places the decree of election and reprobation, before the decree to create man and to permit the origin of sin by man's self-determination. ἐλεεῖ] see comment on ver. 15. σκληρύνει] Compare Deut. ii. 30; Ex. iv. 21; xi. 10; Josh. xi. 20; Isa. lxiii. 17. It is the opposite of ἐλεεῖ. Not to show mercy to a man is, in St. Paul's use of the word, to "harden" him. To harden is, not to soften. Hardening is not the efficient action of God, since Pharaoh is said to have hardened his own heart, Ex. viii. 15, 32; ix. 34; x. 16. The agency of God in hardening is inaction, rather than action. The Holy Spirit does not strive at all with the human will (Gen. vi. 3), and so permits the already sinful man to confirm himself in sin, by pure and unhindered self-determination. The restraints of conscience, and of the providential circumstances amidst which the man lives, may continue, but are overborne by the sinful will. This is the negative aspect of the hardening. But besides this, there may be a positive withdrawal of these restraints. This is punitive action, intended as retribution for past resistance of restraining circumstances and influences. See the explanation of παρέδωκεν in Rom. i. 24. In the instance of Pharaoh, the hardening included both of these features. God left the king of Egypt to his self-will, and also withdrew the restraints that tended to check it. The charge of necessity, in such a reference is absurd. No more unhindered liberty can be conceived of, than this. The human will is left severely alone, to find the reason and source of its impulse wholly within itself. Sin is a more intense and wilful form of self-determination than holiness is; because, unlike the latter, it is the product of the human will in its *solitary* action, without any internal influence from God. "If hardness follows upon God's withholding his softening grace, it is not by any efficient and causative act of God, but from the natural hardness of man. When God hardens a man, he only leaves him to his stony heart. God infuseth not any sin into his creatures, but forbears to infuse his grace, and to restrain their lusts, which, upon the withdrawal of restraints, work impetuously. When a man that hath bridled in a high-mettled horse from running, hath given him the reins; or a huntsman takes off the string that held the dog, and lets him run after the hare, are they the efficient cause of the motion of the one, or the other? No, but the mettle and strength of the horse, and the natural inclination of the hound: both of which are left to their own motions, to pur-

ρύνει. [19] ἐρεῖς μοι οὖν Τί οὖν ἔτι μέμφεται; τῷ γὰρ βουλήματι αὐτοῦ τίς ἀνθέστηκεν;

sue their own natural instincts." Charnocke, Holiness of God. "Five times it is said that God hardened Pharaoh's heart; three times that Pharaoh hardened his own heart. Pharaoh, then, was hardened differently by God, from what he was by himself. He hardened his own heart by wilfully resisting Moses, and despising God, and the judgments of God. God hardened his heart, by not converting his already hard heart into a heart of flesh." Pareus, in loco. "The perdition of sinners," says Calvin (Instit. III. xxiii. 8), "depends upon the divine predestination in such a manner that the cause and matter of it are found in themselves."

VER. 19. An objection not of the Jew exclusively, but of the unbeliever generally. It is suggested by the preceding statements concerning God's compassionating one man and "hardening" another, as he pleases. οὖν] in view of what has been said, in verses 15–18. ἔτι] "still:" after having "hardened," i. e. βουλήματι] not θελήματι (Mat. vi. 10): the *decree* in distinction from the *desire* or inclination of God; his secret as distinguished from his revealed will; the will of good pleasure, in distinction from the will of complacency. These two wills may be contrary to each other; as in the case when God decreed the sin of Adam. This sin was contrary to the divine will, in the sense of the divine desire or inclination, because God forbad it; but was in accordance with the divine will, in the sense of the divine decision. God decreed what he hated and prohibited. The question, "Who hath resisted his will?" does not refer to that will which is spoken of in the Lord's Prayer: "Thy will (θέλημα) be done on earth as it is in heaven." This latter will is equivalent to the moral law (Rom. ii. 18), and is resisted by every man. Pha-

20 ὦ ἄνθρωπε, μενοῦνγε σὺ τίς εἶ ὁ ἀνταποκρινόμενος τῷ θεῷ; μὴ ἐρεῖ τὸ πλάσμα τῷ πλάσαντι Τί με ἐποί-

raoh himself had resisted it. But it refers to that will which is never the object of prayer, viz.: the unconditional decree of God, which cannot be resisted, and the success of which is entirely disconnected with a creature's petitions. The distinction between the will of desire and the will of decree is illustrated in the human sphere by the difference between inclination and volition. A man frequently opposes the inclination of his will, by a volition of his will. He decides to do what he is disinclined to do. ἀνθέστηκεν] the perfect with a present signification: "who resists, or can resist?" The objector does not dispute the fact that the divine decree is irresistible, but alleges that in the instance of "hardening" just mentioned it is *causative* and *necessitating* in its nature. Why should God punish a sin of which he is himself the author? is his inquiry. This is the πρῶτον ψεῦδος, in all anti-predestinarian objections.

VER. 20 begins St. Paul's reply to the allegation which is latent in the preceding question, viz.: that the doctrine of election and reprobation is *fatalism*. He first directs attention to the general relation of man to God. The idea of God as the absolutely Perfect requires that his justice and righteousness should be presupposed under all circumstances. If there be an apparent conflict between the judgment of the Creator and that of the creature, it must be assumed that the latter and not the former is in error. This appeal to the transcendental idea of God, is frequent in St. Paul's writings. Compare Rom. iii. 4. μενοῦνγε] is good-naturedly ironical: "yes, forsooth." σὺ τίς εἶ] is contemptuous, but not bitterly so: "homunculus quantulus es." The immense distance between the finite creature and the infinite Creator suggests the phraseology. The difficult problems in the Divine government are to be approached with reverence toward God, and the presumption that he is righteous in all his ways. ἀνταποκρινόμενος] "to enter into a dispute with:" involving an irreverent equalizing of man with God. πλάσμα] the Apostle continues the reference to the transcendent superiority of God, by noticing the fact that he is the former and disposer, and man the thing formed and disposed. Creation ex nihilo is not meant here. This would require κτίσις. The term πλάσμα designates only the plastic act of the moulder. The whole sinful mass of mankind lies in the hand of God, like clay in the hand of the potter. Compare Isa. xxix. 16; xlv. 9. Also Ecclesiasticus xxxiii. 13. ἐποίησας] is explanatory of πλάσαντι, denoting the fashioning of something already in existence, and not the creation of substance from nonentity. "Shall the clay say to him that *fashioneth* [not createth] it?" Isa. xlv. 9. The clay is already in existence having certain definite properties, and is merely shaped into a certain form by the potter. The potter's agency imparts none of the qualities of clay to the vessel. Similarly, mankind is viewed as already in existence, and as having the definite characteristic of sin produced by *its own* agency, and *as such*, is either elected or reprobated. "It is to be borne in mind, that Paul does not, here, speak of the right of God over his creatures as *creatures*, but as *sinful* creatures" (Hodge, in loco). The question to which the Apostle directs his answer, is not: "Why hast thou made me a sinner?" but: "Why hast thou left me in sin?" The only answer to the first question that he would have given, would be to deny the alleged fact. Many of the anti-predestinarian objections proceed upon the supposition that the first of these questions is the one to be answered, and that the problem of the predestinarian is to reconcile reprobation with a *causative* agency of God in the origin and continuance of sin. For exam-

ησας οὕτως; [21] ἢ οὐκ ἔχει ἐξουσίαν ὁ κεραμεὺς τοῦ πηλοῦ ἐκ τοῦ αὐτοῦ φυράματος ποιῆσαι ὃ μὲν εἰς τιμὴν σκεῦος, ὃ δὲ εἰς ἀτιμίαν;

ple, Philippi (ix. 33) says, "If the guilt of Israel's rejection lies in its unbelief, the absolute predestination of God cannot be regarded as its cause. It is impossible for God to require what he himself refuses, and to punish what he himself causes." This is an erroneous view of predestination. The unbelief is *self*-originated, and invincible by the self. God decides not to overcome it in a particular individual, and thereby predestines him to perdition. The complaint of the objector really is, that God does not save him from his sin. To which the reply is, that God may rightfully do as he pleases in such a case. οὕτως] denotes the condition of one like Ishmael and Esau, whom God "hardened" by not "having mercy" upon him.

VER. 21 continues the reasoning, by explaining the figure of the potter in verse 20. ἐξουσίαν] the right and prerogative, Mat. xxi. 23; 1 Cor. viii. 9. αὐτοῦ φυράματος] the selfsame mass of clay, having properties not originated by the potter. The figure of the potter (Jer. xviii. 3–6) describes God as a Savior, not as a Creator. St. Paul is discussing, here, the liberty of God in respect to delivering Jews and Gentiles generally (represented by Jacob, Esau, and Pharaoh), not from the consequences of his creative and causative agency, but of their own self-determination. As a mass or "lump," by the action of free will they are all sinful and guilty. The mode and manner in which this has occurred, has been described in Rom. v. 12, sq. The doctrine of election and reprobation stands, or falls, with that of the sin in Adam. The voluntary, unnecessitated origin of sin must be conceded. The whole species having become evil and guilty before God, by its own act (πάντες ἥμαρτον), he has the same right to pardon and sanctify a portion of the species, and to pass by, or, technically, to "hate" the remainder of it, that the potter has to mould one sort of vessel out of one part of the lump of clay, and another sort of vessel from another part. "In the sovereignty here asserted, it is God as a moral governor, and not God as a creator, who is brought into view. It is not the right of God to create sinful beings in order to punish them, but his right to deal with sinful beings according to his good pleasure, that is here asserted" (Hodge, in loco). In the instances in which the metaphor of the clay and potter is employed by Isaiah and Jeremiah, it is applied to the Jews as "an *unclean* thing." Compare Isa. lxiv. 6, 8. τιμὴν and ἀτιμίαν] denote the destined uses of the vessels, respectively. Compare 2 Tim. ii. 20, 21. ὃ μὲν σκεῦος] the relative is put for the article in antithetic sentences. Compare 1 Cor. xi. 21. (Winer, 105.)

Verses 22–29 contain a further defence of the divine economy of redemption, in the election of some and the reprobation of others, upon two grounds: 1. That God shows forbearance and patience toward the non-elect, in enduring their sin which is so abominable in his sight, and in delaying their punishment when strict justice requires their immediate and swift destruction. The non-elect are treated better than they deserve, and, therefore, have no just ground of complaint against God. 2. That God desires to show, during this period of forbearance and delay of punishment, his mercy toward the elect.

VER. 22 is a conditional interrogative sentence, the apodosis of which is not expressed, but is suggested by ἀνταποκρινόμενος τῷ θεῷ in verse 20: "If the fact is as follows, will you reply against God?" Compare John vi. 62; Acts xxiii. 9. εἰ] if, as is the fact. δὲ] is adversative (Winer), not transi-

22 εἰ δὲ θέλων ὁ θεὸς ἐνδείξασθαι τὴν ὀργὴν καὶ γνωρίσαι τὸ δυνατὸν αὐτοῦ ἤνεγκεν ἐν πολλῇ μακροθυμίᾳ σκεύη ὀργῆς κατηρτισμένα εἰς ἀπώλειαν,

tive (Meyer). The argument here is of a different nature from that in verses 20, 21. That was founded upon the idea of God, and the optional nature of mercy. This is founded upon the ill desert of man, and the divine patience in reference to it. Consequently, something more than a transition from one topic to another of the same kind is indicated by the particle. θέλων] "inclined:" "willing" (Eng. Ver.) is inadequate. See comment on ver. 19. The mere permission of God is not meant; nor the purpose of God: which would require βουλεύων; but the deep and strong desire: a will that was so profound and intense as to require that self-restraint which is denominated the patience and long-suffering of God (ii. 4). The phrase θέλων ἐνδείξασθαι οργὴν denotes the spontaneity of the divine holiness, "the fierceness and wrath of Almighty God" against sin (Rev. xix. 15), which is held back by the divine compassion, upon the ground of the ἱλαστήριον. See comment on iii. 25. The participle is here employed limitatively, καίτοι being understood (Winer, 344): "although inclined." Notwithstanding the immanent and eternal indignation of God against the wickedness of men like Tiberius and Cæsar Borgia, there was in their history a long-continued and strange forbearance to punish them. This is sometimes so marked, as to be painful to the human conscience, leading men to cry out: "How long, O Lord, how long?" If God bears patiently for a time with such persons, not destroying them at the first moment, but deferring the punishment prepared for them, what ground for complaint have they before the bar of eternal justice? And the reasoning that is true in reference to Tiberius and Borgia, is true substantially, in reference to every non-elect sinner.

The difference is only one of degree in sin (1 Tim. i. 15). The principle is the same. Every non-elect man will have been treated by God better than he deserved. In this divine self-restraint, God evinces kindness even toward those whose obstinate self-determination in sin he does not think proper to overcome by special grace. δυνατὸν] the exercise of retributive justice is an exertion of omnipotence. ἤνεγκεν] is general in its reference, like σκληρύνει in verse 18, and not to be referred particularly to Pharaoh. πολλῇ] the divine patience and forbearance toward the sin of the non-elect is very great, especially when the sensitiveness of the divine holiness in respect to sin is considered. To bear with sin is easy for the deity of Epicurus, but not for the living God of Israel. The stoic Antoninus asks: "Can the gods, who are immortal, bear without indignation, for the continuance of so many ages, with such and so many sinners, yea not only so but also take such care of them that they want nothing; and dost thou so grievously take on as one that could bear with them no longer: thou that art but for a moment of time; yea, thou that art one of those sinners thyself?" Meditations vii. 41. σκεύη] is anarthrous, because no particular individuals are meant, but the class, generally, of the reprobated. ὀργῆς] the genitive of quality: objects of wrath. Compare τέκνα ὀργῆς, Eph. ii. 3. κατηρτισμένα] 1. used adjectively: "fit for" (Chrysostom, Theodoret, Theophylact, De Wette, Tholuck, Lange). This is favored by the change to another word (προητοίμασεν), and another tense, in verse 23, where the elect are spoken of. 2. Used participially: "prepared for:" by themselves (Grotius, Bengel); by God (Augustine, Calvin, Meyer). This last explanation must be connected with the Augustino-Calvinistic doctrine of the permissive decree. The divine agency in reprobation is not regarded as causative of sin. ἀπώλειαν] endless perdition: the θάνατος of v. 12.

23 καὶ ἵνα γνωρίσῃ τὸν πλοῦτον τῆς δόξης αὐτοῦ ἐπὶ σκεύη ἐλέους, ἃ προητοίμασεν εἰς δόξαν; 24 οὓς καὶ ἐκάλεσεν ἡμᾶς οὐ μόνον ἐξ Ἰουδαίων ἀλλὰ καὶ ἐξ ἐθνῶν,

VER. 23 continues the vindication of God, by giving an additional reason for the divine patience and forbearance. καὶ] "and also:" supply ἤνεγκεν ἐν πολλῇ, etc. If God had invariably visited sin with immediate retribution, in accordance with the promptings of immaculate holiness, there would have been no opportunity for the manifestation of his mercy toward the elect. In this case, there could have been no elect: all must have been reprobated and punished. δόξης] the divine excellence generally, with particular reference, here, to the attribute of mercy. Compare Eph. iii. 16. ἐπὶ] denotes the exuberant overflow *upon* the objects of mercy. προητοίμασεν] 1. "predestined," as in Eph. ii. 10. 2. "prepared." The latter is preferable, because of the previous figure of the potter, and of the kindred word κατηρτισμένα applied to the non-elect. The vessels of compassion are prepared for heaven by the grace of God. The divine agency, in this case, is direct efficiency. The decree is efficacious. God works in man, "both to will, and to do," Phil. ii. 13. If the second explanation is adopted, the preposition in the verb refers to the preparation as being prior to the enjoyment of the glory. δόξαν] heavenly glory.

VER. 24. οὓς] relates to σκεύη ἐλέος, and is masculine, with ἡμᾶς, by attraction. ἐκάλεσεν] See comment on viii. 30. ἐξ Ἰουδαίων] election applies to the Jews, in accordance with the previous affirmation "that they are not all Israel which are of Israel" (ix. 6). καὶ] the elect are taken from the Gentiles also, as well as from the Jews.

VER. 25 proves, from the Old Testament, that vessels of mercy are to be chosen out of the Gentiles. The quotation

25 *ὡς καὶ ἐν τῷ Ὡσηὲ λέγει Καλέσω τὸν οὐ λαόν μου λαόν*
μου καὶ τὴν οὐκ ἠγαπημένην ἠγαπημένην, 26 *καὶ ἔσται ἐν τῷ*
τόπῳ οὗ ἐρρέθη αὐτοῖς Οὐ λαός μου ὑμεῖς, ἐκεῖ κληθήσονται

is from Hosea ii. 25, and is not exactly literal either from the Hebrew or from the Septuagint. The order of the clauses is reversed. In the prophecy, the reference is to the ten tribes; but as they had been excluded from the theocracy, and so were virtually heathen, the apostle regards them as the type of the Gentiles universally. *οὐ λαόν*] "*οὐ* combined with nouns into one idea, obliterates their meaning altogether:" Winer, 476, who cites, Rom. x. 19; 1 Pet. ii. 10; Thucid., i. 137; v. 50; Eurip., Hippol., 196. *οὐκ ἠγαπημένην*] is the Septuagint (ver. 23) rendering of לֹא רֻחָמָה. The Hebrew רָחַם signifies to show mercy, so that, as in ix. 13, compassion and not complacency is the feeling intended.

VER. 26 is taken from Hosea i. 10, almost literally from the Septuagint (ii. 1), and is combined with the preceding quotation from the prophet, so as to make one connected sentence. Such combinations are frequent in Rabbinical citations from the Old Testament. *ἔσται*] should have no comma after it, because it is not Paul's but the prophet's word. *τόπῳ*] refers, in Hosea, to Palestine, where the threat of reprobation from the theocracy, and the promise of future restoration to it, was spoken to the ten tribes. But as the Apostle has made the ten tribes the type of the Gentiles, the "place," here, must be the Gentile lands. The heathen, hitherto externally reprobated (*οὐ λαός*), are to be called into the kingdom of God all over the world. *κληθήσονται*] not merely named, but called with the "calling" of viii. 30.

VER. 27. The Old Testament citations in verses 25, 26, prove the election of a part of the Gentiles (*ἐξ ἐθνῶν*: ver.

υἱοὶ θεοῦ ζῶντος. 27 *Ἠσαΐας δὲ κράζει ὑπὲρ τοῦ Ἰσραήλ*
Ἐὰν ᾖ ὁ ἀριθμὸς τῶν υἱῶν Ἰσραὴλ ὡς ἡ ἄμμος τῆς

24); the Apostle now quotes from the Old Testament to prove the reprobation of a part of the Jews. This, for the Jew, would be a more offensive tenet than even the calling of the Gentiles. "Paul now proceeds to the second point, with which he was unwilling to begin his reasoning, lest he should too much exasperate their minds. And it is not without a wise device, that he introduces Isaiah as crying out in wonder, not as merely narrating, in order that he might excite more attention." Calvin, in loco. There is a recasting and combination of the original passages, as in the preceding citation. δὲ] is adversative: not only is the election of the Gentiles taught in the Old Testament, *but*, also, the reprobation of the Jews. κράζει] loud proclamation. Compare John, i. 15. ὑπὲρ] is equivalent to περί, in later Greek, with verbs of narration. ἐὰν ᾖ, etc.] The quotation is from Isa. x. 22: following the Septuagint, which differs only slightly from the Hebrew. ὑπόλειμμα] is supported by ℵAB Lachm., Tisch., Tregelles; the Sept., Receptus, with DEF have κατάλειμμα. The word is emphatic: "the remnant *only*." σωθήσεται] this is the Septuagint rendering of יָשׁוּב, "will return." The primary reference of the prophet was to the return of the Jews from the Babylonian exile; it is applied by St. Paul to Christ's redemption.

VER. 28 continues the citation, taking the words from Isa. x. 23. The reading without the bracketed words is supported by ℵAB Peshito, Copt., Æth., Lachm., Tisch., Tregelles; with the bracketed words, by the Receptus, Sept., DEF, Vulg. The general doctrine is the same with either reading; and is well given in the English Version: "for he shall finish the work, and cut it short in righteousness: be-

θαλάσσης, τὸ ὑπόλειμμα σωθήσεται. [28] λόγον γὰρ συντελῶν καὶ συντέμνων [ἐν δικαιοσύνῃ· ὅτι λόγον συντετ-

cause a short work will the Lord make upon the earth." The execution of the divine decree of reprobation will be short, sharp, and decisive. There is no vacillation in the mind of God, when he has once decided. The present condition of the Jews, as a people, is a proof that Esau and those whom he represents find no μετανοίας τόπον: no "way to change the mind" (Eng. Ver. margin) of God, "though they seek it carefully with tears" (Heb. xii. 17). The Septuagint rendering, which St. Paul adopts, departs considerably from the Hebrew text; and commentators themselves differ much in their renderings. Meyer's version is as follows: "Destruction is determined upon, and inflowing righteousness (i. e. retribution); for, destruction and (punitive) decision will the Lord Jehovah Sabaoth make in the midst of the whole land." λόγον] the word of threatening, as in Heb. iv. 12: the reprobating decree; hence, the result of the word: the reprobating *work* (Eng. Ver., Beza, Melanch., Calvin). In the New Testament, λόγος, like the Hebrew דָּבָר (Jer. xliv. 4; 2 Sam. xi. 18), is sometimes equivalent to *res*, *factum*. Compare Mat. xix. 11; Mark i. 45; ix. 10; Luke i. 4. Schleusner, in voce. συντελῶν and συντέμνων] denote the energy and swiftness of the divine action: the first refers to the complete accomplishment of the work; and the last to the winding up and ending of it. The two participles are adjuncts of κύριος. δικαιοσύνῃ] denotes retributive justice (iii. 25). This reprobating work is grounded wholly in law and equity; and objections against it are objections against law and equity. It is subsequently (xi. 22) denominated "severity:" i. e. the strict and exact enforcement of righteousness. There is no compassion (χρηστότης, xi. 22) in it. The question whether God may reprobate a portion of the human

μημένον] ποιήσει κύριος ἐπὶ τῆς γῆς. [29] καὶ καθὼς προείρηκεν Ἠσαΐας, Εἰ μὴ κύριος Σαβαὼθ ἐγκατέλιπεν ἡμῖν σπέρμα, ὡς Σόδομα ἂν ἐγενήθημεν καὶ ὡς Γόμορρα ἂν ὡμοιώθημεν.

race, is simply the question whether he may be the God of retribution (xii. 19).

VER. 29. An additional quotation from Isaiah (i. 9), in proof of the reprobation of a part of the Jews. It is verbatim from the Septuagint, which translates שָׂרִיד (= survivor), by *σπέρμα*. *προείρηκεν*] 1. "has previously said," in an earlier chapter (Erasmus, Calvin, Beza, Grotius). 2. "has prophesied" (Tholuck, Meyer). The latter rendering requires a comma after *καί*. *Σαβαὼθ*] the host of heaven, angelic and starry: mind and matter. This epithet is chosen, because election is an act of sovereignty. *σπέρμα*] not vegetable (Hodge), but animal. It denotes the same as *τὸ ὑπόλειμμα* (ver. 27): only a small number. *ὡς Σόδομα*] had none been elected *ἐξ Ἰουδαίων* (ver. 24), and all been rejected, the case of the Jews would have been like that of Sodom and Gomorrah.

Verses 30 and 31 summarize the facts brought out in the previous discussion respecting election and reprobation: viz., that the Gentiles who have hitherto had no theocratic privileges and no outward call, are now the objects of God's spiritual election; and the Jews who have hitherto had such theocratic privileges and the outward call, are now the objects of God's spiritual reprobation. Not that every Gentile without exception is individually elected, and every Jew individually reprobated. The apostle is speaking of the general condition of things, at the time he is writing. The Gentiles were then coming to Christ in multitudes, while the Jews in multitudes were rejecting him (Acts xxviii. 24–28). The general attitude of heathenism was believing; that of

30 *Τί οὖν ἐροῦμεν; ὅτι ἔθνη τὰ μὴ διώκοντα δικαιοσύνην κατέλαβεν δικαιοσύνην, δικαιοσύνην δὲ τὴν ἐκ πί-*

Judaism was unbelieving. This state of things, so far as the Jews were concerned, the apostle teaches, was not always to continue (xi. 25–32).

VER. 30. τί οὖν ἐροῦμεν] "What, then, is to be inferred," from the statements in verses 6–29. Compare viii. 31; xi. 7. ἔθνη] is anarthrous, to denote not the heathen without exception, but some of the heathen. μὴ διώκοντα] the figure of a race, as in Phil. iii. 12. There was no strenuous pursuit, in paganism, after conformity to law, and the happiness resulting from it. Paganism was sunk in sin, in the manner described in i. 18–32, and had no hope of a blessed immortality (Eph. ii. 2, 3, 11, 12). δικαιοσύνην] is anarthrous, and denotes here, subjective righteousness, or personal obedience of the law. Compare vi. 13, 16, 18–20. The moral perfection required by the law was not an object aimed at by the Gentile. κατέλαβεν] to lay hold upon, or acquire. Phil. iii. 12, 13. Though the Gentile did not seek righteousness, yet he got it. δικαιοσύνην] has the same subjective signification as in the preceding instance, *but is followed by an explanation.* δικαιοσύνην δὲ] St. Paul now explains how the Gentile obtained a righteousness that he did not "run after," and of what sort it is. It was the "righteousness without works," and came to him through that electing act of God which has been described. God called him, and faith in Christ's ἱλαστήριον was the consequence (viii. 30). In this way he laid hold upon a righteousness that was *equivalent* to the perfect subjective righteousness required by the moral law, though not identical with it. This difference and equivalency is marked by the adversative particle δὲ, and the explanatory clause τὴν ἐκ πίστεως: showing that the righteousness here specified is not the same in kind with that denoted by δικαιοσύνην in the two

στεως, 31 *Ἰσραὴλ δὲ διώκων νόμον δικαιοσύνης εἰς νόμον*
οὐκ ἔφθασεν. 32 *διατί; ὅτι οὐκ ἐκ πίστεως, ἀλλ᾽ ὡς ἐξ*

previous instances. See the comment on the same particle, and qualifying clause, in iii. 22. The substance of the whole statement in this verse is, that the Gentiles who did not pursue after inherent righteousness, obtained, by God's electing compassion, imputed righteousness; they who did not attempt to earn salvation, had it given to them outright.

VER. 31 is a continuation of the sentence begun in verse 30. δὲ] is adversative, showing that the Jews did, and obtained, exactly the opposite of what the Gentiles did, and obtained. νόμον δικαιοσύνης] 1. for δικαιοσύνην νόμου, by Hebraistic transposition: Acts v. 20, Rom. vii. 24 (Chrysost., Theodoret, Calvin, Beza, Bengel). 2. the genitive of authorship: "a law that justifies" (Tholuck, Rückert, Meyer, Philippi). 3. νόμον δικαιοσύνης in the first instance, is the Mosaic moral law, and in the second, is the law of faith, iii. 27 (Flatt, De Wette). The first of these interpretations is preferable. The δικαιοσύνη νόμου is the perfect personal righteousness prescribed and required by the law, and is the same as the δικαιοσύνη of verse 30. The Jews pursued after this, and did not obtain it. The Gentiles did not pursue after this, and obtained its *equivalent.* εἰς νομον] (without δικαιοσύνης) is the reading of ℵABDE Copt., Lachm., Tisch., Tregelles. The Peshito, Vulgate, Receptus, KL add δικαιοσύνης. It is implied, even if not expressed; because the same thing is meant, as in the preceding clause. The repetition is for the sake of emphasis. ἔφθασεν] is equivalent to κατέλαβεν, in verse 30. It denotes acquisition or attainment. Compare Phil. iii. 16.

VER. 32. Assigns the reason why the Jews did not lay hold upon and obtain the perfect righteousness required by the law: viz., because they adopted the method of works.

ἔργων· προσέκοψαν γὰρ τῷ λίθῳ τοῦ προσκόμματος,
33 *καθὼς γέγραπται Ἰδοὺ τίθημι ἐν Σιὼν λίθον προσκόμ-*
ματος καὶ πέτραν σκανδάλου, καὶ ὁ πιστεύων ἐπ' αὐτῷ οὐ
καταισχυνθήσεται.

This method, as St. Paul has abundantly shown, fails in the case of sinful man, 1. because there is no expiation of sin; 2. there is no inward and spiritual obedience of the law. Neither justification nor sanctification are possible, if they are "sought not by faith, but by the works of the law." διατί] sc. εἰς νόμον δικαιοσύνης οὐκ ἔφθασεν. ἐκ πίστεως] sc. ἐδίωξαν νόμον δικαιοσύνης. The Jews could have obtained the righteousness required by the law, by exercising faith in Christ. ἀλλ'] sc. ἐδίωξαν. ὡς] They pursued after the righteousness, "as if" it could be obtained in this way. Compare 2 Cor. iii. 5. γὰρ] introduces a proof of the preceding statement, drawn from an actual fact in the history of the Jews. λίθῳ] a figure for Christ *crucified:* the doctrine of vicarious atonement, the nucleus of this Epistle, is specially meant. The history of the Christian religion shows that this is the most offensive to human pride of all the Christian dogmas. See Luke ii. 34; 1 Cor. i. 23. The figure of stumbling agrees well with the previous use of διώκειν.

Ver. 33. This stumbling was foretold by Isaiah (viii. 14; xxviii. 16). The two verses are blended: "God declares that he would be to the people of Judah and of Israel, for a rock of offence, at which they should stumble and fall. Since Christ is that God who spoke by the prophets, this prophecy is fulfilled in Christ" (Calvin, in loco). Compare 1 Pet. ii. 6–8. καταισχυνθήσεται] is the Septuagint rendering of יָחִישׁ (= to flee, from fear). "This is subjoined for the consolation of the godly; as though he had said: Because Christ is called the stone of stumbling, there is no reason that we should dread him; for he is appointed for life to believers" (Calvin, in loco). Compare v. 5.

The 32d verse is a highly important one, because it brings to notice *the difference between election and reprobation.* According to the preceding statements of St. Paul, men are elected, and saving faith in Christ is the consequence. Election does not presuppose faith. There is no faith prior to the electing act of God, and consequently faith must be produced by this act. Faith is the gift of God (Eph. ii. 8). Hence faith is only the secondary instrumental cause of salvation. But, in the 32d verse, man's unbelief and rejection of Christ is assigned as the primary and efficient cause of perdition, and, consequently, the divine act of reprobation as the secondary and occasional cause. In the instance of reprobation, there is unbelief *already existing;* for reprobation supposes the existence of sin. Consequently, the reprobating act does not (like the electing act) *originate* any new moral quality in the man. It merely lets an existing quality, viz.: unbelief, continue. Reprobation is, therefore, not the efficient and guilty cause of perdition, but only the occasional and innocent cause of it. St. Paul repeats the same truth in xi. 20: "Well: because of *unbelief* they were broken off."

The facts, then, in St. Paul's theory of reprobation are as follows: God does nothing to save the non-elect sinner. His action is inaction. God passes the man by, in the bestowment of regenerating grace. He has a right to do so, because he does not owe this grace to any man. The divine inaction, or preterition, is the occasional cause of the sinner's perdition: the efficient cause being the obstinate self-determination of the human will; as a man's doing nothing to prevent a stone from falling, is the occasional cause of its fall, the efficient cause being gravitation. If this self-determination in sin were superable by the human will itself, the inaction of God in reprobation would not make the man's perdition certain. Although God had decided to do nothing to save him, he might save himself. But this obstinate self-determination to evil is insuperable by the human will (John viii. 34; Rom. viii. 7). Consequently, mere inaction, or doing nothing, on the part of God, results in an everlasting self-determination to sin, on the part of man. The doctrine of reprobation is necessarily connected with that of self-originated sin, and bondage in sin. Viewed in this connection, there is no foundation for the charge of fatalism, frequently made by anti-predestinarian exegetes, of which the following extract from Meyer (in loco) is an example. "The contents of Rom. ix. 6–29, in themselves considered, certainly exclude the notion of a divine decree that is conditioned by the self-determination of the human will, or of an absolute agency of God that depends upon that of the individual man; but, at the same time, they equally exclude the fatalistic determinism, the *tremendum mysterium* of Calvin, which, as Augustine's theory had previously done, robs man of his self-determination and freedom in respect to salvation, and makes him the passive object of the arbitrary and absolute will of God."

God is the author of salvation, because he elects; but he is not the author of perdition, because he reprobates. In the first instance, he is efficiently active, by his Spirit and word; in the second instance, he is permissively inactive. If John Doe throw himself into the water, and is rescued by Richard Roe, the statement would be that he is saved because Richard Roe rescued him. But if John Doe throw himself into the water and is not rescued by Richard Roe, the verdict of the coroner would be suicide, and not homicide: "Drowned because he threw himself in," and not: "Drowned, because Richard Roe did not pull him out." Compare Hosea xiii. 9.

CHAPTER X

1 Ἀδελφοί, ἡ μὲν εὐδοκία τῆς ἐμῆς καρδίας καὶ ἡ δέη-
σις πρὸς τὸν θεὸν ὑπὲρ αὐτῶν εἰς σωτηρίαν. 2 μαρτυρῶ

St. Paul, in this chapter, enters into an examination of the reason mentioned in ix. 32 why the Jews did "not attain to the righteousness of the law:" viz., because they sought it through their own personal obedience (ἐξ ἔργων), and not by trust in Christ's vicarious obedience (ἐκ πίστεως). The Apostle proves, chiefly by Old Testament citations, that the efficient and meritorious cause of the perdition of the Jews was their unbelief in, and rejection of Christ, the promised Messiah and Redeemer.

Ver. 1. St. Paul repeats his assurance of deep interest in the Jews. Compare ix. 1–5. εὐδοκία] does not, primarily, denote desire (Chrysost., Theodoret, De Wette, Olshausen), but kindness and compassion (Augustine: bona voluntas; Calvin: benevolentia; Meyer). Compare Eph. i. 5; Phil. i. 15; ii. 13. It is the word which designates the feeling in God that prompts his election of individual sinners. See comment on ix. 13. St. Paul has the same benevolent compassion for his unbelieving Christ-rejecting brethren "according to the flesh." δέησις] the compassion prompts the prayer, which is a desire. Bengel remarks: "Non orasset Paulus, si absolute reprobati essent." This would be true, provided the fact of their absolute reprobation had been *revealed* to Paul. In this case, prayer would be forbidden, as it is in the case of

γὰρ αὐτοῖς ὅτι ζῆλον θεοῦ ἔχουσιν, ἀλλ' οὐ κατ' ἐπίγνω-
σιν· [3] ἀγνοοῦντες γὰρ τήν τοῦ θεοῦ δικαιοσύνην, καὶ τὴν
ἰδίαν δικαιοσύνην ζητοῦντες στῆσαι, τῇ δικαιοσύνῃ τοῦ

the "sin unto death" (1 John v. 16). But as no such revelation had been made, the Apostle's prayer would have been natural and proper, even though it were a fact in the divine mind that the subjects of the prayer were reprobated. The divine decree is not the guide of human supplication, but the benevolent feeling of the pious heart. Since no man knows what the divine decree is, and who the reprobate are, the prayer for the salvation of men must be indiscriminate, and for all without exception. Moreover, there is no alternative but to pray either for all men, or for none. In his ignorance of the divine purpose, the Christian, must pray for all, in order to pray for any. αὐτῶν] instead of τοῦ Ἰσραήλ, is the reading of ℵABDEF Peshito, Vulg., Coptic, Lachm., Tisch. εἰς σωτηρίαν] denotes the end aimed at in the prayer.

VER. 2 gives the reason, introduced by γὰρ, for the compassion and the prayer. θεοῦ] the genitive of the object: "for God." Compare John ii. 17; Acts xxi. 20; xxii. 3; Gal. i. 14. As examples of false zeal for God, see John xvi. 2; Acts xxvi. 9–11. ἐπίγνωσιν] the preposition is intensive (i. 32): the zeal was not founded upon a clear and discriminating knowledge.

VER. 3 explains the clause, οὐ κατ' ἐπίγνωσιν. ἀγνοοῦντες] 1. to misconceive: implying some knowledge that is vitiated by the fault of the person, as in ii. 4; 1 Cor. xiv. 38 (Wolfius, De Wette, Tholuck, Lange). 2. to be entirely ignorant of (Meyer). The first is the true explanation, as verses 19–21 prove. The Old Testament contains the doctrine of "God's righteousness," in connection with that of the Messiah (iii. 21);

and the Jew was acquainted with it. But he modified and perverted it. Had the Jew been utterly ignorant upon this subject, as the Gentile was, he would not have been chargeable with a greater guilt than that which rests upon the Gentile (ii. 9, 12). At the same time, the unbelief connected with this culpable and inexcusable ignorance is not so intense a form, as that which is accompanied with a clear and conclusive knowledge, such, for example, as is possessed by the lost spirits in perdition. St. Paul mentions this fact, as one reason why he feels as he does toward his Jewish brethren. "He perceived that they had fallen through ignorance, and not through malignancy of mind" (Calvin in loco). Compare Christ's words in Luke xxiii. 34, and St. Paul's statement respecting himself in 1 Tim. i. 13. *θεοῦ δικαιοσύνην*] the genitive of authorship: the gratuitous and imputed righteousness which God bestows. See comment on i. 17; iii. 21. *ἰδίαν δικαιοσύνην*] personal righteousness accruing from actual personal obedience. Compare Phil. iii. 9. It is the same that is meant by *δικαιοσύνην τὴν ἐκ νόμου* in verse 5: the righteousness *ἐξ ἔργων* (ix. 32), as distinguished from the righteousness *χωρὶς ἔργων* (iv. 6). *ζητοῦντες στῆσαι*] they strenuously endeavored to establish, or make valid before the bar of justice and reward, this personal righteousness. The attempt was a failure, for the reason, 1. that there is no *ἱλαστήριον*, no atonement for sin, in such a species of righteousness; and, 2. the obedience itself was not the spiritual and perfect service required by both conscience and the decalogue. The rendering of the English Version: "going about to establish" is felicitous, implying the toilsomeness and futility of the attempt. *ὑπετάγησαν*] middle signification: the gratuitous imputed "righteousness of God" is conceived of as a divine arrangement, or ordinance, to which self-submission is due from every sinful man to whom it is made known. All legal endeavor is hostility to evangelical requirement. He who

θεοῦ οὐχ ὑπετάγησαν. [4] *τέλος γὰρ νόμου Χριστὸς εἰς δικαιοσύνην παντὶ τῷ πιστεύοντι.* [5] *Μωϋσῆς γὰρ γράφει τὴν δικαιοσύνην τὴν ἐκ νόμου, ὅτι ὁ ποιήσας αὐτὰ ἄνθρω-*

would work out a personal righteousness rejects Christ's righteousness. The "worker" excludes the "believer" (iv. 4, 5).

VER. 4 mentions an additional proof, introduced by γὰρ, that the unbelieving Jew had not submitted himself to the "righteousness of God." In rejecting Christ, as prophet, priest and king, he rejected this righteousness. τέλος] is highly emphatic by position: 1. the end in the sense of *termination*, or ceasing to exist and operate: Christ abolished the law, as the means of justification, vi. 14; vii. 4, 6; Eph. ii. 15 (Augustine, Luther, De Wette, Tholuck, Olshausen, Fritzsche, Meyer, Hodge); 2. the end, in the sense of the *aim:* Christ is the goal to which the Old Testament law, both ceremonial and moral, conducts, Gal. iii. 24; Col. ii. 17 (Chrysost., Theodoret, Grotius, Beza, Bengel); 3. the end, in the sense of *fulfilment:* Christ vicariously meets all the requirements of the law, both as penalty and precept, xiii. 10; 1 Tim. i. 5 (Origen, Erasmus, Calvin, Calovius, Wolfius). As the statement relates to Christ, the centre and substance of the Gospel, all of these explanations may be combined. Christ is the τέλος, in each and every sense here mentioned. If a single explanation is to be adopted, the last is preferable, as agreeing with the tenor of the Epistle. The passages cited above show that St. Paul sometimes uses τέλος in the sense of πλήρωμα. See, also, Mat. v. 17. εἰς δικαιοσύνην] the purpose of Christ's fulfilment of the law: viz., that the believer might be δίκαιος in every respect before the divine law. τῷ πιστεύοντι] is emphatic, and qualifies παντὶ: not every man without exception, but every believing man.

VER. 5 begins the proof from the Old Testament, that salvation is by faith in Christ's vicarious obedience, and not by man's personal obedience. γράφει] writes of, or describes. ὅτι] is recitative. The citation is from the Septuagint rendering of Lev. xviii. 5. Compare Nehem. ix. 29; Ezek. xx. 21; Gal. iii. 12. The "righteousness which is of the law" is the same as "their own righteousness," in verse 3. ποιήσας] denotes *perfect* obedience, external and internal, like ἐργαζόμένος in iv. 4. See comment. αὐτὰ] is omitted by ℵADE, Vulg., Coptic, Tisch.; is supported by BFGL, Sept., Peshito, Recept., Lachm. αὐτῇ] is the reading of ℵAB Vulg., Coptic, Lachm., Tisch., Tregelles; αὐτοῖς is that of Sept., DEFL Peshito, Receptus. The first refers to the righteousness; the latter, to the "statutes and judgments" mentioned in the passage in Leviticus.

VER. 6 begins another quotation from Moses (Deut. xxx. 11–14), the purpose of which is to describe the "righteousness of faith," as the opposite of the "righteousness which is of the law." The apostle substitutes "righteousness of faith" for "commandment," in the original passage (because the latter term is used *comprehensively*, of the *whole* doctrine of God which Moses was inspired to teach), and, personifying it, represents it as describing the way of life. Several views are taken. 1. The original passage is Messianic. Moses is here prophetically describing the evangelical righteousness by faith in the Messiah; as in Leviticus xviii. 5 (quoted in verse 5) he describes the legal righteousness, or that of perfect personal obedience (Calvin, Pareus, Olshausen, Fritzsche, Reiche). 2. St. Paul accommodates or adapts the language of Moses, which primarily refers only to the law and legal righteousness, to the gospel and evangelical righteousness (Chrysost., Luther, Beza, Rosenmüller, Tholuck, Rückert, Hodge). 3. The Apostle allegorizes the

passage, and somewhat violently wrests it from its original meaning, which has no connection with the doctrine of justification by faith (De Wette, Meyer). The first view agrees best with the nature of the argument, which endeavors to prove the doctrine of justification from the Old Testament. Unless the words of Moses really teach this doctrine, the citation is logically worthless. That Moses understood and taught the gospel as well as the law, is proved by Luke xxiv. 27; John v. 46; Acts iii. 22–26; xxvi. 22, 23; Rom. iii. 21. He also taught all that Abraham understood and taught; and Abraham, the apostle has already shown, was divinely instructed respecting justification by faith (iv. 1–22). "Moses is speaking not concerning the law alone, but concerning the *whole* doctrine which he was inspired and commanded to teach to the children of Israel. This was not legal merely and only, but comprehended, also, evangelical truths and promises. He exhorts the people to observe his teaching (which he designates by two words: מִצְוָה, commandment, and חֻקָּה, statute), because it was not secret, and difficult to be understood, but plain and clear. But this alone would not make the legal commandment *easy to be obeyed.* The gracious promise of mercy and help from God must be connected with it, in order to this. The gospel was associated with the law, in the doctrine of Moses viewed as a system of truth, and an entire whole. God promises to circumcise the heart of his people, and of their seed, that they may love the Lord their God with all their heart and soul, and that they may live (Deut. xxx. 6). This association of law with grace is seen clearly in the ritual and ceremonial part of the Mosaic institute. And it is indicated in the passage quoted by St. Paul, by the words, 'In thy mouth, and in thy heart.' As law, the doctrine of Moses was in the mouth; as grace it was in the heart." Pareus in loco. Similarly, Calvin remarks (in loco), "If Moses spake of the law only, it had been

πος ζήσεται ἐν αὐτῇ. [6] ἡ δὲ ἐκ πίστεως δικαιοσύνη οὕτως λέγει· Μὴ εἴπῃς ἐν τῇ καρδίᾳ σου Τίς ἀναβήσεται εἰς τὸν οὐρανόν; τοῦτ' ἔττιν Χριστὸν καταγαγεῖν· [7] ἢ Τίς καταβήσεται εἰς τὴν ἄβυσσον; τοῦτ' ἔστιν Χριστὸν ἐκ νεκρῶν ἀναγαγεῖν. [8] ἀλλὰ τί λέγει; Ἐγγύς σου τὸ ῥῆμά ἐστιν,

a frivolous argument; since the law of God is no more easy to be done when it is put before our eyes, than when it is set at a distance. Therefore he means not the law only, but all the doctrine of God, which comprehends the Gospel under it." This interpretation agrees with the statement in the opening of the Epistle (i. 2), that God, in the Old Testament, "pre-announced the gospel concerning his Son Jesus Christ, by his prophets." εἴπῃς ἐν τῇ καρδίᾳ] to speak inwardly is, to think, Ps. xiv. 1; Mat. iii. 9. Thought is internal language; and language is external thought. Thought and language are two modes of the same thing. τίσ ἀναβήσεται] the question of unbelief, regarding the incarnation: as if Christ had not already come upon earth. St. Paul does not here, or in the succeeding verses, conform exactly to the original phraseology, because he is quoting ad sensum. He indicates this, by not introducing the quotation by the usual formula, Μωϋσῆς γράφει (ver. 5), or λέγει ἡ γραφὴ (ix. 17).

VER. 7. τίς καταβήσεται] a second question of unbelief, regarding the resurrection: as if Christ had not risen from the dead. ἄβυσσον] the equivalent of Sheol, and Hades, when these are used in the sense of the grave (Gen. xxxvii. 35; Ps. xlix. 15; Acts ii. 27, 31); and not in the sense of a place of retributive torment (Deut. xxxii. 22; Job. xxi. 13; Ps. ix. 17; Prob. v. 5; Mat. xi. 23; xvi. 18; Luke xvi. 22–26; Rev. i. 18; iii. 7; xx. 13, 14). τοῦτ' ἔστιν, etc.] the clause explains the meaning of the descent into the abyss.

VER. 8. ἀλλὰ τί λέγει] sc. ἡ δικαιοσύνη πίστεως. The utter-

ἐν τῷ στόματί σου καὶ ἐν τῇ καρδίᾳ σου· τοῦτ' ἔστιν τὸ ῥῆμα τῆς πίστεως ὃ κηρύσσομεν. [9] ὅτι ἐὰν ὁμολογήσῃς

ance of the righteousness of faith is directly contrary to what the unbeliever "says in his heart." Unbelief raises objections and makes difficulties; faith gets rid of them in a mass, by resting in the omnipotence of God as promised and pledged in Christ. Its utterance is that of the Apostle before Agrippa: "Why should it be thought a thing incredible, that *God* should raise the dead?" (Acts xxvi. 8). ἐγγύς] is strongly emphatic, by position. To obtain eternal life by laying hold upon a perfect righteousness close at hand, like that of Christ, is a far shorter and nearer way than to pursue after it (διώκειν, ix. 30), up and down through all space, in a prolonged and wearing personal effort that is baffled at every point, and proves in the end to have been utterly worthless and useless for the purpose aimed at. ἐν τῷ στόματί, etc.] the clause explains ἐγγύς. The revealed doctrine, or fact (ῥῆμά), of the righteousness of faith, is in its own nature both theoretic and practical, truth and life (John vi. 63). Hence, it is not merely a word in the mouth, but a principle in the heart. As such, it is as nigh and close to man, as his own consciousness itself. πίστεως] is the genitive of the object, and explains the nature of the word, or doctrine, taught by Moses, and re-affirmed by St. Paul. It is addressed to faith, and requires faith. Under the old economy, this faith was trust in the divine Redeemer as revealed to Adam and Abraham in the "Seed of the Woman;" and to Moses and the Prophets in the Messiah. Under the new economy, it is trust in Jesus Christ. κηρύσσομεν] denotes a public proclamation: the plural refers to the apostles and evangelists, and the ministry generally.

VER. 9. ὅτι] 1. is explanatory, denoting the purport of

ἐν τῷ στόματί σου κύριον Ἰησοῦν, καὶ πιστεύσῃς ἐν τῇ καρδίᾳ σου ὅτι ὁ θεὸς αὐτὸν ἤγειρεν ἐκ νεκρῶν, σωθήσῃ·

the ῥῆμα (Vulgate, Eng. Ver., Beza). 2. is logical, giving a proof: "because" (Tholuck, De Wette, Meyer, Stuart, Alford). The last is preferable, because the subject-matter of the doctrine or word preached, is not the subjective act of faith and confession, but the objective suffering and obedience of Christ. The preacher's great theme is Christ himself, and not the believer's trust in him. ὁμολογήσῃς] public confession before men, Mat. x. 32, 33; xvi. 16–19; 1 Tim. vi. 13. στόματι] corresponds with στόματι in verse 8: the "word" must be "in the mouth." κύριον] is a predicate: "as Lord;" there is a reference to ἀναβήσεται, in verse 6. The ascension of Christ into heaven implies his original divinity, and descent from heaven. The word κύριος is the Septuagint rendering of Jehovah, and any Jew who publicly confessed that Jesus of Nazareth was "Lord," would be understood to ascribe the divine nature and attributes to him. It is also the Old Testament term for the Son of God, and the Messiah; and when Christ himself asserted that he was the Son of God, and the Messiah, he was charged with blasphemy (Mat. xxvii. 63–66), and with equalizing himself with God (John xi. 24, 30, 33). πιστεύσῃς] denotes that inward act which is outwardly confessed: faith is the "word in the heart," antithetic to confession, which is the "word in the mouth" (verse 8). Faith and confession are two modes of the same thing: viz., the new divine life in the soul. Christian confession is as truly a gracious and holy act, as Christian faith. Hence the two are inseparable. There is no genuine faith if there is an aversion and unwillingness to confess faith. A man who is ashamed of Christ does not savingly believe in him. There may be saving faith when, owing to providential reasons, it is impossible to confess it publicly; but in this case there is

10 καρδίᾳ γὰρ πιστεύεται εἰς δικαιοσύνην, στόματι δὲ ὁμο-
λογεῖται εἰς σωτηρίαν. 11 λέγει γὰρ ἡ γραφή Πᾶς ὁ πι-

a *desire* to confess the faith of the heart, and the desire is the will, and the will, in the sight of God, is the deed (2 Cor. viii. 12). καρδίᾳ] corresponds with καρδίᾳ in verse 8. ἤγειρεν] looks back to καταβήσεται in verse 7. Faith has special reference to the atoning death, and triumphant resurrection of Jesus the Lord. σωθήσῃ] corresponds to ζήσεται, in verse 5. The salvation obtained under the gospel, is equivalent to the life that would have been obtained under the law, had man perfectly kept the law.

VER. 10 is an emphatic repetition of the necessity of confession and faith, in order to salvation. The order is now reversed, because this is the true order: faith being the root, confession the branch, Mat. xii. 34; 2 Cor. iv. 13. St. Paul, in the preceding statement, had followed the order of Moses. πιστεύεται] the passive is employed for the sake of abstract universality. δικαιοσύνην] "righteousness without works," or gratuitous justification. σωτηρίαν] is the result and issue of justification. The meaning, of course, is not that faith is the instrumental cause of justification, and confession that of salvation. This is to divide the indivisible. Salvation supposes justification, and confession supposes faith. Each, therefore, may stand for the other. St. Paul could have said: "With the heart, faith is exercised unto salvation, and with the mouth, confession is made unto justification;" because sincere confession is meant, and this implies faith.

VER. 11 contains another citation from the Old Testament (Isa. xxviii. 16) in the Septuagint version, in proof that faith is a saving act. The passage has already been quoted, in ix. 33. πᾶς] is not in the Hebrew, or the Septuagint, but is implied in ὁ πιστεύων. αὐτῷ] refers to Christ, in

στεύων ἐπ' αὐτῷ οὐ καταισχυνθήσεται. [12] *οὐ γὰρ ἐστιν διαστολὴ Ἰουδαίου τε καὶ Ἕλληνος· ὁ γὰρ αὐτὸς κύριος πάντων, πλουτῶν εἰς παντας τοὺς ἐπικαλουμένους αὐτόν.* [13] *Πᾶς γὰρ ὃς ἂν ἐπικαλέσηται τὸ ὄνομα κυρίου σωθή-*

St. Paul's application of the passage. The original justifies this application; for, the "precious corner stone" there spoken of is the Messiah. See Mat. xxi. 42. καταισχυνθήσεται] See comment on v. 5.

VER. 12 explains πᾶς in the preceding verse. οὐ διαστολὴ] No difference, i. e., in respect to salvation by faith and confession. Compare iii. 22. ὁ αὐτὸς] is the subject, and κύριος the predicate (Meyer). De Wette regards ὁ αὐτὸς κύριος as the subject, as in the English Version. The term κύριος refers to Christ (Origen, Chrysost., Wolfius, Bengel, Tholuck, De Wette, Rückert, Fritzsche, Meyer, Philippi). It is referred to God, by Theodoret, Theophyl., Pareus, Grotius, Ammon, Reiche, Umbreit. The first is best, as the Apostle speaks of Christ in both the preceding and following verses. "Christ, according to Phil. ii. 11, is a Being who is to be worshipped as Lord of all; to whom ἐπικαλεῖσθαι is referred in 1 Cor. i. 2, Acts ii. 21, ix. 14, xxii. 16; and to whom χάρις is ascribed in Rom. i. 5, v. 15, 2 Cor. xiii. 13." (De Wette, in loco.) Meyer adopts the Arian distinction between calling upon God the Father as God in the absolute sense, and upon Christ as the mediator between the Father and man. πλουτῶν] is a term descriptive of the divine fulness, which is attributed to Christ, in Coloss. ii. 9. Compare Rom. v. 15; Eph. iii. 8. εἰς] "towards," or "in reference to."

VER. 13. A quotation (without λέγει ἡ γραφή) from Joel ii. 32, according to the Septuagint. γαρ] does not belong to the citation, but introduces it. The sentiment is kindred to that of verse 11. He who believes in Christ shall not be dis-

σεται. [14] πῶς οὖν ἐπικαλέσωνται εἰς ὃν οὐκ ἐπίστευσαν;
πῶς δὲ πιστεύσωσιν οὗ οὐκ ἤκουσαν; πῶς δὲ ἀκούσονται
χωρὶς κηρύσσοντος; [15] πῶς δὲ κηρύξωσιν ἐὰν μὴ ἀποστα-
λῶσιν; καθὼς γέγραπται Ὡς ὡραῖοι οἱ πόδες τῶν εὐαγ-

appointed; and he who calls upon Christ shall be saved. Faith and prayer are cognate acts. Prayer to Christ for mercy and salvation is an act by which faith in Christ shows itself. The deity of Christ is implied in the fact that he is the Being upon whom universal man must call, in prayer, for eternal salvation.

VER. 14. The assertion that men must universally supplicate Christ for salvation, suggests the necessity of universally preaching Christ, in order to this. Hence, the gospel requires the Christian ministry. οὖν] a deduction from verse 13. ἐπικαλέσωνται] (ἐπικαλέσονται, Rec.) has the same subject as ἐπικαλέσηται, in verse 13, viz.: Jews and Greeks indiscriminately. κηρύσσοντος] public and official proclamation. The Christian herald was called and set apart for ministerial service, i. 1, 5; Acts xiii. 3; 1 Tim. iv. 14.

VER. 15. κηρύξωσιν] is the reading of ℵABDEL Lachm., Tisch., Tregelles. The Receptus has κηρύξουσιν. The notion of possibility is denoted more strongly by the aorist subjunctive, than by the future indicative: "How can they preach." ἀποσταλῶσιν] namely, by Christ, by whose command they preach (ver. 17). γέγραπται] in Isa. lii. 7. The citation is given freely from the Septuagint. The original is a prophecy concerning the whole future of Messiah's kingdom. This includes all the temporal deliverances of God's people; but these are only secondary to the spiritual deliverance. The return from the Babylonian exile, to which there may be a reference, is only symbolical of something far greater, to which St. Paul here refers it. The messengers who announce the

γελιζομένων [εἰρήνην, τῶν εὐαγγελιζομένων] τὰ ἀγαθά.
16 ἀλλ' οὐ πάντες ὑπήκουσαν τῷ εὐαγγελίῳ. Ἠσαΐας γὰρ
λέγει Κύριε, τίς ἐπίστευσεν τῇ ἀκοῇ ἡμῶν;

good news of the end of the earthly captivity, are typical of the gospel messengers. ὡραῖοι] timely, or seasonable (ὥρα). Compare Eccl. iii. 11. As the essence of beauty is proportion and exact adjustment, the rendering of the English Version ("beautiful") is correct. The words in brackets are wanting in ℵABC Sahid., Coptic, Æthiopic, Lachm., Tisch., Tregelles; and found in DEFL Vulgate, Peshito, Receptus. εἰρήνην and ἀγαθά] denote the spiritual peace, and benefits of the gospel.

Ver. 16 directs attention to the fact that notwithstanding there is this universal proclamation of the gospel, there is not a universal belief of the gospel. The apostle does not permit his reader to lose sight of man's unbelief, and hardness of heart. 'αλλ'] "although messengers were sent to preach, *yet*," etc. Compare v. 14. πάντες] refers to both Jews and Gentiles; because the prophet Isaiah, whom he cites, speaks of the gospel in relation to the entire world of mankind. The previous discussion of election and reprobation has likewise shown that there are believers and unbelievers among both Jews and Greeks. ὑπήκουσαν] denotes willing subjection, and not merely the assent of the understanding. Compare vi. 17; 2 Thess. i. 8. The aorist is historical: they did not obey, during the preaching, i. e. (Alford). γὰρ] introduces the proof from Isaiah liii. 1. St. John (xii. 38) quotes the same passage as descriptive of the reception which Christ's preaching met with. In the complaint of the prophet concerning the unbelief of the Jews of his day, the apostle finds a prophesy of the unbelief of both Jews and Gentiles in the latter day. ἀκοῇ] that which is heard: the

17 *ἄρα ἡ πίστις ἐξ ἀκοῆς, ἡ δὲ ἀκοὴ διὰ ῥήματος Χριστοῦ.*

"message." Yet, not the abstract message; but the message as preached and heard.

VER. 17 is a summary recapitulation, introduced by ἄρα ("accordingly"), of what has been said in verses 14–16. The line of remark, in these verses, shows that saving faith depends upon the knowledge of gospel truth; and the universal knowledge of this truth among mankind depends upon Christ's appointment of a ministry to preach it. ἀκοῆς] not the act of hearing (Rückert, De Wette, Philippi), but the thing heard: the message as proclaimed, as in verse 16 (Tholuck, Meyer, Hodge). The act itself of hearing, if it were believing hearing, would be the same as faith; and if it were unbelieving hearing, then faith could not be said to "come" by means of it. ῥήματος Χριστοῦ] is the reading of ℵBCDE Vulgate, Sahidic, Coptic, Lachm., Tisch., Tregelles. The Receptus AL, Peshito, read θεοῦ. 1. The "revelation" of Christ, in the subjective sense of the act of revealing. The gospel message (ἀκοη), as contained in both the Old and New Testaments, is the product of divine inspiration (Calvin, Tholuck). 2. The "commission," or command of Christ, Mat. xxviii. 19; Acts i. 8; Eph. iv. 8, 11 (Beza, Meyer, Hodge). The last is preferable, particularly if Χριστοῦ be adopted as the reading. That ρημα has this signification, is seen in Luke iii. 2. It is also favored by the immediately preceding context, which has spoken of the sending and hearing of gospel messengers. "Accordingly, then, faith cometh through the truth as preached; and the truth is preached by the command of Christ." If θεοῦ be adopted, there would be more reason for the first explanation of ῥήματος; and the meaning would be: "Faith cometh through the truth; and the truth by the inspiration of God."

18 *ἀλλὰ λέγω, μὴ οὐκ ἤκουσαν; μενοῦνγε Εἰς πᾶσαν τὴν γῆν ἐξῆλθεν ὁ φθόγγος αὐτῶν, καὶ εἰς τὰ πέρατα τῆς οἰκου-*

VER. 18 mentions a possible excuse for unbelieving men generally, viz., that some of them may have been excluded by God, like the heathen under the old economy, from hearing the gospel message, and gives the refutation of it. ἀλλὰ] "although faith cometh, etc., *yet.*" Compare ver. 16. λέγω] the Apostle himself suggests the excuse. ἤκουσαν] sc. τὴν ἀκοην. The subject of the verb is not merely the Jews (Tholuck, Meyer, Philippi), but the Gentiles also (Calvin, Fritzsche, Hodge). See the explanation of πάντες in verse 16. μενοῦνγε] not in irony, as in ix. 20, but in emphatic earnest. φθόγγος] is the vibration of a musical string. αὐτῶν] refers to the preachers who have been sent forth διὰ ῥήματος Χριστοῦ. The extract is from the Septuagint of Ps. xviii. 5 (Eng. Ver., xix. 4). St. Paul accommodates a passage which refers originally to natural religion, to revealed religion. He does not introduce it by the usual formula, λέγει ἡ γραφή. πέρατα] the "frontiers." ῥήματα αὐτῶν] is the same thing that is denoted by ἀκοῇ ἡμῶν in verse 16. St. Paul could say, in his day, that the gospel had had a universal proclamation, and "was preached to every creature which is under heaven" (Coloss. i. 23), in the same sense that the preacher of the present day can say it. The separating wall between Jew and Gentile had been broken down, Christianity was for the whole human race, and Christ's ῥῆμα was: "Go preach to every creature." If the fact that many nations and peoples had not actually heard the preacher's voice, was a reason why he should refrain from saying that Christianity is the religion of universal man, it is a reason why the modern preacher should refrain from saying it. The Apostle replies to the suggestion, that unbelief may be excusable because some may be excluded by divine arrangements from hearing it, that the

μένης τα ῥήματα αὐτῶν. [19] *ἀλλὰ λέγω, μὴ Ἰσραὴλ οὐκ ἔγνω; πρῶτος Μωϋσῆς λέγει Ἐγὼ παραζηλώσω ὑμᾶς ἐπ'*

gospel is as wide and all-embracing as the race. Compare Coloss. i. 6. Calvin's explanation is as follows: "God from the beginning manifested his divinity to the Gentiles, though not by the preaching of men, yet by the testimony of creation. For though the gospel was then silent among them, yet the whole workmanship of heaven and earth did speak, and make known its author by its preaching. It hence appears, that the Lord, even during the time in which he conferred the favor of his covenant to Israel, did not yet so withdraw from the Gentiles the knowledge of himself, but that he ever kept alive some sparks of it among them. He indeed manifested himself more particularly to his chosen people, so that the Jews might be justly compared to domestic hearers, whom he familiarly taught as it were by his own mouth; yet as he spoke to the Gentiles at a distance by the voice of the heavens, he showed by this prelude that he designed to make himself known, at length, to them also."

VER. 19 mentions a second possible excuse for the unbelieving Jews: viz., that they may have been ignorant of the fact that the gospel was intended for the heathen, and finding that God was extending it to them might infer that he had revoked his previous covenant with Abraham and his seed. This excuse is refuted by Scripture citations, which show that the original promise to Abraham included "all the nations of the earth" (Gen. xxii. 18). ἀλλὰ] See comment on verse 18. λέγω] as in verse 18. Ἰσραὴλ] this alleged excuse does not apply to men universally, but only to the Jews. ἔγνω] 1. "Did not the Jews know the gospel?" (Chrysost., Calvin, Beza, Philippi). 2. "Did not the Jews know that they were to be rejected?" The connection, in this case, is

οὐκ ἔθνει, ἐπ' ἔθνει ἀσυνέτῳ παροργιῶ ὑμᾶς. 20 *Ἠσαΐας*
δὲ ἀποτολμᾷ καὶ λέγει Εὑρέθην τοῖς ἐμὲ μὴ ζητοῦσιν,

with the thought in verse 21 (Aquinas, Pareus, Rosenmüller, Tholuck, Stuart, Hodge). 3. "Did not the Jews know that the promise to Abraham was universal in its nature?" (Fritzsche, De Wette, Meyer, Alford). The last explanation is preferable, because it is closely connected with the immediately preceding and following citations from the Old Testament. πρῶτος] Moses is first in the list of witnesses. λέγει] the quotation is from Deut. xxxii. 21, almost verbatim from the Septuagint. God threatened the Israelites, on account of their idolatry, that he would show favor to the Canaanites, and thereby excite their jealousy, as they, by their idolatry, had awakened his. St. Paul explains this as typical of the blessing of the Gentiles, and the displeasure of the Jews therewith. παραζηλώσω] emulation is the general conception in the word, as in xi. 11, 14 (Schleusner, in voce). This may assume the form of jealousy, as here, and in the passage in Deuteronomy; or of anger, as in 1 Cor. x. 22. ἐπ'] "over," or "on account of." οὐκ ἔθνει] לֹא עָם: "a no-people." See the explanation of οὐ λαόν, in ix. 25. Only God's people come up to the idea of a people in the full sense. Compare 1 Pet. ii. 10. ἀσυνέτῳ] the folly of idolatry is meant. Compare i. 21, 22.

Ver. 20. δὲ] marks the transition to another witness, but with a somewhat adversative sense. There is a contrast between Moses and Isaiah, in respect to the tone of the testimony. ἀποτολμᾷ] is not adverbial, but has the force of a verb. "He dares to speak out, and tell the whole truth" (Theophylact). Compare κράζει, in ix. 27. The quotation is given freely from the Septuagint of Isa. lxv. 1. The parallel clauses are transposed. The original reference of the prophecy is to the Gen-

ἐμφανὴς ἐγενόμην τοῖς ἐμὲ μὴ ἐπερωτῶσιν. [21] πρὸς δὲ τὸν Ἰσραὴλ λέγει Ὅλην τὴν ἡμέραν ἐξεπέτασα τὰς χεῖράς μου πρὸς λαὸν ἀπειθοῦντα καὶ ἀντιλέγοντα.

tiles. The prophet announces, in verse 1, that God will say, "Behold me," to "a nation not called by his name;" and in verse 2 gives the reason, viz.: the conduct of his "rebellious people." The original reference of the first verse to the Jews themselves, and only its typical reference to the Gentiles, by St. Paul (Meyer and others), implies that Israel could properly be described as a nation that had not been called by the name of Jehovah. See Alexander, in loco.

VER. 21. πρὸς] 1. "against:" adversus (Erasmus, Calvin, Beza, Grotius); 2. "to" (Vulgate, Luther, Rückert, Meyer); 3. "in reference to" (Wolfius, Tholuck, De Wette, Fritzsche, Philippi). The last is best, because in the preceding verse Isaiah has spoken in reference to the Gentiles, and now speaks in another reference, which is marked by δὲ. ἐξεπέτασα] the outstretched arms express the compassion and yearning appeal of God. Compare Prov. i. 24; Ezek. xviii. 31, 32; Hosea xi. 8. ἀπειθοῦντα καὶ ἀντιλέγοντα] the present participle denotes the constant mood and temper. The Jews did not merely oppose, but contradicted. In answer to the compassionate invitation of God, they said: "We will not." Meyer, in loco. Compare Mat. xxiii. 37.

CHAPTER XI

[1] *Λέγω οὖν, μὴ ἀπώσατο ὁ θεὸς τὸν λαὸν αὐτοῦ; μὴ γένοιτο· καὶ γὰρ ἐγὼ Ἰσρηλείτης εἰμί, ἐκ σπέρματος*

In this chapter, St. Paul first proves that the reprobation of the Jews, previously described, is not a *total* reprobation. God has elected and saved some of them; it is only a portion that he has passed by, or "hardened." Verses 1–10. The Apostle, then, in the second place, shows that this reprobation is not a *finality* in and of itself. It is a means to an end, and a part of a benevolent plan. God does not reprobate some of the Jews for the mere sake of reprobating, but as instrumental to the salvation of the Gentiles. And when this end has been attained, then the Jews themselves as a body shall be brought into the church, and "all Israel shall be saved." Verses 10–32.

Ver. 1. λέγω οὖν] looks back, not to the statements in chapter x. respecting the calling of the Gentiles and the universality of the gospel (Meyer and others), but to what the Apostle has said in chapter ix. concerning reprobation, and especially the reprobation of the Jews (Rom. ix. 6–33). The erroneous inference, introduced by οὖν, which he refutes, relates to the harsher and more offensive side of his dogmatic teaching. ἀπώσατο] signifies "to thrust out entirely:" an utter and total rejection, without any exceptions, is meant. Compare Ps. xciv. 13. The Apostle would not have what he has previously said respecting the reprobation of the Jews to

'Αβαάμ, φυλῆς Βενιαμείν. 2 *οὐκ ἀπώσατο ὁ θεὸς τὸν λαὸν αὐτοῦ ὃν προέγνω. ἢ οὐκ οἴδατε ἐν Ἡλίᾳ τί λέγει*

be so understood, as to imply the abrogation of the covenant formerly made with Abraham, and that the Jews were now entirely alienated from the kingdom of God. The reprobation spoken of is only of a portion of the people: "blindness in *part* is happened to Israel" (verse 25). ἐγὼ] Paul had been elected (Acts ix. 15), and this proves that the reprobation was not sweeping and total. 'Ισραηλείτης] a descendant of Jacob and not of Esau. Βενιαμείν] this tribe together with Judah constituted the theocratic people, after the Exile. These particulars demonstrate that the apostle was thoroughly and completely a Jew. Compare Phil. iii. 5.

VER. 2. λαὸν] 1. The spiritual people, as in ix. 6; Gal. vi. 16. (Origen, Aug., Chrys., Luther, Calvin, Pareus, Hodge). 2. The theocratic people (De Wette, Tholuck, Meyer, Philippi, Stuart, Lange, Alford). The last is preferable, because this is the meaning of λαὸν in verse 1, the sentiment of which St. Paul is refuting. He is speaking most commonly in this chapter, of the nation as a whole, out of which, he says, a part are spiritually elected, so that the nation as a whole are not rejected. It would be superfluous, to assert and endeavor to prove that the spiritual people of God are not "thrust out entirely." προέγνω] is used in the Hebrew signification, "to elect," as in viii. 29. The "people" being the theocratic people, the election here meant is the outward call. St. Paul lays stress upon the fact of the external election of the nation, as a proof that there could not have been a spiritual reprobation of *all* the individuals composing it. It is improbable, that having given to the Jews the Mosaic law, moral and ceremonial, together with the Levitical priesthood, and the divine oracles, God would not effectually call any of

ἡ γραφή ; ὡς ἐντυγχάνει τῷ ϑεῷ κατὰ τοῦ Ἰσραήλ, 3 Κύριε, τοὺς προφήτας σου ἀπέκτειναν, τὰ ϑυσιαστήριά σου
κατέσκαψαν, κἀγὼ ὑπελείφϑην μόνος, καὶ ζητοῦσιν τὴν
ψυχήν μου. 4 ἀλλὰ τί λέγει αὐτῷ ὁ χρηματισμός ; Κατέλιπον ἐμαυτῷ ἑπτακισχιλίους ἄνδρας, οἵτινες οὐκ ἔκαμψαν

them. The outward call, in such a case, would be inexplicable. ἢ] "or," in case you are not convinced by this. ἐν Ἡλίᾳ] in the section, or narrative, relating to Elijah. Compare Mark xii. 26. ἐντυγχάνει] signifies to plead either for or against; the preposition κατὰ shows that the latter is intended here: viz.: "to complain of."

Ver. 3. The passage is freely cited from the Septuagint rendering of 1 Kings xix. 10, 14. ἀπέκτειναν] namely, the Israelites by the command of Ahab and Jezebel, 1 Kings xviii. 4, 13, 17. ϑυσιαστήριά] the plural is explained by the fact, that after the revolt from Judah, the ten tribes could not go up to Jerusalem to offer sacrifice, and consequently erected altars for this purpose. This had been forbidden (Lev. xvii. 8, 9; Deut. xii. 13); but when a central and appointed place of sacrifice could not be had, altars upon "high places" were permitted to pious worshippers, 1 Kings iii, 2–4. κατέσκαψαν] "to raze from the ground." μόνος] sc. τῶν προφήτων.

Ver. 4. χρηματισμός] the divine response to the complaint. Compare Mat. ii. 12. It is found in 1 Kings xix. 18, and varies slightly from both the Septuagint and Hebrew. κατέλιπον ἐμαυτῷ] "I have reserved for myself." ἑπταχισχιλίους] "Though this stands for an indefinite number, it was yet the Lord's design to specify a large multitude. Since, then, the grace of God prevails so much in an extreme state of things, let us not lightly give over to the devil all those whose piety

γόνυ τῇ Βάαλ. 5 *οὕτως οὖν καὶ ἐν τῷ νῦν καιρῷ λεῖμμα κατ' ἐκλογὴν χάριτος γέγονεν·* 6 *εἰ δὲ χάριτι, οὐκέτι ἐξ*

does not openly appear to us" (Calvin in loco). τῇ Βάαλ] בַּעַל = lord or ruler: a Phenician deity, identical with the Chaldean Bel, or Belus. It was the male generative principle, symbolized by the sun; with which was associated the female generative principle, symbolized by Ashtoreth, or the Grecian Astarte. The use of the feminine article is explained: 1. by supposing that Astarte is included, and that Baal is thus androgynous (Reiche, Olshausen, Philippi). 2. by contempt (Gesenius, Tholuck). 3. to agree with εἰκονι, understood (Erasmus, Beza, Grotius, Bengel). The Septuagint in this place reads τῷ; but uses the feminine article in 1 Sam. vii. 4; Hosea ii. 8; Zeph. i. 4. The Apocrypha also employs the feminine.

Ver. 5. St. Paul applies the election in Elijah's day to the election under the gospel-dispensation. οὕτως] in conformity with this occurrence in Elijah's time. λεῖμμα] corresponds to κατέλιπων, and is identical with ὑπόλειμμα in ix. 27. χάριτος] is the genitive of source. Respecting the fact itself, it is said in Acts xxi. 20, that there were "tens of thousands of believing Jews." Compare iii. 3; xi. 17, where "some" (τινες) are spoken of as unbelieving, implying that others were believers. This "remnant" sustains the same relation to the "people" spoken of in verses 1 and 2, that 'Ισραηλ does to οἱ ἐξ 'Ισραήλ, in ix. 6; and the "children of God" to the "children of the flesh," in ix. 8. The fact that in Elijah's time, and in the Apostle's time, God called with his effectual calling, a multitude from out of that larger body whom he had called only with the outward calling, proved that God had not totally reprobated the Jewish people.

Ver. 6 is explanatory. St. Paul, again, as he had previ-

ἔργων, ἐπεὶ ἡ χάρις οὐκέτι γίνεται χάρις [εἰ δὲ ἐξ ἔργων, οὐκέτι ἐστὶ χάρις, ἐπεὶ τὸ ἔργον οὐκέτι ἐστὶν ἔργον]·
7 τί οὖν; ὃ ἐπιζητεῖ Ἰσραήλ, τοῦτο οὐκ ἐπέτυχεν, ἡ δὲ

ously done in ix. 11, 16, takes particular pains to show that this election is not founded upon man's prior obedience, as the reason and cause of it. The natural heart is legal, and desires to merit salvation. Hence, the necessity of reiterating, that man does not earn and merit the electing compassion of God, by works of his own. χάριτι] sc. λεῖμμα γέγονεν. ἔργων] denotes perfect works: sinless obedience, such as the law requires. See explanation of iv. 4. οὐκέτι] sc. γέγονεν. γίνεται] is used instead of ἔστι, because an alteration is meant: ἔστι would denote the intrinsic nature of a thing, which is unchangeable. If this election were upon the ground of obedience, then mercy would be converted into justice: "gratia nisi gratis sit, gratia non est." (Aug.). The clause in brackets is wanting in ℵACDE Sahid., Copt., Vulg., Erasmus, Griesbach, Lachm., Tisch., Tregelles. It is supported by BL Peshito, Receptus.

Ver. 7. τί οὖν] sc. ἐροῦμεν: a deduction from verses 2–6. The thought is similar to that in ix. 30, 31. ἐπιζητει] is like διώκων, in ix. 31. The preposition is intensive, and the present tense denotes continuous effort. The Jewish people as a nation (Ἰσραήλ) labored in a legal manner to obtain eternal life, and failed. ἐκλογὴ] is that part of the Jewish people, designated as λεῖμμα, who sought after eternal life by faith in the promised Messiah. But this faith itself was the gift of God (Eph. ii. 8). ἐπέτυχεν] commonly takes the genitive (the Receptus reads τούτου); but may be followed by the accusative. Compare Plato's Republic, iv. 431 c. λοιποὶ] the remainder of the Jews: the τινες of iii. 3; xi. 17. ἐπωρώθησαν] is derived from πῶρος: the osseous cement formed in a

ἐκλογὴ ἐπέτυχεν· οἱ δὲ λοιποὶ ἐπωρώθησαν, [8] καθάπερ γέγραπται Ἔδωκεν αὐτοῖς ὁ θεὸς πνεῦμα κατανύξεως, ὀφθαλμοὺς τοῦ μὴ βλέπειν καὶ ὦτα τοῦ μὴ ἀκούειν, ἕως

broken bone. Hence, "to become callous;" as in Mark. vi. 52; viii. 17; John xii. 40. This word, in the Septuagint of Job xvii. 7, is translated in the English Version by, "became dim;" and in 2 Cor. iii. 14 by, "were blinded," as it is also in this passage. As St. Paul, in ix. 18, has described reprobation by σκληρύνει, this would be a reason for adopting the etymological rendering. But the succeeding explanation of the term, in verse 8, favors the second signification. The word relates to both the understanding and the will. For the relation of the human to the divine agency, in the case, see the explanation of σκληρύνει, in ix. 18. Calvin's explanation (in loco) is one of the few passages in his writings which subject him to the charge of supra-lapsarianism.

VER. 8 contains a proof from the Old Testament: the citation is a combination of Deut. xxix. 4 with Isa. xxix. 10, freely according to the Sept. ἔδωκεν] denotes not only permission, but the punitive withdrawal of restraints. See explanation of παρέδωκεν, in i. 24. κατανύξεως] "stupefaction" Religious apathy and lethargy show that God has ceased to strive with the man, and has left him to himself. Compare Eph. iv. 19. This word, in the Septuagint, sometimes has the signification of exasperation: an angry and embittered spirit. Luther and Calvin give it this meaning. τοῦ μὴ βλέπειν] 1. the descriptive genitive: "eyes of not seeing," i. e., that do not see (Grotius, Fritzsche, Philippi). 2. the genitive of purpose (Meyer). The latter agrees best with ἔδωκεν. ἕως τῆς, etc.] is best connected with ἔδωκεν, as a part of the quotation.

τῆς σήμερον ἡμέρας. [9] *καὶ Δαυεὶδ λέγει Γενηθήτω ἡ τράπεζα αὐτῶν εἰς παγίδα καὶ εἰς θήραν καὶ εἰς σκάνδαλον καὶ εἰς ἀνταπόδομα αὐτοῖς,* [10] *σκοτισθήτωσαν οἱ ὀφθαλμοὶ αὐτῶν τοῦ μὴ βλέπειν, καὶ τὸν νῶτον αὐτῶν διαπαντὸς συγκαμψον.*

VER. 9 gives another proof, from Ps. lxix. 22, 23, that a part of the Jewish people had been judicially blinded. The citation varies somewhat from the Septuagint. The psalm is Messianic, as is proved by comparing verses 9 and 21 with John ii. 17; Mat. xxvii. 34, 48; John xix. 29, 30. What David said concerning the enemies of the Messiah, or the unbelieving Jews, in his time, is applicable to them in all time. γενηθήτω] In the Hebrew, the future is employed, which the Septuagint renders by the imperative. Some regard it as the intensive future, so that there is a prophecy that these things shall certainly happen to the enemies of Christ. But it may be taken as an imprecation, uttered by David speaking as the inspired organ of God. The Supreme Judge can authorize a prophet to pronounce his punitive judgment for him, as he can a human magistrate to inflict punitive justice for him (xiii. 4). τράπεζα] is put for earthly enjoyments: while they are eating and drinking, in fancied security. παγίδα] the snare by which the wild beast is caught. θήραν] the quarry, or heap of game: this is neither in the Hebrew nor the Septuagint, but an addition by the apostle. σκάνδαλον] is the Septuagint word for the classical σκανδάληθρον, or stick to which the bait is tied, in a trap.

VER. 10. νῶτον, etc.] The Hebrew is, "make their loins continually to shake." St. Paul follows the Septuagint version. σύγκαμψον] God is the agent. The reference is not to Roman slavery, but to spiritual. These citations from the Old Testament prove that the spiritual rejection of a por-

11 Λέγω οὖν, μὴ ἔπταισαν ἵνα πέσωσιν; μὴ γένοιτο· ἀλλὰ τῷ αὐτῶν παραπτώματι ἡ σωτηρία τοῖς ἔθνεσιν, εἰς

tion of the Jewish nation was known and foretold, from the beginning of Jewish history.

VER. 11 begins a new paragraph, in which the apostle mentions a reason for the reprobation of a part of the Jews. οὖν] in reference to the "blinding," just proved by Scripture citations. Compare verse 1. ἔπταισαν] the subject is the λοιποὶ, of verse 7, who do not belong to the "election." Compare James ii. 10; iii. 2; 2 Pet. i. 10. πέσωσιν] is emphatic: "did they stumble merely that they might *fall?*" Had God no end to accomplish by this reprobation? παραπτώματι] the dative of the means: here, the occasional cause. The connection is with ἔπταισαν. This word invariably denotes a culpable and punishable act (Rom. v. 15–18; Mat. vi. 14). Hence, reprobation is consistent with the doctrine of personal responsibility and guilt. The "fall" of the unbeliever is also the "transgression" of the unbeliever. σωτηρία] sc. γέγονεν. As actual instances, in which the rejection of the gospel by the Jews led to its acceptance by the Gentiles, see Acts xiii. 43–49; xxiii. 28. The same thing is foretold, in Isa. xlix. 4–6; Mat. xxi. 43. The rejection of the gospel by the Jews facilitated its progress in the Gentile world, in the following manner: 1. The opposition of the Jews to the preaching of the doctrine of the Messiah to the Gentiles, made the apostles more determined and earnest to do so. See 1 Thess. ii. 14–16. 2. The Jewish-Christians attempted to force the ceremonial law upon the Gentile-Christians, and this resulted in a more spiritual understanding and universal spread of the Christian religion. Had the Jewish Christians been more numerous in the Primitive Church, the ceremonial law might have been a "heavy yoke," for a

τὸ παραζηλῶσαι αὐτούς. 12 εἰ δὲ τὸ παράπτωμα αὐτῶν πλοῦτος κόσμου καὶ τὸ ἥττημα αὐτῶν πλοῦτος ἐθνῶν, πόσῳ μᾶλλον τὸ πλήρωμα αὐτῶν. 13 ὑμῖν δὲ λέγω τοῖς ἔθνεσιν. ἐφ' ὅσον μὲν οὖν εἰμὶ ἐγὼ ἐθνῶν ἀπόστολος, τὴν διακονίαν μου δοξάζω, 14 εἴπως παραζηλώσω μου τὴν σάρκα καὶ

longer time than it was (Acts xv. 10). εἰς τὸ] is telic. The attainment of the providential design is reserved for the future. The Jews, as yet, have not been beneficially affected by the evangelizing of the Gentile. They still stand in a hostile attitude to Christianity. παραζηλῶσαι] to waken, not "jealousy" (Eng. Ver.) but, "emulation."

Ver. 12. δὲ] is transitive: "now." πλοῦτος] sc. γέγονε. The Gentile world is enriched, indirectly, by the falling away of the Jews. ἥττημα] is not classical, but found in the Sept., Isa. xxxi. 8; 1 Cor. vi. 7: not "minority," referring to the small number of Jewish believers (Chrysost., Theod., Erasmus, Beza, Bengel, Olsh.); but "diminution," or loss (impoverishment): the equivalent of ἀποβολὴ in verse 15. (De Wette, Meyer, Hodge). πλήρωμα] not "majority," antithetic to "minority;" but "gain," antithetic to "diminution," or loss. If the rejection of the Jews has proved to be such a blessing to the Gentiles, then much more their future restoration will be a blessing to them. αὐτῶν] sc. πλοῦτος ἐθνῶν γένησεται: subjective genitive, as in the two previous instances: "their fall," and, "their loss," and "their gain."

Ver. 13, and 14, guard the Gentiles against a false inference from the foregoing, viz.: that the apostle felt no interest in the Jews. ἐφ' ὅσον] not temporal, quamdiu, Mat. ix. 15; but quatenus, "in so far as," Mat. xxv. 40. μὲν] the correlative δὲ is not expressed, but implied: "I magnify my office, indeed, *but* I wish to stimulate my brethren." (Meyer). δοξάζω] "I praise," i. e. highly estimate. εἴπως] "if so be

σώσω τινὰς ἐξ αὐτῶν. [15] εἰ γὰρ ἡ ἀποβολὴ αὐτῶν καταλ-
λαγὴ κόσμου, τίς ἡ πρόσληψις εἰ μὴ ζωὴ ἐκ νεκρῶν;
[16] εἰ δὲ ἡ ἀπαρχὴ ἁγία, καὶ τὸ φύραμα· καὶ εἰ ἡ ῥίζα

that:" he is not absolutely certain, yet is hopeful that the more he urged the evangelization of the Gentile, the more he should savingly benefit the Jews. σάρκα] the equivalent of σπέρμα Ἀβραάμ, in ix. 7.

VER. 15 is a conclusion from verses 13, 14, similar to that in verse 12 from verse 11. ἀποβολὴ] the "rejection" of the Jew, spoken of in ix. 27, 29; x. 21; xi. 7. καταλλαγὴ] the heathen, through faith in Christ, are reconciled to God, v. 11. The Jewish reprobation is the occasional cause of the Gentile reconciliation. πρόσληψις] is the contrary of ἀποβολὴ: spiritual election and effectual calling is meant. ζωὴ ἐκ νεκρῶν] Compare vi. 13; Luke xv. 24. Not the resurrection of the body, which is to follow the conversion of the Jews, and the bringing in of the fulness of the Gentiles (Origen, Theodoret, Chrysost., Anselm, De Wette, Tholuck, Meyer); but spiritual life, and all the blessings of redemption (Calvin, Bengel, Philippi, Hodge). The argument is this: If the reprobation of the Jews, who as the outwardly called might naturally have been expected to be the inwardly called, results in such a blessing to the heathen world, then certainly the inward call itself must result in the greatest possible blessing to the Jews themselves.

VER. 16. δὲ] is transitive, introducing a reason for expecting the πρόσληψις of the Jew: namely, that the Jews were the chosen people of God. ἀπαρχὴ] sc. φυράματος. The allusion is to the offering of the first fruits of the earth: not generally, however, of grain, grapes, etc., but of kneaded meal, or dough, Numb. xv. 19–21. The "first fruits" represent: 1. the patriarchs Abraham, Isaac, and Jacob, in distinction from the rest of the people, τὸ φύραμα (Greek Fathers, Erasmus, Calvin, Grotius, Tholuck, Olshausen, De Wette, Meyer, Philippi, Hodge). 2. the elect Jews: "if some were elected, the rest may be" (Ambrose, Anselm, Rosenmüller). The first is the true explanation, as verse 28 shows. ἁγία] not in the spiritual sense of holy, but of consecration, or outward separation to the service of God. Compare Mat. iv. 5; vii. 6; Luke ii. 23; 1 Cor. vii. 14. ῥίζα and κλάδοι] are only another figure for the same things represented by the "first fruits" and the "lump." The Jewish patriarchs and their descendants all stood in the same covenant relation to God, as the chosen people (Deut. vii. 8, 9; Luke i. 55). The restoration of the Jews, and their admission into the Christian Church, is to be anticipated because of this original relation. The fact of the external call justifies the expectation of the internal. Not that the former is the ground of the latter, or that the latter necessarily and in every single instance follows from the former. Spiritual election does not rest upon the fact that the individual has the outward means of grace, any more than upon his works or personal merit; but solely upon the decision of God (ix. 15, 16). Nevertheless, the fact of the outward call is a valid reason for expecting, and hoping for the inward call. This expectation may not be realized invariably. It was not in the case of the Jews, some of whom were passed by, in the bestowment of saving grace, and continued in unbelief. God has liberty and sovereignty, in respect to regenerating grace, yet the general economy of redemption warrants the belief that he will follow the outward call with the inward; and that those who are externally "holy," shall be made spiritually so. In regard to electing grace, as connected with the outward call and the use of means, the individual must not insist upon absolute certainty beforehand, but must proceed upon the ground of strong probability, as does the farmer in the sowing of grain.

ἁγία, καὶ οἱ κλάδοι. 17 *εἰ δέ τινες τῶν κλάδων ἐξεκλάσθησαν, σὺ δὲ ἀγριέλαιος ὢν ἐνεκεντρίσθης ἐν αὐτοῖς καὶ συνκοινωνὸς τῆς ῥίζης καὶ τῆς πιότητος τῆς ἐλαίας ἐγένου,*

VERSES 17–20 warn the Gentile-Christians against self-exaltation because they have been elected, while Jews have been rejected. *τινες*] not all, but only a fraction of the entire number of the Jews. Compare iii. 3; xi. 25. *σὺ*] the Gentile-Christian. *ἀγριέλαιος*] is used here as an adjective, to denote the species: an entire tree is never grafted in. In verse 24, the word is used as a noun. *ἐν αὐτοῖς*] 1. "in," or "upon them": taking their place. (Beza, De Wette, Olsh.) 2. "among them" (Grotius, Fritzsche, Philippi, Meyer). The first is preferable, because of the subsequent warning against boasting over the branches that had been broken off. There is no need to press the comparison, and explain by the custom of grafting the wild-olive (oleaster) into the cultivated, for the purpose of strengthening the latter. "It often happens that though the olive trees thrive well, yet they bear no fruit. These should be bored with an auger, and a green graft or slip of a wild olive-tree be put into the hole; thus, the tree being as it were impregnated with fruitful seed, becomes more fertile." (Columella, de Re Rustica, v. 10.) Only the general figure of grafting is to be considered. As a graft shares in the qualities of the stock, so the Gentiles, who were wild-olive by nature (verse 24); that is, were aliens from the commonwealth of Israel and strangers from the covenants of promise (Eph. ii. 12); obtained a part in the blessings of the gospel and the church. The Jews were the channel of good to the Gentiles, as the olive-tree is to the graft. *ῥίζης καὶ πιότητος*] the Gentiles partook of the root and fatness of the olive-tree, when they entered into a spiritual participation of the blessings of the Abrahamic covenant.

18 μὴ κατακαυχῶ τῶν κλάδων· εἰ δὲ κατακαυχᾶσαι, οὐ σὺ
τὴν ῥίζαν βαστάζεις ἀλλὰ ἡ ῥίζα σέ. 19 ἐρεῖς οὖν Ἐξεκλάσθησαν κλάδοι ἵνα ἐγὼ ἐνκεντρισθῶ. 20 καλῶς· τῇ ἀπιστίᾳ
ἐξεκλάσθησαν, σὺ δὲ τῇ πίστει ἕστηκας. μὴ ὑψηλὰ φρόνει,

VER. 18. κατακαυχῶ] "to assert superiority over." Compare James ii. 13; iii. 14. κλάδων] not the Jewish people as a whole (Meyer), but the branches broken off (Chrys., Erasm., De Wette). εἰ δὲ] "but if, as thou shouldest not." ῥίζα] sc. βαστάζει: "thou, too, art only a branch;" a branch is not self-sustaining. Compare John xv. 4.

VER. 19. οὖν] with reference to the reason, given in verse 18, for not boasting. κλάδοι] is anarthrous, to denote some branches, not all. ἐγὼ] is emphatic, implying a proud self-reliance.

VER. 20. καλῶς] sc. ἐρεῖς: the fact is conceded, but not the inference drawn from it. ἀπιστίᾳ] the dative of the reason: "on account of," Gal. vi. 12. Unbelief was the reason of this rejection of a part of the Jews. Not that there was a greater degree of unbelief in their case, than in that of those Jews who were elected. This may or may not have been the fact. But there was unbelief, because there was sin, in the heart of these persons, and God decided not to overcome it. See comment on ix. 18, 33. τῇ πίστει] trust in Christ's vicarious righteousness is the method by which the elect stand, both before the bar of God and in the path of duty. ἕστηκας] the perfect signification is to be emphasized: "thou hast stood, up to this time." To "stand," is the contrary of that apostasy which is figuratively described by ἐξεκλάσθησαν, and literally by πεσόντας in verse 22. The two terms, "standing" and "falling," are found together in xiv. 4. ὑψηλὰ φρόνει] (ℵAB Lachm., Tisch.) denotes the same self-sufficient feeling

ἀλλὰ φοβοῦ· [21] εἰ γὰρ ὁ θεὸς τῶν κατὰ φύσιν κλάδων οὐκ ἐφείσατο, [μήπως] οὐδὲ σοῦ φείσεται.

expressed in the ἐγὼ of verse 18. Compare xii. 16. φοβοῦ] signifies the contrary feeling: viz.: self-distrust and reliance upon another. The apostle teaches that there is no security for the Gentile, any more than for the Jew, but in humility and trust in Christ. Unbelief and self-righteousness, in either instance, result in perdition.

VER. 21 contains a reason why these Gentiles who had been grafted in, should not presume upon their spiritual election, and "be wise in their own conceits" (ver. 25). If they vaingloriously trusted in their election, as the Jews had in their theocratic privileges, they would meet with the same treatment with the Jews. κατὰ φύσιν] natural, and not grafted branches (ver. 17). Christ (Mat. viii. 12) affirms that some of "the children of the kingdom shall be cast out into outer darkness." There was more probability of a divine indulgence toward the original covenant people, than toward the heathen. But there had been no such indulgence toward the Jews, and of course there would not be with the Gentiles. μήπως] is omitted in ℵABC Lachm., Tisch., Tregelles. οὐδὲ σοῦ φείσεται] the hypothesis, here, of the casting off of the elect Gentile by God who has elected him, does not prove that such an event will actually occur. The children of God are warned against apostasy, as one of the means of preventing apostasy. The holy and filial fear of falling is one of the means of not falling. He who has no such fear, because he presumes upon his election, will fall. Hence the promise, "I will put my fear in their hearts, in order that they may not depart from me" (Jer. xxxii. 40). Augustine explains: "in order that they may persevere." Though the perseverance of the believer is a certainty for God, yet it is

22 ἴδε οὖν χρηστότητα καὶ ἀποτομίαν τοῦ θεοῦ· ἐπὶ μὲν τοὺς πεσόντας ἀποτομία, ἐπὶ δὲ σέ χρηστότης θεοῦ, ἐὰν ἐπιμένῃς τῇ χρηστότητι· ἐπεὶ καὶ σὺ ἐκκοπήσῃ.

not so for the believer himself, unless he has the assurance of faith. Past failures in duty, much remaining corruption, and strong temptations to sin, cause him to feel very uncertain respecting his good estate. He is more fearful sometimes, that he shall be lost, than he is certain that he shall be saved. He may therefore, consistently, be warned against self-deception and apostasy. Compare Heb. vi. 4–9; John xv. 6. "By such threatenings, God does not render the salvation of believers a matter of doubt, as though the elect were in danger of excision (for the apostle immediately asserts that the gifts of God are without repentance; and Christ affirms that it is impossible that the elect should perish), but he applies incitements, that he may keep them in duty, and from sin. These threatenings, moreover, are addressed to the visible church as a body. Some members of this body are false members. The threat of excision is therefore proper and necessary for the church as a whole, although it would not apply to those who are true members. Neither would it be proper to infer that a true member may fall from grace, because the whole visible body is warned against apostasy. The seven churches of Asia were cut off for unbelief, but it does not follow that the true members in those churches were cut off" (Pareus, in loco).

Ver. 22 is a deduction, more immediately from verses 17 and 21, and more remotely, from the whole course of reasoning respecting election and reprobation. The rejection of some (τινες) of the Jews, and the election of some (σὺ) of the Gentiles, is an impressive example of the divine justice and mercy. χρηστότητα] the divine compassion. See comment on ii. 4. ἀποτομίαν] is found only here in the New Testament. It signifies severe and exact justice: the opposite of compassion. It has already been alluded to in συντέμνων, ix. 28. When God refrains from manifesting mercy, he manifests justice; because he must do one thing or the other. He is holy and just when he leaves the sinful will to its self-determination, and punishes it for its self-determination. To complain of justice, or "to reply against God" on account of it (ix. 20), is both a moral and a logical absurdity. πεσόντας] the reprobated Jews (xi. 11); the branches broken off for unbelief (ver. 20). ἀποτομία] sc. ἔστιν. The nominative is supported by ℵABC Lachm., Tisch., Tregelles; the accusative, by DL Receptus. χρηστότης θεοῦ] sc. ἐστίν. This is the reading of ℵABCD Lachm., Tisch., Tregelles. ἐὰν ἐπιμένῃς τῇ χρηστότητι] to "continue in the divine goodness," is to continue to trust in it: to continue in faith. After regeneration, the human will co-operates with the Holy Spirit, and growth in grace is conditioned upon fidelity upon the part of the believer. He must work out his own salvation in connection with God, who also works in him to will and to do (Phil. ii. 12, 13). Hence the exhortation of Christ to the believer, "Abide in me, and I will abide in you" (John xv. 4); and the warning, "If a man abide not in me he is cast forth as a branch, and is withered." (John xv. 6). The same truth is taught, here, by St. Paul. The divine compassion will continue to be exercised towards the believer, if he continues to rely upon it. Compare Coloss. i. 23. But if he deserts the method of grace, and relies upon his own works and personal merit, divine justice will take the place of compassion, and there will be, in his case as in that of the Jew, rejection instead of election: "thou also shalt be cut off." The case is a hypothetical one, like that in verse 21, for the purpose of illustrating the doctrine of salvation by faith, and does not necessarily imply actuality. Whether, in fact, an elect person ever fails to "continue in God's compassion," and is "cut off" by his justice, must be decided by the teachings of Scripture upon this particular point. They are explicit in the negative. See John x. 28, 29; xvii. 12; xviii. 9; Rom. xi. 29; Phil. i. 6; Heb. vi. 9; 1 Pet. i. 5; Jude 24. Anti-predestinarian exegetes find in these hypothetical propositions respecting "continuing," and "being cut off," an argument against predestination and irresistible grace, and a proof of the defectibility of grace, and of the repetition of conversion (Meyer, in loco). But they confound the development of holiness with the origin of it; progressive sanctification with regeneration. The first alone is made to depend upon the co-operation of the believer. The last depends solely upon the divine will, and is unconditioned by the creature. "We understand now," says Calvin in loco, "in what sense Paul threatens those with excision whom he has already asserted to have been grafted into the hope of life through God's election. For, first, though this cannot happen to the elect, they have yet need of such warning, in order to subdue the pride of the flesh; which being strongly opposed to their salvation, needs to be terrified with the dread of perdition. As far, then, as Christians are illuminated by faith, they hear, for their assurance, that the calling of God is without repentance; but as far as they carry about them the flesh which wantonly resists the grace of God, they are taught humility by this warning, 'Take heed lest thou too be cut off.'" Another explanation of these passages, is to refer them to the Gentile world as a whole; and the meaning then is, that if any portion of the Gentiles do not believe in Christ, they will be rejected, as the unbelieving Jews have been (Hodge).

VER. 23 contains an hypothesis of the opposite kind, introduced by δὲ, viz.: that if the reprobated Jew should not

23 κἀκεῖνοι δέ, ἐὰν μὴ ἐπιμένωσιν τῇ ἀπιστίᾳ, ἐνκεντρισθήσονται· δυνατὸς γάρ ἐστιν ὁ θεὸς πάλιν ἐνκεντρίσαι

persist in unbelief, but should exercise faith in Christ, he would be saved. This also, like the preceding supposition, is introduced for the purpose of illustrating by an extreme example the truth which St. Paul is so desirous of impressing, that salvation is by faith in Christ, and not by the works of the law. There is nothing that would prevent the salvation even of a reprobate, provided he should believe on the Lord Jesus Christ. Trust in atoning blood is all-prevalent with God; so much so, that if we could suppose it to come into existence by the action of the non-elect himself, it would save him. That such a case does not occur, and cannot from the nature of sin and the human will, is proved by those numerous passages which teach the self-originated bondage of the sinner, and that faith is the gift of God. A similar example of the supposition of something that is neither actual nor possible, for the purpose of vividly and strongly illustrating the subject under discussion, is found in 1 Cor. xiii. 1–3. Here, the extreme supposition is made that there is Christian faith without Christian love. κἀκεῖνοι] "even those" natural branches which God "broke off" (verse 20), and "did not spare" (verse 21): the same as the πεσόντας (ver. 22). ἐὰν μὴ ἐπιμένωσιν, etc.] corresponds to ἐὰν ἐπιμένῃς, etc. (ver. 22). Should the reprobated come to have the same spirit with the elected, he would obtain the same blessing with him: he would be "grafted in." δυνατὸς] God is able to graft them in again. St. Paul does not say that the non-elect are able to graft themselves in again. He who rejected them, could still elect them, if he so pleased. πάλιν] not a second time in reference to the *inward*, but to the outward call. This non-elect Jew belonged to the chosen people. The outward call, in his case, was followed by the internal reprobation.

αὐτούς. [24] *εἰ γὰρ σύ ἐκ τῆς κατὰ φύσιν ἐξεκόπης ἀγριελαίου καὶ παρὰ φύσιν ἐνεκεντρίσθης εἰς καλλιέλαιον, πόσῳ μᾶλλον οὗτοι οἱ κατὰ φύσιν ἐνκεντρισθήσονται τῇ ἰδίᾳ ἐλαίᾳ.*
[25] *Οὐ γὰρ θέλω ὑμᾶς ἀγνοεῖν, ἀδελφοί, τὸ μυστήριον*

Hence, if God (who is "able" to do this) should reverse his rejection, and spiritually elect him, this would be a second grafting in: the first ingrafting having been only the theocratic election. The apostle does not suppose the loss of regenerating grace, and a second bestowment of it.

VER. 24. γὰρ] connects with κἀκεῖνοι ἐνκεντρισθήσονται, and introduces a reason for the preceding statement respecting re-engrafting. σὺ] the Gentile-Christian. κατὰ φύσιν] qualifies ἀγριελαίου, and denotes the original nature and qualities of the tree. παρὰ φύσιν] grafting modifies the natural development of a branch, and is, in so far, contrary to nature. καλλιέλαιον] is anarthrous, to denote the species. οἱ κατὰ φύσιν] sc. ὄντες. Fritzsche reads οἵ, making it a relative. ἰδίᾳ] the spiritual election of a member of the theocracy is more natural and probable, on the face of it, than that of a pagan; as olive upon olive, is more homogeneous than oleaster upon olive.

VER. 25. St. Paul passes now to a prediction concerning the future of the Church, as composed both of Jews and Gentiles. Verses 25–32 constitute one of the most important prophecies in the New Testament. γὰρ] is connective only: equivalent to etenim (Winer, 448). οὐ θέλω ἀγνωεῖν] a litotes, employed to direct special attention (Rom. i. 13; 1 Cor. x. 1; xii. 1; 2 Cor. i. 8; 1 Thess. iv. 13). ὑμᾶς] you Gentile-Christians. μυστήριον] not in the pagan sense of an esoteric doctrine known only to the initiated, but in the Christian sense of a doctrine that requires a divine revelation in order to be known. Compare Rom. xvi. 5; 1 Cor.

τοῦτο, ἵνα μὴ ἦτε ἐν ἑαυτοῖς φρόνιμοι, ὅτι πώρωσις ἀπὸ μέρους τῷ Ἰσραὴλ γέγονεν, ἄχρις οὗ τὸ πλήρωμα τῶν ἐθνῶν

ii. 7–10; xv. 51; Eph. iii. 4, 5. The divine purpose respecting the future evangelization and salvation of the Jewish people and the heathen world, must be divulged by God himself. ἐν ἑαυτοῖς] is the reading of AB Peshito, Recep., Lachm., Tregelles: παρ' ἑαυτοῖς is supported by ℵCDL Tisch. Compare xii. 16. If the latter be adopted, the sense is: "before yourselves" (as judges), i. e.: in your own estimation (Winer, 395). φρόνιμοι] denotes false wisdom, as in Rom. xii. 16; 1 Cor. iv. 10; 2 Cor. xi. 19; and this is accompanied with pride. The apostle is still warning the Gentile Christian against the self-righteous spirit spoken of in verses 18–21. πώρωσις] See comment on xi. 7. ἀπὸ μέρους] does not qualify πώρωσις (to denote a partial in distinction from a total hardening: Calvin); but γέγονεν (De Wette, Meyer, Hodge), or else τῷ Ἰσραήλ (Fritzsche). The reprobation is total, whenever it occurs, but it does not occur to every individual of the nation. The qualification is extensive, not intensive; denoting the number of the hardened, not the degree of the hardening. The reprobate are only a part of the Jews. ἄχρις οὗ] implies a time when the present apostasy and rejection of the mass of the Jews will cease. τὸ πλήρωμα] the great body of the Gentiles: universitas, multitudo, ingens concursus ethnicorum (Calvin, Fritzsche, Stuart, Hodge); not the mere supplement from the Gentiles, to take the place of the unbelieving Jews (Olshausen, Philippi). Πλήρωμα is applied in the sense of a great majority, to the Jews, in verse 12; and this "fulness" is defined in verse 26, by πᾶς: the nation generally. εἰσέλθῃ] sc. εἰς τὴν ἐκκλησίαν. The church, as the etymology implies, are the elect. The "fulness" of the Gentiles constitutes a definite but immense number, whom God foreknew, called, and justified in the

εἰσέλθῃ, 26 καὶ οὕτως πᾶς Ἰσραὴλ σωθήσεται, καθὼς γέγραπται Ἥξει ἐκ Σιὼν ὁ ῥυόμενος, ἀποστρέψει ἀσε-

manner previously described by the apostle. St. Paul, here, asserts the Christianization of the globe, prior to the Christianization of the Jews. In neither case, however, is it necessary to suppose the regeneration of every individual without exception. Yet, the terms πλήρωμα and πᾶς, applied to the elect, imply that the non-elect will be comparatively few.

VER. 26. οὕτως] i. e. after the fulness of the Gentiles has entered into the church. πᾶς Ἰσραὴλ] 1. the spiritual Israel, composed of elect Jews and Gentiles together, as in Rom. ix. 6; Gal. vi. 6 (Aug., Theodoret, Luther, Calvin). The connection is against this: for, the apostle having spoken of the "fulness" of the Gentiles, is now describing the "fulness" of the Jews, in contrast with it. 2. the elect Jews, but constituting only a small number brought into the church from time to time: the ὑπόλειμμα of ix. 27; xi. 5 (Bengel, Olshausen, Philippi). According to this view, the nation as a whole is not to be restored. 3. the great mass or body of the nation, who are to be converted after the evangelization of the Gentile world (Beza, Rückert, Fritzsche, Tholuck, De Wette, Meyer, Hodge). The last is the correct view, because πᾶς is the opposite of ἀπὸ μέρους. Prior to the entrance of the fulness of the Gentiles into the church, the Jews "in part" (xi. 25; οἱ λοιποι, xi. 7; τινες, xi. 17) are blinded. Only a remnant of them are among the spiritually elect. The nation as a whole is reprobate. But when the fulness of the Gentiles shall have come into the church, this state of things will be reversed. The nation as a whole (πᾶς Ἰσραὴλ) will then be spiritually elect and "saved," and only a fraction (τὸ μέρος) spiritually rejected. γέγραπται] the citation is given freely from the Septuagint of Isa. lix. 20. The apostle does

βείας ἀπὸ Ἰακώβ· 27 *καὶ αὕτη αὐτοῖς ἡ παρ' ἐμοῦ διαθήκη, ὅταν ἀφέλωμαι τὰς ἁμαρτίας αὐτῶν.* 28 *κατὰ μὲν τὸ εὐαγ-*

not obtain his knowledge of the future of the church from this passage, but from his own inspiration. He confirms his own prediction by the language of Isaiah. ἐκ Σιὼν] the Redeemer shall come from the people of Israel, whose capital is Zion. The Septuagint reads ἕνεκεν Σιὼν, "*for* Zion," which agrees with the Hebrew. ὁ ῥυόμενος] is the Septuagint rendering of גּוֹאֵל, the Messiah. ἀποστρέψει] denotes the converting power of Christ. Compare Luke i. 16, 17. St. Paul follows the Septuagint. In the Hebrew, the whole passage reads as follows: "A redeemer shall come to (or, for) Zion, and to (or, for) the converts from transgression, in Jacob." The apostle teaches, that the deliverance alluded to by the prophet, is not confined to the "remnant," or small fraction that has been spoken of, but refers to the future conversion of the nation as a whole.

VER. 27 is cited freely from the Septuagint of Isa. lix. 21, in combination with a clause from Isa. xxvii. 9. It describes the nature of the covenant of God with his church, in order to show what is involved in the future conversion and restoration of the Jews. St. Paul distinctly teaches that the conversion of the Gentile world, as a whole, must take place before that of the Jews, as a whole; but he gives no clue to the time when it will occur, because no clue was given to him. The μυστήριον, or fact itself, was revealed to him, but not the time and season, which is unrevealable, according to Acts i. 7.

VERSES 28–32 recapitulate what has been said, in verses 11–27, concerning the temporary rejection and final election of the Jews. κατὰ εὐαγγέλιον] denotes the point of view: "having respect to the gospel:" i. e. the spread of the gospel.

γέλιον ἐχθροὶ δι' ὑμᾶς, κατὰ δὲ τὴν ἐκλογὴν ἀγαπητοὶ διὰ τοὺς πατέρας· [29] ἀμεταμέλητα γὰρ τὰ χαρίσματα καὶ ἡ

Compare the use of εὐαγγέλιον for εὐαγγελίζεσθαι, in i. 1. ἐχθροὶ] is best regarded as passive: "treated as enemies by God." The subject is suggested by αὐτῶν in verse 27: viz.: the Jews as unbelieving and rejected. The elliptical word with ἐχθροὶ is θεοῦ (Meyer), not εὐαγγέλιον (Pareus, Fritzsche), or Παυλου (Theodoret, Luther). δι' ὑμᾶς] one purpose of the rejection of a part of the Jews was, that the entrance of the Gentiles into the church might be facilitated and hastened. κατὰ τὴν ἐκλογὴν] "having respect to the church of Christ," that total mass which is to be called out of all nations, the Jews included: ἐκλογή is here equivalent to ἐκκλησία. ἀγαπητοὶ] denotes the love of compassion, not of complacency. See comment on ix. 13. God loved, that is compassionated, these Jews who are sinners and "enemies of God." διὰ τούς πατέρας] Compare xi. 16. Notwithstanding his rejection of a portion of the Jews, God still remembers his covenant with Abraham, and purposes to bring into the church the great body of his descendants.

VER. 29 contains a proof, introduced by γὰρ, that the Jews are "beloved." ἀμεταμέλητα] Compare Heb. xii. 17. The word is emphatic by position, and denotes the unchangeableness of the divine purpose. The promise to Abraham and his seed (Gen. xvii. 7) will not be revoked. χαρίσματα] the effects of the call. κλῆσις] the particular act of election: the cause of the χαρίσματα. Calvin regards the "gifts and calling," here spoken of, as referring only to the theocratic privileges and election; and this is favored by the preceding context, which speaks of the relation of the Jewish patriarchs to their descendants: a relation like that between the "first fruits" and the "lump," and between the "root" and the

κλῆσις τοῦ θεοῦ. [30] ὥσπερ γὰρ ὑμεῖς ποτὲ ἠπειθήσατε τῷ
θεῷ, νῦν δὲ ἠλεήθητε τῇ τούτων ἀπειθείᾳ, [31] οὕτως καὶ
οὗτοι νῦν ἠπείθησαν, τῷ ὑμετέρῳ ἐλέει ἵνα καὶ αὐτοὶ νῦν

"branches" (xi. 16). Pareus extends the meaning further, and makes the "gifts and calling" to be individual and spiritual, including faith, remission of sins, and salvation. The sentiment of the passage is true in reference to both national and individual election.

VERSES 30 and 31 constitute a single sentence, and are a reiteration and confirmation, introduced by γὰρ, of the teaching in verses 11–27. ὑμεῖς] you Gentiles. ποτὲ] "formerly:" before the gospel was preached to you. ἠπειθήσατε] "disbelieved," and consequently "disobeyed," in the manner described in i. 18 sq. The conduct agrees with the creed. νῦν] since the gospel has been preached to you. ἠλεήθητε] the Gentiles became the objects of the divine compassion (ἔλεος), by being called, justified, and sanctified, in the manner previously described. ἀπειθείᾳ] is the dative of the instrument. The unbelief of the Jew was the occasional cause of the faith of the Gentile (xi. 11–14). οὗτοι] the unbelieving Jews. ἠπείθησαν] sc. θεῷ. The unbelief of the Jew differed from that of the heathen, in that it related to God as revealed in Christ; the heathen unbelief had respect to God as revealed only in nature and the human soul (i. 18 sq.). The Jew disobeyed, by rejecting grace; the Gentile, by transgressing law. ὑμετέρῳ] is objective in its force: "the compassion shown to you." ἐλέει] is not to be connected with ἠπείθησαν (Vulgate, "non crediderunt in vestram misericordiam," Luther, Lachm., Lange), but with ἐλεηθῶσιν (Eng. Ver., De Wette, Meyer, Philippi, Alford, Hodge). The construction of ἐλέει in the apodosis is like that of ἀπειθείᾳ in the protasis; because the two words are antithetic. St. Paul

ἐλεηθῶσιν· [32] συνέκλεισεν γὰρ ὁ θεὸς τοὺς πάντας εἰς ἀπείθειαν ἵνα τοὺς πάντας ἐλεήσῃ. [33] ὢ βάθος πλούτου

might have written τῇ ὑμετέρῃ πίστει. ἵνα ἐλεηθῶσιν] is placed after τῷ ὑμετέρῳ ἐλέει, for the sake of emphasizing the latter. Compare 1 Cor. ix. 15; 2 Cor. ii. 4; Gal. ii. 10. As the Gentiles, viewed as a whole, obtained the benefits of redemption, instrumentally, through the unbelief of the Jews, so the Jews, viewed as a whole, will hereafter obtain the benefits of redemption, instrumentally, through the belief of the Gentiles.

VER. 32 confirms the statement in verses 30, 31. συνέκλεισεν] compare Gal. iii. 22, 23. The literal and classical signification is: "to shut in," or "inclose," Luke v. 6. In later Greek, it is used metaphorically, and signifies, "to deliver up to the power of," Ps. xxxi. 8; Ps. lxviii. 50 (Sept.). Several explanations are given: 1. God declares and proves all men to be sinners. He includes ("concludes," Eng. Ver.) all in a sinful estate. He shuts them up in this class, and makes them conscious that they belong to it. To "shut up" an opponent, by an argument, is to convict him. (Chrysost., Theod., Pareus, Grotius, Wetstein, Wolfius). 2. He permits them to sin (Origen, Rosenmüller, Tholuck). 3. He judicially withdraws restraints, and gives them over to sin, as in i. 24; ix. 18 (Calvin, De Wette, Meyer). The objection to this latter explanation is, that judicial blindness is the most intense degree of sin, and is the characteristic of a particular class of mankind; while the connection requires a characteristic that is universal, and common to all (πάντας). It is not the fact of great sin, but of sin, that is in the mind of the writer. The first explanation is the best. God charges all men with sin, and convicts them of it. "God," says Pareus, "has included all men in sin, by manifesting, accusing, and condemning unbelief, but not by producing or approving it." The sentiment is kindred to that in iii. 9, 10: "Jews and Gentiles are all under sin; there is none righteous, no, not one." And the same with that in v. 12: "all have sinned." τοὺς πάντας] both Jews and Gentiles: the two classes into which the writer has divided mankind, and which have been the subject of his reasoning. Compare iii. 9. ἀπείθειαν] see the explanation of ἀπειθεία in verse 30. St. Paul here refers the sin of the heathen and of the Jew, to unbelief: the former to unbelief in God abstractly; the latter to unbelief in God in Christ. ἵνα τοὺς πάντας ἐλεήσῃ] the purpose of God in declaring and evincing that all men are sinners, is that he may save them from sin. Conviction is in order to conversion. It is a means only, and not an end in itself. Universal salvation, in the sense of the salvation of every individual, is not taught here; because πάντας refers to classes, not to individuals; to ὑμεῖς and οὗτοι in verses 30 and 31: viz.: Gentiles and Jews. Sin is not confined to either class (iii. 9), nor is salvation. Redemption is co-extensive with the race. The gospel is offered to all. That it is rejected by some, is proved by ix. 7, 27, 29, 31, 32; x. 3; xi. 7–10, 22. Meyer finds, here, a purpose on the part of God to save all Jews and Gentiles without exception, but this purpose is defeated by the self-will of individuals. This contradicts viii. 29, 30; ix. 16, 18, 21.

VER. 33 begins an utterance of praise in view of the compassion of God, as shown in the justification and sanctification of sinners. βάθος] may denote either the unsearchableness (Philippi), or the exuberant fulness (Meyer). 1. To be connected with the three following genitives (Chrysost., Grotius, Bengel, Rosenmüller, Tholuck, De Wette, Olshausen, Fritzsche, Philippi, Meyer, Hodge). 2. To be connected only with πλούτου; the two following genitives being exe-

καὶ σοφίας καὶ γνώσεως θεοῦ· ὡς ἀνεξερεύνητα τὰ κρίματα αὐτοῦ καὶ ἀνεξιχνίαστοι αἱ ὁδοὶ αὐτοῦ. [34] *τίς γὰρ ἔγνω νοῦν κυρίου; ἢ τίς σύμβουλος αὐτοῦ ἐγένετο;* [35] *ἢ τίς*

getical (Luther, Calvin, Beza, Reiche, Eng. Ver.). If the first is chosen, πλούτου must have the secondary signification of "mercy" (x. 12), or of "resources." If the second is chosen, πλούτου has its literal meaning of "abundance." This is preferable. The tautology of the clause, "depth of riches" is explained by the great emphasis and wonder in the mind of the writer. σοφίας] refers to the end aimed at, by the divine mind. γνώσεως] refers to the means employed for the attainment of the end. κρίματα] the decisions or determinations of God, in this plan of salvation: particularly those which relate to the election of some, and the rejection of others. ἀνεξιχνίαστοι] the etymon is ἴχνος, a track, or footprint. The divine decisions being self-moved, and wholly internal, are not traceable by the finite intellect. Compare Job v. 9; ix. 10; xxvi. 14. ὁδοὶ] the paths, in which the footprints are not visible.

VER. 34 cites Isa. xl. 13, in proof of the preceding statement. It is nearly literal from the Septuagint. The first clause refers to γνῶσις, and the second to σοφία (Theodoret, Fritzsche, Meyer).

VER. 35 continues the Old Testament proof from Job xli. 3 (Eng. Ver. 11). St. Paul follows the Hebrew text, which is mistranslated by the Seventy (xli. 2). "Had man first given to God something for which he could claim a recompense, then the divine wisdom would not be free and inexplicable, but determined and conditioned by human action, and therefore within the reach and cognizance of human calculation." Philippi in loco. In the whole matter of the forgive-

προέδωκεν αὐτῷ, καὶ ἀνταποδοθήσεται αὐτῷ; [36] ὅτι ἐξ
αὐτοῦ καὶ δι' αὐτοῦ καὶ εἰς αὐτὸν τὰ πάντα· αὐτῷ ἡ δόξα
εἰς τοὺς αἰῶνας, ἀμήν.

ness of sin and gratuitous justification, no man first gives to God, and as a consequence of such gift is repaid by God.

VER. 36 answers the question in verse 35, by implication, in the negative. "No one first gave," etc., "because," etc. ὅτι] introduces the reason. ἐξ αὐτοῦ] out of, or *from* God, as the source. The reference is to creative power. δι' αὐτοῦ] *through* God's continual working. The reference is to providential preservation, Heb. i. 3. εἰς αὐτὸν] *to* God as the ultimate end. τὰ πάντα] all the divine acts and their consequences, in the three great spheres of creation, providence, and redemption. These are intended to manifest the divine excellence, and thereby to promote the worship and glory of God by the creature. Some commentators find the trinitarian distinctions, in this use of the prepositions, as in 1 Cor. viii. 6; Coloss. i. 16 (Augustine, Hilary, Olshausen, Philippi). Tholuck, in the 4th edition of his commentary on Romans, remarking upon Olshausen's assertion that the relation of Father, Son, and Spirit is expressed in this passage, observes: "And who can dispute this, when the apostle elsewhere describes the Father as the causal principle, the Son as the Mediator, the Spirit as the principle immanent in the church?" In the 5th edition, however, he denies the trinitarian reference. δόξα] sc. εἴη. The term denotes the honor and homage due to God, from the creature. Compare Gal. i. 5; Eph. iii. 21. εἰς τοὺς αἰῶνας] absolute eternity: the plural is intensive.

CHAPTER XII

1 Παρακαλῶ οὖν ὑμᾶς, ἀδελφοί, διὰ τῶν οἰκτιρμῶν τοῦ θεοῦ, παραστῆσαι τὰ σώματα ὑμῶν θυσίαν ζῶσαν ἀγίαν εὐάρεστον τῷ θεῷ, τὴν λογικὴν λατρείαν ὑμῶν,

St. Paul, having completed his statement of the doctrine of gratuitous justification, passes, in the remainder of the Epistle, to consider the duties that grow out of a justified state and condition. He deduces the principles of Christian ethics and morality from the evangelical system itself. Christian ethics differs from pagan ethics, in respect: 1. to its greater extent; and 2. to the underlying motive. The former includes duties toward God, the people of God, and mankind at large. The latter is restricted to the relations of man to man. Christian ethics finds its motive in the sense of the divine mercy in Christ, and the consciousness of redemption ; the motive of pagan ethics is prudential only; either that of fear, or of self-interest.

The apostle, with some transposition of topics, owing to the rapid and energetic movement of his thought, enunciates the duties of the Christian believer under the following heads: 1. Duties to God and the Church: xii. 1–13; xiv. 1–xv. 13; xvi. 17–20; 2. Duties to the State: xiii. 1–7; 3. Duties to Society: xii. 14–21; xiii. 8–14. He then concludes with personal references, greetings, and benediction: xv. 14–xvi. 16; xvi. 21–27.

Ver. 1. *παρακαλῶ*] "Moses jubet: apostolus hortatur." Bengel in loco. *οὖν*] draws an inference, not from xi. 35, 36

(Tholuck, Meyer), but from the whole discussion of the righteousness of God, in chapters i.–xi. (Calvin, Bengel, De Wette, Philippi, Hodge). St. Paul founds the ensuing ethics and morality upon the foregoing doctrines of justification, sanctification, and election. Compare Eph. iv. 1; 1 Thess. iv. 1. διὰ] "through," or "by means of." The preposition implies that the *motive* to obey the exhortations that follow, lies in the divine mercy exercised toward redeemed sinners in the manner described. Their gratitude for the compassion of God in their redemption would impel them to Christian service. οἰκτιρμῶν] is the Septuagint translation of רַחֲמִים, "bowels." It denotes the divine compassion for man, who as sinful is exposed to the divine wrath. See the explanation of ἠγάπησα in ix. 13, and of ἐλεήσω in ix. 15. παραστῆσαι] is the classical term to denote the laying of the sacrificial victim on the altar. σώματα] not the body in distinction from the soul (Fritzsche, Meyer); nor the sensuous nature (Köllner); but the entire man (Beza, De Wette, Philippi, Stuart, Hodge). Compare vi. 12, 13. The body, in distinction from the soul, could not be offered as a "rational" and spiritual sacrifice. θυσίαν] not a propitiatory sacrifice, but the sacrifice of praise and thanksgiving, Heb. xiii. 15, 16. ζῶσαν] "abominabile est, cadaver offerre." Bengel. ἁγίαν] "consecrated," Luke ii. 23; John xvii. 19. τῷ θεῷ] is the adjunct of εὐάρεστος. Compare Phil. iv. 18; Eph. v. 2; Heb. xiii. 16. τὴν λογικὴν λατρείαν] is in apposition with the entire sentence παραστῆσαι . . . τῷ θεῷ; because only the self-consecration (not the θυσία) could be denominated a λατρεία, or cultus. λογικὴν] "that is, having in it nothing bodily, nothing tangible, nothing sensible" (Chrysostom). Œcumenius explains by "bloodless." St. Peter (ii. 2) speaks of λογικὸν γάλα: milk suited to the mind. Athenagoras denominates the true knowledge of God and the sincere prayers of Christians a λογική λατρεία. "The believer's rational service to

2 καὶ μὴ συνχηματίζεσθαι τῷ αἰῶνι τούτῳ, ἀλλὰ μεταμορφοῦσθαι τῇ ἀνακαινώσει τοῦ νοός, εἰς τὸ δοκιμάζειν ὑμᾶς τί τὸ θέλημα τοῦ θεοῦ, τὸ ἀγαθὸν καὶ εὐάρεστον καὶ

God consists not, like the theocratic cultus, in material oblations, but in inward rational self-consecration, both as to soul and body." Philippi in loco. Compare John iv. 23, 24; 1 Pet. ii. 5.

VER. 2. συνχηματίζεσθαι] with μεταμορφοῦσθαι is the reading of ADEFG Griesbach, Lachm.; and is adopted by De Wette, Meyer, Philippi, Alford. The Receptus with א (which reads μεταμορφοῦσθαι) BL Peshito, Itala, Vulgate, Tischendorf, read συνχηματίζεσθε and μεταμορφοῦσθε. The first is preferable, because a second dependent sentence connected with παρακαλῶ is easy and natural; and because א itself has the infinitive in the second instance, suggesting that the imperative in the first instance, in this ms., may be a mistake of the scribe. The difference between σχῆμα and μορφή, in these two verbs, is that between the outward shape and the inward organic structure. Compare Phil. ii. 6–8, where μορφή denotes the divine essence of the Logos, and σχῆμα the human figure or shape that was assumed. In this passage, however, there is no need to press this distinction. Christians are exhorted not to fashion themselves upon the scheme or model of this world. αἰῶνι τούτῳ] is the same as ὁ ἐνεστὼς αἰών, Gal. i. 4; and ὁ νῦν αἰών, Eph. ii. 2. It is the contrary of ὁ αἰών ὁ ερχόμενος, Luke xviii. 30; and ὁ αἰών ὁ μέλλων, Mat. xii. 32. The difference between the two is identical with that between time and eternity; the transient and the everlasting state of existence. See comment on vi. 22. The New Testament everywhere represents the present temporary world in which man is living, as under the dominion of sin and Satan, " the prince of this world." Compare

John xiv. 30; xv. 18, 19; xvi. 8, 11, 20, 33; xvii. 9, 14, 16; Gal. i. 4; Eph. ii. 3; vi. 5; 1 John ii. 15–17; iii. 1, 13; iv. 4, 5; v. 4, 5; vi. 19. A "worldly" spirit is a selfish and wicked spirit. The true distinction between the church and the world is, that the former fashions itself upon the "scheme" of the future and the everlasting; the latter upon that of the present and fleeting moment. Believers, though in "this world" are not a part of it. According to the inspired view and theory, the profane and secular world is immoral. Merely human civilization is luxury, and luxury is sin. The worldly centres of civilization are centres of evil. Babylon is the symbol of them, Rev. xviii. 2–24. *μεταμορφοῦσθαι*] is middle: "to transform yourselves." The believer, being regenerate, co-operates with the Holy Spirit in sanctification, and hence may be urged to holy activity. Were he "dead in sin," such a command would be inconsistent. Compare the command to self-renewal (not self-regeneration), in Eph. iv. 23. *ἀνακαινώσει*] is the instrumental dative. By means of his progressive sanctification, the believer is transformed from the one scheme of life, to the other. This text proves that the *νοῦς*, equally with the sensuous nature, is affected by apostasy, and requires regeneration and sanctification. After *νοός*, the Receptus ℵEL Peshito, Æthiopic, Vulgate, have *ὑμῶν*: it is omitted by ABDF Lachm., Tisch., Tregelles. *εἰς τὸ δοκιμάζειν*] "in order to test," and thereby to understand. One design, though not the only one, of increasing sanctification, is that the believer may distinguish between what pleases and what displeases God. Clearness of moral perception, and tenderness of conscience, result from growth in grace. Compare Eph. v. 10; Phil. i. 10; Heb. v. 14. *τὸ θέλημα*] the objective will, or the divine law (ii. 18; 1 Thess. iv. 3). The Vulgate, Chrysostom, and others, understand by it, the subjective will of God: the divine inclination or desire. But in this case, it would be needless to describe it

τέλειον. [3] λέγω γὰρ διὰ τῆς χάριτος τῆς δοθείσης μοι παντὶ τῷ ὄντι ἐν ὑμῖν, μὴ ὑπερφρονεῖν παρ' ὃ δεῖ φρονεῖν, ἀλλὰ φρονεῖν εἰς τὸ σωφρονεῖν, ἑκάστῳ ὡς ὁ θεὸς ἐμέρισεν

as εὐάρεστον. An act of will is of course willing; and a desire is pleasing. τὸ ἀγαθὸν, etc.] is in apposition, and describes the divine law or will.

VER. 3. λέγω] denotes, here, a command or injunction, as in Mat. v. 34, 39, 44. γὰρ] "namely," i. e., in accordance with the preceding exhortation in verses 1 and 2. χάριτος] the grace conferred on him for the apostolic office. Compare i. 5; xv. 15; 1 Cor. xv. 9, 10; Gal. i. 15, 16; Eph. iii. 7, 8; 1 Tim. i. 12. This gave St. Paul authority. The word of the apostles has the same weight as the word of their Master, Luke x. 16. παντὶ, etc.] every individual, without exception. ὑπερφρονεῖν . . φρονεῖν . . σωφρονεῖν] Compare, for the paronomasia, 1 Cor. xi. 31, 32; xiii. 6, 7, 13. φρονεῖν is the base: to mind; to mind overmuch; to mind wisely. "Illud peccat in excessu per superbiam; istud est justum de se et aliis judicium: hoc vero significat modestiam." Wetstein. "Mind" (φρήν) is employed in the sense of temper or disposition. Christians are first of all exhorted to the principal grace of Christianity: viz., humility, or a right mental attitude of the creature before the Creator. This is the particular grace which Christ singles out of his own absolute and perfect character, for imitation by his disciples, Mat. xi. 29; xviii. 2–4. ἑκάστῳ] is placed before instead of after ὡς, for emphasis. Compare 1 Cor. iii. 5; vii. 17. ὡς] denotes proportion. πίστεως] faith in Christ. Justifying faith is the gift of God, according to his election. It has a variety of degrees and graces (μέτρον), 1 Cor. xii. 4 sq.; Eph. iv. 7, 16. Some are called to a more distinguished service in the church than others; and the personal estimate which

μέτρον πίστεως. 4 καθάπερ γὰρ ἐν ἑνὶ σώματι πολλὰ
μέλη ἔχομεν, τὰ δὲ μέλη πάντα οὐ τὴν αὐτὴν ἔχει πρᾶξιν,
5 οὕτως οἱ πολλοὶ ἓν σῶμά ἐσμεν ἐν Χριστῷ, τὸ δὲ καθ' εἷς

the believer should have concerning himself should be exactly proportioned to the gifts which he has received. To think neither too much nor too little of the grace of God within the soul, is one of the most difficult of all duties. For instances of its performance by St. Paul, see 1 Cor. ii. 1–4; iv. 9–13; xv. 10; 2 Cor. xi. 5, 23–33; xii. 2–13. The apostle makes humility to be the foundation of Christian ethics and morality. The pagan ethics is vitiated, even in its best form as seen in the Platonic philosophy, and still more in the Stoic, by egotism, or the disposition ὑπερφρονεῖν παρ' ὃ δεῖ φρονεῖν.

VER. 4. The Church is described under the figure (common also in classical writers) of an organic body. Compare 1 Cor. xii. 12 sq. There is reciprocity of action in an organism; so that no one part is independent of the others. This excludes a proud self-reliance. Only that which is self-existent and isolated is excused from humility. Meekness and lowliness of spirit would be unsuitable to God, but is necessarily required in all created and dependent beings. πρᾶξιν] "function." No one member can discharge all the bodily functions; it is confined to its own office. "If the whole body were an eye, where were the hearing?" 1 Cor. xii. 17.

VER. 5. οἱ πολλοὶ] the multitude of Christian individuals. ἓν σῶμά ἐν Χριστῷ] justifying faith unites each believer to Christ, and thus the multitude of units becomes a unity. This union is so intimate with Christ the Head, that the unity itself, or the Church, in one instance, is actually denominated "Christ," 1 Cor. xii. 12. Compare Eph. i. 23;

ἀλλήλων μέλη. [6] ἔχοντες δὲ χαρίσματα κατὰ τὴν χάριν τὴν δοθεῖσαν ἡμῖν διάφορα, εἴτε προφητείαν, κατὰ τὴν ἀναλογίαν τῆς πίστεως,

iv. 15, 16, 23; Coloss. i. 18; ii. 19. τὸ δὲ] is the reading of ℵABDFG Lachm., Tisch. The Receptus reading, ὁ δὲ is supported only by EL. καθ' εἷς] is a solecism not uncommon in later Greek. Compare Mark xiv. 19; John viii. 9; Rev. xxi. 21. The regular form, καθ' ἕνα, occurs in 1 Cor. xiv. 31; Eph. v. 33. The meaning of the clause is: "But in respect to (τὸ: i. e., κατά τὸ) our individual relation (καθ' εἷς), we are members of one another."

VER. 6. ἔχοντες] is not a descriptive adjunct of ἐσμεν in verse 5, and separated from it only by a comma (Lachm., Tisch., De Wette, Reiche), but begins a new hortatory sentence (Eng. Ver., Beza, Griesbach, Olshausen, Fritzsche, Meyer, Philippi, Hodge). δὲ] "now," is transitive to the exhortation, which is founded upon the preceding statement that believers are the recipients of divine gifts, and are members of one another. χαρίσματα] the gifts are specified below, and presuppose faith in Christ. Unbelievers never have them. διάφορα] the difference in the gifts is due to God the Holy Spirit, who "divideth to every man severally as he will," 1 Cor. xii. 11. προφητείαν] the enumeration of the gifts now begins. The gift of prophecy was more than the ability to expound the Old Testament, especially the prophetical books (Zwingli, Calvin, and elder Lutheran exegetes). "The New Testament idea of the prophetic office is essentially the same as that of the Old Testament. Prophets are men who, inspired by the Spirit of God, remove the veil from the future (Rev. i. 3; xxii. 7, 10; John xi. 51; Acts xi. 27, 28; xxi. 10, 11, compare 1 Pet. i. 10); make known concealed facts of the present, either in discovering the secret will of God (Luke i.

67 sq.; Acts xiii. 1 sq.; Eph. iii. 5), or in disclosing the hidden thoughts of man (1 Cor. xiv. 24, 25), and bringing into light his unknown deeds (Mat. xxvi. 68; Mark xiv. 65; Luke xxii. 64; John iv. 19); and dispense to their hearers instruction, comfort, exhortation in animated, powerfully impassioned language going far beyond the ordinary limits of human discourse (Mat. vii. 28, 29; Luke xxiv. 19; John vii. 40; Acts xv. 32; 1 Cor. xiv. 3, 4, 31)." Philippi in loco. The difference between an apostle (who is also a prophet, Eph. ii. 20; iii. 5), and a prophet was, that the former office was more comprehensive than the latter, and its inspiration was abiding, while that of the latter was occasional and transient. *κατὰ τὴν ἀναλογίαν τῆς πίστεως*] sc. *προφητεύωμεν*. 1. Subjective faith is meant. The clause is equivalent to *κατὰ μέτρον πίστεως*. The prophet must be true and sincere, communicating only what God has revealed to him (Origen, Chrysost., Ambrose, Bengel, De Wette, Tholuck, Meyer). 2. The objective rule of faith is meant. The individual prophecy must harmonize with that body of doctrine which has come down from the beginning, 1 Cor. iii. 11; xiv. 37; xv. 3; Gal. i. 8, 9; 1 John iv. 6 (Aquinas, Luther, Calvin, Pareus, Flatt, Klee, Umbreit, Philippi, Hodge). The latter is preferable, because in this connection the apostle would be more likely to exhort to accuracy in the teaching than to sincerity. The latter might be presumed, as a matter of course; but there might be mistakes made by a sincere man. That *πίστις* is used in the New Testament in the objective signification of a creed, or rule of faith, is proved by Gal. i. 8; vi. 16; Phil. iii. 16; 1 Tim. iv. 1; vi. 20; 2 Tim. i. 13, 14; iii. 15, 16, 18; iv. 3; Titus i. 4, 9; ii. 1, 6, 10. And that such a test was required, to protect the church from the heterodoxy of false prophets is proved by Mat. xxiv. 11, 24; 1 Thess. v. 19–21; 1 Tim. iv. 1; 1 John iv. 1. This injunction of St. Paul is the key to systematic theology. No al-

7 *εἴτε διακονίαν, ἐν τῇ διακονίᾳ, εἴτε ὁ διδάσκων, ἐν τῇ διδασκαλίᾳ,* 8 *εἴτε ὁ παρακαλῶν, ἐν τῇ παρακλήσει, ὁ μεταδιδοὺς, ἐν ἁπλότητι, ὁ προϊστάμενος, ἐν σπουδῇ, ὁ ἐλεῶν, ἐν ἱλαρότητι.*

leged Christian tenet can be correct which conflicts with other Christian tenets. All Christian truth must be consistent with Christianity. For example, the deity of Christ supposes the doctrine of the trinity; monergistic regeneration involves the doctrine of election; and an infinite atonement for sin, by God-incarnate, logically implies an infinite penalty for sin.

VER. 7. διακονίαν] not "ministry" in the general sense of any ecclesiastical office whatever, as in 1 Cor. iii. 5; 2 Cor. vi. 4; Eph. iii. 7; vi. 21; Coloss. i. 7, 23; 1 Tim. iv. 6 (Chrysost., Luther), but in the restricted sense of the diaconate (De Wette, Meyer, Philippi). The writer is enumerating particular gifts and offices in the church. The deacons had charge of the external affairs of the church; the care of the poor, the sick, etc., Acts vi. 1–3; Phil. i. 1; 1 Tim. iii. 8–13. ἐν τῇ διακονίᾳ] sc. ὦμεν: employed intensively, as in 1 Tim. iv. 15. Compare the "totus in illis" of Horace. The deacon must do his work thoroughly. ὁ διδάσκων] the "teacher" is distinguished from the prophet, in 1 Cor. xii. 28; Eph. iv. 11. The latter implied inspiration; the former only the common knowledge of a devout and disciplined Christian mind. The office of "teacher" corresponded, probably, to that of the modern "preacher." ἐν τῇ διδασκαλίᾳ] sc. ἔστω: in the intensive sense, as above.

VER. 8. ὁ παρακαλῶν] "exhortation" is addressed more to the heart, and "teaching" to the understanding; yet neither can be separated from the other. They were not two offices, consequently, but were united in one person.

See 1 Cor. xiv. 31; Titus i. 9. But a talent for one or the other form of instruction generally predominates in an individual. *ἐν τῇ παρακλήσει*] sc. *ἔστω*: in the intensive sense, as above. *ὁ μεταδιδοὺς*] 1. the official giving of the funds of the church, by the deacon. 2. the private charity of the individual believer. The first view is preferable, because the writer is enumerating the offices of the church. The second view is favored, however, by the fact that *μεταδιδόναι* is employed to denote private benevolence, in Luke iii. 11; Eph. iv. 28, while official distribution is denoted by *διαδιδόναι*, in Acts iv. 35; and also by the adjunct *ἐν ἁπλότητι*. "Sincerity" is more naturally referred to a private, than to an official act. De Wette combines the two views: "the apostle here, as in the use of *ἐλεῶν* which is commonly referred to the deacon's care of the sick, extends the scope of the official *χάρισμα*, so as to include the common agency of the church member also." *ἐν ἁπλότητι*] for the explanation, see Mat. vi. 2 sq.; Luke vi. 30–35. All ostentation, and mercenary motive, is excluded. *ὁ προιστάμενος*] not the person who had charge of the strangers, like Phœbe, xvi. 2 (Bengel, Vitringa, Stuart); but the president, or overseer, elsewhere denominated *ἐπίσκοπος, πρεσβύτερος, ποιμήν* (Calvin, Rothe, Philippi, Hodge). See, in proof, 1 Thess. v. 12; 1 Tim. iii. 4, 5; v. 17. The standing designation of the bishop or presbyter, in the primitive church, was *ὁ προεστώς*. Compare Justin Martyr, i. 67. The gift requisite for the office is the *χάρισμα κυβερνήσεως*, 1 Cor. xii. 28. *ἐν σπουδῇ*] with zeal and earnestness: all perfunctory service is excluded. *ὁ ἐλεῶν*] the deacon's service of attendance upon the sick and suffering is primarily in view, because the apostle is speaking of official gifts; yet the exhortation is applicable to the private Christian. An injunction to the performance of Christian duty may have a principal reference, and yet not an exclusive one. *ἐν ἱλαρότητι*] with "hilarity." A cheerful spon-

9 ἡ ἀγάπη ἀνυπόκριτος· ἀποστυγοῦντες τὸ πονηρόν, κολ-
λώμενοι τῷ ἀγαθῷ. 10 τῇ φιλαδελφίᾳ εἰς ἀλλήλους φιλό-

taneity and alacrity is meant. Pity should be impulsive, and not an effort; an inclination, and not a volition. Compare 2 Cor. ix. 7; Philemon 14.

VER. 9. St. Paul passes, now, from the duties of church officers, to those of church members generally. Christian ethics is now viewed in its individual and private aspects. ἡ ἀγάπη ἀνυπόκριτος] sc. ἔστω. Compare 2 Cor. vi. 6; 1 Pet. i. 22. Genuine morality is founded in inclination, or affection. An act that is not prompted by real pleasure in the act is not of the nature of virtue. It is, more or less, insincere and hypocritical. The particular moral affection that underlies true ethics is love, and hence St. Paul begins with this. "Love is the fulfilling of the law," xiii. 10; and "the bond of perfectness," Coloss. iii. 14; because if this feeling exists in the soul, all the external acts required by the law will follow naturally and necessarily. If there be supreme love of God in the heart, all duties toward God will be discharged. If there be the love of the neighbor as of the self, all duties toward mankind will be performed. It is to be noticed, that the affection of love is here, as elsewhere, the object of a command; which shows that the moral affections are modes of the will. But that this command to love may be obeyed, the human will itself must be enabled "to will" (Phil. ii. 13), by the Holy Spirit; because the affection of love is the deep and central determination of the will, and not a mere volition or resolution. ἀποστυγοῦντες . . κολλώμενοι] sc. ἐστέ. These participial clauses we regard as exegetical of the preceding exhortation to sincere love, and punctuate accordingly. Pure Christian love manifests itself in two phases: the ethical recoil from moral evil, and the cleaving to moral good. The

στοργοι· τῇ τιμῇ ἀλλήλους προηγούμενοι. [11] *τῇ σπουδῇ μὴ ὀκνηροί· τῷ πνεύματι ζέοντες, τῷ κυρίῳ δουλεύοντες,*

former, full as much as the latter, evinces the sincerity of the affection. Indifference toward sin, and especially an indulgent temper toward it, proves that there is no real love of holiness. The true measurement of a man's love of God, is the intensity with which he hates evil. Compare Ps. xcvii. 10. The ethics produced by the sentimental idea of God and of moral evil, is "easy virtue." Chrysostom, Theodoret, and Theophylact explain the preposition in *ἀποστυγοῦντες* as intensive: *σφόδρα μισεῖν; εκ ψυχῆς μισεῖν.* The word *κολλάω* denotes the closest possible adherence. Compare Luke x. 11.

Ver. 10. *τῇ φιλαδελφίᾳ*] is the dative of reference. Brotherly love, in the New Testament, is a highly prominent phase of love in general. Compare 1 Thess. iv. 9; Heb. xiii. 1; 1 Pet. i. 22; 2 Pet. i. 7. *φιλόστοργοι*] sc. *ἐστέ.* The *στόργη* is the *tenderest* form of affection, because founded in the physical nature and in blood-relationship; and similar should be the affection of Christian toward Christian. *τῇ τιμῇ ἀλλήλους προηγοῦμενοι*] this participial clause, also, is explanatory of the preceding exhortation: "in regard to showing honor, preceding one another;" i. e., going before one another (Luke xxii. 47), either as an example, or as anticipating. Brotherly affection is manifested particularly in the desire that a fellow Christian be honored, rather than one's self.

Ver. 11. *τῇ σπουδῇ* is the dative of reference. "Zeal" is strenuous energy in the execution of anything. It is not to be restricted, here, to preaching, or any one Christian duty; but denotes the Christian temper, in respect to all duties. St. Paul, in the context, mentions a number of them. *μὴ ὀκνηροί*] sc. *ἔστε.* "In regard to zeal, be not lazy" (Luther). *ζέοντες*] sc. *ἔστε.* This and the following participial clauses

12 τῇ ἐλπίδι χαίροντες, τῇ θλίψει ὑπομένοντες, τῇ προσευχῇ προσκαρτεροῦντες, 13 ταῖς χρείαις τῶν ἁγίων κοινωνοῦντες, τὴν φιλοξενίαν διώκοντες.

are exegetical of the injunction not to be sluggish. πνεύματι] denotes the temper or disposition. Compare Acts xviii. 25. κυρίῳ] is supported by ℵABL Peshito, Copt., Æth., Vulgate, Receptus, Beza, Lachm., Tisch., Tregelles. Codices DFG, Griesbach, Mill, read καιρῷ. But the injunction to "serve the time," or to "accommodate one's self to the time," is the maxim of worldly policy, rather than of Christianity. Christians are to make the best *use* of time (Eph. v. 16), but are not to serve it. δουλεύοντες] sc. ἔστε. This clause discriminates true from false zeal, which serves self, or man, rather than the Lord.

VER. 12. The three exhortations in this verse are connected with each other, and involve an earnest and zealous Christian spirit. ἐλπίδι] is the dative of the ground or motive: "on account of hope." Christian love is the ground of Christian joy, as heathen despair is the ground of heathen sorrow, 1 Thess. iv. 13 (Philippi). θλίψει] the dative of the state or condition. ὑπομένοντες] denotes patient endurance. See comment on ii. 7. προσκαρτεροῦντες] signifies unremitting attention. Compare Luke xviii. 7; Acts i. 14; Eph. vi. 18; Coloss. iv. 2; 1 Thess. v. 17. Continual prayer is requisite in order patiently to endure earthly trials and sorrows; and patient endurance is impossible without the glad hope of an ultimate deliverance from trials.

VER. 13. Christian zeal is now described in its outward exhibition toward fellow believers. χρείαις] the reading μνείαις, supported only by DF, is probably a corruption introduced by the later "commemoration" of saints, and is almost universally rejected. κοινωνοῦντες] may have the

[14] *Εὐλογεῖτε τοὺς διώκοντας ὑμᾶς· εὐλογεῖτε, καὶ μὴ καταρᾶσθε.* [15] *χαίρειν μετὰ χαιρόντων, κλαίειν μετὰ κλαι-*

transitive signification: "to impart," Gal. vi. 6; but the intransitive meaning: "to partake," is the prevalent one in the New Testament. See Rom. xv. 27; Phil. iv. 15; 1 Tim. v. 22; Heb. ii. 14; 1 Pet. iv. 13; 2 John 11. Christians, by sympathy and zealous endeavor to relieve, are to make the needy condition of their brethren *common* (κοινός) to themselves. φιλοξενίαν] hospitality is often enjoined in the New Testament. See Heb. xiii. 2; 1 Tim. v. 10; Titus i. 8; 1 Pet. iv. 9. The poverty of the early church, and the lack of inns, made this form of brotherly love uncommonly necessary. διώκοντες] the needy must be sought out and followed after; not merely received when they present themselves. "*Sectantes*, ut hospites non modo admittatis, sed quæratis" (Bengel).

VER. 14. St. Paul now turns to the duties relating to society generally, and the unsanctified world. εὐλογεῖτε, etc.] the words of Christ (Mat. v. 44; Luke vi. 28) were probably in the mind of the writer. Similar references to the Sermon on the Mount occur in the apostolic epistles. Compare Rom. ii. 19; 1 Cor. iv. 12, 13; vii. 10; James iv. 9; v. 12; 1 Pet. iii. 9, 14; iv. 14. διώκοντας] "Christi causa" (Bengel). καταρᾶσθε] "ne animo quedem" (Bengel). Such an exhortation as this would not apply to fellow Christians, but to persecuting Jews and Pagans.

VER. 15. χαίρειν and κλαίειν] sc. ὑμᾶς δεῖ. The infinitive is used for the imperative, when emphasis and precision are desired in the command. The two verbs are contrasted in John xvi. 20; 1 Cor. vii. 30. Respecting this injunction, Chrysostom remarks that it is easier to weep with those that weep, than to rejoice with those that rejoice; because nature

ὄντων, [16] *τὸ αὐτὸ εἰς ἀλλήλους φρονοῦντες. μὴ τὰ ὑψηλὰ φρονοῦντες, ἀλλὰ τοῖς ταπεινοῖς συναπαγόμενοι· μὴ γίνεσθε φρόνιμοι παρ' ἑαυτοῖς.* [17] *μηδενὶ κακὸν ἀντὶ κακοῦ ἀπο-*

itself prompts the former, but envy stands in the way of the latter.

VER. 16. φρονοῦντες] sc. ἔστε. This clause we regard as explanatory of the preceding injunction, and punctuate accordingly. "Be of the same mind or temper, in regard to one another: accord with the joy or the grief, as the case may be." Real and perfect sympathy with his fellow man is the duty of a Christian. τὰ ὑψηλὰ] riches, honor, office, etc. φρονοῦντες] denotes the disposition and aspiration of the mind. Compare xi. 20. ταπεινοῖς] is best regarded as neuter, as the opposite of ὑψηλὰ (Calvin, Beza, De Wette, Fritzsche, Meyer, Philippi). συναπαγόμενοι] sc. ἔστε. The word signifies, "to be carried or drawn away with," Gal. ii. 13; 2 Pet. iii. 7. Men naturally are carried away with the pride of life; but Christians should be attracted rather by its lowly circumstances and conditions. Compare the injunction to the rich "to *rejoice*, in that he is made low," James i. 10. παρ' ἑαυτοῖς] See comment on xi. 25. Those who are wise "before themselves," or in their own estimation merely, are self-conceited. This clause is to be connected with the preceding, being kindred in sentiment and explanatory.

VER. 17. μηδενὶ] is universal: Jew or Gentile, Christian or Pagan. ἀποδιδόντες] sc. ἔστε. Compare Mat. v. 39; 1 Thess. v. 15; 1 Pet. ii. 23; iii. 9. The doctrine of the Pharisees was exactly contrary. See Mat. v. 38, 43. The precept not to render evil for evil is taught by Socrates (Crito, 49). But Socrates could not impart the disposition to obey the precept. Hermann (on Sophoclis Philoct., 679) states the

διδόντες, προνοούμενοι καλὰ ἐνώπιον πάντων ἀνθρώπων.
18 εἰ δυνατόν, τὸ ἐξ ὑμῶν, μετὰ πάντων ἀνθρώπων εἰρηνεύον-

common doctrine of Grecian morality as follows: "Nec laudant Græci, si quis iniquis æquus est, sed virtutem esse censent æquis æquum, iniquum autem iniquis esse." προνοούμενοι, etc.] Compare 2 Cor. viii. 21. This clause is to be connected with the preceding injunction, as explanatory of it. The participle has a limiting force: "*yet* being mindful of (or exhibiting) things honorable in the sight of all men." The command to submit to wrongs, and not to render evil for evil, is to be obeyed not in a pusillanimous manner, but with Christian dignity. Thomas Paine, in reference to the injunction of our Lord to turn the other cheek to the smiter, charges Christianity with "the spirit of a spaniel," asserting that it destroys proper self-respect, and renders man indifferent to insult and affronts. St. Paul guards here against such an interpretation of this unique command, peculiar to the Christian religion alone. καλὰ] not "honest" (Eng. Ver.), but "honorable": the "honestum" in Cicero's use of the word. There is no reference to an honest provision for domestic necessities.

VER. 18. εἰ δυνατόν] the possibility of being at peace with all men is partly subjective, and partly objective; depending partly upon the Christian, and partly upon the world. It may be necessary for the believer to discharge duty, or to bear witness to the truth; and this may exasperate the unbeliever. "Be friends of all men, if it be possible; if it is not possible upon both sides, then at all events be friendly upon your own part" (Grotius). Respecting the *objective* possibility in the case, Calvin remarks that "it is not possible that there should be perpetual peace between the soldiers of Christ, and the sinful world whose prince is Satan." τὸ

τες, [19] μὴ ἑαυτοὺς ἐκδικοῦντες, ἀγαπητοί, ἀλλὰ δότε τόπον τῇ ὀργῇ· γέγραπται γὰρ Ἐμοὶ ἐκδίκησις, ἐγὼ ἀνταποδώσω, λέγει κύριος.

ἐξ ὑμῶν] sc. κατά: "as regards what *proceeds* from you." It is not the same as τὸ κατ' ἐμέ (i. 15): "my ability."

VER. 19 is to be connected with verse 18, as epexegetical. One way whereby to live peaceably with all men is, not to revenge one's own wrongs. δότε τόπον τῇ ὀργῇ] The change in the construction from the participial imperative to the regular imperative is for the sake of greater precision and emphasis. 1. ὀργῇ denotes the wrath of God: "give place to, or make way for, the divine retribution" (Chrysost., August., Calvin, De Wette, Tholuck, Meyer, Philippi, Hodge). This agrees with the preceding injunction, not to take vengeance into one's own hand; and with the succeeding explanatory clause, "Vengeance is mine, I will repay, saith the Lord." 2. ὀργῇ denotes the believer's wrath: "give time to wrath," that is, "allow it to subside inwardly" (Semler, Stuart). In support of this explanation is cited the Latin phrase, "darent iræ spatium," Livy, ii. 56; viii. 32; Lactant, De Ira, 18. But in these places, spatium is temporal, denoting a space of *time;* while τόπος denotes place only: a space in which to operate. 3. ὀργῇ denotes the adversary's wrath: "allow him to vent his rage" (Morus, Jowett, Wordsworth). This, like the first explanation, agrees with the meaning of δότε τόπον: compare Luke xiv. 9; Judges xx. 36; but not with either context. Moreover, it would be a merely prudential, not an ethical injunction. St. Paul, here, represents it as a Christian duty to desire that divine justice be administered by the Divine Being. To object to retribution as measured out by the Supreme Judge is unethical, and immoral. The Christian should not have the slightest desire to administer justice himself, particularly in reference to his own wrongs; but he should rejoice in the fact that an unerring and impartial Ruler will render to every man according to his deeds. "Personal injury, so far as it is merely injury to himself, the Christian is unconditionally to forgive. But so far as it is injury to the divine holiness as well; to the right that God has willed and the ordinance that God has established; he is to desire the recompense due to it, i. e., its punishment, in order to make reparation to this holy and inviolable ordinance. He is not merely to commit to God, but also to beseech from God, the revelation of his judicial righteousness to the glory of his holy name, in presence of wilful dishonor done to that name, whether the dishonor be done by himself, or by another. The apostolic dictum in this passage does not set aside, but confirms the prayers against enemies, in the so-called imprecatory psalms. Compare Luke ix. 5; 2 Thess. i. 6; 2 Tim. iv. 14; 1 Pet. ii. 23; Rev. vi. 10, and the striking remarks of Hengstenberg in his Commentary on the Psalms, III., app. lxx." (Philippi in loco). γέγραπται] in Deut. xxxii. 35. St. Paul adds λέγει κύριος. Compare xiv. 11; 1 Cor. xiv. 21; 2 Cor. vi. 17. ἐμοὶ] Compare Heb. x. 30. The dative of possession, here, implies exclusiveness: "to me only." The infliction of retribution, or punishment in distinction from chastisement, belongs to God alone. Punishment, in the restricted and proper sense, is solely for *requital*, and does not aim at the improvement of the criminal. Consequently, punishment is in its own nature *endless*, and the Supreme Being is the only one who may inflict it. Man has no right to punish except as it is delegated to him, in the office of a magistrate. In this case, man discharges a divine and not a human function.

VER. 20 is a citation from Prov. xxv. 21, 22, literally from the Septuagint, which agrees with the Hebrew. ἀλλὰ ἐὰν is

20 ἀλλὰ Ἐὰν πεινᾷ ὁ ἐχθρός σου, ψώμιζε αὐτόν· ἐὰν διψᾷ, πότιζε αὐτόν· τοῦτο γὰρ ποιῶν ἄνθρακας πυρὸς σωρεύσεις ἐπὶ τὴν κεφαλὴν αὐτοῦ. 21 μὴ νικῶ ὑπὸ τοῦ κακοῦ, ἀλλὰ νίκα ἐν τῷ ἀγαθῷ τὸ κακόν.

supported by ℵAB Copt., Vulg., Lachm., Tisch. ἐὰν οὖν is the reading of DEL Peshito, Æth. ἀλλὰ] "do not wreak your revenge, *but*, on the contrary," etc. If οὖν be adopted, then the injunction in this verse is a deduction from the fact that retribution belongs exclusively to God. ἄνθρακας, etc.] gives the motive for showing kindness to an enemy. "Coals of fire" is a metaphor for keen anguish. Compare the Arabic phrases, "coals in the heart," and "fire in the liver." Explanations: 1. The remorse awakened by this unmerited kindness, resulting, perhaps, in repentance (Origen, Augustine, Jerome, Ambrose, Erasmus, Luther, Wolfius, Bengel, Tholuck, De Wette, Olshausen, Fritzsche, Philippi, Hodge, Alford). 2. The divine retribution, resulting from surrendering the case into God's hands (Chrysostom, Theodoret, Theophylact, Beza, Grotius, Wetstein, Hengstenberg). The first is preferable, because the "coals of fire" are immediately connected with the "feeding" and "giving drink."

Ver. 21. τοῦ κακοῦ] the enemy's evil, i. e. "Do not allow yourself to be overcome by the wickedness of your adversary; as would be the case, if you suffered yourself to be exasperated by him to personal revenge." ἀλλὰ, etc.] "*but*, on the contrary, overcome your enemy's wickedness by your kindness, which will awaken his remorse and sorrow." This verse recapitulates the sentiment of verses 19 and 20.

CHAPTER XIII

[1] *Πᾶσα ψυχὴ ἐξουσίαις ὑπερεχούσαις ὑποτασσέσθω. οὐ γάρ ἐστιν ἐξουσία εἰ μὴ ὑπὸ θεοῦ, αἱ δὲ οὖσαι ὑπὸ*

THE apostle passes now, in verses 1–7, to the Christian's duties toward the State. He may have been led to this, in part, by the seditious and revolutionary temper of the Jew, which showed itself occasionally in open rebellion against the Roman authority, Acts v. 37. But the principal reason was of a general nature. He would lay down principles for the Church universal, in all time, and in reference to government in the abstract.

VER. 1. πᾶσα ψυχὴ] is equivalent to πᾶς ἄνθρωπος. Compare ii. 9. ἐξουσίαις ὑπερεχούσαις] "authorities above, or over him." The idea of sovereignty and supremacy is implied. Government supposes an authority higher than that of the governed. Law is superior to the subject of law. Compare 1 Tim. ii. 2; 1 Pet. ii. 13. ὑποτασσέσθω] denotes voluntary self-subjection. Compare Luke ii. 51; 1 Cor. xvi. 16; Eph. v. 22 sq.; Titus ii. 5. Unwilling obedience to the government is not Christian virtue. οὐ γάρ, etc.] assigns the reason for obeying the civil authority: viz., because of its divine origin. Even bad governments are not excepted: "there is *no* authority, except by and from God." The fact that an earthly government may be corrupt and tyrannical does not disprove the divine origin of government; any more than the fact that parents may be unfaithful to their duties proves that the family is not divinely originated; or the fact that a particular church may become corrupt proves that the church is not divine in its source. St. Paul, however, does not teach, here, that *any* degree of tyranny, whatever, is to be submitted to by a Christian. If the government attempt to force him to violate a divine command, for example to desist from preaching the gospel, or to take part in pagan worship, he must resist even unto death. See Acts iv. 19; v. 29. Most of the apostles suffered martyrdom for this principle. But in respect to "things pertaining only to this life" (1 Cor. vi. 4), and in cases in which the rights of conscience and religious convictions were not infringed upon, both Christ and his apostles taught that injustice, and even tyranny, should be submitted to, rather than that revolutionary resistance be made. And this, because merely earthly liberty, and the rights of property, are of secondary consideration. The same rule applies to the relation of the individual to the State, in this case, that applies to the relation between man and man. If a Christian is defrauded of his property by a fellow believer, he ought to "take the wrong, and suffer himself to be defrauded," rather than "go to law one with another," 1 Cor. vi. 7. In like manner, in regard to merely worldly good, the Christian should forego his rights and allow himself to be ill-treated even by the government under which he lives, rather than organize a rebellion and bring on war with its untold evils. Political freedom is one of the most valuable of merely earthly blessings; and political slavery is one of the greatest of merely earthly evils. Yet Christ and his apostles nowhere teach or imply, that either individual or organized action was justifiable, even under the tyranny of Rome, in order to obtain the former, or abolish the latter. On the contrary, they dissuade from and forbid it. Compare Mat. xvii. 24–27; xxii. 17–21; 1 Cor. vii. 21, 22; 1 Tim. vi. 1. ὑπὸ] is the reading of ℵABL Lachm., Tisch., Tregelles; ἀπό

θεοῦ τεταγμέναι εἰσίν. 2 ὥστε ὁ ἀντιτασσόμενος τῇ ἐξου-
σίᾳ τῇ τοῦ θεοῦ διαταγῇ ἀνθέστηκεν· οἱ δὲ ἀνθεστηκότες
ἑαυτοῖς κρῖμα λήψονται. 3 οἱ γὰρ ἄρχοντες οὐκ εἰσὶν
φόβος τῷ ἀγαθῷ ἔργῳ, ἀλλὰ τῷ κακῷ. θέλεις δὲ μὴ φο-

that of DEF Receptus. οὖσαι] is the reading of ℵABDF Copt., Æth., Vulg.; the Receptus with EL Peshito add ἐξουσίαι, which is superfluous, being understood as matter of course. The word denotes an "actually existing" authority: a government de facto, though possibly not de jure, in all respects. τεταγμέναι] the fact that a civil government is organized, and in actual operation, is an evidence that God has so appointed, in his providence. The plural implies that there are varieties in the forms of human government. "Christianity gives its sanction not exclusively to *one* definite form of government, but to the form of government actually subsisting at any time, and guards it against revolutionary attempts." Philippi in loco.

Ver. 2. ὥστε] "so that;" as a consequence from the fact that the existing authorities are ordained by God. ἀντιτασσόμενος] denotes primarily a drawing up in battle array, but is here employed in the general signification of opposition, or resistance. Compare Acts xviii. 6; James iv. 6. ἀνθέστηκεν] is equivalent to ἀντιτάσσεται. Compare ix. 19. κρῖμα] the condemnation of God, i. e., whose ordinance they have resisted.

Ver. 3 connects with verse 1 (Calvin, Tholuck, Philippi, Hodge), and assigns an additional reason for obedience, viz., that government is not only an ordinance of God, but a *beneficial* ordinance. Meyer connects with verse 2, so that verse 3 explains the *mode* in which God condemns, viz., through the civil authority. ἀγαθῷ ἔργῳ, etc.] is supported by ℵABDF Copt., Lachm., Tisch., Tregelles. The Receptus,

βεῖσθαι τὴν ἐξουσίαν; τὸ ἀγαθὸν ποίει, καὶ ἕξεις ἔπαινον ἐξ αὐτῆς· [4] θεοῦ γὰρ διάκονός ἐστιν σοὶ εἰς τὸ ἀγαθόν. ἐὰν δὲ τὸ κακὸν ποιῇς, φοβοῦ· οὐ γὰρ εἰκῇ τὴν μάχαιραν φορεῖ· θεοῦ γὰρ διάκονος ἐστιν ἔκδικος εἰς ὀργὴν τῷ τὸ κακὸν πράσσοντι. [5] διὸ ἀνάγκη ὑποτάσσεσθαι, οὐ μόνον διὰ τὴν ὀργήν, ἀλλὰ καὶ διὰ τὴν συνείδησιν. [6] διὰ τοῦτο γὰρ

with EL Peshito, reads τῶν ἀγαθων ἐργῶν, etc. δὲ] is transitive: "now, do you desire," etc. Luther, Tholuck, Philippi, Lange, construe as a hypothetical sentence: "Thou desirest not to be afraid of the authority. I put the case." ἔπαινον] Compare 1 Pet. ii. 14. Grotius remarks that at the time when St. Paul wrote this, Nero was not persecuting the Christians. But the principle is a general one. "Damnatio malorum laus est bonorum" (Pelagius).

VER. 4. διάκονός ἐστιν] sc. ἡ ἐξουσία· εἰς τὸ ἀγαθόν] "for your advantage," in the way of praise and protection. Compare 1 Tim. ii. 2. εἰκῇ] not for mere show, but for use, when required. μάχαιραν] the sword is the symbol of the magistrate's power to put to death. ἔκδικος] sc. ὤν: not "revenger" (Eng. Ver.), but "avenger," in modern English. In the earlier usage, retributive justice was denominated both "revenging," and "vindictive." εἰς ὀργὴν] i. e., εἰς τὸ ἐπιφέρειν ὀργὴν. "Wrath" is here put for its effect, viz.: punishment.

VER. 5 contains an inference, introduced by διὸ, from the statements in verses 1–4. ἀνάγκη] denotes a moral necessity founded in the nature both of government and of man. ὑποτάσσεσθαι] is middle: "to submit yourselves." διὰ τὴν ὀργήν] a prudential motive is allowable. The fear of punishment, like "the respect to the recompense of reward" (Heb. xi. 26), has its proper place in morals. It is, however, a subordinate place. ἀλλὰ καὶ διὰ τὴν συνείδησιν] the command of

καὶ φόρους τελεῖτε· λειτουργοὶ γὰρ θεοῦ εἰσὶν εἰς αὐτὸ
τοῦτο προσκαρτεροῦντες. 7 ἀπόδοτε πᾶσιν τὰς ὀφειλάς,

conscience is the principal reason for voluntary subjection to lawful authority. But as conscience is the voice of God in the soul, this reason for obedience is equivalent to that given in 1 Pet. ii. 13: "submit yourselves to every ordinance of man διὰ τὸν κύριον."

VER. 6 is best connected, not with verses 1–4 (Calvin, De Wette, Philippi), but with verse 5 (Meyer). τοῦτο] viz.: the fear of punishment, and the command of conscience. γὰρ] supposes an ellipsis; viz., "you are thus submitting yourselves, *for* you are paying taxes." καὶ] "also," in addition to other acts of obedience to the government. τελεῖτε] is not imperative (Eng. Vers., Tholuck, Stuart, Hodge), but indicative (Chrysost., Theophylact, Vulgate, Calvin, Beza, De Wette, Meyer, Lange, Philippi). Were it imperative, the sentence would have been introduced by οὖν rather than γὰρ, which does not well agree with the imperative. And furthermore, the command to pay tribute, is given, by way of reiteration and emphasis, in the next verse. To pay taxes is one of the most conclusive evidences of submission to the government. λειτουργοὶ θεοῦ] is the predicate. The subject is οἱ understood, referring to ἄρχοντες in verse 3. λειτουργὸς is a term that denotes the temple service of the priests, Heb. i. 7; viii. 2. It is here applied to the tax-gatherers, who as officers of a government that has been ordained of God are, in this sense, his attendants or "ministers." γὰρ] introduces the reason why they are paying tribute. τοῦτο] viz.: the collection of taxes. προσκαρτεροῦντες] denotes steady attention. Compare xii. 12.

VER. 7 summarizes and repeats, for the sake of emphasis, the exhortations in verses 1–6. ἀπόδοτε] is followed by οὖν

τῷ τὸν φόρον τὸν φόρον, τῷ τὸ τέλος τὸ τέλος, τῷ τὸν φόβον τὸν φόβον, τῷ τὴν τιμὴν τὴν τιμήν.

8 Μηδενὶ μηδὲν ὀφείλετε, εἰ μὴ τὸ ἀλλήλους ἀγαπᾶν· ὁ γὰρ ἀγαπῶν τὸν ἕτερον, νόμον πεπλήρωκεν. 9 τὸ γὰρ οὐ

in the Peshito, Receptus, FL; which is omitted by ℵBD Copt., Lachm., Tisch., Tregelles. τῷ] sc. ἀπαιτοῦντι, which, as Meyer remarks, wiil suit φόβον and τιμὴν, as well as φόρον and τέλος; because magistrates (to whom πᾶσι refers) require or demand respect and honor. φόρον] "tribute" is the land and capitation tax, Luke xx. 22. τέλος] "custom" (vectigalia) is the tax on merchandise. The apostle mentions taxes first in the order, because he has already singled this out as an evidence of submission to the civil authority, and also, perhaps, because of the Jewish disposition to dispute this demand from a Gentile government. Compare Mat. xvii. 24–27; xxii. 17. φόβον and τιμὴν] denote the honor due to judges and the higher civil authorities.

Ver. 8 begins a new paragraph (verses 8–14), in which the writer returns to the duty of Christians toward society generally, which was previously spoken of in xii. 14–21. μηδενὶ] is universal, including both the church and the world. Indebtedness must be discharged toward all mankind. εἰ μὴ ἀγαπᾶν] "By its very nature, love is a duty which when discharged is not discharged; since he does not truly love who loves for the sake of ceasing from loving, and in order to relieve himself from the duty of love." Philippi. Similarly, Augustine remarks: "Love is still due, even when it has been rendered, because there will never be a time when it is not to be rendered. The obligation to love is not nullified, but multiplied, by the bestowment of love." ὁ γὰρ, etc.] Compare Mat. xxii. 37–40.

Ver. 9 corroborates the statement in verse 8, by showing

μοιχεύσεις, οὐ φονεύσεις, οὐ κλέψεις, οὐκ ἐπιθυμήσεις, καὶ εἴ τις ἑτέρα ἐντολή, ἐν τῷ λόγῳ τούτῳ ἀνακεφαλαιοῦται, ἐν τῷ Ἀγαπήσεις τὸν πλησίον σου ὡς σεαυτόν. [10] ἡ ἀγάπη τῷ πλησίον κακὸν οὐκ ἐργάζεται· πλήρωμα οὖν νόμου ἡ ἀγάπη. [11] καὶ τοῦτο εἰδότες τὸν καιρόν, ὅτι ὥρα ἤδη ὑμᾶς

that all the particular statutes of the decalogue relating to one's fellow man are summed in the command, to love him as one's self. οὐ κλέψεις] is followed by οὐ ψευδομαρτυρήσεις in ℵ Copt., Æth., Receptus; which is omitted in ABDEFGL Peshito, Sahidic, Lachm., Tisch. εἴ τις ἑτέρα ἐντολή] sc. ἐν τῷ νόμῳ ἐστίν. ἀνακεφαλαιοῦται] is "recapitulated," or "brought under one head" (κεφαλή). ἐν τῷ] ("namely") is omitted in BFG Itala, Vulgate, and bracketted by Lachm., and Tregelles; it is found in ℵADL Tisch. σεαυτόν] FGL Receptus read ἑαύτον, which is sometimes used for the second person. See Winer in loco.

VER. 10. κακὸν οὐκ ἐργάζεται] St. Paul employs the negative form, because of the negatives in the statutes he has cited. But the positive is implied: "Love doeth good" (χρηστεύεται), 1 Cor. xiii. 4. οὖν] introduces the conclusion drawn from the preceding analysis of the law, viz.: that love is the complete fulfilment of the law. The doctrine of justification by works finds no support in this text; because it does not settle the question of fact, whether any man, in a perfect manner, loves God supremely and his neighbor as himself.

VER. 11. καὶ τοῦτο] "and this too," or "especially." τοῦτο refers to the injunction in verse 8 with the explanation in verses 9 and 10. It introduces the motive to obey which follows. There is no need of supplying ποιῶμεν or ποιεῖτε (Bengel, Tholuck). Compare 1 Cor. v. 6, 8; Eph. ii. 8; Phil. i. 28; Heb. xi. 12. The more common usage in the classics is καὶ ταῦτα. εἰδότες] "since," or "because" we know. τὸν

καιρόν] the "period": not *χρόνος*, time generally. The peculiarity of the season or period is meant. *ὥρα*] sc. *ἐστίν*: the "hour," or particular point, in the period. *ἤδη*] "now, at length," without waiting any longer. Compare *ἤδε ποτὲ*, i. 10. It qualifies *ἐγερθῆναι*. *ὑμᾶς*] is the reading of ℵABC, Tisch. The Receptus, DEFGL, Peshito, Vulg., Sahidic, Coptic, Lachm. read *ἡμᾶς*. *ὕπνου*] sleep is a common figure for the apathy of sin. Compare Eph. v. 14; 1 Thess. v. 6. Believers having remainders of sin have remainders of spiritual lethargy, against which they must watch and strive. *γὰρ*] introduces the reason why it is the hour for them to awake. *ἡμῶν*] may be connected with *σωτηρίαν* (Vulgate, Eng. Ver., Luther, Hodge); or with *ἐγγύτερον* (Calvin, Meyer, Philippi, who cite x. 8). *σωτηρία*] 1. The completion of redemption in eternity, in sinless perfection and the glorified body (Theodore Mops., Calvin, Calovius, Flatt, Stuart, Hodge). 2. The second advent of Christ, when believers shall be made perfect and clothed with the resurrection body (De Wette, Olshausen, Meyer, Philippi, Lange, Alford). The first explanation is preferable, because *ἐπιφάνεια* and *παρουσία* are the settled terms for the advent, and there is no instance in which *σωτηρία* is put for it. The apostle exhorts believers to watchfulness, because they are nearer the end of the Christian race and fight than they were when they first began it. If they had made no progress, but were as far off from the goal as ever, they would have no motive to struggle. "Nearer is salvation now, to us, than at that time when we began to believe." Calvin in loco. The second view, however, may be adopted, without maintaining that St. Paul mistakenly expected the Parousia in his own life-time, as is asserted by De Wette and Meyer. Philippi, who explains *σωτηρία* by the Lord's second coming, remarks that the rapid spread of Christianity may have given St. Paul reason to hope that the Lord's return might occur in his own day, but did not give him the certainty

ἐξ ὕπνου ἐγερθῆναι· νῦν γὰρ ἐγγύτερον ἡμῶν ἡ σωτηρία ἢ ὅτε ἐπιστεύσαμεν. 12 *ἡ νὺξ προέκοψεν, ἡ δὲ ἡμέρα ἤγ-*

that it would; because the particular time of this advent is expressly stated to be unrevealed, and absolutely unknown to man, Mark xiii. 32. "The Parousia known as objectively near in the divine view, might also have seemed to be subjectively near in human expectation. But there would be an error in identifying the latter with the former. No sooner did this error appear, than the apostles at once corrected it, 2 Thess. ii. 1 sq.; 2 Pet. iii. 1 sq. Had St. Paul been asked whether he knew if he or any of his contemporaries would survive till the return of Christ, with the same inspired certainty with which he knew the general fact of that return, he would have replied in the negative." Similarly Alford remarks, that "the fact that the nearness or the distance of the day of Christ's coming was unknown to the apostles, in no way affects the prophetic announcements of God's Spirit by them, concerning its preceding and accompanying circumstances. The 'day and the hour' formed no part of their inspiration; the details of the event did." Similarly Tholuck. *ὅτε ἐπιστεύσαμεν*] when we believed in Christ, and became Christians, Acts xix. 2; 1 Cor. iii. 5.

VER. 12. *ἡ νὺξ*, etc.] the night is the time for sleep, and for sin, because of the darkness, 1 Thess. v. 7. *ἡ δὲ ἡμέρα*] the day is the time for work, and for holiness, because of the light, Job xxiv. 15–17; John iii. 19–21; 1 Thess. v. 5, 8. "The time of sin and sorrow is nearly over (*προέκοψεν*), and that of holiness and happiness is at hand (*ἤγγικεν*)." Hodge in loco. The other explanation of *σωτηρία* fails here: the apostle could not with certainty say that the Parousia was "at hand," in the sense of occurring in the life-time of those to whom he wrote. But, since the believer's death brings

γικεν. ἀποθώμεθα οὖν τὰ ἔργα τοῦ σκότους, ἐνδυσώμεθα δὲ τὰ ὅπλα τοῦ φωτός. 13 ὡς ἐν ἡμέρᾳ εὐσχημόνως περιπατήσωμεν, μὴ κώμοις καὶ μέθαις, μὴ κοίταις καὶ ἀσελ-

him into perfect holiness and blessedness, he could speak of "salvation," in the ordinary New Testament use of the term, as being certainly "at hand." ἀποθώμεθα] is the opposite of ἐνδυσώμεθα, and represents the works of darkness as night-garments, which on the approach of day are to be taken off. οὖν] namely, because of the approaching holiness and blessedness of the next life, which the believer will so soon enter upon. That this is one of the most powerful and effective motives for resisting sin, the perusal of Howe's "Blessedness of the Righteous" will convince any one. δὲ] is the reading of ABCD Copt., Griesbach, Lachm., Tisch. It denotes merely the contrast. The Receptus, with FL Peshito, reads καὶ; א omits the conjunction altogether. ὅπλα] the figure is changed from clothing to armor, because of the fight to which believers are exhorted. Compare Eph. vi. 13 sq.

VER. 13. εὐσχημόνως] becomingly; with decorum, 1 Cor. vii. 35; xiv. 40; 1 Thess. iv. 12. κώμοις καὶ μέθαις] night revellings and carousals, Gal. v. 21; 1 Pet. iv. 3. κοίταις καὶ ἀσελγείαις] venery and wantonness. "Abstract nouns in the plural denote the various expressions, evidences, outbreaks, and concrete manifestations generally, of the quality expressed by the singular." Winer in loco. The first two terms relate to sins of gluttony and drunkenness; the last two, to sins of licentiousness. They are naturally connected: "sine Cerere et Baccho Venus friget." Ovid. They are also sins of the night: "nox et amor vinumque nihil moderabile suadent." Ovid, Amor., I. v. 59. That St. Paul was compelled to warn Christian believers against this class of sins, does not prove that the primitive Christian life and charac-

γείαις, μὴ ἔριδι καὶ ζήλῳ, [14] ἀλλὰ ἐνδύσασθε τὸν κύριον Ἰησοῦν Χριστόν, καὶ τῆς σαρκὸς πρόνοιαν μὴ ποιεῖσθε εἰς ἐπιθυμίας.

ter was as a whole inferior to that of the modern church. The paganism from which the first Christians had been converted left habits of life that could not be instantaneously and entirely extirpated. In estimating the energy of divine grace in the soul, the line of Burns is to be remembered:

"We know not what's *resisted*."

The primitive church was more under the influence of the "lust of the flesh" than of the "pride of life;" the modern church is more under the influence of the "pride of life" than of the "lust of the flesh." But pride is as great a sin, in the sight of God, as sensuality. This should be considered, in forming an estimate of some of the modern missionary churches. ἔριδι καὶ ζήλω] quarrelling and jealousy are naturally connected with the vices just mentioned. The Memoirs of fashionable and court life, like those of St. Simon and Grammont illustrate this.

VER. 14. ἐνδύσασθε τόν κύριον] the figure denotes the most intimate union and appropriation. See Gal. iii. 27; Eph. iv. 24; Coloss. iii. 10, 12; Luke xxiv. 49; 1 Cor. xv. 53, 54; 2 Cor. v. 3; 1 Thess. v. 8; Job xxix. 14; Isa. li. 9; Ezek. xxvi. 16. Compare also Homer's δύσεο δ' ἀλκήν, Il. xix. 36. σαρκὸς] 1. is employed in the physical sense, to denote the sensuous nature ("die lebendige Materie des σῶμα," Meyer), in distinction from the rational. The apostle does not forbid all provision for the flesh, but only such provision as is lustful. "He does not forbid to drink, but to get drunk; he does not forbid marriage, but fornication" (Chrysost., Luther, Calvin, De Wette, Meyer, Philippi). 2. σάρξ is employed in the ethical signification of the whole man as corrupt; so that a total prohibition of a provision for the flesh is meant (Eng. Ver., Fritzsche, Stuart, Hodge, Alford). The latter view is favored by the general signification of σάρξ in this Epistle. St. Paul employs the term to denote, not the sensuous in distinction from the rational nature, but the entire man; and not that which is created and innocent, but that which is fallen and sinful. Compare viii. 3–9, 12 et alia. πρόνοιαν μὴ ποιεῖσθε] is equivalent to μὴ προνοεῖσθε: "do not provide for." Compare xii. 17; 1 Tim. v. 8. εἰς ἐπιθυμίας] denotes the intention: "so that lusts may be excited." Compare Mat. v. 28. Sinful lusts are the natural characteristics of the sinful σάρξ. There are remainders of σάρξ in the believer (chapters vii., viii.), and he must not do anything to stir them up. These were the verses that struck the eye of Augustine when the voice said to him: "Tolle, lege." Confessions, viii. 12.

CHAPTER XIV

St. Paul now resumes the consideration of the believer's duties toward the Church, which was interrupted in xii. 14 by a transition to his duties toward Society. He continues the subject down to xv. 13. The particular duty which he considers relates to *differences of opinion*, among believers, *respecting points not essential to salvation.* The difference of sentiment related to abstinence from flesh (verses 2, 21), from wine (verse 21), and the observance of Jewish sacred days (verse 5). The principal views are the following: 1. The "weak in faith" held that the Mosaic law respecting flesh, wine, and sacred days, was still obligatory upon Christians (Origen, Chrysost., Theodoret, Jerome, Calovius, Reiche). 2. The "weak in faith," though believing that the Mosaic ceremonial statutes were no longer binding, yet thought that abstinence from the sacrificial-flesh and libation-wine of the pagan, sold in the market, was obligatory (Clem. Alex., Ambrose, Augustine, Michaelis, Flatt, Neander, Tholuck, Philippi). This view is favored by a comparison with 1 Cor. viii. 10; x. 19–23, where the same needless but well-intended scrupulousness appears. 3. The third view places the abstinence upon both grounds (Erasmus, Rückert, De Wette). This latter is preferable, because all the data cannot be brought under either view alone. Both Jewish and Gentile-Christians are advised and enjoined by St. Paul. The Jewish-Christian who was "weak in the faith" relied upon Christ's sacrifice for justification (otherwise he would not have even a weak *faith*); but from his previous education and training in Judaism, and an imperfect apprehension of Christianity (xv. 1; 1 Cor. viii. 7, 10, 11), supposed that the distinction between clean and unclean meats, and sacred and secular days, was still valid and should be observed. His error was not legalism proper, but *asceticism.* Had he, with the carnal Jew, maintained that salvation depended upon the observance of the ceremonial law, the apostle would have spoken in the language of stern condemnation, as he does in Gal. i. 6; ii. 3–5, 14–17; v. 1, 2. Some of the Gentile-Christians, on the other hand, remembering the abominations of that idolatry from which they had been converted, supposed that contact with paganism in any form whatever must be avoided, and hence abstained from sacrificial meat and wine offered for sale. These also were evangelical though "weak" believers; relying for salvation upon Christ, but lacking the spiritual insight to perceive that "an idol is nothing in the world" (1 Cor. viii. 4). Upon both sides then, Jewish and Gentile, there were conscientious scruples, which though not really valid, were yet to be respected. From St. Paul's point of view, there was "nothing unclean of itself" (xiv. 14), and an idol was a nonentity to which the believer ought to have not the slightest reference; yet St. Paul expressly says that he shall respect the scruples of such of his brethren as were not yet sufficiently enlightened to see as he saw (xiv. 21, 22; 1 Cor. viii. 13). It must not be supposed that these "weak brethren" constituted a majority of the Roman church. The great body of both Jewish and Gentile believers in the congregation, probably, held the views of the apostle himself, and were "strong" in the faith (xv. 1).

VER. 1. πίστει] justifying faith. These persons, though relying upon Christ for salvation, were weakened in their reliance by fears and anxieties, which led them to ascetic

[1] *Τὸν δὲ ἀσθενοῦντα τῇ πίστει προσλαμβάνεσθε, μὴ εἰς διακρίσεις διαλογισμῶν.* [2] *ὃς μὲν πιστεύει φαγεῖν*

opinions and practices. There is in believers generally more or less of this legal element, which interferes with boldness and assurance of faith. It is seen in the experience of a devout Roman Catholic like Pascal. It arises from "the want of an intelligent and firm conviction of the gratuitous nature of justification, and of the spirituality of the gospel." Hodge in loco. προσλαμβάνεσθε] More than reception into the church is meant; for the weak brother was already in the church. "Welcome him to your affectionate and helpful acquaintance and communion." διακρίσεις διαλογισμῶν] "decisions of questions:" διακρίνειν signifies to pass judgment, Mat. xvi. 3; to decide, 1 Cor. vi. 5. Compare also 1 Cor. xii. 10; Heb. v. 14. διαλογισμός denotes speculations (i. 21; 1 Cor. iii. 20), or disputings (Phil. i. 14). The "strong" should not attempt to decide the points of difference between themselves and the "weak," by inviting the "weak" to discuss them with them. "Non sumentes vobis dijudicandas ipsorum cogitationes." Grotius. By waiving the matters in dispute, and dwelling upon the cardinal truth of faith in Christ, they would in the end convert the weak brother into a strong one. The history of the early Jewish-Christians shows, that by this kindly and forbearing mode of treatment they were either brought over to a full and free evangelism and were merged in the church, like the Nazarenes, or else lapsed down upon an anti-evangelical and hostile position, like the Ebionite.

VER. 2 describes the difference between the strong and the weak believer. πιστεύει] is equivalent to πίστιν ἔχει: "he has such a faith that he eats." Compare Acts xiv. 9. ὁ δὲ] not ὃς δε: "the other" (compare verse 5); but ὁ ἀσθενῶν:

πάντα, ὁ δὲ ἀσθενῶν λάχανα ἐσθίει. [3] *ὁ ἐσθίων τὸν μὴ ἐσθίοντα μὴ ἐξουθενείτω· ὁ δὲ μὴ ἐσθίων τὸν ἐσθίοντα μὴ κρινέτω· ὁ θεός γὰρ αὐτὸν προσελάβετο.* [4] *σὺ τίς εἶ ὁ κρίνων ἀλλότριον οἰκέτην; τῷ ἰδίῳ κυρίῳ στήκει ἢ πίπτει·*

"the weak." λάχανα ἐσθίει] the weak brother ate bread and vegetable food, and no flesh of unclean animals, no meat offered to idols, and no meat of clean animals on the sacred days (Reiche, Neander, Tholuck, Philippi). Meyer interprets the phrase as excluding flesh altogether.

VER. 3 gives the rule for both parties. ἐξουθενείτω] denotes disdain or contempt for the weak brother, as narrow and superstitious. ὁ δὲ μὴ] is the reading of ℵABCD Lachm., Tisch. The Receptus, with EL Peshito, Sahidic, Æth., Vulgate, reads καὶ ὁ μὴ. κρινέτω] the weak brother must not pass a condemning judgment upon the strong, as lacking in Christian earnestness and fidelity. γὰρ] introduces the reason, viz.: because Christ has received the "strong" as a true disciple.

VER. 4. σὺ τίς εἶ] Compare ix. 20; James iv. 12. ὁ κρίνων] refers to μὴ κρινέτω, verse 3, and consequently to the weak in faith (Meyer, Philippi), and not to both parties (Tholuck, Hodge). ἀλλότριον οἰκέτην] judgment of a servant belongs to the master alone; who in this case is God, and not man. στήκει] to stand in the judgment is to be acquitted. Compare Ps. i. 5; Luke xxi. 36; Rev. vi. 17. πίπτει] to fall in the judgment is to be condemned; causa cadere. σταθήσεται] is more comprehensive in its signification, here, than in the preceding clause. It denotes not merely the pronunciation of a favorable judgment, but also support in that course of life and conduct which results in a favorable judgment. The "strong" shall be enabled by God's grace to stand in faith and obedience, and thereby in the final judgment. Compare

σταθήσεται δέ, δυνατεῖ γὰρ ὁ κύριος στῆσαι αὐτόν. [5] ὃς μὲν κρίνει ἡμέραν παρ' ἡμέραν, ὃς δὲ κρίνει πᾶσαν ἡμέραν· ἕκαστος ἐν τῷ ἰδίῳ νοῒ πληροφορείσθω. [6] ὁ φρονῶν τὴν

1 Cor. x. 12. δυνατεῖ γὰρ] is the reading of ℵABCDF Lachm., Tisch., Tregelles. Compare 2 Cor. xiii. 3. The Receptus, with L, reads δυνατὸς γάρ ἐστιν. κύριος] is the reading of ℵABC Peshito, Sahidic, Coptic, Æth., Lachm., Tisch., Tregelles. The Receptus, with DEFL, reads θεός.

Ver. 5 relates to the second point of difference, the observance of the Jewish fasts and festivals. παρ'] has a comparative force, as in i. 25; Luke xiii. 2; Heb. 1. 4. "One judges that one day is above, or superior to another." St. Paul refers, here, to the ordinary Jewish sacred days, as in Gal. iv. 10; Col. ii. 16. The Lord's day was never regarded by the apostles, or by the Primitive Church, as a common Jewish festival; and, consequently, this and the following statements have no reference to the Christian Sabbath, as some (Philippi, Alford) maintain. The Jewish Sabbath itself was distinguished from the other sacred days of Judaism, by being made a part of the moral law, or decalogue, while the secondary holy-days were provisions of the ceremonial law only. πᾶσαν ἡμέραν] sc. ἴσην εἶναι (not παρά). ἰδίῳ νοῒ πληροφορείσθω] this is the general principle of action, in reference to points not essential to salvation. "One man should not be forced to act according to another man's conscientious scruples, but every one should be satisfied in his own mind, and be careful not to do what he thinks to be wrong." Hodge in loco.

Ver. 6 assigns the reason, introduced by γὰρ, for the preceding rule of action, viz.: that the particular person, whether he be weak or strong in the faith, has reference to the Lord in what he does, and believes that he is serving

ἡμέραν κυρίῳ φρονεῖ. καὶ ὁ ἐσθίων κυρίῳ ἐσθίει, εὐχαριστεῖ γὰρ τῷ θεῷ· καὶ ὁ μὴ ἐσθίων κυρίῳ οὐκ ἐσθίει καὶ εὐχαριστεῖ τῷ θεῷ. 7 οὐδεὶς γὰρ ἡμῶν ἑαυτῷ ζῇ, καὶ

him by his particular course of conduct. If this be the believer's actual conviction, he must not be despised for his scruples, if he is one of the "weak," or censured for his freedom, if he is one of the "strong." κυρίῳ] for the service and honor of the Lord. The reference is to Christ, as verse 9 shows (Meyer, Philippi). After φρονεῖ, the Receptus, with L Peshito, Eng. Ver., adds the clause καὶ ὁ μὴ φρονῶν τὴν ἡμέραν κυρίῳ οὐ φρονεῖ. It is omitted by ℵABCDEFG Copt., Æth., Lachm., Tisch., Tregelles. εὐχαριστεῖ] refers to the thanks given before the meal, Deut. viii. 10; Mat. xiv. 19; xv. 36; xxvi. 26; 1 Cor. x. 30; 1 Tim. iv. 4, 5. κυρίῳ οὐκ ἐσθίει] the abstinence, as well as the partaking, is out of regard to the honor and service of Christ. καὶ εὐχαριστεῖ] the thanksgiving in this case is, of course, not for the meat which is not eaten, but for the "herbs" which are. This meal, like the other, is accompanied with thanksgiving to God.

Ver. 7. ἑαυτῷ] the dative of advantage, like κυρίῳ. No Christian lives for his own honor and service. The greater includes the less. Life and death stand for the sum total of human existence. Whoever has devoted himself to the Lord completely, has of course devoted himself to him in the details of eating and abstinence. The reference is not to the objective fact that life and death are in the Lord's hand, which is true of the unbeliever as well as of the believer; but to the subjective *purpose*, and its execution, of consecrating the whole existence, which is true only of the believer. ἀποθνήσκει] Compare Phil. i. 20; Rev. xiv. 13. The believer serves Christ in his death, as truly as in his life. To die in faith honors the Redeemer as much as does any active

οὐδεὶς ἑαυτῷ ἀποθνήσκει· [8] ἐάν τε γὰρ ζῶμεν, τῷ κυρίῳ
ζῶμεν, ἐάν τε ἀποθνήσκωμεν, τῷ κυρίῳ ἀποθνήσκομεν.
ἐάν τε οὖν ζῶμεν ἐάν τε ἀποθνήσκωμεν, τοῦ κυρίου ἐσμέν.
[9] εἰς τοῦτο γὰρ Χριστὸς ἀπέθανεν καὶ ἔζησεν, ἵνα καὶ
νεκρῶν καὶ ζώντων κυριεύσῃ. [10] σὺ δὲ τί κρίνεις τὸν

service for him. "Eadem ars moriendi, quæ vivendi." Bengel.

VER. 8 repeats in a positive form, and emphasizes, what has been said in a negative form, in verse 7. ἐάν τε, etc. . . ἐάν τε, etc.] "both if," etc. . . "and if," etc.: in one case as much as in the other. τοῦ κυρίου] is the genitive of possession. The thrice-repeated κυρίος indicates the "divine majesty and power of Christ." Bengel. These words were the dying utterance of Edward Irving.

VER. 9. The Receptus, with DL Peshito, Eng. Ver., reads ἀπέθανεν καὶ ἀνέστη καὶ ἀνέζησεν; the reading in the text is supported by ℵABC Copt., Æth., Lachm., Tisch., Tregelles. This verse gives the reason why believers belong to Christ, viz.: because Christ by his sacrificial life and death for them acquired a title to them. ἀπέθανεν] as an ἱλαστήριον, i. e. Compare iii. 25. ἔζησεν] as antithetic to ἀπέθανεν, is here equivalent to ἀνέζησεν (which accounts for the Receptus reading); as in Rev. iv. 8; 2 Cor. iv. 10; Rom. v. 10. By his death and resurrection, Christ obtained his lordship. ἵνα] denotes the divine purpose. νεκρῶν καὶ ζώντων] deceased and living believers. Christ's dominion over his people is not interrupted by their death. Compare Mat. xxii. 32. If Christ is Lord of his people, not only when living but also when dead, it follows that they are under obligation to serve him both in death and in life.

VER. 10, σὺ δὲ] this is addressed to the "weak," who passes a censure upon the freedom of the "strong" in faith.

ἀδελφόν σου; ἢ καὶ σὺ τί ἐξουθενεῖς τὸν ἀδελφόν σου; πάντες γὰρ παραστησόμεθα τῷ βήματι τοῦ θεοῦ. [11] γέγραπται γάρ Ζῶ ἐγώ, λέγει κύριος, ὅτι ἐμοὶ κάμψει πᾶν γόνυ, καὶ πᾶσα γλῶσσα ἐξομολογήσεται τῷ θεῷ. [12] ἄρα οὖν

καὶ σὺ] this is addressed to the "strong," who was prone to despise the "weak" in faith. πάντες γὰρ, etc.] assigns the reason why the one should not censure, or the other despise, viz.: that both are to stand before the divine tribunal, where neither will be the other's superior. Compare verse 4. θεοῦ] is the reading of ℵABCDEFG Copt., Lachm., Tisch, Tregelles; the Receptus, L, Peshito, Vulg., read Χριστοῦ. De Wette, Tholuck, Philippi, and Hodge contend for the latter. The ms. authority decidedly favors the former, and the early versions the latter. Polycarp also (Philipp. 6) says πάντες δεῖ παραστῆναι τῷ βήματι τοῦ Χριστοῦ. The phrase βῆμα τοῦ Χριστοῦ is found in 2 Cor. v. 10; and θρόνος τοῦ υἱοῦ τοῦ ανθρώπου in Mat. xxv. 31. The pronunciation of the final judgment is the official act of the Son, and not of the Father, Mat. vii. 22, 23; John v. 22; Acts xvii. 31.

VER. 11 proves by quotation from the Old Testament, that every one must stand before the judgment-seat of God. γέγραπται] in Isa. xlv. 23. The citation is considerably varied from the Septuagint. ζῶ ἐγώ] the Sept. has κατ' ἐμαυτοῦ ὀμνύω. Compare Num. xiv. 21, 28; Deut. xxxii. 40. "By my life, I asseverate that to me every knee shall bow." ἐξομολογήσεται τῷ θεῷ] the Sept. reads ὀμεῖται πᾶσα γλῶσσα τὸν θέον, which agrees with the Hebrew. ἐξομολογήσεται does not mean, here, the confession of sin (Chrysost., Theophylact), which would require the accusative of the object (Matt. iii. 6; Acts xix. 18; James v. 16), but the *praise* of God, as the final judge, Rom. xv. 9; Mat. xi. 25; Luke x. 21 (Meyer, Philippi). Compare Phil. ii. 11.

ἕκαστος ἡμῶν περὶ ἑαυτοῦ λόγον δώσει τῷ θεῷ. [13] μηκέτι
οὖν ἀλλήλους κρίνωμεν, ἀλλὰ τοῦτο κρίνατε μᾶλλον, τὸ μὴ

Ver. 12 is an inference (introduced by ἄρα οὖν: "accordingly then"), for the sake of emphatic repetition, from verses 4, 10, 11. The emphatic word is θεῷ. Every one owes an account to *God*, not man, and therefore will not be judged by man. δώσει] is the reading of ℵACEL Tisch. The Receptus, with BDFG Lachm., Tregelles, reads ἀποδώσει. Compare Luke xvi. 2; Heb. xiii. 17; 1 Pet. iv. 5. The same authorities which support ἀποδώσει omit οὖν.

Ver. 13. St. Paul, in the first clause of this verse, founds an exhortation to *both* parties (ἀλλήλους), upon the preceding statements respecting God as the only judge, and then in the last clause passes to a duty of the "strong" toward the "weak;" viz.: not to hinder or injure him in the Christian life, by the exercise of personal liberty in regard to the disputed points. The apostle continues to discuss the subject of the right use of Christian liberty, down to verse 23. κρίνωμεν] has the same meaning as in verses 4, 10. Though the "weak" in faith has hitherto been represented as the censorious person, yet crimination naturally leads to recrimination, and both the weak and strong are warned. τοῦτο κρίνατε μᾶλλον] "determine this, rather." κρινεῖν is here employed, by antanaclasis, in a different sense from its use in the previous clause. In the first instance, it signifies, to pass a judicial sentence; in the second, it signifies, to form a moral judgment, or to prescribe a rule of action for one's self: to "determine," or "resolve," as in 1 Cor. ii. 2; vii. 37; 2 Cor. ii. 1. τὸ μὴ, etc.] this sentence is made equivalent to a substantive by the neuter article, and explains τοῦτο. Compare 2 Cor. ii. 1. πρόσκομμά] is an obstacle against which the foot of the traveller strikes. σκάνδαλον] is a part of a trap. See comment on

τιθέναι πρόσκομμα τῷ ἀδελφῷ ἢ σκάνδαλον. [14] οἶδα καὶ πέπεισμαι ἐν κυρίῳ Ἰησοῦ ὅτι οὐδὲν κοινὸν δι' ἑαυτοῦ, εἰ

xi. 9. The strong in the faith must not, by recklessly following his own convictions as to what is allowable in disputed matters, put anything in the path of a fellow disciple that will ensnare him, or cause him to stumble and fall.

VER. 14 teaches that the strong believer is really in the right, so far as the abstract question in dispute is concerned, but that this does not authorize him to disregard the conscientious scruples of the weak believer. πέπεισμαι ἐν κυρίῳ] strengthens οἶδα. St. Paul's knowledge is an absolutely sure conviction, founded upon his communion with Christ. In this way, he is "fully persuaded in his own mind" (verse 5). κοινὸν] corresponds to the classical βέβηλον, "profane." It denotes what is unclean according to the ceremonial law, Lev. xi. ἑαυτοῦ] is the reading of the Receptus, which is supported by ℵBC Vulg., Tisch. The reading αυτου is supported by ADEFGL: which is accented ἀυτοῦ (him), by Theodoret (who refers it to Christ), Bengel, Lachm., Tregelles, Meyer; and αὑτοῦ (itself), by Griesbach, Knapp, Matthiæ, De Wette, Philippi. The first and last are supported by Chrysostom's explanation, τῇ φύσει. There is nothing unclean per se. It is made so only by a positive statute. Compare Mat. xv. 11; Acts x. 14, 15, 28. εἰ μὴ] is equivalent to ἀλλά, and refers to the whole clause, οὐδὲν κοινὸν δι' ἑαυτοῦ (De Wette, who cites Mat. xii. 4; Gal. ii. 16). Meyer, Philippi, Fritzsche, and Winer, on the contrary, give it the literal meaning of "except," connecting it with οὐδὲν κοινόν alone. These grammarians explain εἰ μὴ by "nisi," in Mat. xii. 4; Gal. i. 7, 19; ii. 16. λογιζομένῳ] signifies, as usual in the Epistle, to "reckon," or "account." ἐκείνῳ] is strongly emphatic; compare Mark vii. 15, 20; 2 Cor. x. 18. "The dis-

μὴ τῷ λογιζομένῳ τι κοινὸν εἶναι, ἐκείνῳ κοινόν. [15] εἰ γὰρ
διὰ βρῶμα ὁ ἀδελφός σου λυπεῖται, οὐκέτι κατὰ ἀγάπην
περιπατεῖς. μὴ τῷ βρώματί σου ἐκεῖνον ἀπόλλυε, ὑπὲρ οὗ

tinction between clean and unclean meats is no longer valid. So far, the Gentile converts are right. But they should remember that those who consider the law of the Old Testament on this subject as still binding, cannot with a good conscience disregard it. The simple principle here taught is, that it is wrong for any man to violate his own sense of duty." Hodge in loco.

VER. 15. εἰ γὰρ] is the reading of ℵABCDEFG Vulg., Copt., Griesbach, Lachm., Tisch., Tregelles. The Receptus, with L Peshito, reads εἰ δέ. Tholuck, Meyer, Lange, Alford, Wordsworth, Jowett adopt the first; De Wette, Philippi, Hodge prefer the second. The first must be chosen, upon diplomatic considerations, though the more difficult of explanation. Verse 15 may be connected with verse 13: "do not put a stumbling block, etc., *for*, if, on account of meat," etc. This makes verse 14 parenthetical, which is objectionable. Or, verse 15 may be connected with the last clause of verse 14, by supplying the ellipsis: "there is good reason for mentioning this exception, *for*, etc." (Meyer). The other reading is easily explained: "there is nothing unclean of itself, *but* if, on account of meat, etc." βρῶμα] the "unclean" meat eaten by the strong believer. λυπεῖται] 1. is "filled with remorse," being emboldened to eat against his scruples (De Wette, Meyer). 2. is spiritually "injured" (Philippi). The latter is favored by the following ἀπόλλυε, and by the classical (not New Testament) use of the word. βρώματι] the eating of "unclean" meat, as before. ἀπόλλυε] denotes the *tendency* of such a course of action, on the part of the strong in faith. Such an example is not helpful and saving,

Χριστὸς ἀπέθανεν. [16] *μὴ βλασφημείσθω οὖν ὑμῶν τὸ ἀγαθόν.* [17] *οὐ γάρ ἐστιν ἡ βασιλεία τοῦ θεοῦ βρῶσις καὶ πό-*

but injurious and destructive. To encourage a fellow disciple to violate his conscience, and thereby to fill him with remorse, will end in his ruin, if persisted in. But it does not follow that it will be persisted in. On the contrary, see verse 4. See also the comment on xi. 21, 22. Bengel and Philippi find in this verse "a dictum probans for the possibility of apostasy." ἀπέθανεν] "do not think more of your food, than Christ thought of his life." Bengel.

VER. 16. βλασφημείσθω] "to be evil spoken of." Compare ii. 24; 1 Tim. vi. 1; Titus ii. 5; 2 Pet. ii. 2. τὸ ἀγαθόν] 1. Your Christian liberty, 1 Cor. x. 29, 30 (Grotius, Calvin, Tholuck, Hodge). This makes ὑμῶν refer to the "strong" alone. 2. The Christian faith, or the gospel (Chrysost., Luther, Bengel, Philippi). 3. The Christian church, or the kingdom of God, ver. 17 (Meyer). The second or third is preferable to the first, because the "evil speaking" is evidently from outside of the church, and the "good thing" is something belonging to the church as a whole, and not to a portion of it. This is also favored, by the reading ἡμῶν, instead of ὑμῶν, which is found in DEFG Peshito. St. Paul exhorts both the "weak" and the "strong" not to give occasion, by their disputes and contentions with one another, to the heathen world, to speak evil of the Christian religion and church. Compare 1 Cor. x. 32.

VER. 17 assigns a motive, introduced by γὰρ, for avoiding the reproaches of the world. ἡ βασιλεία τοῦ θεοῦ] This phrase is equivalent to ἡ βασιλεία, simply; or ἡ βασιλεία τοῦ Χριστοῦ, or τῶν οὐρανῶν, or τοῦ οὐρανοῦ. As this kingdom has both an objective and a subjective side, is both visible and invisible, the phrase sometimes denotes: 1. the Christian life in the

σις, ἀλλὰ δικαιοσύνη καὶ εἰρήνη καὶ χαρὰ ἐν πνεύματι
ἁγίῳ· [18] ὁ γὰρ ἐν τούτῳ δουλεύων τῷ Χριστῷ εὐάρεστος τῷ

soul, as in this passage, and 1 Cor. iv. 20; Mat. vi. 33; Luke xviii. 21. 2. the Christian church in which it is embodied: either in its present earthly form, Mat. xiii. 24–30; xvi. 19; or its future heavenly, Mat. vii. 21; 1 Cor. vi. 9; xv. 50; Gal. v. 21; Eph. v. 5; or, both together, Mat. iii. 2; vi. 10; Coloss. i. 13; iv. 11. βρῶσις καὶ πόσις] the kingdom of God does not consist in eating or not eating, drinking or not drinking particular things. Christianity is not ceremonialism. Hence, they should not, by their disputes about ceremonial observances, provoke the reproaches of unbelievers. δικαιοσύνη, εἰρήνη, and χαρὰ] are employed, not in the ethical sense of uprightness, peace with men, and enjoyment of life as the consequence (Chrysost., Grotius, Fritzsche, Meyer), but in the dogmatic sense of justification, reconciliation with God, and spiritual joy (Calvin, Pareus, Calovius, Rückert, De Wette, Tholuck, Philippi, Hodge). This is the use of these terms throughout the Epistle, and the adjunct, "in the Holy Ghost," agrees with it. "Since the object is, to state in what the *essence* of God's kingdom consists, no derivative and accidental characteristics can be meant, but only those which are primary and essential." Philippi. At the same time, it must be remembered that the ethical virtues grow naturally and necessarily out of the evangelical δικαιοσύνη, and are inseparable from it. See the preceding statements, in chapters vi.–viii., respecting the connection between sanctification and justification, or of morality with faith. De Wette, consequently, combines both explanations. ἐν πνεύματι ἁγίῳ] is connected with χαρὰ only. Compare Acts xiii. 52; Gal. v. 22; 1 Thess. i. 6.

VER. 18 is a confirmation, introduced by γὰρ, of the state-

θεῷ καὶ δόκιμος τοῖς ἀνθρώποις. [19] ἄρα οὖν τὰ τῆς εἰρήνης διώκωμεν καὶ τὰ τῆς οἰκοδομῆς τῆς εἰς ἀλλή-

ment in verse 17 respecting the nature of the kingdom of God. τούτῳ] is the reading of ℵABCDFG, Vulg., Sahidic, Coptic, Lachm., Tisch., Tregelles. The Receptus, EL, Peshito, read τούτοις. Some (De Wette, Hodge) refer τούτῳ to πνεύματι ἁγίῳ, by whose assistance the believer serves Christ. Meyer takes it collectively, as referring to the fact stated in verse 17, "in accordance with which" the believer serves Christ. It is simpler to supply some word like τρόπῳ: "he who serves Christ in this manner." The reference of τούτοις would, of course, be to δικαιοσύνη, εἰρήνη, and χαρὰ. εὐάρεστος] denotes complacency. God takes pleasure in one who serves Christ in the evangelical manner described. The legalist is not well-pleasing to God, because "whatsoever is not of *faith* is sin" (verse 23). δόκιμος] is "approved of" by men, and thus gives them no occasion to "speak evil of" the Christian religion, and the kingdom of God.

VER. 19 is an exhortation, in the form of an inference from verses 17, 18, to attain the end proposed in verse 16. ἄρα οὖν] "accordingly then." διώκωμεν] is the reading of CDE Receptus; and διώκομεν that of ℵABFGL, Lachm., Tisch. The latter is the most strongly supported, but we retain the former, because ἄρα οὖν does not agree with the indicative ("accordingly then, we are pursuing." Lachmann makes it an interrogation: "accordingly then, are we pursuing?"), and the vowels ω and ο are liable to be exchanged by a scribe. The term denotes a strenuous pursuit, as in ix. 30, 31. οἰκοδομῆς] the figure denotes establishment and advance in the Christian life. Christian character is a structure built upon Christ, who is the foundation (1 Cor. iii. 2), and the chief corner-stone (Eph. ii. 20). εἰς ἀλλήλους] the edification

λους. [20] μὴ ἕνεκεν βρώματος κατάλυε τὸ ἔργον τοῦ θεοῦ. πάντα μὲν καθαρά, ἀλλὰ κακὸν τῷ ἀνθρώπῳ τῷ διὰ προσκόμματος ἐσθίοντι· [21] καλὸν τὸ μὴ φαγεῖν

is mutual. The "strong" by his fraternal forbearance finally leads the "weak" to a better view of Christian liberty, and the "weak" by his conscientiousness preserves the "strong" from laxity of conscience.

VER. 20 is an exhortation to the "strong," similar to that in verse 15. κατάλυε] to loosen and pull down: the figure of the edifice is still retained. ἔργον τοῦ θεοῦ] the edification is God's work. "Ye are God's building," 1 Cor. iii. 9. The reference is not to faith, or any particular grace, but to the believer himself: "fratrem, quem deus fecit fidelem." Estius. πάντα καθαρά] is a repetition of the affirmation that "there is nothing unclean of itself," in verse 14. μὲν] followed by ἀλλὰ denotes a concession with a guarding clause: "It is indeed true that all things are clean, *but*, etc." κακὸν] i. e., τὸ καθαρόν ἐστίν κακὸν (Meyer). Other ellipses are, πᾶν (Reiche); τὸ βρῶμα (Grotius); τὸ ἐσθίειν (Rückert); τὸ πάντα φαγεῖν (Fritzsche, Philippi). διὰ προσκόμματος] the genitive of occasion: he who eats contrary to his conscientious convictions, by means of (διὰ) the example set by the "strong." This example has previously been denominated a πρόσκόμμα in verse 13. The sentiment is the same as in the last clause of verse 14. Some commentators (Grotius, Bengel, De Wette, Fritzsche, Hodge) refer τῷ ἐσθίοντι to the "strong." In this case, διὰ προσκόμματος must be taken as an adjective, and rendered "offensively," or so as to give offence; which is not so literal, and is contrary to the context.

VER. 21 contains the rule of action for the "strong." καλὸν] sc. σοί ἐστι, 1 Cor. ix. 15. μὴ φαγεῖν, etc.] it is noble and admirable, to practise entire abstinence, rather than an

κρέα μηδὲ πιεῖν οἶνον μηδὲ ἐν ᾧ ὁ ἀδελφός σου προσκόπτει ἢ σκανδαλίζεται ἢ ἀσθενεῖ. 22 σὺ πίστιν ἣν ἔχεις κατὰ σεαυτὸν ἔχε ἐνώπιον τοῦ θεοῦ. μακαρίος ὁ μὴ κρί-

allowable indulgence that works spiritual evil to a fellow Christian. μηδὲ ἐν ᾧ] i. e. μηδὲ ποιεῖν ἐν ᾧ. ἢ σκανδαλίζεται ἢ ἀσθενεῖ] are omitted by ℵAC Peshito, Coptic, Æth., Tisch.; and supported by BDEFGL Vulg., Sahidic, Receptus, Lachm., Tregelles. ἀσθενεῖ] is weakened and made hesitating, in regard to following his conscientious conviction.

Ver. 22. ἣν ἔχεις] is the reading of ℵABC Coptic, Lachm., Tisch., Tregelles. "The faith which thou hast, have it to thyself." The Receptus DEFGL Vulg., Peshito, Sahidic, Æth., omit ἣν. This latter may be construed as concessive: "Thou hast faith, have it to thyself" (Luther, Beza, Fritzsche, Tholuck); or interrogatively: "Hast thou faith? have it to thyself" (Calvin, Grotius, Eng. Ver., De Wette, Philippi, Hodge). πίστιν] the strong faith of St. Paul, which "knows and is persuaded in the Lord Jesus that there is nothing unclean of itself." ἔχε] this faith is not to be given up, but firmly held, because it is founded in the true view of the case in dispute. κατὰ σεαυτὸν] 1. The "strong" may act in accordance with his own convictions in his own private life, whenever his example will not be a snare to the "weak." 2. The "strong" is not ostentatiously to parade his views before those whose scruples are different from his own. ἐνώπιον τοῦ θεοῦ] the "strong" when following his own convictions in private, must remember that though a weak brother is not present as a spectator, yet God is present. This is a salutary check which will prevent Christian liberty from becoming licentiousness. μακάριος, etc.] applies to both the "strong" and the "weak" alike. He is to be felicitated who has no reason to reproach himself for what he does,

νων ἑαυτόν, ἐν ᾧ δοκιμάζει· 23 *ὁ δὲ διακρινόμενος ἐὰν φάγῃ κατακέκριται, ὅτι οὐκ ἐκ πίστεως· πᾶν δὲ ὃ οὐκ ἐκ πίστεως ἁμαρτία ἐστίν.*

whether he eat, or abstain. Happy is he who has a good conscience. κρίνων] denotes a condemnatory sentence, as in Mat. vii. 1; Luke xix. 22; John iii. 17; viii. 26; Rom. ii. 1, 3. δοκιμάζει] what he approves of and permits itself to do: "agendum eligit," Estius; "alloweth," Eng. Ver. Compare i. 28; 1 Cor. xvi. 3.

VER. 23. διακρινόμενος] denotes doubt respecting the rightfulness of an act. Compare iv. 20. The reference is rather to the "weak" believer; but not exclusively so. ἐὰν] if, in spite of his doubt, i. e. κατακέκριται] the act itself condemns him, before God and his own mind. The rendering "damned," of the English Version, is misleading. It is only when persisted in, that such action results in everlasting damnation. ὅτι] assigns the reason for the condemnation. ἐκ πίστεως] sc. ἔφαγε. Two meanings belong to πίστις. 1. Justifying faith, such as has been the theme of the Epistle, i. 17; iii. 25, 26 et passim (Augustine, Calovius). 2. Moral faith, or the conviction of the rectitude of an act (Chrysost., Grotius, De Wette). The connection certainly requires the latter meaning, because the writer is speaking of the necessity of a "full assurance" of the correctness of the course pursued. Vacillation and doubt are forbidden. But since this clear conviction is impossible without faith in Christ, the second meaning must be combined with the first. "Faith, here, is the firm assurance proceeding from justifying faith in Christ." Philippi. "Faith, here, is faith in Christ, so far as it brings moral confidence in regard to the right course of action in a given case." Meyer. "The word faith, is to be taken, here, for a fixed persuasion of the mind, or a firm assurance, yet not that of any kind, but that which is derived from the truth of God." Calvin. "Innuitur ergo ipsa fides, qua fideles censentur, conscientiam informans et confirmans; partim fundamentum, partim norma rectæ actionis." Bengel. δὲ] is transitive: "now." Yet, the sentiment introduced by it is intended to be corroborative of the preceding statement; and hence, as De Wette suggests, γὰρ would have been proper. πίστεως] has the same meaning as in the preceding sentence. Augustine founded his proposition: "omnis infidelium vita peccatum est," upon this clause. "If every action is sin, which does not proceed from the assurance that it is well-pleasing to God, and such assurance itself can only be the result of evangelical faith, it follows that every action is sin that has not such faith as its ultimate source." Philippi. The explanation: "Whatever we do which we are not sure is right, is wrong" (Hodge), does not exhaust the meaning of this important dictum of St. Paul.

CHAPTER XV

[1] Ὀφείλομεν δὲ ἡμεῖς οἱ δυνατοὶ τὰ ἀσθενήματα τῶν ἀδυνάτων βαστάζειν καὶ μὴ ἑαυτοῖς ἀρέσκειν. [2] ἕκαστος ἡμῶν τῷ πλησίον ἀρεσκέτω εἰς τὸ ἀγαθὸν πρὸς οἰκοδομήν· [3] καὶ γὰρ ὁ Χριστὸς οὐχ ἑαυτῷ ἤρεσεν, ἀλλὰ καθὼς γέ-

THIS chapter, down to verse 13, continues the subject of the preceding chapter. Hence Lachmann arranges xv. 1–13 as a part of chapter xiv. Even if this arrangement is adopted, a new paragraph begins here.

VER. 1. δὲ] is transitive: "now." At the same time, the sentiment is inferential in respect to the preceding, as the English Version, "we *then*," etc., implies. ἡμεῖς] the Apostle reckons himself with the "strong," whose views he shared, xiv. 14, 20. ἀσθενήματα] the "infirmities" meant, are the scruples respecting clean and unclean meats, sacrificial flesh, and libation-wine. βαστάζειν] to bear, in the sense of forbear: to tolerate. Compare Gal. vi. 2, 5. ἑαυτοῖς ἀρέσκειν] self-gratification is the contrary of self-denial, which is the leading trait in the Christian religion, Mat. x. 37–39; xvii. 24.

VER. 2. τὸ ἀγαθὸν] what is spiritually useful and beneficial. Compare τὸ συμφέρον, 1 Cor. x. 33. The "pleasure" is not to be of any kind whatever, but only that which is profitable. πρὸς] "with a view to," as in iii. 26. οἰκοδομήν] see comment on xiv. 19.

VER. 3 assigns the reason for the preceding exhortation. καὶ] "even" Christ, etc. Χριστὸς οὐχ, etc.] Compare 2 Cor.

γραπται Οἱ ὀνειδισμοὶ τῶν ὀνειδιζόντων σε ἐπέπεσαν ἐπ' ἐμέ. 4 *ὅσα γὰρ προεγράφη, εἰς τὴν ἡμετέραν διδασκαλίαν ἐγράφη, ἵνα διὰ τῆς ὑπομονῆς καὶ διὰ τῆς παρακλήσεως*

viii. 9; Eph. v. 25; Phil. ii. 5 sq.: 1 Pet. ii. 21; Heb. xii. 2, where Christ is presented as an example of living for others, and not for himself. ἀλλὰ] requires no supplementary word, like ἐγένετο, or ἐποίησεν (Grotius). Christ is introduced directly, as speaking the words of the Psalm (Meyer, Philippi). The quotation is literal from the Septuagint of Ps. lxix. 9. The psalm is Messianic, and verses 22, 23, have been quoted in xi. 9. 10. See the comment. ὀνειδιζόντων σε] Christ, by receiving upon himself the revilings of God's enemies, proved that he did not live for self-gratification.

VER. 4 evinces the propriety of the preceding quotation. προεγράφη] refers to the Messianic matter of the Old Testament, like προεπηγγείλατο in i. 2. B reads ἐγράφη, here, and inserts πάντα after it. ἡμετέραν] us Christians. διδασκαλίαν] denotes a union of instruction and admonition. ἐγράφη] is the reading of ℵBCDEFG Peshito, Vulg., Copt., Æth., Lachm., Tisch., Tregelles. The Receptus AL read προεγράφη. ἵνα] denotes the end for which the Scriptures were given. ὑπομονῆς and παρακλήσεως] are both to be connected with γραφῶν: the power to endure temptation and afflictions (comment on v. 3), and spiritual comfort (comment on i. 12), are produced by the knowledge of the divine word. διὰ] before τῆς παρακλήσεως is the reading of ℵABCL Peshito, Æth., Griesbach, Lachm., Tisch., Tregelles. It is omitted by DEFG Vulg., Copt., Receptus. τὴν ἐλπίδα] the article denotes the well-known Christian hope of future blessedness. Compare v. 2. ἔχωμεν] not, "to hold on upon" (Beza), but, "to have," or "possess" (De Wette, Meyer, Philippi). ἐλπίδα is subjective, as in Acts xxiv. 15; 2 Cor. x. 15; Eph. ii.

τῶν γραφῶν τὴν ἐλπίδα ἔχωμεν. 5 ὁ δὲ Θεὸς τῆς ὑπομονῆς καὶ τῆς παρακλήσεως δῴη ὑμῖν τὸ αὐτὸ φρονεῖν ἐν
ἀλλήλοις κατὰ Χριστὸν Ἰησοῦν, 6 ἵνα ὁμοθυμαδὸν ἐν ἑνὶ
στόματι δοξάζητε τὸν Θεὸν καὶ πατέρα τοῦ κυρίου ἡμῶν

12; 1 Thess. iv. 13; 1 John iii. 3. The effect of the patience and comfort derived from the Scriptures is a cheering personal hope of eternal life.

Ver. 5, together with verse 6, continues the subject, but in the form of a prayer to God. δὲ] is transitive: "now." Θεὸς τῆς, etc.] God is the author and source of patience and consolation; the Scriptures are the instrument which he employs. Compare Θεὸς τῆς ἐλπίδος, xv. 13; and Θεὸς τῆς εἰρήνης, xv. 33; Phil. iv. 9; 1 Thess. v. 23; Heb. xiii. 20. δῴη] is the Hellenistic form, instead of the Attic δοίη. Compare 2 Tim. i. 16, 18. The strong and steady unanimity spoken of is a gift of God. τὸ αὐτὸ φρονεῖν] Compare xii. 16; Phil. ii. 2. "Unanimity in doctrine is not meant, here, but in feeling and action. Common patience and common consolation, in common tribulations, are the source and cement of unity, especially when the tribulation consists in reviling and persecution on the part of God's enemies (verse 3), which is a summons to God's friends, to stand together all the more firmly." Philippi. κατὰ Χριστὸν] according to the will (not the example) of Christ, like κατὰ Θέον, viii. 27. The oneness of his people was a strong desire of Christ, John xvii. 21–23.

Ver. 6. ἵνα] denotes the end intended by this unanimity, viz.: God's praise and glory. ὁμοθυμαδὸν] unanimously, and in a body, Acts. i. 14. ἐν ἑνὶ στόματι] is the outward expression of ὁμοθυμαδὸν. Oneness of feeling and purpose results in oneness of speech. τὸν Θεὸν καὶ πατέρα τοῦ κυρίου, etc.] Compare 2 Cor. i. 3; xi. 31; Eph. i. 3; Coloss. i. 3; 1 Pet. i. 3. "In all these passages, τοῦ κυρίου belongs only to πατήρ, and not to θεός, as is shown by the passages in which God is described as ὁ θεὸς καὶ πατήρ, without the addition of the genitive τοῦ κυρίου ἡμῶν Ἰησοῦ Χριστοῦ, 1 Cor. xv. 24; Eph. v. 20; Coloss. iii. 17; James i. 27; iii. 9. The praise is first of all defined as a δοξάζειν τὸν θεὸν, the standing designation (Mat. ix. 8; Mark ii. 12; Luke ii. 20; v. 25, 26; vii. 16; xiii. 13; Acts iv. 21; xi. 18; xxi. 20; Rom. i. 21; xv. 9; 1 Cor. vi. 20; 2 Cor. ix. 13; Gal. i. 24; 1 Pet. ii. 12; iv. 11, 16); and this God is then more precisely defined as Father of the Lord Jesus Christ. He is praised first of all as God in the abstract, and then as Father of Jesus Christ, in which character he has bestowed on men all benefits that call for praise. So Theodoret: ἡμῶν θεὸν ἐκάλεσε τὸν θεὸν, τοῦ δὲ κυρίου πατέρα. On the other hand, the application of τοῦ κυρίου Ἰησοῦ Χριστοῦ to θεὸν and πατέρα together appears utterly without reason, because it is not easy to see why God should be praised directly and simply as the God of Jesus Christ, John xx. 17; Eph. i. 17; Heb. i. 9. But when the Father of the Lord Jesus Christ is praised, indirectly the Son, this Lord Jesus Christ himself, is praised as well, and that with one mind, since he is the one Lord of all, x. 12; xiv. 6–9." Philippi in loco. Meyer agrees with this interpretation, and observes: "It ought not to have been objected to this interpretation, that the form of expression in this case must either have been τὸν θεὸν ἡμῶν καὶ πατέρα Ἰησοῦ Χριστοῦ, or else τὸν θεὸν τὸν πατέρα Ἰησοῦ Χριστοῦ. Either of these would be the expression of *another* idea. But as St. Paul has here expressed himself, τόν binds the conceptions of *God* and *Father of Christ* in unity." This interpretation is adopted, also, by the English Version, De Wette, Stuart. The other interpretation is supported by Grotius, Bengel, Rückert, Fritzsche. Tholuck, Hodge, and Alford, are undecided.

VER. 7. διὸ] "on which account," viz.: in order that this

'Ιησοῦ Χριστοῦ. [7] διὸ προσλαμβάνεσθε ἀλλήλους, καθὼς καὶ ὁ Χριστὸς προσελάβετο ὑμᾶς εἰς δόξαν τοῦ θεοῦ. [8] λέγω γὰρ Χριστὸν διάκονον γενέσθαι περιτομῆς ὑπὲρ ἀληθείας θεοῦ, εἰς τὸ βεβαιῶσαι τὰς ἐπαγγελιας τῶν πατέ-

unanimous praise may be rendered. προσλαμβάνεσθε] receive to your affectionate fellowship, as in xiv. 1. ἀλλήλους] the exhortation is addressed both to the "strong" and the "weak." καθὼς ὁ Χριστός] if Christ could welcome you to his communion, you, surely, can welcome each other to your own communion. ὑμᾶς] is the reading of ℵACEFGL Peshito, Vulg., Copt., Æth., Lachm., Tisch., Tregelles. The Receptus, with BD, reads ἡμᾶς. εἰς δόξαν τοῦ θεοῦ] is best connected with Χριστὸς προσελάβετο, as the nearer antecedent, and on account of the contents of verses 8, 9. Christ received you Jews and Gentiles, in order that the veracity and mercy of God might be honored, and in this way God be glorified.

VER. 8 explains how Christ "received" them. λέγω] "I wish to say," i. e., "I mean:" a common way, in St. Paul's writings, of beginning an explanation. Compare 1 Cor. i. 12; Gal. v. 16. γὰρ] is the reading of ℵABCDEFG Vulg., Copt., Griesb., Lachm., Tisch., Tregelles. It has the signification "namely," as in Mat. i. 18 (Receptus). The Receptus, with L Peshito, reads δὲ. Χριστὸν] is the reading of ℵABC Copt., Æth., Lachm., Tisch. The Receptus Peshito, DEFG read 'Ιησοῦν Χριστὸν. γενέσθαι] is the reading of BCDFG Lachm., Tregelles. Tischendorf, with ℵAEL, reads γεγενῆσθαι. διάκονον περιτομῆς] Christ became a servant of the circumcised Jews, in condescending to become their Messiah and Saviour. Compare Mat. xx. 28. περιτομὴ denotes the circumcised, as opposed to τὰ ἔθνη, in verse 9. Compare iii. 26; iv. 12; Gal. ii. 7; Eph. ii. 11. ὑπὲρ ἀληθείας] in behalf of God's veracity. εἰς τὸ βεβαιῶσαι, etc.] in fulfilling, by his

ρων, ⁹ τὰ δὲ ἔθνη ὑπὲρ ἐλέους δοξάσαι τὸν θεόν, καθὼς γέγραπται Διὰ τοῦτο ἐξομολογήσομαί σοι ἐν ἔθνεσιν καὶ τῷ ὀνόματί σου ψαλῶ, ¹⁰ καὶ πάλιν λέγει Εὐφράνθητε ἔθνη μετὰ τοῦ λαοῦ αὐτοῦ. ¹¹ καὶ πάλιν λέγει Αἰνεῖτε πάντα τὰ ἔθνη τὸν κύριον, καὶ ἐπαινεσάτωσαν αὐτὸν πάν-

incarnation, God's promise to the patriarchs respecting the "Seed of the Woman," Christ established the divine truthfulness. Compare Luke i. 55; Acts iii. 25; Rom. ix. 4; Gal. iii. 8.

VER. 9. τὰ δὲ ἔθνη δόξάσαι] 1. depends upon λέγω: "I mean, that the Gentiles *have* praised," by their conversion, i. e. (De Wette, Rückert); or *should* praise (Calvin, Grotius, Tholuck, Philippi); or *praise* (Vulgate, Luther, Fritzsche, Hodge). 2. is co-ordinate with βεβαιῶσαι and depends upon εἰς τὸ: "in order that the Gentiles might praise," etc. (Eng. Ver., Meyer). The last is preferable. ὑπὲρ] = περί: "in respect to," or "for." γέγραπται] in Ps. xviii. 49, according to the Sept. διὰ τοῦτο] belongs to the quotation, and does not refer back to the preceding statement. ἐξομολογήσομαί] signifies "to praise," as in xiv. 11. The original speaker is David, who is the type of Christ, who promises to glorify God among the Gentiles.

VER. 10. πάλιν] in another passage, viz.: Deut. xxxii. 43, according to the Sept. The Hebrew reads: "Rejoice O ye nations, his people." λέγει] sc. ἡ γραφή, suggested by γέγραπται, verse 9.

VER. 11. πάλιν λέγει] is the reading of Lachmann, with BDEFG Peshito. Tischendorf, with ℵACL Vulgate, omits λέγει. ἐπαινεσάτωσαν] is supported by ℵABCDE Lachm., Tisch., Tregelles. The Receptus FGL read ἐπαινέσετε. The term is stronger in meaning than αἰνεῖτε: "laud him" (Eng.

τες οἱ λαοί. 12 καὶ πάλιν Ἠσαΐας λέγει Ἔσται ἡ ῥίζα τοῦ
Ἰεσσαί, καὶ ὁ ἀνιστάμενος ἄρχειν ἐθνῶν, ἐπ' αὐτῷ ἔθνη
ἐλπιοῦσιν. 13 ὁ δὲ θεὸς τῆς ἐλπίδος πληρώσαι ὑμᾶς πάσης
χαρᾶς καὶ εἰρήνης ἐν τῷ πιστεύειν, εἰς τὸ περισσεύειν ὑμᾶς
ἐν τῇ ἐλπίδι ἐν δυνάμει πνεύματος ἁγίου.
14 Πέπεισμαι δέ, ἀδελφοί μου, καὶ αὐτὸς ἐγὼ περὶ ὑμῶν,

Ver.). The citation is from Ps. cxvii. 1, according to the Septuagint, which agrees with the Hebrew.

VER. 12. Ἠσαΐας λέγει] in xi. 10. St. Paul follows the Sept. The Hebrew reads: "And in that day shall be a root of Jesse, which stands for a banner to the nations; unto it shall the Gentiles turn." ῥίζα τοῦ Ἰεσσαί] Rev. v. 5; xxii. 16; Isa. xi. 1. Christ is a shoot from the stock of David; the royal stock itself having been cut down. ἐπ'] denotes recumbency and rest upon. ἐλπιοῦσιν] "Hope in Christ, is a proof of Christ's divinity." Calvin. "Previously, the Gentiles were without hope, Eph. ii. 12." Bengel.

VER. 13 concludes the section with an invocation, similar to that in verse 5. δὲ] is transitive: "now." ἐλπίδος] God is the God of hope, as he is of patience and consolation (verse 5). πάσης] is anarthrous, to denote all possible kinds of joy and peace. The reading in the text is supported by ℵACDEL Lachm., Tisch., Tregelles. BFG read πληροφορήσαι ὑμᾶς ἐν πάσῃ χαρᾷ καὶ εἰρήνῃ, ἐν τῷ πιστεύειν ὑμᾶς ἐν τῇ ἐλπίδι, etc. πιστεύειν] faith is the source of joy and peace. ἐν δυνάμει] denotes the element in which, and the energy by which: "in and by." See on i. 24.

VER. 14 begins a statement of the reason why St. Paul writes to the Roman church, viz.: because it is composed chiefly of Gentiles, and he has been appointed to preach chiefly to the Gentiles. πέπεισμαι] denotes strong convic-

ὅτι καὶ αὐτοὶ μεστοί ἐστε ἀγαθωσύνης, πεπληρωμένοι πάσης γνώσεως, δυνάμενοι καὶ ἀλλήλους νουθετεῖν· 15 τολμηρότερον δὲ ἔγραψα ὑμῖν ἀπὸ μέρους, ὡς ἐπαναμιμνήσκων

tion, as in viii. 38; xiv. 14. Notwithstanding the earnest exhortation to duty, which might look as if he doubted their Christian character, he nevertheless has confidence in them. δέ] is not transitive (Meyer), but adversative. "*But*, although I have thus admonished you, I am convinced," etc. καὶ αὐτὸς ἐγὼ] "I myself also:" the same person who has exhorted them. καὶ αὐτοὶ] "You yourselves, also:" spontaneously, without being exhorted. ἀγαθωσύνης] kindness, or good-will, so as to be conciliatory toward each other. γνώσεως] knowledge of Christian truth, particularly respecting the universality of the gospel. ℵB Tisch. read τῆς γνώσεως. νουθετεῖν] fraternal admonition is meant, Acts xx. 31; 1 Cor. iv. 14.

Ver. 15. τολμηρότερον] this adjective is used adverbially: "more boldly" than was to be expected, considering my confidence in your good spirit, and insight of truth. AB read τολμηροτέρως. δὲ] is adversative: "however." ὑμῖν] is followed by ἀδελφοὶ, in DEFGL Peshito, Vulg., Receptus. ἀπὸ μέρους] 1. qualifies τολμηρότερον: "somewhat too boldly" (Peshito, Grotius, Hodge). 2. qualifies ἔγραψα: "I have written boldly, in places:" e. g., xii. 2; xiii. 11 sq.; xiv. (De Wette, Meyer, Lange, Philippi). The latter is preferable. "The boldness consists in having exhorted them as if they were his own church, although he was not the founder." Lange. ἐπαναμιμνήσκων] "reminding you again." The apostle does not assume that he is teaching them what they were totally ignorant of, but is reiterating what they already know. This refers to those passages in the epistle that relate to their duties toward God, society, and the church;

ὑμᾶς διὰ τὴν χάριν τὴν δοθεῖσάν μοι ἀπὸ τοῦ Θεοῦ 16 εἰς τὸ
εἶναί με λειτουργὸν Χριστοῦ Ἰησοῦ εἰς τὰ ἔθνη, ἱερουρ-
γοῦντα τὸ εὐαγγέλιον τοῦ Θεοῦ, ἵνα γένηται ἡ προσφορὰ
τῶν ἐθνῶν εὐπρόσδεκτος, ἡγιασμένη ἐν πνεύματι ἁγίῳ.
17 ἔχω οὖν τὴν καύχησιν ἐν Χριστῷ Ἰησοῦ τὰ πρὸς τὸν

and not to those new revelations of truth which he makes in this epistle. διὰ τὴν χάριν, etc.] gives the reason for the action mentioned in the sentence τολμηρότερον . . ὑμᾶς. χάριν] is the grace of the apostolate, i. 5.

VER. 16. εἰς τὸ εἶναί . . ἔθνη] specifies the purpose for which the apostolical grace was given him. εἰς ἔθνη] "with reference" to the Gentiles. ἱερουργοῦντα] 1. ministering as a priest. The apostle discharged a priestly function in reference to the gospel, in preaching it. The gospel was, metaphorically, an oblation (Luther, Erasmus, Tholuck, Meyer). 2. Consecrating the gospel (Aug., Calvin). 3. Being employed in the gospel: operans evangelii (Beza, Pareus). The first is preferable, because εὐαγγέλιον = εὐαγγελίζεσθαι, as in i. 1; xv. 19. ἵνα γένηται ἡ προυσφορὰ, etc.] denotes the purpose of this discharge of a priestly function. "It is the priesthood of the Christian pastor, to sacrifice men, as it were, to God, by bringing them to obey the gospel; and not, as the Papists vaunt, by offering up Christ to reconcile men to God. Paul does not give, here, the name of priest to the pastors of the Church as a perpetual title, but employs the term metaphorically, in order to set forth the honor of the ministry." Calvin. ἐθνῶν] genitive of apposition: the Gentiles themselves are the offering. ἐν πνεύματι] the offering has no value, except through the sanctification of the Holy Spirit.

VER. 17. οὖν] draws an inference from verses 15, 16. τὴν καύχησιν] *the* glory which I have; *my* glorying, John v. 34,

θεόν· [18] οὐ γὰρ τολμήσω τι λαλεῖν ὧν οὐ κατειργάσατο
Χριστὸς δι' ἐμοῦ εἰς ὑπακοὴν ἐθνῶν, λόγῳ καὶ ἔργῳ, [19] ἐν

36; Rom. iii. 27. The article is omitted by the Receptus ℵAL; is supported by BCDEFG Lachm., Tisch., Tregelles. ἐν Χριστῷ] the glorying is not in himself per se, but in himself as in Christ, viii. 1; 1 Cor. xv. 31. τὰ πρὸς τὸν θεόν] sc. κατά: in respect to things that have a view, or reference, to the kingdom and cause of God, on earth.

Ver. 18 proceeds to explain what the writer means, by saying that he has a reason for glorying. γὰρ] introduces the explanation. οὐ τολμήσω] "I will never be so presuming;" there is a reference to τολμηρότερον, in verse 15. λαλεῖν] not in the bad sense, "to prate about," but, simply, "to say" or "state." οὐ κατειργάσατο] "has *not* accomplished." These are the emphatic words in the sentence (Meyer, Philippi), and not Χριστὸς (Theodoret, Olsh., Fritzsche, Tholuck, Hodge). The negative is put for the positive: "I speak of what Christ has actually accomplished through me." Glorying in his official labors has a good ground, for he has had real success. εἰς ὑπακοὴν] "in order to produce obedience." Compare i. 5. λόγῳ καὶ ἔργῳ] denotes the instrumentalities employed by the apostle, Acts vii. 22; 2 Cor. x. 11.

Ver. 19. σημείων καὶ τεράτων] refer to ἔργῳ, in verse 18. The genitive denotes an emanating source: an awakening impression proceeded from the miracles. For the miracles wrought by St. Paul, see Acts xiv. 3; xv. 12; xvi. 16 sq.; xix. 11 sq.; xx. 10 sq.; 2 Cor. xii. 12. "σημεῖα καὶ τέρατα are miraculous, divine operations in the world of physical nature, appointed by God as signs of higher relations, in order to excite the attention of men," Philippi. The latter term is a more precise definition of the former, when the two are employed together. ἐν δυνάμει πνεύματος] is to be referred, not to

δυνάμει σημείων καὶ τεράτων, ἐν δυνάμει πνεύματος ἁγίου, ὥστε με ἀπὸ Ἱερουσαλὴμ καὶ κύκλῳ μέχρι τοῦ Ἰλλυρικοῦ

δυνάμει σημείων, but to κατεργάσατο Χριστὸς . . λόγω καὶ ἔργω. Compare 1 Cor. ii. 4. ἁγίου] is the reading of ACDEFG Vulg., Copt., Griesb., Lachm., Tregelles. The Receptus, ℵL, Peshito, Æth., Tisch., read θεοῦ. B reads πνεύματος only. ὥστε, etc.] mentions the result of the working of Christ in him. ἀπὸ Ἱερουσαλὴμ] St. Paul labored three years in Damascus and Arabia (Acts ix. 20 sq.; Gal. i. 17 sq.), before he appeared in Jerusalem; but as these were disciplinary and preparatory, he reckons from Jerusalem as the starting-point of his apostolic work. It was here that he joined the apostolic college, Acts. ix. 28, 29; xxii. 18. καὶ κύκλῳ] sc. τῆς Ἱερουσαλὴμ. Compare Mark iii. 34; vi. 36; Luke ix. 12. 1. The circuit or vicinity: not the immediate neighborhood, which would be trivial to mention, but Arabia, Syria, and Cilicia (Gal. i. 21; Acts ix. 30; xi. 25 sq.), constituting a circle of which Jerusalem was the centre (De Wette, Meyer, Philippi, Alford). 2. An arc of a circle described by starting from Jerusalem across Syria, Asia Minor, Troas, Macedonia, and Greece, as far as Illyria (Chrysost., Theodoret, Theophylact, Flacius). The latter, says Philippi, would be too ostentatious. μέχρι τοῦ Ἰλλυρικοῦ] St. Paul begins at Jerusalem, the south-east terminus a quo, and goes to Illyria, the north-west terminus ad quem. Illyria was the division line between the Eastern and Western Roman Empire. Meyer and Philippi regard Illyria as not merely the point which the apostle reached in his missionary labors, but as one of the countries, not enumerated in Acts, in which he preached the gospel. "This preaching probably happened during the journey mentioned in Acts xx. 1–3." Philippi. πεπληρωκέναι] "have fulfilled [the work of preaching] the gospel:" "have fully preached the gospel," Eng. Ver. Compare Coloss. i. 25.

πεπληρωκέναι τὸ εὐαγγέλιον τοῦ Χριστοῦ. [20] οὕτως δὲ φιλοτιμούμενον εὐαγγελίζεσθαι οὐχ ὅπου ὠνομάσθη Χριστός, ἵνα μὴ ἐπ' ἀλλότριον θεμέλιον οἰκοδομῶ, [21] ἀλλὰ καθὼς

εὐαγγέλιον is equivalent to εὐαγγελίζεσθαι, as in i. 1. The apostle had completely discharged his apostolic function of introducing Christianity into these countries, and founding churches. He does not mean that there was no more work to be done in these regions by preachers of the gospel. "He has completely *spread* the Gospel." Lange.

Ver. 20 states the principle adopted by St. Paul in his apostolic labor. οὕτως δὲ] "But, in such a manner." φιλοτιμούμενον] is the reading of ℵACEL Peshito, Receptus, Tisch.; φιλοτιμοῦμαι is that of BDFG Lachm., Tregelles. The word literally signifies, "to pursue zealously, so as to obtain honor thereby." It was a point of honor, with St. Paul (Meyer). Such a motive, however, is foreign to the apostle, and only the general notion of earnest endeavor is meant, as in 2 Cor. v. 9; 1 Thess. iv. 11. If the participial form is adopted, it depends upon ὥστε με . . πεπληρωκέναι: "but endeavoring earnestly to preach the gospel, in such a manner," etc. οὐχ ὅπου, etc.] explains οὕτως, negatively. ὠνομάσθη] not, "called upon," or "worshipped," but "known," simply. The reference is to heathen, or utterly unevangelized regions. St. Paul does not mean to say that he would never labor to instruct and edify existing churches, by "imparting some spiritual gift" to them (i. 11). This very letter to the Roman church proves the contrary. But he never would select as a field for the founding of new churches one that had already been occupied by another apostle. ἀλλότριον] "belonging to another person," 2 Cor. x. 15.

Ver. 21. ἀλλά] introduces the positive explanation of οὕτως. γέγραπται] in Isa. lii. 15: quoted literally from the Septuagint,

γέγραπται Οἷς οὐκ ἀνηγγέλη περὶ αὐτοῦ ὄψονται, καὶ οἳ οὐκ ἀκηκόασιν συνήσουσιν. [22] διὸ καὶ ἐνεκοπτόμην τὰ πολλὰ τοῦ ἐλθεῖν πρὸς ὑμᾶς, [23] νυνὶ δὲ μηκέτι τόπον ἔχων ἐν τοῖς κλίμασι τούτοις, ἐπιποθίαν δὲ ἔχων τοῦ ἐλθεῖν πρὸς ὑμᾶς ἀπὸ πολλῶν ἐτῶν, [24] ὡς ἂν πορεύωμαι εἰς

which agrees substantially with the Hebrew. The subject, in the original connection, is the Gentile nations, or the Gentile nations and kings together. περὶ αὐτοῦ] is an addition by the LXX., referring to "my servant," in Isa. lii. 13. ἀκηκόασιν] sc. τὸ εὐαγγέλιον, suggested by εὐαγγελίζεσθαι, in verse 20, and ἀναγγέλη, in verse 21.

VER. 22 begins to describe the plan of his present journey. διὸ] "for this reason," viz.: because he had been occupied in preaching the gospel in unevangelized regions. τὰ πολλά] is the reading of ℵACL Vulg., Receptus, Tisch., Tregelles. Lachmann, with BDEFG, reads πολλάκις. The meaning is: "in most cases," "for the most part." This was not the sole reason (compare 1 Thess. ii. 18), but the principal one.

VER. 23. τόπον] "scope," or opportunity for apostolic labor in founding new churches. Compare xii. 19. κλίμασι] "regions," or "districts;" namely, from Jerusalem to Illyria, verse 19. Compare 2 Cor. xi. 10; Gal. i. 21. πολλῶν is supported by ℵADEFGL, Receptus, Tisch.; ἱκανῶν is the reading of BC Lachm.

VER. 24. ὡς ἂν] (L Recept., ὡς ἐάν): "whensoever." Σπανίαν] the Greek Iberia, and Latin Hispania. It was a Roman province, with many Jewish residents, and thus well adapted for evangelistic work. That St. Paul executed his purpose to go to Spain, is affirmed by those who maintain the traditional view of a second Roman imprisonment, and denied by

τὴν Σπανίαν (ἐλπίζω γὰρ διαπορευόμενος θεάσασθαι ὑμᾶς καὶ ὑφ' ὑμῶν προπεμφθῆναι ἐκεῖ, ἐὰν ὑμῶν πρῶτον ἀπὸ μέρους ἐμπλησθῶ).
25 νυνὶ δὲ πορεύομαι εἰς Ἱερουσαλὴμ

those who, like Wieseler, reject this. After Σπανίαν, the Receptus, with L, inserts ἐλεύσομαι πρὸς ὑμᾶς; which is omitted by ℵABCDEFG Peshito, Vulg., Copt., Æth., Griesbach, Mill, Lachm., Knapp, Tisch., Tregelles. Such a preponderance of manuscript and editorial authority makes it necessary to reject the clause, although it renders the construction very difficult. γὰρ] is supported by ℵABCDEL Copt., Receptus, Lachm., Tisch., Tregelles; and omitted by FG Peshito, Æth., Griesbach. The weight of authority requires its adoption, though it still more complicates the structure, if ἐλεύσομαι etc. is rejected. We adopt Lachmann's punctuation and parenthesis, as on the whole dealing best with the difficulties in the case. Tischendorf places a colon after Σπανίαν. διαπορευόμενος] The Apostle intended no long stay, but only a rapid passage through the city of Rome, because the Christian church was already established there. ὑφ'] is the reading of ℵACL Receptus, Tisch., Tregelles; ἀφ' ("from your city") is the reading of BDEFG Lachmann. The first agrees best with other passages in which the persons who escort the apostle are spoken of. Compare Acts xv. 3; 2 Cor. i. 16. ἐκεῖ] instead of ἐκεῖσε. "After verbs of motion, the adverb of rest expresses the *object* of the motion. To be escorted *thither*, in order to be *there*. Compare John xi. 8." Philippi. ἀπὸ μέρους] "in some degree:" non quantum vellem, sed quantum licebit. Grotius. ὑμῶν ἐμπλησθῶ] spiritually filled, or satisfied, by personal intercourse. It is the same as the "comforting together by mutual faith," in i. 12.

VER. 25, in Lachmann's arrangement, is closely connected with the first clause of verse 24: the νυνὶ δὲ of verse 23 being

διακονῶν τοῖς ἁγίοις. [26] εὐδόκησαν γὰρ Μακεδονία καὶ Ἀχαΐα κοινωνίαν τινὰ ποιήσασθαι εἰς τοὺς πτωχοὺς τῶν ἁγίων τῶν ἐν Ἱερουσαλήμ. [27] εὐδόκησαν γάρ, καὶ ὀφειλέται εἰσὶν αὐτῶν· εἰ γὰρ τοῖς πνευματικοῖς αὐτῶν ἐκοι-

resumed in verse 25. The writer does not finish what he intended to say when he began the sentence, "Whenever I go into Spain." He first interrupts himself by the thought expressed in the parenthesis, and then, instead of returning to the sentence and completing it, adds, "But now I am [not going to Spain but] going to Jerusalem," etc. εἰς Ἱερουσαλὴμ] This was the apostle's fifth journey to Jerusalem, Acts xxi. 15, 17. The first journey is mentioned in Acts ix; the second, in xi. 30; the third, in xv.; the fourth, in xviii. 21. διακονῶν] the service consisted first, in taking up the collection, and then, in conveying it to the poor brethren at Jerusalem. The present tense denotes the present continuance of the service. Respecting this collection, see Acts xxiv. 17; 1 Cor. xvi. 3; 2 Cor. ix. 1, 2.

VER. 26 gives the reason, introduced by γὰρ, why he has to render this service. εὐδόκησαν] (ηὐδόκησαν, ℵB Tisch.) Compare Luke xii. 32; Rom. x. 1; 1 Cor. i. 21; Gal. i. 15. κοινωνίαν] literally, communion, or fellowship. As a charitable gift is an expression of this, the word came to have the technical signification of "contribution." πτωχοὺς . . ἐν Ἱερουσαλήμ] the church at Jerusalem was particularly needy, as the wealth and culture of the Jews at the national centre was antagonistic to Christianity.

VER. 27. εὐδόκησαν] (ηὐδόκησαν, ℵA Tisch.) is repeated, in order to add the remark, that this voluntary resolve was at the same time the discharge of a Christian obligation. πνευματικοῖς αὐτῶν] the blessings of the gospel had passed from

νώνησαν τὰ ἔθνη, ὀφείλουσιν καὶ ἐν τοῖς σαρκικοῖς λειτουργῆσαι αὐτοῖς. [28] τοῦτο οὖν ἐπιτελέσας καὶ σφραγισάμενος αὐτοῖς τὸν καρπὸν τοῦτον, ἀπελεύσομαι δι' ὑμῶν εἰς Σπανίαν· [29] οἶδα δὲ ὅτι ἐρχόμενος πρὸς ὑμᾶς ἐν πληρώματι εὐλογίας Χριστοῦ ἐλεύσομαι. [30] παρακαλῶ δὲ ὑμᾶς, ἀδελφοί, διὰ τοῦ κυρίου ἡμῶν Ἰησοῦ Χριστοῦ καὶ διὰ τῆς ἀγάπης τοῦ πνεύματος, συναγωνίσασθαί μοι ἐν ταῖς προσευχαῖς

the mother-church at Jerusalem to the Gentiles. σαρκικοῖς] material good. The higher spiritual gift demands, certainly, the smaller temporal gift, in return. Compare 1 Cor. ix. 11.

VER. 28. τοῦτο] this business of "ministering." σφραγισάμενος] not literally: "having carried the money sealed" (Erasmus, Calvin), or, "having assured them by letter and seal, as to the delivery of the money" (Michaelis); but figuratively: "having put them in secure possession." Compare the English "consign," from consignare. ἀπελεύσομαι] namely, from Jerusalem. δι' ὑμῶν] through your city, 2 Cor. i. 16.

VER. 29. οἶδα] expresses strong conviction. ἐν] "endowed with," or "full of." Compare ἐν λύπῃ, in 2 Cor. ii. 1. εὐλογίας] is followed by τοῦ εὐαγγελίου τοῦ, in L Peshito, Vulgate, Receptus. These words are omitted by ℵABCDEFG Copt., Æth., Lachm., Tisch., Tregelles.

VER. 30. St. Paul now asks the prayers of the Roman brethren, with reference to his impending journey: a frequent request of his, 2 Cor. i. 11; Phil. i. 19; Philemon 22. διὰ] denotes the motive. Compare xii. 1. ἀγάπης] is subjective: the love wrought in the believer by the Holy Spirit, Gal. v. 22. "He appeals not only to their love of Christ, but to their love for himself, as a fellow Christian." Hodge. συναγωνίσασθαί] prayer is a struggle (ἀγῶν) with God (Gen. xxxii. 24 sq.), and against inward and outward spiritual foes

ὑπὲρ ἐμοῦ πρὸς τὸν θεόν, [31] ἵνα ῥυσθῶ ἀπὸ τῶν ἀπειθούντων ἐν τῇ Ἰουδαίᾳ καὶ ἡ διακονία μου ἡ εἰς Ἱερουσαλὴμ εὐπρόσδεκτος τοῖς ἁγίοις γένηται, [32] ἵνα ἐν χαρᾷ ἐλθὼν πρὸς

(Luke xiii. 24). Compare Coloss. i. 29; ii. 1; iv. 12. πρὸς τὸν θεόν] is connected with προσευχαῖς.

VER. 31. ἵνα] denotes the object of the prayer. ῥυσθῶ ἀπὸ τῶν ἀπειθούντων] the Jews were unbelievers in the gospel (and thus disobedient to God), and bitter opponents of St. Paul as the preacher of the gospel. For instances, see Acts xiv. 2; xxi. 27; 2 Cor. xi. 24. καὶ] is followed by ἵνα, only in the Receptus EL. διακονία] is the reading of ℵACEL Peshito, Copt., Æth., Recept., Tisch., Tregelles; δωροφορία is the reading of BDFG Lachm. The former agrees best with διακονῶν, in verse 25. εἰς] denotes the destination of the "ministry." This is the reading of ℵACE Recept., Tischendorf. Lachmann, with BDFG, reads ἐν. εὐπρόσδεκτος] The Acts of the Apostles and the Epistle to the Galatians show that, owing to Judaistic prejudices, there was some jealousy toward the apostle to the Gentiles, in the church at Jerusalem. St. Paul desires to have this removed, so that his service shall be "entirely acceptable." ἁγίοις] notwithstanding their jealousy of him, he recognizes them as fellow-believers, and denominates them "saints."

VER. 32. ἵνα] denotes the final aim of the prayer, viz.: that he might have a prosperous meeting with the Roman church. The prayer, in this particular, was not granted, for he went to Rome as a prisoner, Acts xxiii. 11; xxviii. 14, 16. ἐλθὼν] is the reading of ℵAC, Copt., Lachm., Tisch. The Receptus, DEFGL, Peshito, Vulgate, Æth., read ἔλθω. θεοῦ] is found in ACL, Peshito, Vulgate, Copt., Receptus, Tischendorf. Lachmann, with B, reads κυρίου Ἰησοῦ. ℵ reads Ἰησοῦ Χριστοῦ. DEFG read Χριστοῦ Ἰησοῦ. St. Paul elsewhere em-

ὑμᾶς διὰ θελήματος θεοῦ συναναπαύσωμαι ὑμῖν. 33 ὁ δὲ θεὸς τῆς εἰρήνης μετὰ πάντων ὑμῶν. ἀμήν.

ploys θεοῦ in connection with θέλημα. Compare i. 10; 1 Cor. i. 1; iv. 19; 2 Cor. i. 1; viii. 5; Eph. i. 1; Coloss. i. 1; 2 Tim. i. 1. This would be the only instance of the phrase, "by the will of Christ." συναναπαυσωμαι ὑμῖν] "That I may be refreshed together with you." The word literally means, "to obtain a rest." Spiritual rest and refreshment is meant, as in 1 Cor. xvi. 18; 2 Cor. vii. 13. These words are found in ℵACL, Receptus, Lachm. (1st ed.), Tischendorf. B and Lachm. (2d ed.) omit them. DE read ἀναψυξω μεθ' ὑμῶν. FG read ἀναψύχω μεθ' ὑμῶν. If ἔλθω is adopted, καὶ must be supplied before συναναπαυσωμαι.

Ver. 33 is a common formula of invocation, often employed by St. Paul. Compare xvi. 20; 2 Cor. xiii. 11; Phil. iv. 9; 1 Thess. v. 23; 2 Thess. iii. 16; Heb. xiii. 20. εἰρήνης] refers, not to the differences among the Roman brethren (Grotius, Calvin), nor to his own conflicts (Meyer); but to Christian peace, simply (Philippi). ἀμήν] is found in ℵBCDEL, Peshito, Vulgate, Copt., Æth., Recept., Tisch. It is omitted in AFG, and bracketted by Lachmann and Tregelles.

CHAPTER XVI

[1] *Συνίστημι δὲ ὑμῖν Φοίβην τὴν ἀδελφὴν ἡμῶν, οὖσαν διάκονον τῆς ἐκκλησίας τῆς ἐν Κεγχρεαῖς,* [2] *ἵνα προσ-*

This chapter is composed chiefly of St. Paul's salutations (verses 3–16), and those of his companions (verses 22–24).

Ver. 1. συνίστημι] "I recommend," 2 Cor. v. 12; x. 12, 18. She is both introduced to them, and commended to their affectionate reception. Φοίβην] from Phœbus (Apollo), which is found as a proper name in Martial, iii. 89. Phœbe is found in Suetonius (Augustus, 65). The original idolatrous reference of the name had disappeared, like that of the days of the English week, and hence Christians made no change in their names in such cases. ἀδελφὴν] she is first recommended as a fellow-believer. διάκονον] owing to the rigid separation of the sexes, females in the early church performed the duties of the diaconate, in caring for the sick, poor, and strangers, of the female portion of the church. Pliny, in his celebrated epistle (x. 97), alludes to "duæ ancillæ quæ ministræ dicebantur." Phœbe was probably a widow; because, according to Greek manners, she could not have been mentioned as acting in the independent manner described, if either her husband had been living, or she had been unmarried. Conybeare. Κεγχρεαῖς] the eastern port of Corinth, about seventy stadia distant. Compare Acts xviii. 18.

Ver. 2. προσδέξησθε] denotes fraternal reception, like προσλαμβάνεσθε, in xiv. 1; xv. 7. ἀξίως τῶν ἁγίων] either, "as it

δέξησθε αὐτὴν ἐν κυρίῳ ἀξίως τῶν ἁγίων, καὶ παραστῆτε αὐτῇ ἐν ᾧ ἂν ὑμῶν χρῄζῃ πράγματι· καὶ γὰρ αὐτὴ προστάτις πολλῶν ἐγενήθη καὶ ἐμοῦ αὐτοῦ.

3 Ἀσπάσασθε Πρίσκαν καὶ Ἀκύλαν τοὺς συνεργούς μου ἐν Χριστῷ Ἰησοῦ, 4 οἵτινες ὑπὲρ τῆς ψυχῆς μου τὸν ἑαυτῶν τράχηλον ὑπέθηκαν, οἷς οὐκ ἐγὼ μόνος εὐχαριστῶ

becomes saints to receive saints," or "as saints should be received." The first is preferable with reference to ἐν κυρίῳ. παραστῆτε, etc.] "assist her," etc. This may refer, either to official business for the church, or to some personal business of her own. αὐτὴ] "she herself" (not αὕτη, "this one"). This accentuation of Bengel, Lachmann, and Tischendorf, suggests more strongly the motive for the assistance. Compare 1 Cor. xvi. 10; Phil. ii. 29 sq. προστάτις] is not used technically here of an office, as καὶ ἐμοῦ αὐτοῦ shows; but in the sense of a succorer, or benefactor. See the explanation of προϊστάμενος, in xii. 8.

Ver. 3. Πρίσκαν] (2 Tim. iv. 19) is the reading of ℵABCDEFG, Vulg., Copt., Bengel, Griesbach, Knapp, Lachm., Tisch., Tregelles. The Receptus, Peshito, Æth., have Πρίσκιλλαν (Acts xviii. 2), which is the diminutive of Πρίσκαν, like Livia and Livilla, Drusa and Drusilla. From Acts xviii. 2 sq., 18, 26; 1 Cor. xvi. 19; Rom. xvi. 3; 2 Tim. iv. 19, it appears that Aquila was a native of Pontus, and was driven, with his wife, by the persecution of the Jews by Claudius, from Rome to Corinth, whence he emigrated to Ephesus, and thence to Rome again, and finally to Ephesus again. συνεργούς] a deaconess is a "fellow laborer" with an apostle. That the labor included religious teaching, as well as merely diaconal service, is proved by Acts xviii. 26.

Ver. 4. τράχηλον ὑπέθηκαν] sc. ὑπὸ τὸν σίδηρον. This is to be taken figuratively, in the sense of exposure to great peril

ἀλλὰ καὶ πᾶσαι αἱ ἐκκλησίαι τῶν ἐθνῶν, 5 καὶ τὴν κατ'
οἶκον αὐτῶν ἐκκλησίαν. ἀσπάσασθε Ἐπαίνετον τὸν ἀγαπητόν μου, ὅς ἐστιν ἀπαρχὴ τῆς Ἀσίας εἰς Χριστόν. 6 ἀσπάσασθε Μαρίαν, ἥτις πολλὰ ἐκοπίασεν εἰς ὑμᾶς. 7 ἀσπά-

for the purpose of preserving the apostle's life. This may have occurred on such occasions as the tumults at Corinth and Ephesus, mentioned in Acts xviii. 12 sq.; xix. 23 sq. ἐκκλησίαι τῶν ἐθνῶν] sc. εὐχαριστουσι: i. e., for preserving me, the apostle of the Gentiles, xi. 13.

VER. 5. κατ' οἶκον αὐτῶν εκκλησίαν] Compare 1 Cor. xvi. 19; Coloss. iv. 15; Philemon 2. Before the erection of churches, the Christian congregations met in private houses. The phrase does not mean, "their house-hold, the church" (Origen, Chrysost., Flatt). This would be ὁ ἅγιος οἶκος. Ἐπαίνετον] none of the names in verses 5–15 occur elsewhere in the New Testament, with the exception, perhaps, of Ῥοῦφος (Mark xv. 21). Patristic tradition makes these persons to belong to the seventy disciples (Luke x. 1), and to have been bishops and martyrs. ἀπαρχὴ] the first convert. Ἀσίας] Asia Minor; proconsular Asia; Asia cis Taurum. This is the reading of ℵABCDFG, Vulg., Copt., Æth., Mill, Bengel, Griesbach, Lachm., Tisch. The Receptus, L, Peshito, read Ἀχαΐας, which conflicts with 1 Cor. xvi. 15, unless Epenetus was a member of the family of Stephanas. εἰς Χριστὸν] "with respect to Christ."

VER. 6. Μαρίαν] is the reading of ABC, Copt., Lachm., Tregelles. Tischendorf, ℵDEFGL, Recept., read Μαριάμ. The name indicates a Jewish Christian. ἐκοπίασαν] denotes practical labor (Acts xx. 34, 35; 1 Cor. iv. 12), and not labor in teaching and preaching, which requires the adjunct ἐν λόγῳ καὶ διδασκαλίᾳ (1 Tim. v. 17), or else something in the context which defines it, as in Gal. iv. 11; Phil. ii. 16. The teaching

σασθε Ἀνδρόνικον καὶ Ἰουνίαν τοὺς συγγενεῖς μου καὶ συναιχμαλώτους μου, οἵτινές εἰσιν ἐπίσημοι ἐν τοῖς ἀποσ-

function of women was confined to the instruction of young women, in the fulfilment of their duties as wives and mothers, Titus ii. 3. The public teaching of the congregation by women was prohibited by St. Paul, 1 Cor. xiv. 34, 35. The case of the prophetess was extraordinary, because it rested upon a supernatural gift, Acts xxi. 9; 1 Cor. xi. 5. ὑμᾶς] is the reading of ℵABC, Peshito, Copt., Æth., Griesbach, Lachm., Tisch., Tregelles. The Receptus and L have ἡμᾶς. DEFG have ἐν ὑμῖν. The second reading, though not so well supported as the first, agrees better with the connection. Acts of kindness toward the apostle, rather than toward the Roman congregation, would be a reason for his greeting to Mary.

VER. 7. Ἰουνίαν] Chrysostom and others take this as the accusative of Ἰουνία, a feminine noun, denoting, in this case, either the wife (verse 3), or the sister (verse 15) of Andronicus. Others regard it as a man's name, Junias, an abbreviation of Junianus; in which case it should be written Ἰουνιᾶν. συγγενεῖς] not "countrymen" (De Wette, Olshausen), because there were many other Jews in the congregation to whom salutations might have been sent upon this ground; but "relatives," Mark vi. 4; Luke i. 36, 58; ii. 44; John xviii. 26; Acts x. 24. συναιχμαλώτους] St. Paul was several times imprisoned, 2 Cor. vi. 5; Clement of Rome (1 Cor. 5) says, "seven times." ἐν τοῖς ἀποστόλοις] not "among," in the sense of "of," or "belonging to," the apostles, as Origen, Chrysost., Theodoret, Luther, Calvin, Bengel, Tholuck, explain: giving a wide signification to the term "apostle," so that it denotes all whose labors are not confined to one church, but who plant churches everywhere; but, "honorably known among

τόλοις, οἳ καὶ πρὸ ἐμοῦ γέγοναν ἐν Χριστῷ. [8] *ἀσπάσασθε*
Ἀμπλίαν τὸν ἀγαπητόν μου ἐν κυρίῳ. [9] *ἀσπάσασθε Οὐρ-*
βανὸν τὸν συνεργὸν ἡμῶν ἐν Χριστῷ, καὶ Στάχυν τὸν ἀγα-
πητόν μου. [10] *ἀσπάσασθε Ἀπελλῆν τὸν δόκιμον ἐν Χριστῷ.*
ἀσπάσασθε τοὺς ἐκ τῶν Ἀριστοβούλου. [11] *ἀσπάσασθε*

the apostles." (Beza, Grotius, De Wette, Fritzsche, Meyer, Philippi). When the term "apostle" is applied to others than the Twelve, as in 2 Cor. viii. 23; xi. 13, it is anarthrous. πρὸ ἐμοῦ, etc.] the fact that Andronicus and Junia had been believers of such long standing made them "distinguished." "Venerabilis facit ætas, in Christo maxime." Bengel. γέγοναν] this reading of ℵAB Lachm., Tisch., is the Alexandrine form of γεγόνασιν, which is the reading of CL Receptus.

VER. 8. Ἀμπλίαν] is a Greek contraction from Ampliatus. Tischendorf, ℵABFG, Vulgate, Copt., Æth., read Ἀμπλίατον. The first form is supported by CDEL, Peshito, Receptus, Lachm.

VER. 9. Οὐρβανὸν] Urbanus is a Roman name. συνεργὸν] Compare verse 3. Στάχυν] is a Greek name: literally, a "wheat ear," Mat. xii. 1.

VER. 10. Ἀπελλῆν] compare "Judæus Apella," Horace, Sat., I. i. 100. Origen and Grotius confound this person with Apollos (Acts xviii. 24). δόκιμον] his Christian faith and constancy has been tested and proved. τοὺς ἐκ τῶν Ἀριστοβούλου] the genitive denotes dependence: children, kinsmen, domestics, or slaves may be meant. From the fact that Aristobulus himself receives no greeting, and that τοὺς is used, it is probable that he was not a believer, and that only the believers in his household are meant. Compare τοὺς ὄντας ἐν κυρίῳ, in verse 11.

VER. 11. Ἡρῳδίωνα] is formed from Ἡρῶδες, like Καισαρίων

Ἡρωδίωνα τὸν συγγενῆ μου. ἀσπάσασθε τοὺς ἐκ τῶν Ναρκίσσου τοὺς ὄντας ἐν κυρίῳ. [12] ἀσπάσασθε Τρύφαιναν καὶ Τρυφῶσαν τὰς κοπιώσας ἐν κυρίῳ. ἀσπάσασθε Περσίδα τὴν ἀγαπητήν, ἥτις πολλὰ ἐκοπίασεν ἐν κυρίῳ. [13] ἀσπάσασθε Ῥοῦφον τὸν ἐκλεκτὸν ἐν κυρίῳ, καὶ τὴν μητέρα αὐτοῦ

from Καίσαρ. συγγενῆ] Philippi suggests, from the fact that Herodion is not mentioned with the kinsmen in verse 7, that he belonged to the class of freedmen, or slaves. Ναρκίσσου] "Puto intelligi Narcissum Claudii libertatem (Suet. Claud., 28; Tac. Ann., xii. 57; xiii. 1) in cujus domo aliqui fuerint Christiani." Grotius. So Calvin and Neander. Narcissus died before this epistle was written, but members of his family may have been the persons saluted.

VER. 12. Τρύφαιναν καὶ Τρυφῶσαν] probably two sisters. τὰς κοπιώσας] "quæ laborarunt, etsi nomen habent ἀπὸ τρυφῆς, a deliciis, ut Naëmi." Bengel. Περσίδα] is a name derived from the native country, like Lydia, Syrus, Davus, Geta. ἀγαπητήν] μου is not added, as in verses 5, 8, 9, where men are referred to. Philippi. πολλὰ ἐκοπίασεν] Compare verse 6.

VER. 13. Ῥοῦφον] In Mark xv. 21, Simon of Cyrene is described as the father of Alexander and Rufus. This shows that Rufus must have been highly esteemed in the church, when the evangelist wrote. St. Paul, also, mentions him, here, with special praise. Hence many expositors maintain the identity of the Rufus in Mark xv. 21 and Rom. xvi. 13. ἐκλεκτὸν] not in the sense applicable to all believers, but in the sense of "excellent," "choice:" the French élite. He was distinguished as a Christian. Compare 2 John i. 13. ἐμοῦ] his mother "in the Lord" ("in Israel," Judges v. 7), and, perhaps, by reason of maternal kindness toward him. Compare John xix. 27; 1 Cor. i. 2.

καὶ ἐμοῦ. 14 ἀσπάσασθε Ἀσύγκριτον, Φλέγοντα, Ἑρμῆν,
Πατρόβαν, Ἑρμᾶν, καὶ τοὺς σὺν αὐτοῖς ἀδελφούς. 15 ἀσπάσασθε Φιλόλογον καὶ Ἰουλίαν, Νηρέα καὶ τὴν ἀδελφὴν
αὐτοῦ, καὶ Ὀλυμπᾶν, καὶ τοὺς σὺν αὐτοῖς πάντας ἁγίους.
16 ἀσπάσασθε ἀλλήλους ἐν φιλήματι ἁγίῳ. ἀσπάζονται
ὑμᾶς αἱ ἐκκλησίαι πᾶσαι τοῦ Χριστοῦ.

VER. 14. The persons mentioned in this, and the following verse, were acquaintances of the apostle, but either not so well known, or not so highly distinguished, as the preceding persons mentioned, since no epithets are applied to them. Ἀσύγκριτον] Tischendorf ℵDEFG read Ἀσύνκριτον. Ἑρμῆν, etc.] is the order in ℵABCDFG, Copt., Æth., Lachm., Tisch. The Receptus, with Peshito, Vulg., DEL, have Ἑρμᾶν Πατρόβαν Ἑρμῆν. Origen, Eusebius, Jerome, and others, erroneously take this Hermes for the author of the Pastor. The latter was the brother of the Roman bishop Pius, and lived A.D. 150. σὺν αὐτοῖς] does not refer to assembling for worship, at their house (verse 5), nor to missionary union in evangelistic labor (Reiche), but to common business pursuits and occupations (Fritzsche, Philippi).

VER. 15. Ἰουλίαν] some read Ἰουλιᾶν, which is a contraction of Julianus, and would make the person a man, Julian, instead of a woman, Julia. See on verse 7. Νηρέα] from Νηρεύς, originally a mythological name, like Φοίβην, verse 1. ℵFG read Νηρέαν. Ὀλυμπᾶν] is a contraction from Ὀλυμπιόδωρον. Grotius. τοὺς σὺν αὐτοῖς] their particular associates in life and occupation, as in verse 14. Calvin remarks, respecting these salutations, that "it would have been unseemly to have omitted Peter, in so long a catalogue, if he was then at Rome, as the Romanists assert."

VER. 16. φιλήματι] Compare 1 Cor. xvi. 20; 2 Cor. xiii. 12; 1 Thess. v. 26; 1 Pet. v. 14. The kiss is the Oriental mode

17 ***Παρακαλῶ δὲ ὑμᾶς, ἀδελφοί, σκοπεῖν τοὺς τὰς διχοστασίας καὶ τὰ σκάνδαλα παρὰ τὴν διδαχὴν ἣν ὑμεῖς ἐμά-***

of salutation, as hand-shaking is the Occidental: the men saluting the men, and women the women. Justin Martyr (Apology, i. 65) remarks: "We give each other a kiss, at the close of public worship." πᾶσαι] is the reading of ℵABCDEFG, Peshito, Vulg., Copt., Æth., Griesbach, Mill, Lachm., Tisch. The Receptus omits it. The apostle expresses the common Christian sentiment, or the fellowship of the churches. Or, it may be that he refers to the churches ἐν κύκλῳ τῆς Ἱηρουσαλὴμ, xv. 19.

In verses 17–30, St. Paul returns to the believer's duty in reference to God and the church, in respect to teachers of false doctrine, and disorganizers. "The fact that the Roman epistle is so free from all direct polemical allusions to such teachers, shows that hitherto they had found no entrance into the church." Philippi. Hence, the apostle's exhortation has reference to the future. He would put them upon their guard against the Judaizing Ebionite and the antinomian Gnostic, who were beginning already to make their influence felt in the infant church, both in doctrine and practice.

VER. 17. δὲ] is transitive: "now." σκοπεῖν] "to keep an eye upon," so as to guard against. Compare Phil. iii. 17. τὰς διχοστασίας] the article denotes "the well-known dissensions." The reference is to differences in both doctrine and practice, because the latter originate in the former. τὰ σκάνδαλα] the article has the same force as in the preceding instance. σκάνδαλα denotes the occasions or causes of the διχοστασία. See comment on xi. 9; xiv. 13. What they were, is explained in the context. παρὰ] "contrary to." τὴν διδαχὴν] the teaching which they had received from the

ϑετε ποιοῦντας, καὶ ἐκκλίνετε ἀπ' αὐτῶν· 18 οἱ γὰρ τοιοῦτοι τῷ κυρίῳ ἡμῶν Χριστῷ οὐ δουλεύουσιν, ἀλλὰ τῇ ἑαυτῶν κοιλίᾳ, καὶ διὰ τῆς χρηστολογίας καὶ εὐλογίας ἐξαπατῶσιν

apostles and their συνεργούς. It is the same as τὸν τύπον διδαχῆς, in vi. 17. ἐκκλίνετε ἀπ'] "incline away from," or "avoid:" the contrary of προσλαμβάνεσϑε, in xiv. 1; xv. 7. Beware of their society. As these persons were not members of the church, they could not be excommunicated. Hence, the remark of Grotius, that "there was as yet no regularly constituted church at Rome, otherwise the apostle would have bidden them to excommunicate these false teachers," is erroneous. Chapter xii. 6–8 shows that there was a church organization at Rome.

VER. 18 gives the reason, introduced by γὰρ, for avoiding the false teachers. Χριστῷ] the Receptus, L, Peshito, Copt., read Ἰησοῦ Χριστῷ. οὐ δουλεύουσιν] they *refuse* to serve, as the position of the negative shows. κοιλίᾳ] sc. δουλεύουσιν: they lived a life of pleasure. Departure from truth in doctrine naturally leads to immorality in practice. The intellectual check being gone, the sensual bent is unrestrained. The union of sensuality with heresy is frequently spoken of in the New Testament. Compare Phil. iii. 18, 19; 1 Tim. vi. 3–5; Titus i. 10–12. χρηστολογίας] is used only here, in the New Testament: "dissembling words;" the language of a good man hypocritically used by a bad man. Julius Capitolinus (Vita Pertinacis, 13) defines a "Chrestologus," as one "qui bene loqueretur ut male faceret." Compare 2 Cor. xi. 13, 14. εὐλογίας] "fair speeches," refers rather to flattery. Deceit and flattery are of one species, and may, therefore, be connected with only one article, as here. ἀκάκων] the "guileless," who "having no guile in their own hearts do not expect to find it in others." Philippi.

τὰς καρδίας τῶν ἀκάκων. 19 *ἡ γὰρ ὑμῶν ὑπακοὴ εἰς πάντας ἀφίκετο· ἐφ' ὑμῖν οὖν χαίρω, θέλω δὲ ὑμᾶς σοφοὺς εἶναι εἰς*

VER. 19. γὰρ] Explanations: 1. It introduces a second reason for avoiding false teachers (De Wette, Tholuck, Philippi). Meyer objects to this, that γὰρ is never repeated in a co-ordinate sentence. But see v. 7. 2. It implies that the Roman believers are characterized by this guilelessness which is liable to be imposed upon (Origen, Calvin, Fritzsche, Rückert, Hodge). In this case, ὑπακοὴ is taken to denote an obedient disposition which is liable to be imposed upon, and so is equivalent to ἀκακία. 3. There is an implied antithesis. So far as the Roman brethren are concerned, the apostle knows that by reason of their obedient faith (ὑπακοὴ πίστεως, i. 5, 8), they are not liable to be deceived (Chrysostom, Theodoret, Meyer). "Not without reason do I say 'the hearts of the simple-minded;' for (γὰρ) *you* they will not deceive, because you do not belong to this class." Of these explanations, the third is preferable, because it best agrees with the succeeding context, and ὑπακοὴ has its common signification of "obedience of faith." εἰς πάντας ἀφίκετο] is equivalent to καταγγέλεται ἐν ὅλῳ τῷ κόσμῳ, i. 8. ἐφ' ὑμῖν οὖν χαίρω] is the reading of ℵABCL, Lachm., Tisch., Tregelles. χαίρω οὖν ἐφ' ὑμῖν is that of DFG. The Receptus, Peshito, Copt., read χαίρω οὖν τὸ ἐφ' ὑμῖν. οὖν] because of your well-known faith. θέλω δὲ, etc.] while he has this confidence and joy in them, he yet knows that they are fallible, and gives a mild caution, according to the maxim, "Let him that thinketh he standeth, take heed lest he fall." σοφοὺς] quick to discern. εἰς τὸ ἀγαθόν] in reference to the true doctrine and practice which you have learned (verse 17). ἀκεραίους] (not ἀκακοὺς, as in verse 18): "innocent," or "simple-minded," in the bad sense, as the opposite of σοφούς. For the good sense of the word, see Mat. x. 16; Phil. ii. 15. The apostle would

τὸ ἀγαθόν, ἀκεραίους δὲ εἰς τὸ κακόν. [20] ὁ δὲ θεὸς τῆς εἰρήνης συντρίψει τὸν σατανᾶν ὑπὸ τοὺς πόδας ὑμῶν ἐν τάχει.
ἡ χάρις τοῦ κυρίου ἡμῶν Ἰησοῦ Χριστοῦ μεθ' ὑμῶν.

have them dull and obtuse in reference to evil. τὸ κακόν] the false doctrine of the false teachers. Compare 2 Cor. xiv. 20.

Ver. 20. δὲ] is not transitive (Eng. Ver.), but adversative. "There are these dangers from false teachers, and I have cautioned you; *but*, notwithstanding, the God of peace shall bruise, etc." εἰρήνης] the contrary of the dissensions and divisions spoken of above. συντρίψει] a reference, as many expositors explain, to Gen. iii. 15. σατανᾶν] false teachers are the ministers of Satan, 2 Cor. xi. 5. ἐν τάχει] the early heresies were failures. Ebionitism and Gnosticism were soon crushed out. The preservation of primitive Christianity from the fatal errors that very soon assailed it is one of the most striking of the gracious providences of God toward his church. ἡ χάρις, etc.] is the usual benediction at the end of the Pauline epistles. Compare 2 Cor. xiii. 14; Gal. vi. 18; Phil. iv. 23; 2 Thess. iii. 18, etc. Ἰησοῦ Χριστοῦ] is the reading of ACL, Peshito, Vulgate, Coptic, Æthiopic, Receptus, Lachm. ℵB Tisch. omit Χριστοῦ. The Receptus reads ἀμήν, but this is supported by no uncial ms., and is generally rejected by editors.

Verses 21–23 are a postscript conveying the greetings of St. Paul's companions, kinsmen, and friends, to the Roman church. These persons, very probably, requested the apostle to send their salutations, after he had concluded his epistle. The addition of such a postscript is a strong evidence of genuineness rather than of spuriousness.

Ver. 21. ἀσπάζεται] is the reading of ℵABCDFG, Vulg., Copt., Lachm., Tisch. The Receptus EL read ἀσπάζονται

21 *Ἀσπάζεται ὑμᾶς Τιμόθεος ὁ συνεργός μου, καὶ Λούκιος καὶ Ἰάσων καὶ Σωσίπατρος οἱ συγγενεῖς μου.* 22 *ἀσπάζομαι ὑμᾶς ἐγὼ Τέρτιος ὁ γράψας τὴν ἐπιστολὴν ἐν κυρίῳ.* 23 *ἀσπάζεται ὑμᾶς Γάϊος ὁ ξένος μου καὶ ὅλης τῆς ἐκκλησίας.*

Τιμόθεος] is the well-known companion and helper who is mentioned in all the Pauline epistles, excepting Galatians, Ephesians, and Titus. Compare, also, Acts xvi. 1 sq.; xvii. 14 sq.; xviii. 5; xix. 22; xx. 4. Λούκιος] Origen confounds him with the evangelist Luke. Perhaps he was Lucius of Cyrene, Acts xiii. 1. Ἰάσων] Perhaps Jason of Thessalonica, Acts xvii. 5 sq. Σωσίπατρος] Probably Σώπατρος (Sopater) of Berea, Acts xx. 4. Compare Σωκράτης and Σωσικράτης, Σώστρατος and Σωσίστρατος. οἱ συγγενεῖς] Compare verses 7, 11.

VER. 22. ἀσπάζομαι] the tense changes. Tertius, who has written the epistle thus far, at the dictation of the apostle, now sends his own salutation, by the permission, or perhaps the suggestion, of the apostle: "hoc Pauli vel hortatu vel concessu facile interposuit Tertius." Bengel. As Philippi remarks, it would have been unfitting for St. Paul to send the salutation from Tertius as from a third person, while the latter himself wrote it down. Τέρτιος] Grotius remarks respecting Tertius and Quartus, "Romani hi fuerunt negotiantes Corinthi." Tertius has been incorrectly taken to be Silas, because the Hebrew for tertius (שְׁלִישִׁי) sounds like Silas. But the Greek Σίλας is the contraction of Σιλουανός (Sylvanus). γράψας] St. Paul was accustomed to dictate his epistles, as appears from 1 Cor. xvi. 21; Gal. vi. 11; Coloss. iv. 18; 2 Thess. iii. 17. ἐν κυρίῳ] is an adjunct of ἀσπάζομαι.

VER. 23. The apostle begins again to dictate. Γάϊος] (Caius) is probably the same that is mentioned in 1 Cor. i. 14; since this epistle was written at Corinth. There are, however, three others of this name, in the New Testament,

ἀσπάζεται ὑμᾶς Ἔραστος ὁ οἰκονόμος τῆς πόλεως, καὶ Κούαρτος ὁ ἀδελφός. [24] *ἡ χάρις τοῦ κυρίου ἡμῶν Ἰησοῦ Χριστοῦ μετὰ πάντων ὑμῶν. ἀμήν.*

Acts xix. 29; xx. 4; 3 John 1. ξένος μου] during his first abode in Corinth, the apostle lodged with Aquila and Priscilla, Acts xviii. 1–3; then with Justus, Acts xviii. 7. ἐκκλησίας] Gaius was the "host of the whole church," because he was hospitable to all the members, and his house was the place of worship for them. Ἔραστος] is not the person mentioned in Acts xix. 22; 2 Tim. iv. 20, unless we suppose the apostle in this place to describe him by an office which he formerly held. οἰκόνομος] the quæstor, or keeper of the public money. Κούαρτος] an Italian, as the name Quartus shows. The ordinal numbers, primus, secundus, etc., were employed by the Latins as proper names. ὁ ἀδελφος] not the brother of Erastus, which would require αὐτοῦ, but the Christian brother.

Ver. 24 is a repetition of the benediction in verse 20, and is omitted by ℵABC, Coptic, Æthiopic, Lachm., Tisch., Tregelles. It is found in DEFG, Vulgate, Peshito (after verse 27), Receptus. Meyer retains it, quoting the remark of Wolfius: "Ita hodiernum, ubi epistola *vale* dicto consummata est, et alia paucis commemoranda menti se adhuc offerunt, scribere solemus: *vale iterum*." He also cites 2 Thess. iii. 16, 18, as an instance of the repetition of the benediction. But in this place, the two forms are very different from each other; while in Rom. xvi. 24, it is a verbatim repetition, with the exception of the addition of πάντων.

Ver. 25 begins one of the most carefully constructed and characteristic benedictions, in the Pauline epistles. It is found in ℵBCDE, Vulgate, Peshito, Coptic, Æthiopic, Receptus, Bengel, Lachm., Tisch., and Tregelles. L, nearly 200 of the cursives, the lectionaries, Beza, Griesbach, and

25 Τῷ δὲ δυναμένῳ ὑμᾶς στηρίξαι κατὰ τὸ εὐαγγέλιόν μου καὶ τὸ κήρυγμα Ἰησοῦ Χριστοῦ, κατὰ ἀποκάλυψιν μυστηρίου χρόνοις αἰωνίοις σεσιγημένου, 26 φανερωθέντος

Mill, have it, but place it after xiv. 23. A inserts it both after xiv. 23, and xvi. 24. It is wanting in F (with vacant space after xiv. 24), and in G (with vacant space after xiv. 23). The internal evidence is highly in favor of the genuineness of this benediction, for it is strikingly Pauline in its elements. Marcion, the Gnostic, rejected it upon dogmatic grounds, and his solitary opinion is the main reliance, so far as historical evidence goes, of Baur and the Tübingen school, in their attack upon the genuineness of chapters xv., xvi. Respecting the earlier attacks of Semler and Paulus, De Wette (xvi. 25–27) remarks: "die Gründe für diese Annahmen verdienen keine Widerlegung." δὲ] is transitive: "now." τῷ δυναμένῳ] spiritual strength is not self-derived, but is from God. στηρίξαι] "to render steadfast;" with reference, not merely to the attempts of false teachers, but to faith in the whole evangelical doctrine, as St. Paul has enunciated it in this epistle. Compare i. 11; 1 Thess. iii. 2, 13; 2 Thess. ii. 17; iii. 3. κατὰ το εὐαγγελίον] belongs to στηρίξαι: "in regard to my gospel" (De Wette). The steadfastness has respect to the gospel. God can strengthen them so that they shall not vacillate, and depart from evangelical truth. For the force of κατὰ, see xi. 28. μου] is used officially, as in ii. 16: "of me, an authorized apostle." καὶ] "namely." τὸ κήρυγμα] is exegetical of τὸ εὐαγγελίον: the gospel is the herald's proclamation, or message, respecting Jesus Christ. "Preconium Jesu Christi apellat evangelium." Calvin. Χριστοῦ] not the subjective genitive: Christ's preaching by St. Paul (Meyer), but the genitive of the object: the preaching which has Christ for its theme (Luther, Calvin, De Wette, Tholuck, Philippi). κατὰ] is regarded by Meyer and others as co-ordinate with the preceding κατὰ, and dependent upon στηρίξαι, so that the gospel is denominated an ἀποκάλυψις, in respect to which God is able to strengthen believers. The objection to this is, that the "mystery" referred to, here, is not the gospel itself; which would require the article, as in Eph. iii. 9; Coloss. i. 26; but the fact that the Gentiles are partakers with the Jews in the blessings of redemption. Hence the view of Fritzsche, Rückert, De Wette, Tholuck, and Philippi, is preferable: viz., that κατὰ has the meaning of "conformably to," or "in consequence of," and depends upon the whole clause τῷ δὲ δυναμένῳ ὑμᾶς στηρίξαι. Rückert would supply τὸ γεγενημένον: "which (namely, τὸ κήρυγμα) occurred conformably to the revelation, etc." μυστηρίου] is anarthrous: *a* mystery, viz., relating to the Gentiles. The term "mystery," in the Biblical usage, denotes a truth or fact that requires to be revealed from God, because it cannot be discovered by human investigation and reasoning. It does not necessarily involve something abstruse and difficult to comprehend, though it may involve this. That the gospel was intended for the Gentiles was a "mystery," because it could not be known until God had announced his intention in this particular. But the doctrine of the universality of Christianity is easily enough understood when revealed. The fact that the reprobation of the Jews is to continue until the fulness of the Gentiles has come in was a "mystery," until St. Paul, by inspiration, revealed it (xi. 25 sq.). But there is nothing difficult of apprehension in this revealed fact; though it could not have been known to man, unless St. Paul, or some other inspired man, had made it known. The "mystery" here alluded to is not the gospel (De Wette, Meyer), but the calling of the Gentiles: "mysterium de gentibus concorporatis." Bengel. So Philippi. This has been a prominent feature in the epistle throughout. Compare i. 5, 6, 13–15; iii. 29; iv. 10, 11; ix.

δὲ νῦν διά τε γραφῶν προφητικῶν κατ' ἐπιταγὴν τοῦ αἰωνίου θεοῦ εἰς ὑπακοὴν πίστεως εἰς πάντα τὰ ἔθνη γνωρισ-

24–26, 30; x. 11–13; xi. 11, 13, 30; xv. 9, 12, 15–21. St. Paul was the apostle to the Gentiles, and *his* gospel (εὐαγγέλιόν μου), in an emphatic sense, was that the Gentiles are fellow-heirs of the promise. Accordingly he describes God, in this closing benediction upon a Gentile Church, as one who is able to strengthen them in respect to the truth in Christ, conformably with that purpose of a universal proclamation of this truth which had eternally been in the mind of God, and which he made known at the proper time in the Old Testament scriptures. χρόνοις αἰωνίοις] "during eternal ages:" the dative of duration, Luke viii. 29; Acts viii. 11. The αἰών referred to in this instance, is that in which God exists; which is eternity, and not time. Consequently the "æonian," here, is the eternal. The intensive plural is employed to denote this. See the comment on vi. 23. σεσιγημένου] God had "kept silent" respecting the fact.

VER. 26. νῦν] is antithetic to χρόνοις αἰώνιοις, as φανερωθέντος is to σεσιγημένου. τε] mentions with particularity an additional feature: "and also." γραφῶν προφητικῶν] the Old Testament teaching respecting the universality of the kingdom of Christ. Compare i. 2; xi. 18–20; xv. 9–12. If the "mystery" here spoken of is the plan of redemption in general, the Old Testament would not have been mentioned as the sole, or even the principal instrument in "making it known." The New Testament was a yet more important means. But the Old Testament was particularly needed in order to prove to the gainsaying Jews, that the Gentiles were to be partakers of the Messianic salvation. κατ' ἐπιταγὴν] is to be connected with both φανερωθέντος and γνωρισθέντος. αἰωνίου] is suggested by χρόνοις αἰωνίοις. εἰς υπακοὴν πίστεως] Compare

θέντος, [27] μόνῳ σοφῷ θεῷ διὰ Χριστοῦ Ἰησοῦ, ᾧ ἡ δόξα εἰς τοὺς αἰῶνας τῶν αἰώνων. ἀμήν.

on i. 5. πάντα τὰ ἔθνη] all the Gentiles, in distinction from the Jews, as in i. 5, 13.

VER. 27. σοφῷ] the epithet is chosen with reference to the revelation and announcement of the mystery spoken of. The time and manner are ordered in "manifold wisdom." Compare Eph. iii. 3–10. θεῷ] = τῷ δυναμένῳ, which is resumed by it. διὰ Ἰησοῦ Χριστοῦ] "is to be closely connected with μόνῳ σοφῷ θεῷ, and hence no comma is to be placed after θεῷ: 'To the, through Jesus Christ, only wise God.'" Philippi. The divine wisdom has revealed itself in its highest form, in Jesus Christ. So Meyer, and De Wette; the latter of whom remarks that διὰ Ἰησοῦ Χριστοῦ cannot be connected with δοξα, on account of the intervening ᾧ. The older expositors (Chrysostom, Luther, Beza, Calvin, Grotius, Eng. Ver.) so connect it: "To the only wise God be glory through Jesus Christ." To do this, requires that ᾧ be rejected. But it is found in all the uncials, excepting B, and all the cursives, excepting 33 and 72. ᾧ] 1. Refers to God as wise through Jesus Christ (Meyer). In this case, the dative τῷ δυναμένῳ with its resumption μόνῳ σοφῷ θεῷ, is an anacoluthon. 2. It refers to Χριστοῦ (Tholuck, Philippi). "The apostle," says Philippi, "intended to utter a doxology to the power and wisdom of God the Father; but inasmuch as this wisdom is manifested in Jesus Christ, he transfers the doxology to him, and thus, in blessing the revealer of the divine wisdom, blesses indirectly the God of wisdom himself." Compare 2 Tim. iv. 18; Heb. xiii. 20, 21. 3. ᾧ is a pleonasm, standing for αὐτῷ: "to him, I say" (Stuart, Hodge). δόξα] sc. εἴη.